all
TOGETHER
now

ALL together NOW

the
first
complete
BEATLES
discography
1961--1975

by harry castleman &
walter j. podrazik

BALLANTINE BOOKS · NEW YORK

Library of Congress Catalog Card Number: 75-29523

ISBN 0-345-25680-8-595

This edition published by arrangement with The Pierian Press, Ann Arbor, Michigan

Manufactured in the United States of America

First Ballantine Books Edition: September 1976
Second Printing: January 1977

contents

illustrations

Other

introduction

All Together Now, aside from being the name of a Beatles' song, was the main objective for writing this book. John Lennon, Paul McCartney, George Harrison and Ringo Starr, known collectively as the Beatles, were the most important force in music in the 60's. Other performers of similar stature in their own time have had de-- tailed and complex discographies compiled. The world of rock mu-- sic has always been sadly deficient in this area. We have long felt that an appropriately complete book concerning the Beatles was in order. We waited for such a book to appear. And when none did, we decided to do it ourselves.

A great deal of information about the Beatles has appeared in numerous publications, but none of them presented a complete guide to the group's professional career within one volume.

The main section, called **The Magical Mystery Tour**, details chronologically all of the records the Beatles were associated with as performers, writers and producers. We made a special effort to document the numerous instances in which one of the Beatles worked with other musicians. As much information as possible is included in this disc history, which we believe to be the most com-- plete of its sort ever published.

The section entitled **Linear Notes** serves the double purpose of both index and liner notes. All of the albums and songs released by the Beatles, both individually and as a group, are listed alphabet-- ically. Their work for other artists is listed separately. Whenever possible, we listed musician credits for specific songs (both credited and uncredited). In instances where it was impossible to break down a line--up printed on an album, credits are given following the name of the LP.

The **Beatles From Others** documents a commonly neglected area, the musical heritage upon which the Beatles based their own music. This section traces the history of all the songs the Beatles re-- corded (and many they never released) which were written by other artists.

As an accompanying feature, the **Pandemonium Shadow Show** presents selected recordings by friends, relatives and total strangers which, purposefully or not, were caught up in the general "hoopla" of Beatle merchandising.

The following section, **No, You're Wrong**, debunks a number of well–traveled stories concerning possible Beatle appearances on strange records.

To complete the book, we present, along with a detailed history of bootlegs, complete lists of Apple, Dark Horse, and Ring O' Records, films and books involving the Beatles, and the chart move–ments of their records.

Amidst all these pages of type, one must not forget the corner-stone of this entire subject is, after all, music. Music made up of sound, not print. Music meant to be listened to, not cataloged.

Most groups will never have a book like this published about them but, like it or not, the Beatles are not "just another group." Since something like *All Together Now* was bound to appear, we felt a complete job should be done, and more importantly, that it should be done by people who know and love their music.

ACKNOWLEDGEMENTS

We would like to thank the following for their help in researching and preparing this book.

Businesses and Institutions:

A&M Records
  Bob Garcia, Erika Hirmer
Apple Records
  Tony King, Anita Morgan
Asylum Records
  Sam Sutherland
Capitol Records
  Mickey Diage, Charlotte Nelson
Dark Horse Records
EMI (London)
  Shirley Natanson, Neil Aspinall
ESP Disks
Polydor Ltd. (London)
RCA Records
Shelter Records
  Evan Archerd
United Artists Records
Warner Brothers Records
  Bob Heron, Jo Bergman

The Library of Congress
    Mr. Gerald Gibson, Assistant Head of The Recorded Sound Section
New York Public Library – Rodgers and Hammerstein Collection
    Mr. Gary Gisondi
TGS Associates
    Mr. Ted Schmidt
The Audio Center of the Popular Library at Bowling Green
    University
    Mr. William Schurk
Lennon Music
Richard Perry Productions
Billboard Magazine
    Mr. Dennis Hyland
Melody Maker
    Mr. Ray Coleman
R.I.A.A.
Mal Evans
Dave Herman at WNEW-FM
Peter Cook and Dudley Moore

Friends:

Peter Gibbon
Martin Maloney
Laura Janis
Joyce Kravitz
John O'Leary
Julia Podrazik
Mark Giangrande
Gareth Pawlowski
Skip Groff

Eileen McMahon
John Milward
Carole Cohen
Joe Federici
Bill Small
Mark Guncheon
Mark Nelson
Bill Lastomirsky

Thanks to Tom for putting up with innumerable "final" corrections.

And special thanks to the Democratic National Committee, without
whose air--conditioning none of this would have been possible.

                                   Harry Castleman
                                   Wally Podrazik
                                   August 5, 1975

THE
MAGICAL
MYSTERY
TOUR

The Beatles/1962--1966   **Apple SKBO 3403   (2 LPs)**

Chronological Disc History

This chronology presents, we believe, the complete history of the Beatles on record. It details, with a great deal of accompanying information, all of the records they have been associated with since their debut as a back–up group in 1961. Our focus is on Britain and America, the two main countries in rock music. We made exceptions only for the Beatles' first recordings (in Germany) and for European or Canadian releases which affected the British or American markets.

Early on, we were forced to disregard a fair amount of information heretofore accepted as true. Song writing credits were occasionally filled with pseudonyms, or even conflicting on various records. Titles, too, were sometimes inaccurate. For example, the song called *Kansas City* is, in fact, Little Richard's interpretation of that song, incorporating his own tune *Hey-Hey-Hey-Hey!* into a medley with the original *Kansas City* theme. Timings for individual songs were best considered approximations, due to the technicalities of pressing or the presence of a premature fade-out on a single. In these three areas, we consulted other sources, and the information presented in the chronology reflects, to the best of our knowledge, what is actually on record (as opposed to what the record says it is).

The date listed for a record's release reflects more when the record was first commercially available to the general public than the record company's "official" release date (which occasionally was clearly different from when it was first available to the public). A careful check of calendars will reveal that English records tended to come out on Fridays, while Americans preferred the beginning of the week.

Among the unique features of our chronology are the cataloguing of entries by record, not by song (since Beatle songs appeared in so many different forms); and the concept of a reissue. By denoting reissued material (in all UPPER CASE) we have tried to set off the "first" issuance of a Beatle song, as opposed to its often numerous repackagings. Through this method, one can see which songs on a "new" Beatle album were actually previously released singles, or material out sometime earlier across the Atlantic.

3

We took into consideration the common record company practice of issuing "lead" singles to promote a forthcoming album. In the early years covered, this lead time was usually two weeks or less; by the end of the 60's, it had expanded to four to six weeks. We have used our own judgment in the cases where a single was released technically after an album, but was still generally meant to accompany the album's release.

Along with material released by the four Beatles (either as a group or individually), the chronology includes works by other artists. This is done to trace the equally important aspect of the Beatles as producers, writers and backing musicians. There are, needless to say, literally thousands of versions of Beatle-authored material. Since none of the group had any direct connection with these cover versions, we have ignored all but the instances when one of the Beatles specifically wrote or "gave" one of his songs to another performer.

All the information presented is as exact as we could make it, and is based on conversations with some of those involved and interviews conducted at the time—not just the reading of liner notes.

When dealing with such a large body of works, there are bound to be minor technical differences among various issuings of the same song. The only differences we have denoted are those involving two completely different recordings of the same song.

The version of *Love Me Do* released as a single in Britain (called *version one*) had Ringo playing drums. But, starting with the release of the **Please Please Me** album, an alternate take (with Ringo relegated to the tambourine) was put in its place.

The *Across The Universe* on the **No One's Gonna Change Our World** album was recorded before the version on the **Let It Be** album and is, in fact, a noticeably altered arrangement of the song.

The versions of *Get Back* and *Let It Be* which were on the **Let It Be** album are actually different recordings from those which appeared on the singles.

We have tried to convey the instances in which a reissued song has been either prematurely faded down or had sections electronically edited. A common example of this is seen in the shorter time listed for a single pulled from an album. The version of Ringo's *Oh My My* released as a single is missing 35 seconds of refrain found on the album. Sometimes, however, it's not so clear cut. All of the currently available copies of The Beatles' first recording (*My Bonnie*) do not contain the half minute of spoken intro (in both German and English!) which were found on the first releases. Even more confusing is the case of *I'll Cry Instead* which contains an extra verse on the American soundtrack album and single, but nowhere else.

We found it too cumbersome to denote in the text instances in which later issuance of a song used the basic tracks of the original but had significant portions remixed. In 1963, when the Beatles were becoming world famous, Tony Sheridan rerecorded the vocals of *Sweet Georgia Brown*, leaving intact the instrumental backing recorded by the Beatles in 1961.

We totally ignored a favorite topic among Beatle collectors: recording oddities (the 'hi-hat' beginning of *All My Loving*, the elongated trumpet solo on *Penny Lane*, the 'false starts' on *I'm Looking Through You*, and the like).

For unknown reasons there are numerous and noticeable differences between the stereo and mono versions and between the European and American pressings of many Beatle songs. Capitol Records had a peculiar policy of adding echo or reverb to some of the early Beatle recordings. *I'm Only Sleeping, Money, You Can't Do That* and *She's A Woman* suffer the most from this cross-Atlantic garbling. Along with the generally higher quality of British pressings this has made many Americans go out and buy the English Beatle albums.

The mono/stereo differences are very numerous and nearly impossible to catalogue. There's also the difference between "true" stereo and rechanneled "fake" stereo. The general upshot of this is that you can have up to four "different" recordings of the same take. Since EMI/Capitol have the original tapes of all Beatle recordings separated into separate tracks as far back as **Rubber Soul**, the release of quad mixes is a definite possibility in the future.

5

Some Samples

12.   APR 26, 1963 (UK) Parlophone R 5023
      JUN 10, 1963 (US) Liberty 55586
      by Billy J. Kramer with The Dakotas Prod: George Martin
      A: *Do You Want To Know A Secret*---L-McC---*1:59*
      B: *I'll Be On My Way*---L-McC---*1:38*

113.   FEB 1, 1965 (US) Capitol R 5365 (EP)
      by The Beatles
      4 BY THE BEATLES Prod: George Martin
      side one
        HONEY DON'T---Carl Perkins---*2:56*
        I'M A LOSER---2:31
      side two
        MR. MOONLIGHT---Roy Lee Johnson---*2:35*
        EVERYBODY'S TRYING TO BE MY BABY---Carl Perkins
        ---2:24

121.   JUL 19, 1965 (US) Capitol 5476
      JUL 23, 1965 (UK) Parlophone R 5305
      A side recorded: April 13, 1965
      B side recorded: Late May 1965
      by The Beatles Prod: George Martin
      A: *Help!---2:16*
   *B: *I'm Down---2:30*

221.   SEP 12, 1969 (UK) Decca SKL 5019 (LP)
      by The Rolling Stones Prod: Andrew Loog Oldham
      THROUGH THE PAST, DARKLY (BIG HITS VOL. 2)
      side one
        cut six: *WE LOVE YOU*---Mick Jagger–Keith Richard---*4:39*
        John and Paul: Backing Vocals

263. NOV 23, 1970 (US) Atlantic SD 7202 (LP)
NOV 27, 1970 (UK) Atlantic 2401-004 (LP)
Recorded: June–July 1970
by Steve Stills
  Ringo (as Richie): Drums
STEPHEN STILLS Prod: Steve Stills and Bill Halverson
side two
   cut two: *To A Flame*—Steve Stills—*3:10*
   cut five: *We Are Not Helpless*—Steve Stills—*4:17*

329. SEP 14, 1972 (UK) RCA 2266
by Harry Nilsson Prod: Richard Perry
A: SPACEMAN—Harry Nilsson—*3:33*
   Ringo: Drums
B: YOU'RE BREAKIN' MY HEART—Harry Nilsson—*3:10*
   George: Slide Guitar

449. JUN 2, 1975 (US) RCA JB 10320
JUL 18, 1975 (UK) RCA 2579
by David Bowie Prod: David Bowie and Harry Maslin
A: FAME—Lennon–David Bowie–Luther Andross—*3:30*
B: (right)

The visual code used in the chronology conveys a great deal of information in a very compact space. Using the above sample entries as reference, the following line-by-line guide should clearly explain the style used in this chronological disc history.

first line
The number beginning each entry is the reference number for the Title Index.

The release date is given, followed by the country of release, the record label and record number. If the disc is either an "extended play" (EP) or an album (LP), those letters follow the record number; the record is otherwise understood to be a 45 rpm.

All the releases in both Britain and the United States are listed.

When both countries release exactly the same disc with exactly the same cuts in exactly the same order, the release dates are stacked one over the other. If there are any differences, the releases are listed as separate entries.
on the next line
The recording date is listed if known.
on the next line
The name of the performer is listed.

8

on the next line

The name of the album or EP is listed; the contents are then listed side after side.

Or, the two sides of the single are listed.

General Assumptions:

1. All songs performed by the Beatles are written by Lennon and McCartney unless otherwise stated. (113,121)

In all other cases, the song authorship is spelled out in full. The only authorship abbreviations ever used are: L-McC (12), and combinations of the last names of the Beatles (i.e. McCartney–Starkey, Lennon–Harrison). (449)

2. Producer (Prod) credits are always given and they appear:

After the performer's name if they apply just to the cuts listed from an album or EP (221); or if they apply to a single (12).

After the album or EP title if they apply to the entire disc (113,263).

3. Any Beatle who appears as a backing musician on another performer's recording is listed here only if his presence is the sole reason for the disc being included in the chronological listing (221, 263,329). Otherwise, all such credits should be sought in the Index, where they are listed in complete detail. (449)

The Beatle–as–backing–musician credits which are listed follow the name of the performer (263) if they apply to all cuts listed. If they apply differently to particular cuts, they are listed under the individual cuts (221,329).

Pseudonyms used by the Beatle as a backing musician are listed only for the first entry of a song (263), not on each reissue (329). The pseudonym is always listed in the Title Index.

4. If a Beatle-authored song performed by another artist is included and no Beatle is listed as a backing musician or producer, it has been included because it was specifically "given" to that performer by a Beatle (12).

5. A song appearing in ALL CAPITAL LETTERS is a reissue (a song which has appeared previously on an album or single). Note: cuts released at about the same time in the US and the UK are not reissues; singles which are released at about the same time as the album they are from are also not reissues; but singles released after the album are reissues.

6. A song in parentheses and in all lower case is completely unrelated to any of the Beatles; it is listed simply to show what was on the other side of the Beatle-related song on the single (449).

7. An asterisk * means that the song appeared only on a single and was never subsequently issued in any other form in either the US or the UK (121) as of December 1975.

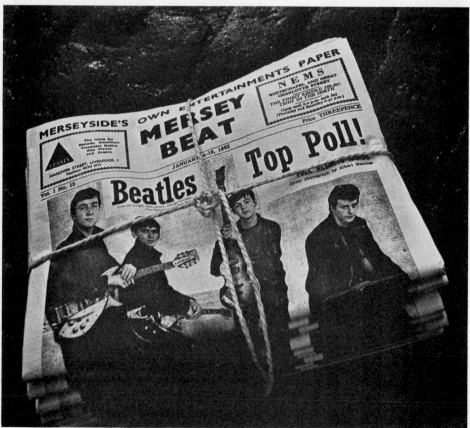

The Beatles -- Circa 1960 -- In The Beginning   **Polydor 24 - 4504   (LP)   partial sleeve front**

1961/62
This
Is Where It All Started

1. JUNE 1961 (GERMANY) Polydor 24 673
    Recorded: May 1961
    by Tony Sheridan and The "Beat Brothers" (=The Beatles)
      Prod: Bert Kaempfert
    A: My Bonnie (Lies Over The Ocean)---Charles Pratt---*2:41*
    B: The Saints (When The Saints Go Marching In)---P.D.---*3:19*

2. SEPT 1961 (GERMANY) Polydor (EP)
    New Songs Recorded: May 1961
    by Tony Sheridan and The "Beat Brothers" (= The Beatles),
      and † The Beatles
    MY BONNIE Prod: Bert Kaempfert
    side one
      MY BONNIE---Charles Pratt---*2:41*
      Why---Tony Sheridan—Bill Crompton---*2:55*
    side two
    †Cry For A Shadow---Lennon—Harrison---*2:22*
      THE SAINTS---P.D.---*3:19*

3. JAN 5, 1962 (UK) Polydor NH 66-833
    Reissued: May 24, 1963 and Feb. 21, 1964
    by Tony Sheridan and The Beatles Prod: Bert Kaempfert
    A: MY BONNIE---Charles Pratt---*2:41*
    B: THE SAINTS---P.D.---*3:19*

4. APR 23, 1962 (US) Decca 31382
    by Tony Sheridan and The "Beat Brothers" (=The Beatles)
      Prod: Bert Kaempfert
    A: MY BONNIE---Charles Pratt---*2:41*
    B: THE SAINTS---P.D.---*3:19*

11

4a. JUNE 1962 (GERMANY) Polydor 237 112 (LP)
by Tony Sheridan and The Beatles
  Prod: Bert Kaempfert
MY BONNIE
side one
  cut one: *MY BONNIE—Charles Pratt—2:41*
side two
  cut one: *THE SAINTS—P.D.—3:19*

5.   OCT 5, 1962 (UK) Parlophone R 4949
Recorded: Sept. 11, 1962
by The Beatles   Prod: George Martin
 *A: Love Me Do (version one)—2:22
 B: P. S. I Love You—2:02

5a. OCTOBER 1962 (GERMANY) Polydor 21485 (EP)
Recorded: May 1961
by Tony Sheridan and The "Beat Brothers" (= The Beatles)
  Prod: Bert Kaempfert
YA-YA
side one
 (ya-ya – part one)
 (ya-ya – part two)
side two
 *Sweet Georgia Brown—Ben Bernie—Maceo Pinkard—
  Kenneth Casey—2:03*
 (skinny minny)

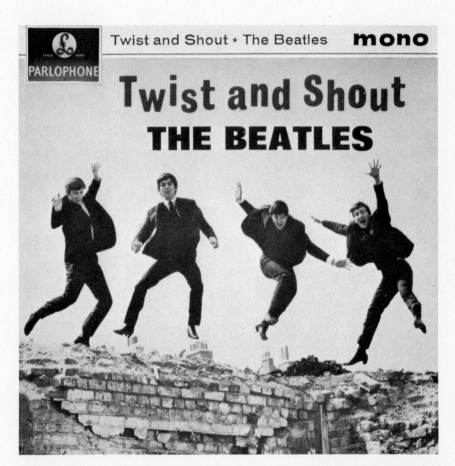

Twist And Shout   Parlophone GEP 8882   (EP)

With The Beatles   **Parlophone PCS 3045   (LP)**

1963

So What's From Liverpool?

6. JAN 11, 1963 (UK) Parlophone R 4983
FEB 25, 1963 (US) Vee Jay VJ 498
Recorded: Nov. 26, 1962
by The Beatles   Prod: George Martin
A: Please Please Me—2:00
B: Ask Me Why—2:24

7. FEB 4, 1963 (CANADA) Capitol of Canada 72076
by The Beatles   Prod: George Martin
*A: LOVE ME DO (version one)—2:22
B: P. S. I LOVE YOU—2:02

8. MAR 22, 1963 (UK) HMV Pop 1136
by Kenny Lynch
*A: Misery—L-McC—2:04
B: (shut the door)

9. MAR 22, 1963 (UK) Parlophone PCS 3042 (LP)
New Songs Recorded: Feb. 11, 1963; except † Sept. 11, 1962
by The Beatles
PLEASE PLEASE ME   Prod: George Martin
side one
I Saw Her Standing There—2:50
Misery—1:43
Anna (Go To Him)—Arthur Alexander—2:56
Chains—Gerry Goffin–Carole King—2:21
Boys—Luther Dixon–Wes Farrell—2:24
ASK ME WHY—2:24
PLEASE PLEASE ME—2:00

side two
†Love Me Do---2:19
  P. S. I LOVE YOU---2:02
  Baby, It's You---Hal David—Burt Bacharach—Barney
    Williams---*2:36*
  Do You Want To Know A Secret---1:55
  A Taste Of Honey---Ric Marlow—Bobby Scott---*2:02*
  There's A Place---1:44
  Twist And Shout---Bert Russell—Phil Medley---*2:32*

10. APR 12, 1963 (UK) Parlophone R 5015
  MAY 27, 1963 (US) Vee Jay VJ 522
  Recorded: March 4, 1963
  by The Beatles Prod: George Martin
  A: *From Me To You---1:49*
  B: *Thank You Girl---2:01*

11. APR 26, 1963 (UK) Parlophone R 5024
  by Duffy Power with The Graham Bond Quartet
  A: I Saw Her Standing There---L-McC---*2:25*
  B: *(farewell baby)*

12. APR 26, 1963 (UK) Parlophone R 5023
  JUN 10, 1963 (US) Liberty 55586
  by Billy J. Kramer with The Dakotas Prod: George Martin
  A: *Do You Want To Know A Secret*---L-McC---*1:59*
  B: *I'll Be On My Way*---L-McC---*1:38*

13. JUL 12, 1963 (UK) Polydor H 21-610 (EP)
  by Tony Sheridan and The Beatles, and † The Beatles
  MY BONNIE Prod: Bert Kaempfert
  side one
    MY BONNIE---Charles Pratt---*2:06*
    WHY---Tony Sheridan—Bill Crompton---*2:55*
  side two
  †CRY FOR A SHADOW---Lennon—Harrison---*2:22*
    THE SAINTS---P.D.---*3:19*

14. JUL 12, 1963 (UK) Parlophone GEP 8882 (EP)
  by The Beatles
  TWIST AND SHOUT Prod: George Martin
  side one
    TWIST AND SHOUT---Bert Russell—Phil Medley---*2:32*
    A TASTE OF HONEY---Ric Marlow—Bobby Scott---*2:02*

side two
DO YOU WANT TO KNOW A SECRET---1:55
THERE'S A PLACE---1:44

15.   JUL 22, 1963 (US) Vee Jay VJLP 1062 (LP)
by The Beatles
INTRODUCING THE BEATLES Prod: George Martin
side one
I SAW HER STANDING THERE---2:50
MISERY---1:43
ANNA (GO TO HIM)---Arthur Alexander---*2:56*
CHAINS---Gerry Goffin—Carole King---*2:21*
BOYS---Luther Dixon—Wes Farrell---*2:24*
LOVE ME DO---2:19
side two
P. S. I LOVE YOU---2:02
BABY, IT'S YOU---Hal David—Burt Bacharach—Barney
   Williams---*2:36*
DO YOU WANT TO KNOW A SECRET---1:55
A TASTE OF HONEY---Ric Marlow—Bobby Scott---*2:02*
THERE'S A PLACE---1:44
TWIST AND SHOUT---Bert Russell—Phil Medley---*2:32*

16.   JUL 26, 1963 (UK) Parlophone R 5049
SEP 23, 1963 (US) Liberty 55626
by Billy J. Kramer with The Dakotas Prod: George Martin
A: Bad To Me—L-McC---*2:18*
B: I Call Your Name---L-McC---*2:00*

17.   JUL 30, 1963 (UK) Piccadilly 7N 35137
by Tommy Quickly Prod: Les Reed
A: Tip Of My Tongue---L-McC---*2:02*
B: (heaven only knows)

18.   AUG 23, 1963 (UK) Parlophone R 5055
SEP 16, 1963 (US) Swan 4152
Recorded: July 1, 1963
by The Beatles Prod: George Martin
A: She Loves You---2:18
B: I'll Get You---2:04

19.   AUG 30, 1963 (UK) Parlophone R 5056
NOV 15, 1963 (US) ATCO 6280
Recorded: July 3, 1963

by The Fourmost
A: *Hello Little Girl*---L-McC---*1:50*
B: *(just in case)*

20. SEP 6, 1963 (UK) Parlophone GEP 8880 (EP)
by The Beatles
THE BEATLES' HITS Prod: George Martin
side one
 FROM ME TO YOU---1:49
 THANK YOU GIRL---2:01
side two
 PLEASE PLEASE ME---2:00
 LOVE ME DO---2:19

21. SEP 27, 1963 (UK) Parlophone R 5065
by Cilla Black
A: *Love Of The Loved*---L-McC---*2:00*
B: *(shy of love)*

22. OCT 25, 1963 (UK) Parlophone GEP 8885 (EP)
by Billy J. Kramer with The Dakotas
THE KRAMER HITS Prod: George Martin
side one
 BAD TO ME---L-McC---2:18
 I CALL YOUR NAME---L-McC---2:00
side two
 DO YOU WANT TO KNOW A SECRET---L-McC---1:59
 I'LL BE ON MY WAY---L-McC---1:38

23. NOV 1, 1963 (UK) Parlophone GEP 8883 (EP)
by The Beatles
THE BEATLES (NO. 1) Prod: George Martin
side one
 I SAW HER STANDING THERE---2:50
 MISERY---1:43
side two
 ANNA (GO TO HIM)---Arthur Alexander---*2:56*
 CHAINS---Gerry Goffin--Carole King---*2:21*

24. NOV 1, 1963 (UK) Parlophone R 5073
NOV 11, 1963 (US) Liberty 55643
Recorded: July 22, 1963
by Billy J. Kramer with The Dakotas Prod: George Martin
A: *I'll Keep You Satisfied*---L-McC---*2:04*
B: *(i know)*

18

25.	NOV 1, 1963 (UK) Decca F 11764
FEB 17, 1964   (US)   London 9641
by The Rolling Stones   Prod: Andrew Loog Oldham
A: I Wanna Be Your Man—L-McC—1:44
B: (stoned)

26.	NOV 8, 1963 (UK) Parlophone PCS 3047 (LP)
by Billy J. Kramer with The Dakotas
LISTEN...   Prod: George Martin
side two
  cut seven: *I CALL YOUR NAME—L-McC—2:00*

27.	NOV 15, 1963 (UK) Parlophone R 5078
FEB 10, 1964   (US)   ATCO 6285
by The Fourmost
A: I'm In Love—L-McC—2:07
B: (respectable)

28.	NOV 22, 1963 (UK) Parlophone PCS 3045 (LP)
NOV 25, 1963   (CANADA)   Capitol Of Canada ST 6051   (LP)
Recorded: July 15, 1963
by The Beatles
WITH THE BEATLES   Prod: George Martin
  (In Canada: **BEATLEMANIA WITH THE BEATLES**)
side one
  It Won't Be Long—2:11
  All I've Got To Do—2:05
  All My Loving—2:04
  Don't Bother Me—Harrison—2:28
  Little Child—1:46
  Till There Was You—Meredith Willson—2:12
  *Please Mr. Postman—Brian Holland—Robert Bateman—Berry
    Gordy—2:34*
side two
  Roll Over Beethoven—Chuck Berry—2:44
  Hold Me Tight—2:30
  You Really Got A Hold On Me—William Robinson—2:58
  I Wanna Be Your Man—1:59
  Devil In Her Heart—Richard B. Drapkin—2:23
  Not A Second Time—2:03
  *Money (That's What I Want)—Berry Gordy—Janie Bradford
    —2:47*

29.   NOV 29, 1963   (UK)   Parlophone R 5084
Recorded: Oct. 19, 1963
by The Beatles   Prod: George Martin
A: I Want To Hold Your Hand—2:24
B: This Boy—2:11

30.   DEC 6, 1963   (FAN CLUB)
Recorded: Oct. 20, 1963
by The Beatles   Prod: George Martin
The Beatles Christmas Record—5:00

31.   DEC 9, 1963   (CANADA)   Capitol Of Canada 72133
by The Beatles   Prod: George Martin
*A: ROLL OVER BEETHOVEN—*Chuck Berry*—2:44*
*B: PLEASE MR. POSTMAN—*Brian Holland—Robert Bateman
    Berry Gordy*—2:34*

Beatles For Sale   (A side)   **Parlophone PCS 3062   (LP)**

Beatles For Sale   (B side)   **Parlophone PCS 3062   (LP)**

Long Tall Sally   Parlophone GEP 8913   (EP)

I Want To Hold   Capitol 5112   (45)
Your Hand/I Saw Her Standing There

The Beatles' Second   Capitol ST 2080   (LP)
Album

I Feel Fine/   Capitol 5327   (45)
She's A Woman

1964
Not A Second Time

32. JAN 13, 1964 (CANADA) Capitol Of Canada ST 6054 (LP)
by The Beatles
TWIST AND SHOUT Prod: George Martin
side one
ANNA (GO TO HIM)---Arthur Alexander---*2:56*
CHAINS---Gerry Goffin---Carole King---*2:21*
BOYS---Luther Dixon---Wes Farrell---*2:24*
ASK ME WHY---*2:24*
PLEASE PLEASE ME---*2:00*
LOVE ME DO---*2:19*
FROM ME TO YOU---*1:49*
side two
P. S. I LOVE YOU---*2:02*
BABY, IT'S YOU---Hal David---Burt Bacharach---Barney
Williams---*2:36*
DO YOU WANT TO KNOW A SECRET---*1:55*
A TASTE OF HONEY---Ric Marlow---Bobby Scott---*2:02*
THERE'S A PLACE---*1:44*
TWIST AND SHOUT---Bert Russell---Phil Medley---*2:32*
SHE LOVES YOU---*2:18*

33. JAN 13, 1964 (US) Capitol 5112
by The Beatles Prod: George Martin
A: I WANT TO HOLD YOUR HAND---*2:24*
B: I SAW HER STANDING THERE---*2:50*

34. JAN 20, 1964 (US) Capitol ST 2047 (LP)
by The Beatles
MEET THE BEATLES! Prod: George Martin
side one
I WANT TO HOLD YOUR HAND---*2:24*
I SAW HER STANDING THERE---*2:50*
THIS BOY---*2:11*

IT WON'T BE LONG—2:11
ALL I'VE GOT TO DO—2:05
ALL MY LOVING—2:04
side two
DON'T BOTHER ME—Harrison—*2:28*
LITTLE CHILD—1:46
TILL THERE WAS YOU—Meredith Willson—*2:12*
HOLD ME TIGHT—2:30
I WANNA BE YOUR MAN—1:59
NOT A SECOND TIME—2:03

35.   JAN 27, 1964   (US)   MGM K 13213
       by Tony Sheridan and The Beatles   Prod: Bert Kaempfert
       A: MY BONNIE—Charles Pratt—*2:06*
       B: THE SAINTS—P.D.—*3:19*

36.   JAN 27, 1964   (US)   Vee Jay VJLP 1062 (LP)
       by The Beatles
       INTRODUCING THE BEATLES   Prod: George Martin
       side one
       I SAW HER STANDING THERE—2:50
       MISERY—1:43
       ANNA (GO TO HIM)—Arthur Alexander—*2:56*
       CHAINS—Gerry Goffin—Carole King—*2:21*
       BOYS—Luther Dixon—Wes Farrell—*2:24*
       ASK ME WHY—2:24
       side two
       PLEASE PLEASE ME—2:00
       BABY, IT'S YOU—Hal David—Burt Bacharach—Barney
          Williams—*2:36*
       DO YOU WANT TO KNOW A SECRET—1:55
       A TASTE OF HONEY—Ric Marlow—Bobby Scott—*2:02*
       THERE'S A PLACE—1:44
       TWIST AND SHOUT—Bert Russell—Phil Medley—*2:32*

37.   JAN 29, 1964   (US)   Liberty 55667
       by Billy J. Kramer with The Dakotas   Prod: George Martin
       A: DO YOU WANT TO KNOW A SECRET—L-McC—*1:59*
       B: BAD TO ME—L-McC—*2:18*

38.   JAN 30, 1964   (US)   Vee Jay VJ 581
       by The Beatles   Prod: George Martin
       A: PLEASE PLEASE ME—2:00
       B: FROM ME TO YOU—1:49

39. JAN 31, 1964 (UK) Decca LK 4577 (LP)
by Various Artists
READY, STEADY, GO
side one
    cut two: *I WANNA BE YOUR MAN*---L-McC---*1:44*
        by The Rolling Stones   Prod: Andrew Loog Oldham

40. JAN 31, 1964 (UK) Polydor NH 52-906
Recorded May 1961; A side vocals rerecorded 1963
by Tony Sheridan and The Beatles Prod: Bert Kaempfert
A: SWEET GEORGIA BROWN--Ben Bernie--Maceo Pinkard--
    Kenneth Casey---*2:03*
B: Nobody's Child---Mel Foree--Cy Coben---*2:58*

41. FEB 3, 1964 (US) MGM SE 4215 (LP)
by Tony Sheridan and The Beatles, and + The Beatles   Prod:
Bert Kaempfert   (Additional cuts by † Tony Sheridan and
The Beat Brothers, and % by The Titans)
**THE BEATLES WITH TONY SHERIDAN AND THEIR
GUESTS**
side one
    MY BONNIE---Charles Pratt---*2:06*
+ *CRY FOR A SHADOW*--Lennon--Harrison---*2:22*
%(johnson rag)
† (swanee river)
%(flying beat)
%(the darktown strutter's ball)
side two
    THE SAINTS---P.D.---*3:19*
%(rye beat)
† (you are my sunshine)
%(summertime beat)
    WHY---Tony Sheridan--Bill Crompton---*2:55*
%(happy new year beat)

42. FEB 7, 1964 (UK) Parlophone GEP 8891 (EP)
by The Beatles
ALL MY LOVING   Prod: George Martin
side one
    ALL MY LOVING---*2:04*
    ASK ME WHY---*2:24*
side two
    MONEY (THAT'S WHAT I WANT)---Berry Gordy--Janie
        Bradford---*2:47*
    P. S. I LOVE YOU---*2:02*

43. FEB 14, 1964 (UK) Parlophone GEP 8892 (EP)
by The Fourmost
THE FOURMOST SOUND
side one
I'M IN LOVE---L-McC---*2:07*
(respectable)
side two
HELLO LITTLE GIRL---L-McC---*1:50*
(just in case)

44. FEB 17, 1964 (CANADA) Capitol Of Canada 72144
by The Beatles Prod: George Martin
A: ALL MY LOVING---*2:04*
B: THIS BOY---*2:11*

45. FEB 26, 1964 (US) Vee Jay VJLP 1085 (LP)
by The Beatles Prod: George Martin (Additional cuts by
Frank Ifield)
**JOLLY WHAT! THE BEATLES AND FRANK IFIELD
ON STAGE**
side one
cut one: *PLEASE PLEASE ME*---*2:00*
cut six: *FROM ME TO YOU*---*1:49*
side two
cut two: *ASK ME WHY*---*2:24*
cut three: *THANK YOU GIRL*---*2:01*

46. FEB 28, 1964 (UK) Polydor NH 52-275
MAR 27, 1964 (US) MGM K 13227
by Tony Sheridan and The Beatles (A side), and The Beatles
(B side) Prod: Bert Kaempfert
A: WHY---Tony Sheridan--Bill Crompton---*2:55*
B: CRY FOR A SHADOW---Lennon--Harrison---*2:22*

47. FEB 28, 1964 (UK) Columbia DB 7225
APR 27, 1964 (US) Capitol 5175
Recorded: Jan. 21, 1964
by Peter and Gordon
A: A World Without Love---L-McC---*2:38*
B: (if i were you)

48. MAR 2, 1964 (US) Tollie 9001
by The Beatles Prod: George Martin
A: TWIST AND SHOUT---Bert Russell--Phil Medley---*2:32*
B: THERE'S A PLACE---*1:44*

49.	MAR 5, 1964 (GERMANY) Odeon 22671
Recorded: Jan. 29, 1964
by The Beatles Prod: George Martin
A: *Komm, Gib Mir Deine Hand*---L-McC–Nicolas–Hellmer
  ---2:23
*B: *Sie Liebt Dich*---L-McC–Nicolas–Montague---*2:16*

50.	MAR 16, 1964 (US) Capitol 5150
MAR 20, 1964 (UK) Parlophone R 5114
A side and B side vocal recorded: Feb. 25, 1964
B side instrumentals recorded: Jan. 29, 1964
by The Beatles Prod: George Martin
A: *Can't Buy Me Love---2:15*
B: *You Can't Do That---2:33*

51.	MAR 20, 1964 (UK) Parlophone GEP 8895 (EP)
by Billy J. Kramer with The Dakotas
I'LL KEEP YOU SATISFIED Prod: George Martin
side one
  I'LL KEEP YOU SATISFIED---L-McC---*2:04*
  (i know)
side two
  (dance with me)
  (it's up to you)

52.	MAR 23, 1964 (US) Vee Jay VJEP 1-903 (EP)
by The Beatles
THE BEATLES Prod: George Martin
side one
  MISERY---1:43
  A TASTE OF HONEY---Ric Marlow–Bobby Scott---*2:02*
side two
  ASK ME WHY---2:24
  ANNA (GO TO HIM)---Arthur Alexander---*2:56*

53.	MAR 23, 1964 (US) Vee Jay VJ 587
by The Beatles Prod: George Martin
A: *DO YOU WANT TO KNOW A SECRET---1:55*
B: *THANK YOU GIRL---2:01*

54.	MAR 30, 1964 (US) Imperial 66027
by Billy J. Kramer with The Dakotas Prod: George Martin
B: *BAD TO ME*---L-McC---*2:18*
A: *(little children)*

55.   APR   6, 1964   (US)   London 9657
by The Rolling Stones   Prod: Andrew Loog Oldham
B: I WANNA BE YOUR MAN---L-McC---*1:44*
A: (not fade away)

56.   APR 10, 1964   (US)   Capitol ST 2080 (LP)
New Songs Recorded: Late Feb. 1964
by The Beatles
THE BEATLES' SECOND ALBUM   Prod: George Martin
side one
  ROLL OVER BEETHOVEN---Chuck Berry---*2:44*
  THANK YOU GIRL---*2:01*
  YOU REALLY GOT A HOLD ON ME---William Robinson
    ---*2:58*
  DEVIL IN HER HEART---Richard B. Drapkin---*2:23*
  MONEY (THAT'S WHAT I WANT)---Berry Gordy—Janie
    Bradford---*2:47*
  YOU CAN'T DO THAT---*2:33*
side two
  Long Tall Sally---Enotris Johnson—Richard Penniman—
    Robert Blackwell---*1:58*
  I Call Your Name---*2:02*
  PLEASE MR. POSTMAN---Brian Holland—Robert Bateman
    —Berry Gordy---*2:34*
  I'LL GET YOU---*2:04*
  SHE LOVES YOU---*2:18*

57.   APR 10, 1964   (UK)   Parlophone GEP 8901 (EP)
by Cilla Black
ANYONE WHO HAD A HEART
side one
  (anyone who had a heart)
  (just for you)
side two
  LOVE OF THE LOVED---L-McC—*2:00*
  (shy of love)

58.   APR 27, 1964   (US)   Tollie 9008
by The Beatles   Prod: George Martin
A: LOVE ME DO---*2:19*
B: P. S. I LOVE YOU---*2:02*

59. MAY 8, 1964 (UK) Phillips BF 1335
by The Strangers with Mike Shannon
*A: *One And One Is Two*---L-McC---*2:10*
B: *(time and the river)*

60. MAY 8, 1964 (UK) Polydor SLPHM 237-622 (LP)
by Various Artists
(Cuts by Tony Sheridan and The Beatles   Prod: Bert
Kaempfert; † The Beatles   Prod: Bert Kaempfert;   % Tony
Sheridan with The Beat Brothers; $ The Beat Brothers;
+ The Jacques Denjean Orchestra; †† Flashes; %% The
Players; $$ The Gerard Poncet Orchestra)
LET'S DO THE TWIST, HULLY GULLY, SLOP, SURF,
LOCOMOTION, MONKEY
side one
$(lantern hully gully)
$(nick nack hully gully)
†*CRY FOR A SHADOW*---Lennon—Harrison---*2:22*
MY BONNIE---Charles Pratt---*2:06*
THE SAINTS---P. D.---*3:19*
WHY---Tony Sheridan—Bill Crompton---*2:55*
+*(be my baby)*
+*(the touch touch)*
side two
††*(ginchy)*
††*(twistarella)*
%%*(sheba)*
$$*(america)*
$$*(if i had a hammer)*
$$*(maria)*
$$*(surf and surf)*
%*(let's slop)*

61. MAY 11, 1964 (US) Capitol ST 2094 (LP)
by Various Artists
(Two cuts by The Beatles   Prod: George Martin)
CHART BUSTERS VOL. 4
side one
cut one: *I WANT TO HOLD YOUR HAND*---*2:24*
side two
cut five: *I SAW HER STANDING THERE*---*2:50*

62. MAY 11, 1964 (CANADA) Capitol Of Canada ST 6063 (LP)
by The Beatles
LONG TALL SALLY Prod: George Martin
side one
  I WANT TO HOLD YOUR HAND---2:24
  I SAW HER STANDING THERE---2:50
  YOU REALLY GOT A HOLD ON ME---William Robinson---
    2:58
  DEVIL IN HER HEART---Richard B. Drapkin---*2:23*
  ROLL OVER BEETHOVEN---Chuck Berry---*2:44*
  MISERY---1:43
side two
  Long Tall Sally---Enotris Johnson—Richard Penniman—
    Robert Blackwell---*1:58*
  I Call Your Name---2:02
  PLEASE MR. POSTMAN---Brian Holland—Robert Bateman
    —Berry Gordy---*2:34*
  THIS BOY---2:11
  I'LL GET YOU---2:04
  YOU CAN'T DO THAT---2:33

63. MAY 11, 1964 (US) Capitol EAP 2121 (EP)
by The Beatles
FOUR BY THE BEATLES Prod: George Martin
side one
  ROLL OVER BEETHOVEN---Chuck Berry---*2:44*
  ALL MY LOVING---2:04
side two
  THIS BOY---2:11
  PLEASE MR. POSTMAN---Brian Holland—Robert Bateman
    —Berry Gordy---*2:34*

64.   MAY 15, 1964   (UK)   Parlophone GEP 8907   (EP)
by Billy J. Kramer with The Dakotas
I'LL KEEP YOU SATISFIED NO. 2   Prod: George Martin
side one
(little children)
(they remind me of you)
side two
(beautiful dreamer)
I CALL YOUR NAME—L-McC—*2:00*

65.   MAY 21, 1964   (US)   Swan 4182
by The Beatles   Prod: George Martin
*A: *SIE LIEBT DICH*—L-McC—Nicolas—Montague—*2:16*
B: *I'LL GET YOU*—*2:04*

66.   MAY 29, 1964   (UK)   Polydor NH 52-317
Recorded: May 1961
by The Beatles (A side), and Tony Sheridan and The Beatles
   (B side)   Prod: Bert Kaempfert
A: *Ain't She Sweet*—Jack Yellen—Milton Ager—*2:12*
B: *If You Love Me, Baby* (also called: *Take Out Some
       Insurance On Me, Baby*)—Charles Singleton—Waldenese
       Hall—*2:52*

67.   MAY 29, 1964   (UK)   Columbia DB 7292
JUN 15, 1964   (US)   Capitol 5211
by Peter and Gordon   Prod: Norman Newell
A: *Nobody I Know*—L-McC—*2:27*
B: *(you don't have to tell me)*

68.   JUN 1, 1964   (US)   ATCO 6302
by Tony Sheridan and The Beatles   Prod: Bert Kaempfert
A: *SWEET GEORGIA BROWN*—Ben Bernie—Maceo Pinkard
       —Kenneth Casey—*2:03*
B: *Take Out Some Insurance On Me, Baby* (also called: *If You
       Love Me, Baby*)—Charles Singleton—Waldenese Hall—*2:52*

69.   JUN 5, 1964 (UK) Columbia SCX 3518 (LP)
by Peter and Gordon
PETER AND GORDON
side one
    cut six: *A WORLD WITHOUT LOVE*—L-McC—*2:38*

70.   JUN 5, 1964 (UK) Decca F 11916
JUL 6, 1964 (US) London 9681
by The Applejacks   Prod: Mike Smith
*A: Like Dreamers Do—L-McC—2:30
B: (everybody fall down)

71.   JUN 8, 1964 (US) Imperial 12267 (LP)
by Billy J. Kramer with The Dakotas
LITTLE CHILDREN Prod: George Martin
side two
    cut one: *DO YOU WANT TO KNOW A SECRET*—L-McC
    —*1:59*
    cut two: *BAD TO ME*—L-McC—*2:18*
    cut three: *I'LL KEEP YOU SATISFIED*—L-McC—*2:04*

72.   JUN 15, 1964 (US) Capitol ST 2115 (LP)
by Peter and Gordon
A WORLD WITHOUT LOVE
side one
    cut one: *A WORLD WITHOUT LOVE*—L-McC—*2:38*

73.   JUN 19, 1964 (UK) Parlophone GEP 8913 (EP)
New Songs Recorded: Late Feb. 1964
by The Beatles
LONG TALL SALLY Prod: George Martin
side one
    LONG TALL SALLY—Enotris Johnson—Richard Penniman
    —Robert Blackwell—*1:58*
    I CALL YOUR NAME—*2:02*
side two
    Slow Down—Larry Williams—*2:54*
    Matchbox—Carl Perkins—*1:37*

74.   JUN 19, 1964 (UK) Polydor 236-201 (LP)
Reissued: Aug. 4, 1967
by Tony Sheridan and The Beatles, and † The Beatles Prod:
Bert Kaempfert (Additional cuts by % Tony Sheridan and
The Beat Brothers)

THE BEATLES' FIRST
side one
†*AIN'T SHE SWEET*—Jack Yellen—Milton Ager—*2:12*
†*CRY FOR A SHADOW*—Lennon—Harrison—*2:22*
%*(let's dance)*
  MY BONNIE—Charles Pratt—*2:06*
  IF YOU LOVE ME, BABY—Charles Singleton—Waldenese
    Hall—*2:52*
%*(what'd i say)*
side two
  SWEET GEORGIA BROWN—Ben Bernie—Maceo Pinkard—
    Kenneth Casey—*2:03*
  THE SAINTS—P.D.—*3:19*
%*(ruby baby)*
  WHY—Tony Sheridan—Bill Crompton—*2:55*
  NOBODY'S CHILD—Mel Foree—Cy Coben—*2:58*
%*(ya ya)*

75.   JUN 26, 1964 (US) United Artists UAS 6366 (LP)
       New Songs Recorded: March—April, 1964; except † *recorded*
         April 16, 1964
       by The Beatles (Additional instrumental cuts by % George
         Martin & Orchestra)
       A HARD DAY'S NIGHT (Original Soundtrack Album)   Prod:
         George Martin
       side one
       †*A Hard Day's Night*—*2:28*
         Tell Me Why—*2:04*
         I'll Cry Instead—*2:06*
       %*(I Should Have Known Better*—L-McC—*2:16)*
         I'm Happy Just To Dance With You—*1:59*
       %*(And I Love Her*—L-McC—*3:42)*
       side two
         I Should Have Known Better—*2:42*
         If I Fell—*2:16*
         And I Love Her—*2:27*
       %*(Ringo's Theme (This Boy)*—L-McC—*3:06)*
         CAN'T BUY ME LOVE—*2:15*
       %*(A Hard Day's Night*—L-McC—*2:00)*

76.   JUL 6, 1964 (US) ATCO 6308
       by The Beatles (A side), and Tony Sheridan and The Beatles
         (B side) Prod: Bert Kaempfert
       A: *AIN'T SHE SWEET*—Jack Yellen—Milton Ager—*2:12*
       B: *NOBODY'S CHILD*—Mel Foree—Cy Coben—*2:58*

77. JUL 10, 1964 (UK) Parlophone PCS 3058 (LP)
New Songs On Side Two Recorded: June 1–3, 1964; except †
by The Beatles
A HARD DAY'S NIGHT Prod: George Martin
side one: Songs from the film *A Hard Day's Night*
 A Hard Day's Night—2:28
 I Should Have Known Better—2:42
 If I Fell—2:16
 I'm Happy Just To Dance With You—1:59
 And I Love Her—2:27
 Tell Me Why—2:04
 CAN'T BUY ME LOVE—2:15
side two
 Anytime At All—2:10
† I'll Cry Instead—1:44
 Things We Said Today—2:35
 When I Get Home—2:14
 YOU CAN'T DO THAT—2:33
 I'll Be Back—2:22

78. JUL 10, 1964 (UK) Parlophone R 5160
by The Beatles Prod: George Martin
A: A Hard Day's Night—2:28
B: Things We Said Today—2:35

79. JUL 10, 1964 (US) Imperial 66048
by Billy J. Kramer with The Dakotas Prod: George Martin
A: I'LL KEEP YOU SATISFIED—L-McC—2:04
B: (i know)

80. JUL 13, 1964 (US) Capitol 5222
by The Beatles Prod: George Martin
A: A Hard Day's Night—2:28
B: I Should Have Known Better—2:42

81. JUL 17, 1964 (UK) Parlophone R 5156
by Billy J. Kramer with The Dakotas Prod: George Martin
A: From A Window—L-McC—1:55
B: (second to none)

82. JUL 20, 1964 (US) Capitol 5234
by The Beatles Prod: George Martin
A: I'LL CRY INSTEAD—2:06
B: I'M HAPPY JUST TO DANCE WITH YOU—1:59

83.   JUL 20, 1964   (US)   Capitol 5235
       by The Beatles   Prod: George Martin
       A: AND I LOVE HER---2:27
       B: IF I FELL---2:16

84.   JUL 20, 1964   (US)   Capitol ST 2108   (LP)
       by The Beatles
       SOMETHING NEW   Prod: George Martin (and Dave Dexter in US)
       side one
         I'LL CRY INSTEAD---1:44
         Things We Said Today---2:35
         Anytime At All---2:10
         When I Get Home---2:14
         SLOW DOWN---Larry Williams---*2:54*
         MATCHBOX---Carl Perkins---*1:37*
       side two
         TELL ME WHY---2:04
         AND I LOVE HER---2:27
         I'M HAPPY JUST TO DANCE WITH YOU---1:59
         IF I FELL---2:16
         KOMM, GIB MIR DEINE HAND---L-McC–Nicolas–Hellmer *---2:23*

85.   JUL 24, 1964   (UK)   Columbia 33SX 1635   (LP)
       Recorded Live: April 19, 1964 at London's Prince Of Wales Theatre
       by Various Artists
       TRIBUTE TO MICHAEL HOLIDAY
       side two
         cut one: *A World Without Love*---L-McC
           by Peter and Gordon

86.   JUL 24, 1964   (UK)   Columbia 8348   (EP)
       by Peter and Gordon   Prod: Norman Newell
       NOBODY I KNOW
       side one
         NOBODY I KNOW---L-McC---*2:27*
         (lucille)
       side two
         (tell me how)
         (long time gone)

87.　JUL 31. 1964　(UK)　Parlophone R 5162
　　　AUG 17, 1964　(US)　Capitol 5258
　　　by Cilla Black　Prod: George Martin
　　　A:　*It's For You*—L-McC—*2:20*
　　　B:　*(he won't ask me)*

88.　AUG 10, 1964　(US)　Oldies 45　OL 149
　　　by The Beatles　Prod: George Martin
　　　A:　*DO YOU WANT TO KNOW A SECRET*—*1:55*
　　　B:　*THANK YOU GIRL*—*2:01*

89.　AUG 10, 1964　(US)　Oldies 45　OL 150
　　　by The Beatles　Prod: George Martin
　　　A:　*PLEASE PLEASE ME*—*2:00*
　　　B:　*FROM ME TO YOU*—*1:49*

90.　AUG 10, 1964　(US)　Oldies 45　OL 151
　　　by The Beatles　Prod: George Martin
　　　A:　*LOVE ME DO*—*2:19*
　　　B:　*P. S. I LOVE YOU*—*2:02*

91.　AUG 10, 1964　(US)　Oldies 45　OL 152
　　　by The Beatles　Prod: George Martin
　　　A:　*TWIST AND SHOUT*—Bert Russell—Phil Medley—*2:32*
　　　B:　*THERE'S A PLACE*—*1:44*

92.　AUG 12, 1964　(US)　Imperial 66051
　　　by Billy J. Kramer with The Dakotas　Prod: George Martin
　　　A:　*From A Window*—L-McC—*1:55*
　　　B:　*I'LL BE ON MY WAY*—L-McC—*1:38*

93.　AUG 24, 1964　(US)　Capitol 5255
　　　by The Beatles　Prod: George Martin
　　　A:　*SLOW DOWN*—Larry Williams—*2:54*
　　　A:　*MATCHBOX*—Carl Perkins—*1:37*

94.　SEP　7, 1964　(US)　Capitol DT 2125　(LP)
　　　by Various Artists
　　　　(Two cuts by The Beatles　Prod: George Martin, and † by
　　　　Peter and Gordon)
　　　THE BIG HITS FROM ENGLAND AND THE USA

side two
   cut one: *CAN'T BUY ME LOVE---2:15*
   cut two: *YOU CAN'T DO THAT---2:33*
†cut three: *A WORLD WITHOUT LOVE---L-McC---2:38*
†cut four: *NOBODY I KNOW---L-McC---2:27*

95.   SEP 11, 1964 (UK) Columbia DB 7356
       SEP 21, 1964 (US) Capitol 5272
       Recorded: Early Aug. 1964
       by Peter and Gordon Prod: Norman Newell
       A: I Don't Want To See You Again---L-McC---1:59
       B: (i would buy you presents)

96.   SEP 28, 1964 (US) Imperial 12273 (LP)
       by Billy J. Kramer with The Dakotas
       I'LL KEEP YOU SATISFIED Prod: George Martin
       side one
          cut one: *I'LL KEEP YOU SATISFIED---L-McC---2:04*
          cut two: *I CALL YOUR NAME---L-McC---2:00*
          cut six: *I'LL BE ON MY WAY---L-McC---1:38*
       side two
          cut one: *FROM A WINDOW---L-McC---1:55*

97.   OCT 1, 1964 (US) Vee Jay VJDX 30 (2 LPs)
       by The Beatles Prod: George Martin (Record One), and The
       Four Seasons (Record Two)
       THE BEATLES VS. THE FOUR SEASONS
       record one: The Beatles' Lineup
       side one
       I SAW HER STANDING THERE---2:50
       MISERY---1:43
       ANNA (GO TO HIM)---Arthur Alexander---*2:56*
       CHAINS---Gerry Goffin--Carole King---*2:21*
       BOYS---Luther Dixon--Wes Farrell---*2:24*
       ASK ME WHY---2:24
       side two
       PLEASE PLEASE ME---2:00
       BABY, IT'S YOU---Hal David--Burt Bacharach--Barney
         Williams---*2:36*
       DO YOU WANT TO KNOW A SECRET---1:55
       A TASTE OF HONEY---Ric Marlow--Bobby Scott---*2:02*
       THERE'S A PLACE---1:44
       TWIST AND SHOUT---Bert Russell--Phil Medley---*2:32*
       record two: The Four Seasons' Lineup
       (Twelve cuts by The Four Seasons)

98.   OCT 5, 1964 (US) ATCO SD 33-169 (LP)
      by Tony Sheridan and The Beatles, and † The Beatles
        Prod: Bert Kaempfert (Additional cuts by % The Swallows)
      AIN'T SHE SWEET
      side one
      †AIN'T SHE SWEET--Jack Yellen—Milton Ager--*2:12*
        SWEET GEORGIA BROWN---Ben Bernie—Maceo Pinkard—
          Kenneth Casey--*2:03*
        TAKE OUT SOME INSURANCE ON ME, BABY--Charles
          Singleton—Waldenese Hall--*2:52*
        NOBODY'S CHILD--Mel Foree—Cy Coben--*2:58*
      %(i wanna be your man)
      %(she loves you)
      side two
      %(how do you do it)
      %(please please me)
      %(i'll keep you satisfied)
      %(i'm telling you now)
      %(i want to hold your hand)
      %(from me to you)

99.   OCT 12, 1964 (US) Vee Jay VJLP 1092 (LP)
      by The Beatles
      **SONGS, PICTURES AND STORIES OF THE FABULOUS
      BEATLES** Prod: George Martin
      side one
        I SAW HER STANDING THERE--*2:50*
        MISERY--*1:43*
        ANNA (GO TO HIM)---Arthur Alexander--*2:56*
        CHAINS---Gerry Goffin—Carole King--*2:21*
        BOYS--Luther Dixon—Wes Farrell--*2:24*
        ASK ME WHY--*2:24*
      side two
        PLEASE PLEASE ME--*2:00*
        BABY, IT'S YOU---Hal David—Burt Bacharach—Barney
          Williams--*2:36*
        DO YOU WANT TO KNOW A SECRET--*1:55*
        A TASTE OF HONEY--Ric Marlow—Bobby Scott--*2:02*
        THERE'S A PLACE--*1:44*
        TWIST AND SHOUT---Bert Russell—Phil Medley--*2:32*

100. OCT 16, 1964 (EUROPE) Parlophone DP 562
JAN 29, 1965 (UK) Parlophone DP 562
by The Beatles Prod: George Martin
A: IF I FELL--2:16
B: TELL ME WHY--2:04

101. OCT 23, 1964 (UK) Parlophone GEP 8916 (EP)
by Cilla Black
IT'S FOR YOU Prod: George Martin
side one
IT'S FOR YOU--L-McC--2:20
(he won't ask me)
side two
(you're my world)
(suffer now i must)

102. OCT 30, 1964 (UK) Columbia DB 7390
by Alma Cogan
*B: I Knew Right Away--Alma Cogan--Stan Foster
Paul: Tambourine
A: (it's you)

103. NOV 4, 1964 (UK) Parlophone GEP 8920 (EP)
by The Beatles
EXTRACTS FROM THE FILM A HARD DAY'S NIGHT
Prod: George Martin
side one
I SHOULD HAVE KNOWN BETTER--2:42
IF I FELL--2:16
side two
TELL ME WHY--2:04
AND I LOVE HER--2:27

104. NOV 6, 1964 (UK) Parlophone GEP 8921 (EP)
by Billy J. Kramer with The Dakotas
FROM A WINDOW Prod: George Martin
side one
FROM A WINDOW--L-McC--1:55
(second to none)
side two
(dance with me)
(the twelfth of never)

105.　NOV 6, 1964 (UK) Parlophone GEP 8924 (EP)
by The Beatles
EXTRACTS FROM THE ALBUM A HARD DAY'S NIGHT
Prod: George Martin
side one
ANYTIME AT ALL---2:10
I'LL CRY INSTEAD---1:44
side two
THINGS WE SAID TODAY---2:35
WHEN I GET HOME---2:14

106.　NOV 23, 1964 (US) Capitol STBO 2222 (2 LPs)
Live cut recorded: Aug. 23, 1964 at The Hollywood Bowl †
by The Beatles; Written and Narrated by John Babcock, Al
Wiman and Roger Christian
THE BEATLES' STORY Prod: Gary Usher and Roger Christian
side one: *12:53*
On Stage With The Beatles---1:03
How Beatlemania Began---1:18
Beatlemania In Action---2:24
Man Behind The Beatles—Brian Epstein---3:01
John Lennon---4:24
Who's A Millionaire?---0:43
side two: *13:07*
Beatles Will Be Beatles---7:37
Man Behind The Music—George Martin---0:47
George Harrison---4:43
side three: *9:18*
A Hard Day's Night—Their First Movie---3:45
Paul McCartney---1:55
Sneaky Haircuts And More About Paul---3:38
side four: *14:36*
†Twist And Shout—Bert Russell—Phil Medley---0:48
The Beatles Look At Life---1:51
"Victims" Of Beatlemania---1:21
Beatle Medley---3:56
Ringo Starr---6:19
Liverpool And All The World!---1:09

107.　NOV 23, 1964 (US) Capitol 5327
NOV 27, 1964 (UK) Parlophone R 5200
Recorded: Early Oct. 1964
by The Beatles Prod: George Martin
A: I Feel Fine---2:20
A: She's A Woman---2:57

108. DEC 4, 1964 (UK) Parlophone PCS 3062 (LP)
Recorded: Late Sept.—Mid Oct. 1964
by The Beatles
BEATLES FOR SALE Prod: George Martin
side one
  No Reply—2:15
  I'm A Loser—2:31
  Baby's In Black—2:02
  Rock And Roll Music—Chuck Berry—*2:02*
  I'll Follow The Sun—1:46
  Mr. Moonlight—Roy Lee Johnson—*2:35*
  medley: 2:30
    Kansas City—Jerry Leiber—Mike Stoller—*1:12*
    Hey—Hey—Hey—Hey!—Richard Penniman—*1:18*
side two
  Eight Days A Week—2:43
  Words Of Love—Buddy Holly—*2:10*
  Honey Don't—Carl Perkins—*2:56*
  Every Little Thing—2:01
  I Don't Want To Spoil The Party—2:33
  What You're Doing—2:30
  Everybody's Trying To Be My Baby—Carl Perkins—*2:24*

109. DEC 11, 1964 (US) Capitol ST 2220 (LP)
by Peter and Gordon
I DON'T WANT TO SEE YOU AGAIN Prod: Norman Newell
side one
  cut one: *I DON'T WANT TO SEE YOU AGAIN*—L-McC—
  1:59
side two
  cut one: *NOBODY I KNOW*—L-McC—*2:27*

110. DEC 15, 1964 (US) Capitol ST 2228 (LP)
by The Beatles
BEATLES '65 Prod: George Martin (and Dave Dexter in US)
side one
  No Reply—2:15
  I'm A Loser—2:31
  Baby's In Black—2:02
  Rock And Roll Music—Chuck Berry—*2:02*
  I'll Follow The Sun—1:46
  Mr. Moonlight—Roy Lee Johnson—*2:35*

side two
    Honey Don't—Carl Perkins—*2:56*
    I'LL BE BACK—*2:22*
    She's A Woman—*2:57*
    I Feel Fine—*2:20*
    Everybody's Trying To Be My Baby—Carl Perkins—*2:24*

111.   DEC 18, 1964 (UK) Columbia 33SX 1660 (LP)
     by Peter and Gordon Prod: Norman Newell
     IN TOUCH WITH PETER AND GORDON
     side one
       cut seven: *I DON'T WANT TO SEE YOU AGAIN*—L-McC—
       1:59

112.   DEC 18, 1964 (FAN CLUB)
     Recorded: Oct. 26–28, 1964
     by The Beatles Prod: George Martin
     Another Beatles Christmas Record—*4:05*

Beatles VI

Capitol ST 2358 (LP)

4 By The Beatles   **Capitol R - 5365 (EP)**

I'm Down/Help   **Capitol 5476 (45)**

I Don't Want To   **Capitol 5371 (45)**
Spoil The Party/Eight Days A Week

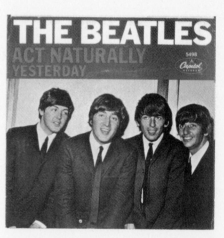

Act Naturally/Yesterday   **Capitol 5498 (45)**

1965

"Harold Wilson?
Isn't He On Decca?"-- Lennon

113. FEB 1, 1965 (US) Capitol R 5365 (EP)
by The Beatles
4 BY THE BEATLES Prod: George Martin
side one
HONEY DON'T---Carl Perkins---*2:56*
I'M A LOSER---*2:31*
side two
MR. MOONLIGHT---Roy Lee Johnson---*2:35*
EVERYBODY'S TRYING TO BE MY BABY---Carl Perkins
---*2:24*

114. FEB 15, 1965 (US) Capitol 5371
by The Beatles Prod: George Martin
A: EIGHT DAYS A WEEK---*2:43*
B: I DON'T WANT TO SPOIL THE PARTY---*2:33*

115. MAR 22, 1965 (US) Capitol ST 2309 (LP)
by The Beatles
THE EARLY BEATLES Prod: George Martin
side one
LOVE ME DO---*2:19*
TWIST AND SHOUT---Bert Russell—Phil Medley---*2:32*
ANNA (GO TO HIM)---Arthur Alexander---*2:56*
CHAINS---Gerry Goffin—Carole King---*2:21*
BOYS---Luther Dixon—Wes Farrell---*2:24*
ASK ME WHY---*2:24*
side two
PLEASE PLEASE ME---*2:00*
P. S. I LOVE YOU---*2:02*
BABY, IT'S YOU---Hal David—Burt Bacharach—Barney
Williams---*2:36*
A TASTE OF HONEY---Ric Marlow—Bobby Scott---*2:02*
DO YOU WANT TO KNOW A SECRET---*1:55*

116.　APR　6, 1965　(UK)　Parlophone GEP 8931 (EP)
　　　by The Beatles
　　　BEATLES FOR SALE　Prod: George Martin
　　　side one
　　　　NO REPLY---2:15
　　　　I'M A LOSER---2:31
　　　side two
　　　　ROCK AND ROLL MUSIC--Chuck Berry---2:02
　　　　EIGHT DAYS A WEEK---2:43

117.　APR　9, 1965　(UK)　Parlophone R 5265
　　　APR 19, 1965　(US)　Capitol 5407
　　　Recorded: Feb. 1965
　　　by The Beatles　Prod: George Martin
　　　A:　Ticket To Ride---3:03
　　　B:　Yes It Is---2:40

118.　JUN　4, 1965　(UK)　Parlophone GEP 8938 (EP)
　　　by The Beatles
　　　BEATLES FOR SALE (NO. 2)　Prod: George Martin
　　　side one
　　　　I'LL FOLLOW THE SUN---1:46
　　　　BABY'S IN BLACK---2:02
　　　side two
　　　　WORDS OF LOVE---Buddy Holly---2:10
　　　　I DON'T WANT TO SPOIL THE PARTY---2:33

119.　JUN 14, 1965　(US)　Capitol ST 2358 (LP)
　　　New Songs Recorded: May 10–11, 1965
　　　by The Beatles
　　　BEATLES VI　Prod: George Martin
　　　side one
　　　　MEDLEY: 2:30
　　　　　KANSAS CITY--Jerry Leiber–Mike Stoller---1:12
　　　　　HEY–HEY–HEY–HEY!---Richard Penniman---1:18
　　　　EIGHT DAYS A WEEK---2:43
　　　　You Like Me Too Much---Harrison---2:34
　　　　Bad Boy---Larry Williams---2:17
　　　　I DON'T WANT TO SPOIL THE PARTY---2:33
　　　　WORDS OF LOVE---Buddy Holly---2:10

side two
WHAT YOU'RE DOING—2:30
YES IT IS—2:40
Dizzy Miss Lizzie—Larry Williams—2:51
Tell Me What You See—2:35
EVERY LITTLE THING—2:01

120.   JUL 5, 1965 (US) Liberty 55806
Recorded: Apr. 1965
by P. J. Proby   Prod: Ron Richards
B: That Means A Lot—L-McC—2:31
A: (let the water run down)

121.   JUL 19, 1965 (US) Capitol 5476
JUL 23, 1965 (UK) Parlophone R 5305
A side recorded: Apr. 13, 1965
B side recorded: Late May 1965
by The Beatles   Prod: George Martin
A: Help!—2:16
*B: I'm Down—2:30

122.   AUG 6, 1965 (UK) Parlophone PCS 3071 (LP)
New Songs on side one recorded: Early Feb.—Early Mar. 1965,
    except †
New Songs on side two recorded: Late May—Early June 1965
by The Beatles
HELP!   Prod: George Martin
side one: Songs from the film Help!
†Help!—2:16
    The Night Before—2:33
    You've Got To Hide Your Love Away—2:08
    I Need You—Harrison—2:28
    Another Girl—2:02
    You're Gonna Lose That Girl—2:18
    TICKET TO RIDE—3:03
side two
    Act Naturally—Johnny Russell—Vonie Morrison—2:27
    It's Only Love—1:53
    YOU LIKE ME TOO MUCH—Harrison—2:34
    TELL ME WHAT YOU SEE—2:35
    I've Just Seen A Face—2:04
    Yesterday—2:04
    DIZZY MISS LIZZIE—Larry Williams—2:51

123.　AUG 13, 1965　(US)　Capitol SMAS 2386　(LP)
by The Beatles　(Additional instrumental cuts † by George
Martin & Orchestra)
HELP! (Original Soundtrack Album)　Prod: George Martin
(and Dave Dexter in US)
side one
†(James Bond Theme---Monty Norman---0:16)
Help!---2:16
The Night Before---2:33
†(From Me To You Fantasy---L-McC---2:03)
You've Got To Hide Your Love Away---2:08
I Need You---Harrison---2:28
†(In The Tyrol---Richard Wagner–arr. Ken Thorne---2:21)
side two
Another Girl---2:02
†(Another Hard Day's Night---L-McC---2:28)
TICKET TO RIDE---3:03
†(The Bitter End---Ken Thorne/You Can't Do That---L-McC---
2:20)
You're Gonna Lose That Girl---2:18
†(The Chase---Ken Thorne---2:24)

124.　AUG 23, 1965　(US)　Liberty LST 7421　(LP)
by P. J. Proby　Prod: Ron Richards
P. J. PROBY
side one
cut one: *THAT MEANS A LOT---L-McC---2:31*

125.　SEP 10, 1965　(UK)　Fontana TF 603
SEP 20, 1965　(US)　Fontana 1525
Recorded: Early Aug. 1965
by The Silkie　Prod: John Lennon and Paul McCartney
A: *You've Got To Hide Your Love Away---L-McC---2:20*
B: *(city winds)*

126.　SEP 13, 1965　(US)　Capitol 5498
by The Beatles　Prod: George Martin
A: *YESTERDAY---2:04*
B: *ACT NATURALLY---Johnny Russell–Vonie Morrison---2:27*

127.　SEP 17, 1965　(UK)　Liberty 10215
by P. J. Proby　Prod: Ron Richards
A: *THAT MEANS A LOT---L-McC---2:31*
B: *(my prayer)*

128. OCT 11, 1965 (US) Capitol Starline 6061
by The Beatles Prod: George Martin
A: TWIST AND SHOUT---Bert Russell--Phil Medley---*2:32*
B: THERE'S A PLACE---*1:44*

129. OCT 11, 1965 (US) Capitol Starline 6062
by The Beatles Prod: George Martin
A: LOVE ME DO---*2:19*
B: P. S. I LOVE YOU---*2:02*

130. OCT 11, 1965 (US) Capitol Starline 6063
by The Beatles Prod: George Martin
A: PLEASE PLEASE ME---*2:00*
B: FROM ME TO YOU---*1:49*

131. OCT 11, 1965 (US) Capitol Starline 6064
by The Beatles Prod: George Martin
A: DO YOU WANT TO KNOW A SECRET---*1:55*
B: THANK YOU GIRL---*2:01*

132. OCT 11, 1965 (US) Capitol Starline 6065
by The Beatles Prod: George Martin
A: ROLL OVER BEETHOVEN---Chuck Berry---*2:44*
B: MISERY---*1:43*

133. OCT 11, 1965 (US) Capitol Starline 6066
by The Beatles Prod: George Martin
A: BOYS---Luther Dixon--Wes Farrell---*2:24*
B: MEDLEY: 2:30
    KANSAS CITY---Jerry Leiber--Mike Stoller---*1:12*
    HEY--HEY--HEY--HEY!---Richard Penniman---*1:18*

134. NOV 22, 1965 (US) Fontana SRF 67548 (LP)
by The Silkie Prod: John Lennon and Paul McCartney
YOU'VE GOT TO HIDE YOUR LOVE AWAY
side one
  cut one: *YOU'VE GOT TO HIDE YOUR LOVE AWAY*--
    L-McC---*2:20*

135. DEC 3, 1965 (UK) Parlophone R 5389
DEC 6, 1965 (US) Capitol 5555
Recorded: Early Nov. 1965
by The Beatles Prod: George Martin
A: We Can Work It Out---*2:10*
A: Day Tripper---*2:37*

136. DEC 3, 1965   (UK)   Parlophone PCS 3075 (LP)
Recorded: Mid Oct.—Early Nov. 1965
by The Beatles
RUBBER SOUL   Prod: George Martin
side one
Drive My Car—2:25
Norwegian Wood (This Bird Has Flown)—2:00
You Won't See Me—3:19
Nowhere Man—2:40
Think For Yourself—Harrison—2:16
The Word—2:42
Michelle—2:42
side two
What Goes On?—Lennon—McCartney—Starkey—2:44
Girl—2:26
I'm Looking Through You—2:20
In My Life—2:23
Wait—2:13
If I Needed Someone—Harrison—2:19
Run For Your Life—2:21

137. DEC 6, 1965   (US)   Capitol ST 2442 (LP)
by The Beatles
RUBBER SOUL   Prod: George Martin
side one
I'VE JUST SEEN A FACE—2:04
Norwegian Wood (This Bird Has Flown)—2:00
You Won't See Me—3:19
Think For Yourself—Harrison—2:16
The Word—2:42
Michelle—2:42
side two
IT'S ONLY LOVE—1:53
Girl—2:26
I'm Looking Through You—2:20
In My Life—2:23
Wait—2:13
Run For Your Life—2:21

138.   DEC   6, 1965   (UK)   Parlophone GEP 8946   (EP)
by The Beatles
THE BEATLES' MILLION SELLERS (also called: **BEATLES'
GOLDEN DISCS**)   Prod: George Martin
side one
   SHE LOVES YOU---2:18
   I WANT TO HOLD YOUR HAND---2:24
side two
   CAN'T BUY ME LOVE---2:15
   I FEEL FINE---2:20

139.   DEC 15, 1965   (US)   Capitol Starline 6076
by Peter and Gordon
A: A WORLD WITHOUT LOVE---L-McC---2:38
B: NOBODY I KNOW---L-McC---2:27

140.   DEC 17, 1965   (FAN CLUB)
Recorded: Oct. 19, 1965
by The Beatles   Prod: George Martin
The Beatles Third Christmas Record---6:26

51

Rain/Paperback Writer   Capitol 5651 **(45)**

Nowhere Man   Parlophone GEP 8952 **(EP)**

1966

Is All This Screaming Necessary?

141.   JAN 10, 1966 (US) Capitol 5579
FEB 11, 1966 (UK) Columbia DB 7834
by Peter and Gordon
A: Woman—Paul McCartney (as Bernard Webb, and as A.
    Smith)—*2:21*
B: (wrong from the start)

142.   FEB 21, 1966 (US) Capitol 5587
by The Beatles   Prod: George Martin
A: NOWHERE MAN—*2:40*
B: WHAT GOES ON—Lennon—McCartney—Starkey—*2:44*

143.   MAR 4, 1966 (UK) Parlophone GEP 8948 (EP)
by The Beatles
YESTERDAY   Prod: George Martin
side one
   YESTERDAY—*2:04*
   ACT NATURALLY—Johnny Russell—Vonie Morrison—*2:27*
side two
   YOU LIKE ME TOO MUCH—Harrison—*2:34*
   IT'S ONLY LOVE—*1:53*

144.   MAR 7, 1966 (US) Capitol ST 2477 (LP)
by Peter and Gordon
WOMAN
side one
   cut one: *WOMAN*—Paul McCartney—*2:21*

145.   MAY 30, 1966 (US) Capitol 5651
JUN 10, 1966 (UK) Parlophone R 5452
A side recorded: Apr. 13, 1966
B side recorded: Late Apr. 1966

by The Beatles   Prod: George Martin
A: *Paperback Writer---2:25*
B: *Rain---2:59*

146.   JUN 17, 1966 (UK)   Columbia SCX 6045 (LP)
by Peter and Gordon
PETER AND GORDON
side one
   cut seven: *WOMAN---Paul McCartney---2:21*

147.   JUN 20, 1966 (US)   Capitol ST 2553 (LP)
New Songs Recorded: Late Apr.—Early May 1966
by The Beatles
"YESTERDAY"...AND TODAY   Prod: George Martin
   (Prepared for release in the USA by Bill Miller)
side one
   DRIVE MY CAR---2:25
   I'm Only Sleeping---2:58
   NOWHERE MAN---2:40
   Dr. Robert---2:14
   YESTERDAY---2:04
   ACT NATURALLY---Johnny Russell—Vonie Morrison---2:27
side two
   And Your Bird Can Sing---2:02
   IF I NEEDED SOMEONE---Harrison---2:19
   WE CAN WORK IT OUT---2:10
   WHAT GOES ON?---Lennon—McCartney—Starkey---2:44
   DAY TRIPPER---2:37

148.   JUL 5, 1966 (US)   Capitol Starline ST 2549 (LP)
by Peter and Gordon
THE BEST OF PETER AND GORDON
side one
   cut one: *A WORLD WITHOUT LOVE---L-McC---2:38*
   cut five: *I DON'T WANT TO SEE YOU AGAIN---L-McC---*
      1:59
side two
   cut one: *WOMAN---Paul McCartney---2:21*

149.   JUL 8, 1966 (UK)   Parlophone GEP 8952 (EP)
by The Beatles
NOWHERE MAN   Prod: George Martin
side one
   NOWHERE MAN---2:40
   DRIVE MY CAR---2:25

54

MICHELLE—2:42
YOU WON'T SEE ME—3:19

150.   AUG 5, 1966 (UK) Parlophone PCS 7009 (LP)
New Songs Recorded: Early April—Mid June 1966
by The Beatles
REVOLVER Prod: George Martin
side one
Taxman—Harrison—2:36
Eleanor Rigby—2:11
I'M ONLY SLEEPING—2:58
Love You Too—Harrison—3:00
Here, There And Everywhere—2:29
Yellow Submarine—2:40
She Said She Said—2:39
side two
Good Day Sunshine—2:08
AND YOUR BIRD CAN SING—2:02
For No One—2:03
DR. ROBERT—2:14
I Want To Tell You—Harrison—2:30
Got To Get You Into My Life—2:31
Tomorrow Never Knows—3:00

151.   AUG 5, 1966 (UK) Parlophone R 5493
AUG 8, 1966 (US) Capitol 5715
by The Beatles   Prod: George Martin
A: Yellow Submarine—2:40
A: Eleanor Rigby—2:11

152.   AUG 5, 1966 (UK) Parlophone R 5489
AUG 29, 1966 (US) ABC 10842
Recorded: Mid July 1966
by Cliff Bennett and The Rebel Rousers   Prod: Paul McCartney
A: Got To Get You Into My Life—L-McC
B: (baby each day)

153.   AUG 5, 1966 (UK) Liberty LEP 2251 (EP)
by P. J. Proby   Prod: Ron Richards
P. J.'s HITS
side one
(hold me)
(together)

side two
   THAT MEANS A LOT—L-McC—*2:31*
   (maria)

154.   AUG 8, 1966 (US) Capitol ST 2576 (LP)
    by The Beatles
    REVOLVER Prod: George Martin (Prepared for release in
    the USA by Bill Miller)
    side one
      Taxman—Harrison—*2:36*
      Eleanor Rigby—*2:11*
      Love You Too—Harrison—*3:00*
      Here, There And Everywhere—*2:29*
      Yellow Submarine—*2:40*
      She Said She Said—*2:39*
    side two
      Good Day Sunshine—*2:08*
      For No One—*2:03*
      I Want To Tell You—Harrison—*2:30*
      Got To Get You Into My Life—*2:31*
      Tomorrow Never Knows—*3:00*

155.   AUG 15, 1966 (US) Metro MS 563 (LP)
    by Tony Sheridan and The Beatles, and † The Beatles Prod:
    Bert Kaempfert (Additional cuts by % Tony Sheridan and
    The Beat Brothers, and $ The Titans)
    THIS IS WHERE IT STARTED
    side one
      MY BONNIE—Charles Pratt—*2:06*
    †*CRY FOR A SHADOW*—Lennon—Harrison—*2:22*
    $*(johnson rag)*
    %*(swanee river)*
    $*(the darktown strutter's ball)*
    side two
      THE SAINTS—P.D.—*3:19*
    $*(rye beat)*
    %*(you are my sunshine)*
    $*(summertime beat)*
      WHY—Tony Sheridan—Bill Crompton—*2:55*

157.   OCT 17, 1966 (US) Clarion 601 (LP)
        by Tony Sheridan and The Beatles, and † The Beatles   Prod:
        Bert Kaempfert (Additional cuts by % The Swallows)
        **THE AMAZING BEATLES AND OTHER GREAT ENGLISH
        GROUP SOUNDS**
        side one
        † AIN'T SHE SWEET---Jack Yellen--Milton Ager---*2:12*
        %(please please me)
        %(from me to you)
            TAKE OUT SOME INSURANCE ON ME, BABY---Charles
                Singleton--Waldenese Hall--*2:52*
            NOBODY'S CHILD---Mel Foree--Cy Coben---*2:58*
        side two
        %(she loves you)
        %(i'm telling you now)
            SWEET GEORGIA BROWN---Ben Bernie--Maceo Pinkard--
                Kenneth Casey--*2:03*
        %(i want to hold your hand)
        %(i wanna be your man)

158.   NOV 18, 1966 (UK) Columbia DB 8061
        by The Escourts   Prod: Paul McCartney
        *A: From Head To Toe---William Robinson--*2:31*
        *B: Night Time---Paddy Chambers---*2:53*

159.   NOV 28, 1966 (US) Clarion 609 (LP)
        by Various Artists
        THE ORIGINAL DISCOTHEQUE HITS
        side one
            cut three: *TAKE OUT SOME INSURANCE ON ME, BABY*
                ---Charles Singleton--Waldenese Hall--*2:52*
                by Tony Sheridan and The Beatles   Prod: Bert Kaempfert

160.   DEC 10, 1966 (UK) Parlophone PCS 7016 (LP)
        by The Beatles
        A COLLECTION OF BEATLE OLDIES   Prod: George Martin
        side one
            SHE LOVES YOU---*2:18*
            FROM ME TO YOU---*1:49*
            WE CAN WORK IT OUT--*2:10*
            HELP!---*2:16*
            MICHELLE---*2:42*
            YESTERDAY---*2:04*
            I FEEL FINE---*2:20*
            YELLOW SUBMARINE---*2:40*

side two
   CAN'T BUY ME LOVE---2:15
   BAD BOY---Larry Williams---*2:17*
   DAY TRIPPER---2:37
   A HARD DAY'S NIGHT---2:28
   TICKET TO RIDE---3:03
   PAPERBACK WRITER---2:25
   ELEANOR RIGBY---2:11
   I WANT TO HOLD YOUR HAND---2:24

161.   DEC 16, 1966 (FAN CLUB)
   Recorded: Nov. 25, 1966
   by The Beatles Prod: George Martin
   The Beatles Fourth Christmas Record---6:40
   Pantomime: Everywhere It's Christmas
   side one: *3:04*
   Song: Everywhere It's Christmas---0:33
   Orowanyna---0:48
    Corsican Choir and Small Choir
   A Rare Cheese---0:33
    Two Elderly Scotsmen
   The Feast---0:44
   The Loyal Toast---0:26
   side two: *3:36*
   Podgy The Bear and Jasper---0:53
   Felpin Mansions: Part One---0:36
    Count Balder and Butler
   Felpin Mansions: Part Two---0:27
    The Count and The Pianist
   Song: Please Don't Bring Your Banjo Back---0:43
   Everywhere It's Christmas---0:03
    Mal Evans
   Reprise: Everywhere It's Christmas---0:54

162.   DEC 23, 1966 (UK) United Artists UP 1165
   Recorded: Dec. 10, 1966
   by The George Martin Orchestra Prod: George Martin
   *A: Love In The Open Air---Paul McCartney---*2:18*
   *B: Theme From "The Family Way"---Paul McCartney---*2:05*

The Beatles

Penny Lane/   **Capitol 5810 (45)**
   Strawberry Fields Forever (A side)

Penny Lane/   **Capitol 5810 (45)**
   Strawberry Fields Forever (B side)

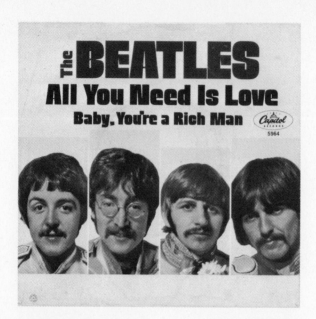

All You Need Is Love/   Capitol 5964   (45)
   Baby You're A Rich Man

Magical Mystery Tour   Parlophone SMMT 1/2   (2 EPs)

1967
It's Lonely At The Top

163.   JAN 6, 1967 (UK) Decca SKL 4847 (LP)
JUN 12, 1967 (US) London MS 82007 (LP)
Recorded: Nov.–Dec. 1966
by The George Martin Orchestra
THE FAMILY WAY (Original Soundtrack Album) Prod:
  George Martin
side one
  Love In The Open Air---Paul McCartney---*13:09*
    cut one: *2:07*
    cut two: *1:10*
    cut three: *1:00*
    cut four: *1:28*
    cut five: *3:26*
    cut six: *3:58*
side two
  Love In The Open Air---Paul McCartney---*11:10*
    cut one: *2:09*
    cut two: *1:19*
    cut three: *1:03*
    cut four: *1:46*
    cut five: *1:00*
    cut six: *2:51*
    cut seven: *1:02*

164.   JAN 27, 1967 (UK) Parlophone PCS 7017 (LP)
by Cliff Bennett and The Rebel Rousers   Prod: Paul McCartney
GOT TO GET YOU INTO OUR LIFE
side one
  cut one: *GOT TO GET YOU INTO MY LIFE*--L-McC

165.   FEB 13, 1967 (US) Capitol 5810
FEB 17, 1967 (UK) Parlophone R 5570
Recorded: Dec. 1966

61

by The Beatles   Prod: George Martin
A: Penny Lane—3:00
A: Strawberry Fields Forever—4:05

166. APR 24, 1967   (US)   United Artists UA 50148
by George Martin & His Orchestra   Prod: George Martin
*A: LOVE IN THE OPEN AIR—Paul McCartney—2:18
B: (bahama sound)

167. MAY 1, 1967   (US)   Capitol Starline 6155
by Peter and Gordon
A: I DON'T WANT TO SEE YOU AGAIN—L-McC—1:59
B: WOMAN—Paul McCartney—2:21

168. JUN 1, 1967   (UK)   Parlophone PCS 7027 (LP)
JUN 2, 1967   (US)   Capitol SMAS 2653 (LP)
Recorded: Early Jan.—Late Apr. 1967, except † Dec. 1966
by The Beatles
SGT. PEPPER'S LONELY HEARTS CLUB BAND   Prod:
George Martin
side one
  Sgt. Pepper's Lonely Hearts Club Band—1:59
  With A Little Help From My Friends—2:46
  Lucy In The Sky With Diamonds—3:25
  Getting Better—2:47
  Fixing A Hole—2:33
  She's Leaving Home—3:24
  Being For The Benefit Of Mr. Kite—2:36
side two
  Within You Without You—Harrison—5:03
† When I'm Sixty-Four—2:38
  Lovely Rita—2:43
  Good Morning Good Morning—2:35
  Sgt. Pepper's Lonely Hearts Club Band (Reprise)—1:20
  A Day In The Life—5:03

169. JUL 7, 1967   (UK)   Parlophone R 5620
JUL 17, 1967   (US)   Capitol 5964
A side recorded: June 25, 1967
B side recorded: May 1967
by The Beatles   Prod: George Martin
A: All You Need Is Love—3:57
B: Baby, You're A Rich Man—3:07

170.   AUG 18, 1967   (UK)   Decca F 12654
         AUG 28, 1967   (US)   London 905
         by The Rolling Stones   Prod: Andrew Loog Oldham
         A: *We Love You*---Mick Jagger–Keith Richard---*4:39*
             John and Paul: Backing Vocals
         B: *(dandelion)*

171.   OCT 13, 1967   (UK)   United Artists UP 1196
         Vocal Recorded: Sept.–Oct. 1966
         by Musketeer Gripweed (John) and The Third Troop
       *A: *How I Won The War*---Ken Thorne
             John: Voice
         B: *(aftermath)*

172.   OCT 20, 1967   (UK)   Marmalade 598-005
         Recorded: Late July 1967
         by The Chris Barber Band
         A: *Catcall*---Paul McCartney
         B: *(mercy mercy mercy)*

173.   NOV 24, 1967   (UK)   Parlophone R 5655
         NOV 27, 1967   (US)   Capitol 2056
         A side recorded: Nov. 4–5, 1967
         by The Beatles   Prod: George Martin
         A: *Hello Goodbye*---*3:24*
         B: *I Am The Walrus*---*4:35*

174.   NOV 27, 1967   (US)   Capitol SMAL 2835   (LP)
         Side one recorded: Sept.–Oct. 1967
         by The Beatles
         MAGICAL MYSTERY TOUR   Prod: George Martin
         side one: Songs from the film *Magical Mystery Tour*
           Magical Mystery Tour---*2:48*
           The Fool On The Hill---*3:00*
           Flying---Lennon–McCartney–Harrison–Starr---*2:16*
           Blue Jay Way---Harrison---*3:50*
           Your Mother Should Know---*2:33*
           I Am The Walrus---*4:35*
         side two
           Hello Goodbye---*3:24*
           STRAWBERRY FIELDS FOREVER---*4:05*
           PENNY LANE---*3:00*
           BABY, YOU'RE A RICH MAN---*3:07*
           ALL YOU NEED IS LOVE---*3:57*

175. DEC 8, 1967 (UK) Parlophone SMMT 1/2 (2 EPs)
by The Beatles
MAGICAL MYSTERY TOUR Prod: George Martin
side one
Magical Mystery Tour—2:48
Your Mother Should Know—2:33
side two
I Am The Walrus—4:35
side three
The Fool On The Hill—3:00
*Flying—*Lennon—McCartney—Harrison—Starkey*—2:16*
side four
*Blue Jay Way—*Harrison*—3:50*

176. DEC 15, 1967 (FAN CLUB)
Recorded: Nov. 28, 1967
by The Beatles Prod: George Martin
Christmas Time Is Here Again!—6:10

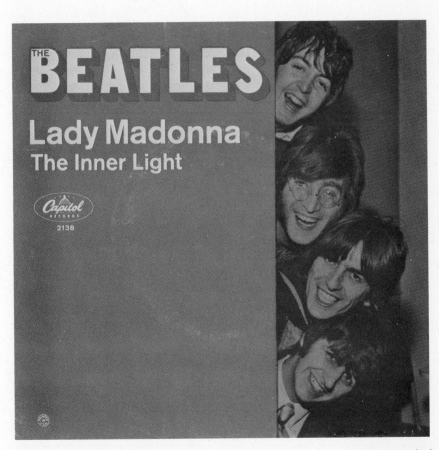

Lady Madonna/The Inner Light   Capitol 2138 (45)

Apple Records, ● in association with Tetragrammaton Records ⬤ rsons   May 1968. Made in Merrie England.

Unfinished Music No. 1: Two Virgins (B side)　　　　　　　**Apple T - 5001**

1968

And God Created Apple

177. MAR 8, 1968 (UK) Parlophone R 5674
      MAY 6, 1968 (US) Bell 726
      Recorded: Feb. 1968
      by Cilla Black   Prod: George Martin
      A: Step Inside Love---L-McC---2:20
      B: (i couldn't take my eyes off you)

178. MAR 8, 1968 (UK) Columbia DB 8379
      by Paul Jones   Prod: Peter Asher
      *A: And The Sun Will Shine---Barry Gibb--Maurice Gibb--
          Robin Gibb
          Paul: Drums
      B: (the dog presides)

179. MAR 15, 1968 (UK) Parlophone R 5675
      MAR 18, 1968 (US) Capitol 2138
      A side recorded: Feb. 3--4, 1968
      B side instrumentals recorded: Jan. 1968 in Bombay
      B side vocals added: Feb. 6, 1968 in London
      by The Beatles   Prod: George Martin
      A: Lady Madonna---2:17
      *B: The Inner Light---Harrison---2:36

180. MAY 17, 1968 (UK) Parlophone PCS 7047 (LP)
      Recorded: Jan. 1968
      by Roger McGough and Mike McGear
      MCGOUGH AND MCGEAR   Prod: Paul McCartney

181. AUG 26, 1968 (US) Apple 2276
      AUG 30, 1968 (UK) Apple R 5722
      A side recorded: July 31--Aug. 1, 1968
      B side recorded: Mid July, 1968

by The Beatles   Prod: George Martin
A: *Hey Jude—7:11*
B: *Revolution—3:22*

182.   AUG 26, 1968   (US)   Apple 1800
SEP   6, 1968   (UK)   Apple 4
Recorded: June 30, 1968
by John Foster and Sons Ltd. Black Dyke Mills Band   Prod:
Paul McCartney
A: Thingumybob—L-McC—1:51
B: Yellow Submarine—L-McC—2:56

183.   AUG 26, 1968   (US)   Apple 1801
AUG 30, 1968   (UK)   Apple 2
Recorded: Mid July 1968
by Mary Hopkin   Prod: Paul McCartney
A: *Those Were The Days—Gene Raskin—5:06*
B: Turn! Turn! Turn! (To Everything There Is A Season)—
Pete Seegar—2:48

184.   AUG 26, 1968   (US)   Apple 1802
SEP   6, 1968   (UK)   Apple 3
Recorded: June 24—June 26, 1968
by Jackie Lomax   Prod: George Harrison
A: *Sour Milk Sea—Harrison—3:51*
B: *The Eagle Laughs At You—Jackie Lomax—2:22*

185.   OCT 11, 1968   (UK)   Liberty LBF 15144
DEC 18, 1968   (US)   Imperial 66345
Recorded: March 1968
by The Bonzo Dog Band   Prod: Paul McCartney (as Apollo C.
Vermouth)
A: *I'm The Urban Spaceman—Neil Innes—2:23*
B: *(canyons of your mind)*

186.   OCT 25, 1968   (ITALY)   Apple 2
by Mary Hopkin   Prod: Paul McCartney
A: Quelli Erand Giorni—Gene Raskin—Dalano—5:06
B: Turn! Turn! Turn! (To Everything There Is A Season)—
Pete Seegar—2:48

187.   NOV   1, 1968   (UK)   Apple SAPCOR 1 (LP)
DEC   2, 1968   (US)   Apple ST 3350 (LP)
English titles recorded: Dec. 1967 in London
Indian titles recorded: Jan. 9—15, 1968 in Bombay

by George Harrison and Band/Indian Orchestra
WONDERWALL MUSIC (Original Soundtrack Album)   Prod:
George Harrison
side one
Microbes—Harrison—*3:39*
Red Lady Too—Harrison—*1:53*
medley: 5:16
Tabla And Pakavaj—Harrison—*1:04*
In The Park—Harrison—*4:08*
medley: 4:14
Drilling A Home—Harrison—*3:07*
Guru Vandana—Harrison—*1:04*
medley: 10:08
Greasy Legs—Harrison—*1:27*
Ski-ing And Gat Kirwani—Harrison—*3:06*
Dream Scene—Harrison—*5:27*
side two
Party Seacombe—Harrison—*4:34*
medley: 5:34
Love Scene—Harrison—*4:16*
Crying—Harrison—*1:14*
Cowboy Museum—Harrison—*1:27*
medley: 4:15
Fantasy Sequins—Harrison—*1:49*
Glass Box—Harrison—*2:21*
On The Bed—Harrison—*1:05*
Wonderwall To Be Here—Harrison—*1:24*
Singing Om—Harrison—*1:54*

188.   NOV 8, 1968 (UK) Parlophone PCS 7065 (LP)
by Cilla Black
THE BEST OF CILLA
side one
cut one: *LOVE OF THE LOVED*—L-McC—*2:00*
side two
cut two: *STEP INSIDE LOVE*—L-McC—*2:20*
cut five: *IT'S FOR YOU*—L-McC—*2:20*

189.   NOV 11, 1968 (US) Apple T 5001 (LP)
Distributed by Tetragrammation Records
NOV 29, 1968 (UK) Apple SAPCOR 2 (LP)
Distributed by Track Records
Recorded: Late May 1968

by John Lennon and Yoko Ono
UNFINISHED MUSIC NO. 1—TWO VIRGINS   Prod: John
Lennon and Yoko Ono
side one
Two Virgins---Lennon—Yoko Ono---*14:02*
  Two Virgins No. 1
  Together
  Two Virgins No. 2
  Two Virgins No. 3
  Two Virgins No. 4
  Two Virgins No. 5
  Two Virgins No. 6
side two
Two Virgins---Lennon—Yoko Ono---*15:00*
  Hushabye Hushabye
  Two Virgins No. 7
  Two Virgins No. 8
  Two Virgins No. 9
  Two Virgins No. 10

190.   NOV 22, 1968   (UK)   Apple PCS 7067/8 (2 LPs)
NOV 25, 1968   (US)   Apple SWBO 101 (2 LPs)
Recorded: May 30—Oct. 14, 1968
by The Beatles
THE BEATLES   Prod: George Martin
side one
Back In The U. S. S. R.---*2:45*
Dear Prudence---*4:00*
Glass Onion---*2:10*
Ob-La-Di, Ob-La-Da---*3:10*
Wild Honey Pie---*1:02*
The Continuing Story Of Bungalow Bill---*3:05*
While My Guitar Gently Weeps---Harrison---*4:46*
Happiness Is A Warm Gun---*2:47*
side two
Martha My Dear---*2:28*
I'm So Tired---*2:01*
Blackbird---*2:20*
Piggies---Harrison---*2:04*
Rocky Racoon---*3:33*
Don't Pass Me By---Starkey---*3:52*
Why Don't We Do It In The Road?---*1:42*
I Will---*1:46*
Julia---*2:57*

side three
Birthday—2:40
Yer Blues—4:01
Mother Nature's Son—2:46
Everybody's Got Something To Hide Except Me And My
*   Monkey—2:25*
Sexy Sadie—3:15
Helter Skelter—4:30
Long, Long, Long—Harrison—3:08
side four
Revolution 1—4:13
Honey Pie—2:42
Savoy Truffle—Harrison—2:55
Cry Baby Cry—3:11
Revolution 9—8:15
Good Night—3:14

191. DEC 6, 1968 (UK) Apple SAPCOR 3 (LP)
Reissued: June 25, 1971
FEB 17, 1969 (US) Apple SKAO 3352 (LP)
Album Recorded: July—Oct. 1968
by James Taylor
JAMES TAYLOR Prod: Peter Asher
side two
cut one: *Carolina In My Mind—James Taylor—3:36*
    Paul: Bass Guitar

192. DEC 20, 1968 (FAN CLUB)
Recorded Separately: Fall 1968
by The Beatles Prod: The Beatles; Edited: Kenny Everett
The Beatles 1968 Christmas Record—7:55
A side: 3:36
B side: 4:19

Unfinished Music   **Zapple ST - 3357**   **(LP)**
No.2: Life With The Lions   **(A side)**

Unfinished Music   **Zapple ST - 3357**   **(LP)**
No.2: Life With The Lions   **(B side)**

Ballad Of John And   **Apple 2531**   **(45)**
   Yoko/Old Brown Shoe

Give Peace A Chance/   **Apple 1809**   **(45)**
   Remember Love

1969

"But If Paul's Alive,
How Did He Die?"

193.   JAN 13, 1969   (US)   Apple SW 153   (LP)
JAN 17, 1969   (UK)   Apple PCS 7070   (LP)
New songs side one recorded: Mid June 1967, except † Mid
  February 1968
by The Beatles   (Additional instrumental cuts % by George
  Martin & Orchestra)
YELLOW SUBMARINE (Original Soundtrack Album)   Prod:
  George Martin
side one
  YELLOW SUBMARINE---2:40
†Only A Northern Song---Harrison---3:23
  All Together Now---2:08
†Hey Bulldog---3:09
  It's All Too Much---Harrison---6:27
  ALL YOU NEED IS LOVE---3:57
side two
%(Pepperland---George Martin---2:18)
%(Medley: Sea Of Time & Sea Of Holes---George Martin---5:16)
%(Sea Of Monsters---George Martin---3:35)
%(March Of The Meanies---George Martin---2:16)
%(Pepperland Laid Waste---George Martin---2:09)
%(Yellow Submarine In Pepperland---L-McC–arr. George Martin
  ---2:10)

194.   FEB   5, 1969   (US)   ATCO SD 7001   (LP)
FEB 28, 1969   (UK)   Polydor 583-053   (LP)
Recorded: Oct. 1968
by Cream
GOODBYE   Prod: Felix Pappalardi
side two
  cut two: *Badge---Harrison–Eric Clapton---2:45*

195.   FEB 21, 1969   (UK)   Apple SAPCOR 5   (LP)
Recorded: Mid Nov. 1968–Mid Jan. 1969
by Mary Hopkin
POST CARD   Prod: Paul McCartney
side one
Lord Of The Reedy River—Donovon Leitch—*2:33*
Happiness Runs (Pebble And The Man)—Donovon Leitch—
2:01
Love Is The Sweetest Thing—Ray Noble—*3:42*
Y Blodyn Gwyn—E. J. Hughes–R. H. Jones—*3:06*
The Honeymoon Song—Mikis Theodorakis–William Sansom
—*2:05*
The Puppy Song—Harry Nilsson—*2:42*
Inchworm (From Hans Christian Andersen)—Frank Loesser
—*2:31*
side two
Voyage Of The Moon—Donovon Leitch—*5:52*
Lullaby Of The Leaves—Joe Young–Bernice Petkere—*2:33*
Young Love—Carole Joyner–Ric Cartey—*2:09*
Someone To Watch Over Me—Ira Gershwin–George Gershwin
Prince En Avignon—Jean Pierre Bourtayre—*3:19*
The Game—George Martin—*2:37*
There's No Business Like Show Business—Irving Berlin—*4:01*

196.   FEB 21, 1969   (UK)   CBS 4041
by The Fourmost   Prod: Paul McCartney
*A: Rosetta—Earl 'Fatha' Hines–Henri Woode
B: (just like before)

197.   MAR   3, 1969   (US)   Apple ST 3351   (LP)
by Mary Hopkin
POST CARD   Prod: Paul McCartney
side one
Lord Of The Reedy River—Donovon Leitch—*2:33*
Happiness Runs (Pebble And The Man)—Donovon Leitch—
2:01
Love Is The Sweetest Thing—Ray Noble—*3:42*
Y Blodyn Gwyn—E. J. Hughes–R. H. Jones—*3:06*
The Honeymoon Song—Mikis Theodorakis–William Sansom
—*2:05*
The Puppy Song—Harry Nilsson—*2:42*
Inchworm (From Hans Christian Andersen)—Frank Loesser
—*2:31*

    Voyage Of The Moon---Donovon Leitch---*5:52*
    Lullaby Of The Leaves---Joe Young–Bernice Petkere---*2:33*
    Young Love---Carole Joyner–Ric Cartey---*2:09*
    THOSE WERE THE DAYS---Gene Raskin---*5:06*
    Prince En Avignon---Jean Pierre Bourtayre---*3:19*
    The Game---George Martin---*2:37*
    There's No Business Like Show Business---Irving Berlin---*4:01*

198.   MAR 17, 1969 (US) ATCO 6668
    APR 3, 1969 (UK) Polydor 2058-285
    UK Reissue: Sept. 21, 1969
    by Cream   Prod: Felix Pappalardi
    A: *BADGE*---Harrison–Eric Clapton---*2:45*
    B: *(what a bringdown)*

199.   MAR 17, 1969 (US) Apple 1805
    by James Taylor   Prod: Peter Asher
    A: *CAROLINA IN MY MIND*---James Taylor---*3:36*
        Paul: Bass Guitar
    B: *(taking it in)*

200.   MAR 21, 1969 (UK) Apple SAPCOR 6 (LP)
    Recorded: Mid Oct. 1968–Jan. 1969
    by Jackie Lomax
    IS THIS WHAT YOU WANT?   Prod: George Harrison
    side one
    Speak To Me---Jackie Lomax---*3:06*
    Is This What You Want?---Jackie Lomax---*2:44*
    How Can You Say Goodbye---Jackie Lomax---*4:13*
    Sunset---Jackie Lomax---*3:54*
    SOUR MILK SEA---Harrison---*3:51*
    I Fall Inside Your Eyes---Jackie Lomax---*3:08*
    side two
    Little Yellow Pills---Jackie Lomax---*4:01*
    Take My Word---Jackie Lomax---*3:55*
    THE EAGLE LAUGHS AT YOU---Jackie Lomax---*2:22*
    Baby You're A Lover---Jackie Lomax---*3:01*
    You've Got Me Thinking---Jackie Lomax---*2:53*
    I Just Don't Know---Jackie Lomax---*2:53*

201.   MAR 28, 1969 (UK) Apple 10
       APR 7, 1969 (US) Apple 1806
       Recorded: Mar. 1–2, 1969
       by Mary Hopkin Prod: Paul McCartney
       A: *Goodbye*---L-McC---*2:23*
       B: *Sparrow*---Bernard Gallagher–Graham Lyle---*3:10*

202.   APR 11, 1969 (UK) Apple R 5777
       MAY 5, 1969 (US) Apple 2490
       Recorded: Late Jan. 1969
       by The Beatles with Billy Preston Prod: George Martin
       A: *Get Back*---*3:11*
       B: *Don't Let Me Down*---*3:34*

203.   MAY 9, 1969 (UK) Zapple 01 (LP)
       MAY 26, 1969 (US) Zapple ST 3357 (LP)
       Side one recorded live: Mar. 2, 1969 at Lady Mitchell Hall,
         Cambridge, England
       Side two recorded: Nov. 4–25, 1968
       by John Lennon and Yoko Ono
       UNFINISHED MUSIC NO. 2: LIFE WITH THE LIONS
        Prod: John Lennon and Yoko Ono
       side one
         "Cambridge 1969"---Lennon–Yoko Ono---*26:30*
          Song For John
          Cambridge 1969
          Let's Go On Flying
          Snow Is Falling All The Time
          Mummy's Only Looking For Her Hand In The Snow
       side two
        No Bed For Beatle John---Lennon–Yoko Ono---*4:45*
        Baby's Heartbeat---Lennon–Yoko Ono---*5:10*
        Two Minutes Silence---Lennon–Yoko Ono---*2:00*
        Radio Play---Lennon–Yoko Ono---*12:35*

204.   MAY 9, 1969 (UK) Zapple 02 (LP)
       MAY 26, 1969 (US) Zapple ST 3358 (LP)
       Side one recorded: Feb. 1969
       Side two recorded: Nov. 1968
       by George Harrison
       ELECTRONIC SOUND Prod: George Harrison
       side one
        Under The Mersey Wall---Harrison---*25:10*
       side two
        No Time Or Space---Harrison---*18:41*

205. MAY 9, 1969 (UK) Apple 11
by Jackie Lomax Prod: Jackie Lomax and Mal Evans (A side);
George Harrison (B side)
A: *New Day*—Jackie Lomax—*3:18*
Ringo: Drums
B: *I FALL INSIDE YOUR EYES*—Jackie Lomax—*3:08*

206. MAY 1969 (US MAIL ORDER) Do It Now Foundation
5000 (LP)
by Various Arists
FIRST VIBRATION
side two
cut two: *NOWHERE MAN*—*2:40*
by The Beatles Prod: George Martin

207. MAY 19, 1969 (US) Apple ST 3354 (LP)
by Jackie Lomax
IS THIS WHAT YOU WANT? Prod: George Harrison, except
† Jackie Lomax and Mal Evans, with Ringo: Drums
side one
Speak To Me—Jackie Lomax—*3:06*
Is This What You Want?—Jackie Lomax—*2:44*
†New Day—Jackie Lomax—*3:18*
Sunset—Jackie Lomax—*3:54*
SOUR MILK SEA—Harrison—*3:51*
I Fall Inside Your Eyes—Jackie Lomax—*3:08*
side two
Little Yellow Pills—Jackie Lomax—*4:01*
Take My Word—Jackie Lomax—*3:55*
THE EAGLE LAUGHS AT YOU—Jackie Lomax—*2:22*
Baby You're A Lover—Jackie Lomax—*3:01*
You've Got Me Thinking—Jackie Lomax—*2:53*
I Just Don't Know—Jackie Lomax—*2:53*

208. MAY 30, 1969 (UK) Apple R 5786
JUN 4, 1969 (US) Apple 2531
A side recorded: Apr. 22, 1969
by The Beatles Prod: George Martin
A: *The Ballad Of John And Yoko*—*2:58*
B: *Old Brown Shoe*—Harrison—*3:16*

209.   JUN 2, 1969 (US) Apple 1807
        B side recorded: Mar. 11, 1969
        by Jackie Lomax   Prod: Jackie Lomax and Mal Evans (A side);
           Paul McCartney (B side)
        A: New Day---Jackie Lomax---*3:18*
              Ringo: Drums
       *B: Thumbin' A Ride---Jerry Leiber–Mike Stoller---*3:58*

210.   JUN 9, 1969 (US) Imperial 12432 (LP)
        by The Bonzo Dog Band   Prod: Paul McCartney
        URBAN SPACEMAN
        side one
           cut one: *I'M THE URBAN SPACEMAN*---Neil Innes---*2:23*

211.   JUN 16, 1969 (US) Capitol 2520
        JUL 18, 1969 (UK) Capitol CL 15604
        Recorded: Feb. 3, 1969
        by The Steve Miller Band   Prod: Glyn Johns and Steve Miller
        A: My Dark Hour---Steve Miller---*3:05*
              Paul (as Paul Ramon): Bass Guitar, Drums and Backing
                 Vocal
        B: (song for our ancestors)

212.   JUN 16, 1969 (US) Capitol SKAO 184 (LP)
        OCT 10, 1969 (UK) Capitol E-ST 184 (LP)
        by The Steve Miller Band
        BRAVE NEW WORLD   Prod: Glyn Johns and Steve Miller
        side two
           cut five: *My Dark Hour*---Steve Miller---*3:05*
              Paul: Bass Guitar, Drums and Backing Vocal

213.   JUN 27, 1969 (UK) Apple 12
        JUL 7, 1969 (US) Apple 1808
        US Reissue: June 26, 1972
        Recorded: Apr. 1969
        by Billy Preston   Prod: George Harrison
        A: That's The Way God Planned It---Billy Preston---*3:22*
        B: What About You?---Billy Preston---*2:07*

214.   JUL 4, 1969 (UK) Apple 13
         JUL 7, 1969 (US) Apple 1809
         A side recorded: June 1, 1969
         by Plastic Ono Band Prod: John Lennon and Yoko Ono
       A: Give Peace A Chance—L-McC—4:49
       B: Remember Love—Yoko Ono—4:01

215.   JUL 7, 1969 (US) ATCO SD 33-291 (LP)
         OCT 24, 1969 (UK) Polydor 583-060 (LP)
         by Cream Prod: Felix Pappalardi
         BEST OF CREAM
         side one
           cut two: *BADGE—Harrison–Eric Clapton—2:45*

216.   JUL 18, 1969 (UK SPECIAL BUSINESS PROMOTION)
           Apple CT 1 (EP)
         by Various Artists
           (By † Jackie Lomax Prod: George Harrison; % Mary Hopkin
             Prod: Paul McCartney; $ The Iveys; + James Taylor)
         WALL'S ICE CREAM
         side one
         $(storm in a teacup)
         +(something's wrong)
         side two
         †LITTLE YELLOW PILLS—Jackie Lomax—4:01
         %HAPPINESS RUNS (PEBBLE AND THE MAN)—Donovon
           Leitch—2:01

217.   AUG 1, 1969 (UK) Liberty LBS 83257 (LP)
         by The Bonzo Dog Band Prod: Paul McCartney
         TADPOLES
         side one
           cut six: *I'M THE URBAN SPACEMAN—Neil Innes—2:23*

218.   AUG 22, 1969 (US) Apple 1810
         AUG 29, 1969 (UK) Apple 15
         Recorded: July 1969
         by Radha Krishna Temple (London) Prod: George Harrison
       A: Hare Krishna Mantra—Traditional–arr. Makunda Das
           Adhikary—3:35
      B: Prayer To The Spiritual Masters—Traditional–arr. Makunda
          Das Adhikary—4:00

219. AUG 22, 1969 (UK) Apple SAPCOR 9 (LP)
SEP 10, 1969 (US) Apple ST 3359 (LP)
Recorded: April–July 1969
by Billy Preston   Prod: George Harrison
THAT'S THE WAY GOD PLANNED IT
side one
  cut one: *Do What You Want*---Billy Preston---*3:40*
  cut three: *Everything's All Right*---Billy Preston–Doris Troy
  ---2:41
  cut four: *She Belongs To Me*---Bob Dylan---*4:06*
  cut five: *It Doesn't Matter*---Billy Preston---*2:37*
  cut six: *Morning Star*---W. C. Handy–Mack David---*3:16*
side two
  cut two: *What About You?*---Billy Preston---*2:07*
  cut three: *Let Us All Get Together Right Now*---Billy Preston
  –Doris Troy---*2:38*
  cut four: *This Is It*---Billy Preston–Doris Troy---*2:38*
  cut six: *That's The Way God Planned It (Parts 1 & 2)*---Billy
  Preston---*5:34*

220. AUG 29, 1969 (UK) Polydor 583-058 (LP)
OCT 6, 1969 (US) ATCO SD-306 (LP)
Recorded: April–May 1969
by Jack Bruce
SONGS FOR A TAILOR   Prod: Felix Pappalardi
side one
  cut one: *Never Tell Your Mother She's Out Of Tune*---Jack
  Bruce–Peter Brown---*3:37*
  George (as L'Angelo Misterioso): Rhythm Guitar

221. SEP 12, 1969 (UK) Decca SKL 5019 (LP)
by The Rolling Stones   Prod: Andrew Loog Oldham
THROUGH THE PAST, DARKLY (BIG HITS VOL. 2)
side one
  cut six: *WE LOVE YOU*---Mick Jagger–Keith Richard---*4:39*
  John and Paul: Backing Vocals

222. SEP 19, 1969 (FRANCE) Apple 16
JUN 15, 1970 (US) Apple 1823
Recorded: Early Aug. 1969
by Mary Hopkin   Prod: Paul McCartney
A: *Que Sera, Sera (Whatever Will Be, Will Be)*---Jay Livingston
  –Ray Evans---*3:04*
B: *Fields Of St. Etienne*---Bernard Gallagher–Graham Lyle---
  3:12

223.   SEP 26, 1969   (UK)   Apple PCS 7088   (LP)
        OCT   1, 1969   (US)   Apple SO 383   (LP)
        Recorded: Early June—Mid Aug. 1969
        by The Beatles
        ABBEY ROAD   Prod: George Martin
        side one
          Come Together---4:16
          Something---Harrison---2:59
          Maxwell's Silver Hammer---3:24
          Oh! Darling---3:28
          Octopus's Garden---Starkey---2:49
          I Want You (She's So Heavy)---7:49
        side two
          Here Comes The Sun---Harrison---3:04
          Because---2:45
          You Never Give Me Your Money---3:57
          Sun King---2:31
          Mean Mr. Mustard---1:06
          Polythene Pam---1:13
          She Came In Through The Bathroom Window---1:58
          Golden Slumbers---1:31
          Carry That Weight---1:37
          The End---2:04
          Her Majesty---0:23

224.   OCT   6, 1969   (US)   Apple 2654
        OCT 31, 1969   (UK)   Apple R 5814
        by The Beatles   Prod: George Martin
        A: SOMETHING---Harrison---2:59
        A: COME TOGETHER---4:16

225.   OCT 17, 1969   (UK)   Apple 19
        OCT 24, 1969   (US)   Apple 1814
        by Billy Preston   Prod: George Harrison
        A: EVERYTHING'S ALL RIGHT---Billy Preston—Doris Troy
             —2:41
        B: (i want to thank you)

226.   OCT 20, 1969   (US)   Apple 1813
        OCT 24, 1969   (UK)   Apple 1001
        A side recorded: Sept. 30, 1969
        by Plastic Ono Band   Prod: John Lennon and Yoko Ono
        A: Cold Turkey---Lennon---4:59
        B: Don't Worry Kyoko (Mummy's Only Looking For A Hand
             In The Snow)---Yoko Ono---4:52

227.   OCT 20, 1969   (US)   Apple SMAX 3361   (LP)
       NOV 7, 1969   (UK)   Apple SAPCOR 11   (LP)
       Recorded: Late Mar.—Early Apr. 1969
       by John Ono Lennon and Yoko Ono Lennon
       WEDDING ALBUM   Prod: John Lennon and Yoko Ono
       side one
          John And Yoko—Lennon—Yoko Ono—*22:23*
       side two
          Amsterdam—Lennon—Yoko Ono—*24:52*

228.   NOV 29, 1969   (UK)   Polydor 582-079   (LP)
       by Various Artists
       HIT '69
       side two
          cut one: *BADGE*—Harrison—Eric Clapton—*2:45*
          by Cream   Prod: Felix Pappalardi

229.   DEC 5, 1969   (UK)   Apple 20
       JAN 12, 1970   (US)   Apple 1815
       Recorded: Sept. 1969
       by Badfinger   Prod: Paul McCartney
       A: *Come And Get It*—Paul McCartney—*2:21*
       B: *(rock of all ages)*

230.   DEC 12, 1969   (UK)   Apple CORE 2001   (LP)
       DEC 12, 1969   (US)   Apple SW 3362   (LP)
       Recorded Live: Sept. 13, 1969 at Toronto's Varsity Stadium
       by The Plastic Ono Band
       **THE PLASTIC ONO BAND—LIVE PEACE IN TORONTO
       1969**   Prod: John Lennon and Yoko Ono
       side one
          Introduction Of The Band—*1:44*
             Kim Fowley: Announcer
          Blue Suede Shoes—Carl Perkins—*2:09*
          Money (That's What I Want)—Berry Gordy—Janie Bradford—
             3:20
          Dizzy Miss Lizzie—Larry Williams—*3:25*
          Yer Blues—L-McC—*3:50*
          Cold Turkey—Lennon—*3:43*
          Give Peace A Chance—L-McC—*3:30*
       side two: *17:38*
          *Don't Worry Kyoko (Mummy's Only Looking For Her Hand
             In The Snow)*—Yoko Ono—*4:44*
          John, John (Let's Hope For Peace)—Yoko Ono—*12:54*

231. DEC 12, 1969 (UK) EMI Star Line SRS 5013 (LP)
Recorded: Feb. 4–8, 1968
by Various Artists
NO ONE'S GONNA CHANGE OUR WORLD
side one
  cut one: *Across The Universe (version one)—3:41*
    by The Beatles   Prod: George Martin

232. DEC 19, 1969 (FAN CLUB)
Recorded Separately: Fall 1969
by The Beatles   Prod: The Beatles; Edited: Maurice Cole
The Beatles Seventh Christmas Record—7:42
A side: 3:34
B side: 4:08

For You Blue/   Apple 2832   (45)
   The Long And Winding Road

You Know My Name/   Apple 2764   (45)
   Let It Be

Instant Karma!/   Apple 1818   (45)
   Who Has Seen The Wind

My Sweet Lord/   Apple 2995   (45)
   Isn't It A Pity

1970

And God Had Indigestion

233. JAN 9, 1970 (UK)   Apple SAPCOR 12 (LP)
FEB 16, 1970 (US)   Apple ST 3364 (LP)
by Badfinger   Prod: Paul McCartney
MAGIC CHRISTIAN MUSIC
side one
cut one: *Come And Get It*---Paul McCartney---*2:21*

234. JAN 30, 1970 (UK)   Apple 21
FEB 16, 1970 (US)   Apple 1817
Recorded: Mid Nov. 1969
by Billy Preston   Prod: George Harrison
A: All That I've Got (I'm Gonna Give It To You)---Billy
Preston—Doris Troy—*3:34*
B: *(as i get older)*

235. FEB 6, 1970 (UK)   Apple 23
A side recorded: Mid Nov. 1969
by Jackie Lomax   Prod: George Harrison (A side); Paul
McCartney (B side)
A: How The Web Was Woven---Clive Westlake—David Most—
3:52
B: THUMBIN' A RIDE---Jerry Leiber—Mike Stoller—*3:58*

236. FEB 6, 1970 (UK)   Apple 1003
FEB 20, 1970 (US)   Apple 1818
A side recorded: Jan. 26, 1970
by John Ono Lennon with The Plastic Ono Band   Prod: Phil
Spector (A side); Yoko Ono Lennon with The Plastic Ono
Band   Prod: John Lennon (B side)
A: *Instant Karma! (We All Shine On)*---Lennon---*3:18*
B: Who Has Seen The Wind?---Yoko Ono---*2:02*

237. FEB 11, 1970 (US) Commonwealth United CU 6004 (LP)
APR 10, 1970 (UK) Pye NSPL 28133 (LP)
by Ken Thorne & Orchestra (Additional cuts by † Badfinger
Prod: Paul McCartney; % Ringo Starr and Peter Sellers)
THE MAGIC CHRISTIAN (Original Soundtrack Album)
side one
†cut two: *Come And Get It*---Paul McCartney---*2:21*
%cut four: *Hunting Scene*---Ken Thorne---*0:25*
   Ringo: Voice
side two
  cut three: *(Come And Get It*---Paul McCartney---*0:46)*

238. FEB 13, 1970 (UK) Apple 24
MAR 16, 1970 (US) Apple 1820
Recorded: Dec. 1969
by Doris Troy   Prod: George Harrison (A side); Doris Troy
(B side)
A: *Ain't That Cute*---Harrison—Doris Troy---*3:48*
*B: *Vaya Con Dios*---Larry Russell—Jack R. Starkey—Inez
   James—Carl Hoff---*3:27*
   George: Guitar

239. FEB 26, 1970 (US) Apple SW 385/SO 385 (LP)
by The Beatles   Prod: George Martin
HEY JUDE (also called: **THE BEATLES AGAIN**)   Prod:
George Martin
side one
  CAN'T BUY ME LOVE---*2:15*
  I SHOULD HAVE KNOWN BETTER---*2:42*
  PAPERBACK WRITER---*2:25*
  RAIN---*2:59*
  LADY MADONNA---*2:17*
  REVOLUTION---*3:22*
side two
  HEY JUDE---*7:11*
  OLD BROWN SHOE---Harrison---*3:16*
  DON'T LET ME DOWN---*3:34*
  THE BALLAD OF JOHN AND YOKO---*2:58*

240. MAR 6, 1970 (UK) Apple 25
MAR 24, 1970 (US) Apple 1821
Recorded: Jan. 1970

by Radha Krishna Temple (London)   Prod: George Harrison
A: *Govinda*—Traditional—arr. Makunda Das Adhikary—*3:18*
B: *Govinda Jai Jai*—Traditional—arr. Makunda Das Adhikary
—*5:58*

241.   MAR 6, 1970   (UK)   Apple R 5833
MAR 11, 1970   (US)   Apple 2764
A side recorded: Late Jan. 1969
B side recorded: Early 1967
by The Beatles   Prod: George Martin
A: *Let It Be*—*3:50*
*B: *You Know My Name (Look Up My Number)*—*4:20*

242.   MAR 9, 1970   (US)   Apple 1819
by Jackie Lomax   Prod: George Harrison
*A: *How The Web Was Woven*—Clive Westlake—David Most—
3:52
B: *I FALL INSIDE YOUR EYES*—Jackie Lomax—*3:08*

243.   MAR 13, 1970   (UK)   Polydor 2384-020 (LP)
by The Chris Barber Band
BATTERSEA RAIN DANCE
side one
   cut five: *CATCALL*—Paul McCartney

244.   MAR 23, 1970   (US)   Shelter SHE 1001 (LP)
APR 24. 1970   (UK)   A&M AMLS 982 (LP)
by Leon Russell
LEON RUSSELL   Prod: Denny Cordell and Leon Russell;
   George: Guitar; Ringo: Drums
side one
   A Song For You—Leon Russell—*4:08*
   Dixie Lullaby—Leon Russell—Chris Stainton—*2:30*
   I Put A Spell On You—Leon Russell—*4:10*
   Shoot Out On The Plantation—Leon Russell—*3:10*
   Hummingbird—Leon Russell—*3:57*
side two
   Delta Lady—Leon Russell—*4:00*
   Prince Of Peace—Leon Russell—Greg Dempsey—*3:05*
   Give Peace A Chance—Leon Russell—Bonnie Bramlett—*2:15*
   Hurtsome Body—Leon Russell—*3:35*
   Pisces Apple Lady—Leon Russell—*2:50*
   Roll Away The Stone—Leon Russell—Greg Dempsey—*3:06*

245.   MAR 27, 1970 (UK) Apple PCS 7101 (LP)
        APR 24, 1970 (US) Apple SW 3365 (LP)
        Recorded: Early Nov.–Mid Dec. 1969, except † Sept. 1969
        and % Feb. 1970
        by Ringo Starr
        SENTIMENTAL JOURNEY Prod: George Martin
        side one
          Sentimental Journey---Bud Green–Les Brown–Ben Homer–
            arr. Richard Perry---*3:27*
        †Night And Day---Cole Porter–arr. Chico O'Farrill--*2:24*
        %Whispering Grass (Don't Tell The Trees)---Fred Fisher–Doris
            Fisher–arr. Ron Goodwin---*2:35*
        %Bye Bye Blackbird---Mort Dixon–Ray Henderson–arr.
            Maurice Gibb---*2:11*
          I'm A Fool To Care---Ted Daffan–arr. Klaus Voorman---*2:39*
        †Star Dust---Hoagy Carmichael–Mitchell Parish–arr. Paul
            McCartney---*3:17*
        side two
        †Blue, Turning Grey Over You---Andy Razof–Thomas 'Fats'
            Waller–arr. Oliver Nelson---*3:19*
        %Love Is A Many Splendoured Thing---Paul Francis Webster–
            Sammy Fain–arr. Quincy Jones---*3:06*
          Dream---Johnny Mercer–arr. George Martin---*2:41*
          You Always Hurt The One You Love---Allan Roberts–Doris
            Fisher–arr. John Dankworth---*2:19*
          Have I Told You Lately That I Love You?---Scott Wiseman–
            arr. Elmer Bernstein---*2:43*
          Let The Rest Of The World Go By---J. Keirn Brennan–Ernest
            R. Ball–arr. Les Reed---*2:54*

246.   APR 17, 1970 (UK) Apple PCS 7102 (LP)
        APR 20, 1970 (US) Apple STAO 3363 (LP)
        Recorded: Nov. 1969–Mar. 1970
        by Paul McCartney
        MCCARTNEY Prod: Paul McCartney
        side one
          The Lovely Linda---Paul McCartney--*0:42*
          That Would Be Something---Paul McCartney---*2:32*
          Valentine Day--Paul McCartney---*1:37*
          Every Night---Paul McCartney---*2:27*
          medley: 2:02
            Hot As Sun---Paul McCartney---*1:28*
            Glasses---Paul McCartney---*0:26*
            Suicide---Paul McCartney---*0:08*
          Junk--Paul McCartney---*1:50*
          Man We Was Lonely--Paul McCartney---*2:50*

side two
 Oo You—Paul McCartney—*2:44*
 Momma Miss America—Paul McCartney—*3:58*
 Teddy Boy—Paul McCartney—*2:28*
 Singalong Junk—Paul McCartney—*2:25*
 Maybe I'm Amazed—Paul McCartney—*3:42*
 Kreen-Akrore—Paul McCartney—*4:04*

247. MAY 4, 1970 (US) Polydor 24-4504 (LP)
 by Tony Sheridan and The Beatles, and † The Beatles Prod:
 Bert Kaempfert (Additional cuts by % Tony Sheridan and
 The Beat Brothers)
 THE BEATLES–CIRCA 1960–IN THE BEGINNING
 side one
 †AIN'T SHE SWEET—Jack Yellen–Milton Ager—*2:12*
 †CRY FOR A SHADOW—Lennon–Harrison—*2:22*
 %(let's dance)
  MY BONNIE—Charles Pratt—*2:06*
  TAKE OUT SOME INSURANCE ON ME, BABY—Charles
   Singleton–Waldense Hall—*2:52*
 %(what'd i say)
 side two
  SWEET GEORGIA BROWN—Ben Bernie–Maceo Pinkard–
   Kenneth Casey—*2:03*
  THE SAINTS—P. D. —*3:19*
 %(ruby baby)
  WHY—Tony Sheridan–Bill Crompton—*2:55*
  NOBODY'S CHILD—Mel Foree–Cy Coben—*2:58*
 %(ya ya)

248. MAY 8, 1970 (UK) Apple PXS 1 (LP)
 Reissued as Apple PCS 7096 on Nov. 6, 1970
 MAY 18, 1970 (US) Apple AR 34001 (LP)
 US Distribution by United Artists Records
 Recorded: Jan. 1969 except † Jan. 3, 1970
 by The Beatles
 LET IT BE (Original Soundtrack Album) Prod: George Martin
 (Jan. 1969) and Phil Spector (Mar. 1970)
 side one
  Two Of Us—*3:33*
  I Dig A Pony—*3:55*
  Across The Universe—*3:51*
  †I Me Mine—Harrison—*2:25*

Dig It---Lennon—McCartney—Harrison—Starkey---*0:51*
Let It Be (version two)---4:01
Maggie Mae---P.D.—arr. Lennon—McCartney—Harrison—
Starkey---*0:39*
side two
I've Got A Feeling---3:38
One After 909---2:52
The Long And Winding Road---3:40
For You Blue---Harrison---*2:33*
Get Back (version two)---3:09

249. MAY 11, 1970 (US) Apple 2832
by The Beatles Prod: George Martin (Jan. 1969) and Phil
Spector (Mar. 1970)
A: *The Long And Winding Road---3:40*
B: *For You Blue*---Harrison---*2:33*

250. JUN 15, 1970 (US) United Artists UAS 5503 (LP)
by Various Artists
PROGRESSIVE HEAVIES
side two
cut five: *I'M THE URBAN SPACEMAN*---Neil Innes---*2:23*
by The Bonzo Dog Band Prod: Paul McCartney

251. JUL 17, 1970 (UK) Liberty LBS 83332 (LP)
AUG 2, 1971 (US) United Artists UAS 5517 (LP)
by The Bonzo Dog Band Prod: Paul McCartney
THE BEAST OF THE BONZOS
side one
cut eight: *I'M THE URBAN SPACEMAN*---Neil Innes---*2:23*

252. AUG 28, 1970 (UK) Apple 28
SEP 21, 1970 (US) Apple 1824
Recorded during "Doris Troy" album sessions
by Doris Troy Prod: Doris Troy
George: Guitar
A: *Jacob's Ladder*---Traditional—arr. Harrison—Doris Troy---
3:18
*B: *Get Back*---L-McC---*3:04*

253. SEP 4, 1970 (UK) Apple 29
Recorded during "Encouraging Words" album sessions
by Billy Preston Prod: George Harrison and Billy Preston
A: *My Sweet Lord*---Harrison---*3:21*
*B: *Long As I Got My Baby*

254.   SEP 11, 1970 (UK) Apple SAPCOR 13 (LP)
NOV 9, 1970 (US) Apple ST 3371 (LP)
Recorded: Dec. 1969—June 1970
by Doris Troy
DORIS TROY   Prod: Doris Troy except † George Harrison
George: Guitar; Ringo: Drums
side one
†AIN'T THAT CUTE---Harrison—Doris Troy---*3:48*
Special Care---Steve Stills---*2:54*
Give Me Back My Dynamite---Harrison—Doris Troy---*4:53*
You Tore Me Up Inside---Doris Troy—Ray Schinnery---*2:27*
Games People Play---Joe South---*3:06*
Gonna Get My Baby Back---Harrison—Starkey—Doris Troy—
Steve Stills---*2:17*
I've Got To Be Strong---Jackie Lomax—Doris Troy---*2:33*
side two
Hurry---Doris Troy—Greg Carroll---*3:10*
So Far---Klaus Voorman—Doris Troy---*4:22*
Exactly Like You---Jimmy McHugh—Dorthy Fields---*3:08*
You Give Me Joy Joy---Harrison—Starkey—Doris Troy—
Steve Stills---*3:38*
Don't Call Me No More---Doris Troy—Ray Schinnery---*2:04*
Jacob's Ladder---Traditional—arr. Harrison—Doris Troy---*3:18*

255.   SEP 11, 1970 (UK) Apple SAPCOR 14 (LP)
NOV 9, 1970 (US) Apple ST 3370 (LP)
Recorded: April—June 1970
by Billy Preston
ENCOURAGING WORDS   Prod: George Harrison and Billy
Preston
side one
Right Now---Billy Preston---*3:13*
Little Girl---Billy Preston---*3:28*
Use What You Got---Billy Preston---*4:21*
My Sweet Lord---Harrison---*3:21*
Let The Music Play---Billy Preston—Joe Greene—Jesse
Kirkland---*2:42*
The Same Thing Again---Billy Preston—Herndon---*4:32*
side two
I've Got A Feeling---L-McC---*2:49*
Sing One For The Lord---Harrison—Billy Preston---*3:47*
When You Are Mine---Billy Preston---*2:44*

I Don't Want You To Pretend---Billy Preston---*2:35*
Encouraging Words---Billy Preston---*3:32*
All Things (Must) Pass---Harrison---*3:38*
You've Been Acting Strange---Billy Preston---*3:20*

256. SEP 14, 1970 (US) ATCO 6780
      Recorded: June 1970
      by Derek and The Dominoes   Prod: Phil Spector
        George: Guitar
      A: *Tell The Truth*---Eric Clapton--Bobby Whitlock---*3:20*
      B: *(roll it over)*

257. SEP 25, 1970 (UK) Apple PAS 10002 (LP)
      SEP 28, 1970 (US) Apple SMAS 3368 (LP)
      Recorded: June 30--July 1, 1970
      by Ringo Starr
      BEAUCOUPS OF BLUES Prod: Pete Drake
      side one
        Beaucoups Of Blues---Buzz Rabin---*2:33*
        Love Don't Last Long---Chuck Howard---*2:44*
        Fastest Growing Heartache In The West---Larry Kingston--
          Fred Dycus---*2:33*
        Without Her---Sorrells Pickard---*2:34*
        Woman Of The Night---Sorrells Pickard---*2:21*
        I'd Be Talking All The Time---Chuck Howard--Larry Kingston
          ---*2:10*
      side two
        $15 Draw---Sorrells Pickard---*3:27*
        Wine, Women And Loud Happy Songs---Larry Kingston---*2:17*
        I Wouldn't Have You Any Other Way---Chuck Howard---*2:57*
        Loser's Lounge---Bobby Pierce---*2:23*
        Waiting---Chuck Howard---*2:54*
        Silent Homecoming---Sorrells Pickard---*3:53*

258. SEP 28, 1970 (US) Capitol ST 563 (LP)
      Repackaged with "Ressurection Shuffle" on July 26, 1971
      FEB 5, 1971 (UK) Capitol EST 563 (LP)
      by Ashton, Gardner and Dyke Prod: Ashton, Gardner & Dyke
      ASHTON, GARDNER AND DYKE (in UK: **THE WORST
        OF ASHTON, GARDNER AND DYKE)**
      side one
        cut two: *I'm Your Spiritual Breadman*---Tony Ashton---*3:16*
          George (as George O'Hara Smith): Guitar

259. OCT 5, 1970 (US) Apple 2969
Recorded: June 30–July 1, 1970
by Ringo Starr   Prod: Pete Drake
A: *Beaucoups Of Blues*---Buzz Rabin---*2:33*
*B: *Coochy-Coochy*---Starkey---*4:48*

260. OCT 26, 1970 (US) Apple 1805
NOV 6, 1970 (UK) Apple 32
by James Taylor   Prod: Peter Asher
A: *CAROLINA IN MY MIND*---James Taylor---*3:36*
     Paul: Bass Guitar
B: *(something's wrong)*

261. NOV 20, 1970 (UK) Polydor 2485-003 (LP)
by Various Artists
SUPERGROUPS VOL. 2
side one
   cut five: *NEVER TELL YOUR MOTHER SHE'S OUT OF
   TUNE*---Jack Bruce–Peter Brown---*3:37*
   by Jack Bruce   Prod: Felix Pappalardi
   George: Rhythm Guitar

262. NOV 23, 1970 (US) Apple 2995
by George Harrison   Prod: George Harrison and Phil Spector
A: *My Sweet Lord*---Harrison---*4:39*
A: *Isn't It A Pity (version one)*---Harrison---*7:10*

263. NOV 23, 1970 (US) Atlantic SD 7202 (LP)
NOV 27, 1970 (UK) Atlantic 2401-004 (LP)
Recorded: June–July 1970
by Steve Stills
   Ringo (as Richie): Drums
STEPHEN STILLS   Prod: Steve Stills and Bill Halverson
side two
   cut two: *To A Flame*---Steve Stills---*3:10*
   cut five: *We Are Not Helpless*---Steve Stills---*4:17*

264. NOV 25, 1970 (US) Columbia M3X 30353 (3 LPs)
News Documentary Narrated by Walter Cronkite
I CAN HEAR IT NOW–THE SIXTIES   Prod: Walter Cronkite
and Fred W. Friendly
side four
   band one: *I WANT TO HOLD YOUR HAND*---*0:38*
   by The Beatles   Prod: George Martin

93

265. NOV 27, 1970 (US) Apple STCH 639 (3 LPs)
NOV 30, 1970 (UK) Apple STCH 639 (3 LPs)
Recorded: Late May—Late Aug. 1970
by George Harrison
ALL THINGS MUST PASS Prod: George Harrison and Phil
Spector
side one
I'd Have You Anytime---Harrison—Bob Dylan---*2:50*
My Sweet Lord---Harrison---*4:39*
Wah-Wah---Harrison---*5:35*
Isn't It A Pity (version one)---Harrison---*7:10*
side two
What Is Life---Harrison---*4:18*
If Not For You---Bob Dylan---*4:27*
Behind That Locked Door---Harrison---*3:03*
Let It Down---Harrison---*4:55*
Run Of The Mill---Harrison---*2:52*
side three
Beware Of Darkness---Harrison---*3:47*
Apple Scruffs---Harrison---*3:03*
Ballad Of Sir Frankie Crisp (Let It Roll)---Harrison---*3:47*
Awaiting On You All---Harrison---*2:44*
All Things Must Pass---Harrison---*3:46*
side four
I Dig Love---Harrison---*4:54*
Art Of Dying---Harrison---*3:35*
Isn't It A Pity (version two)---Harrison---*4:46*
Hear Me Lord---Harrison---*5:46*
record three: *Apple Jam*
side five
Out Of The Blue---Harrison---*11:07*
It's Johnny's Birthday---Harrison---*0:49*
Plug Me In---Harrison---*3:15*
side six
I Remember Jeep---Harrison---*6:59*
Thanks For The Pepperoni---Harrison---*5:26*

266. NOV 30, 1970 (US) Atlantic 2778
JAN 29, 1971 (UK) Atlantic 2091-046
by Steve Stills Prod: Steve Stills and Bill Halverson
B: To A Flame---Steve Stills---*3:10*
Ringo: Drums
A: (love the one you're with)

267.   DEC   3, 1970   (US)   Apple 1826
         by Billy Preston   Prod: George Harrison and Billy Preston
         A: MY SWEET LORD---Harrison---*3:21*
         B: LITTLE GIRL---Billy Preston---*3:28*

268.   DEC 11, 1970   (UK)   Apple PCS 7124 (LP)
         DEC 11, 1970   (US)   Apple SW 3372 (LP)
         Recorded: Early Oct. 1970
         by John Lennon Plastic Ono Band
         JOHN LENNON/PLASTIC ONO BAND   Prod: John Lennon,
          Yoko Ono and Phil Spector
         side one
          Mother---Lennon---*5:29*
          Hold On (John)---Lennon---*1:49*
          I Found Out---Lennon---*3:33*
          Working Class Hero---Lennon---*3:44*
          Isolation---Lennon---*2:48*
         side two
          Remember---Lennon---*4:29*
          Love---Lennon---*3:17*
          Well Well Well---Lennon---*5:52*
          Look At Me---Lennon---*2:49*
          God---Lennon---*4:04*
          My Mummy's Dead---Lennon---*0:48*

269.   DEC 11, 1970   (UK)   Apple SAPCOR 17 (LP)
         DEC 11, 1970   (US)   Apple SW 3373 (LP)
         Recorded: Early Oct. 1970 except † Feb. 1968
         by Yoko Ono Plastic Ono Band
         YOKO ONO/PLASTIC ONO BAND   Prod: John Lennon and
          Yoko Ono
         side one
          Why---Yoko Ono---*5:30*
          Why Not---Yoko Ono---*10:39*
          Greenfield Morning I Pushed An Empty Baby Carriage All
           Over The City---Yoko Ono---*5:40*
         side two
         †AOS---Yoko Ono---*7:06*
          Touch Me---Yoko Ono---*3:40*
          Paper Shoes---Yoko Ono---*8:10*

270. DEC 18, 1970 (US FAN CLUB) Apple SBC 100 (LP)
DEC 18, 1970 (UK FAN CLUB) Apple LYN 2154 (LP)
by The Beatles
THE BEATLES' CHRISTMAS ALBUM (in UK: **FROM THEN
TO US**)   Prod: George Martin except † The Beatles
side one
THE BEATLES CHRISTMAS RECORD (Dec. 1963)—5:00
*ANOTHER BEATLES CHRISTMAS RECORD (Dec. 1964)
—4:05*
*THE BEATLES THIRD CHRISTMAS RECORD (Dec. 1965)
—6:26*
*THE BEATLES FOURTH CHRISTMAS RECORD (Dec.
1966)—6:40*
side two
CHRISTMAS TIME IS HERE AGAIN! (Dec. 1967)—6:10
*†THE BEATLES 1968 CHRISTMAS RECORD (Dec. 1968)
—7:55*
*†THE BEATLES SEVENTH CHRISTMAS RECORD (Dec.
1969)—7:42*

271. DEC 28, 1970 (US) Apple 1827
by John Lennon Plastic Ono Band   Prod: John Lennon, Yoko
Ono and Phil Spector (A side); Yoko Ono Plastic Ono Band
Prod: John Lennon and Yoko Ono (B side)
A: MOTHER—Lennon—3:55
B: WHY—Yoko Ono—5:30

271a. 1970 (HOLLAND) Philips 369 002 PF
by Jotta Herre
A: Penina—Paul McCartney—3:00
B: (north)

The Beatles Christmas Album

Apple SBC 100 (LP)

Early 1970/It   Apple 1831   (45)
Don't Come Easy

Wild Life   Apple SW - 3386   (LP)

Happy Xmas/   Apple 1842   (45)
Listen, The Snow Is Falling

Power To The People/   Apple 1830   (45)
Touch Me

1971

My Sweet Lord,
He's So Fine

272. JAN 15, 1971 (UK) Apple R 5884
      by George Harrison Prod: George Harrison and Phil Spector
      A: *MY SWEET LORD*---Harrison---*4:39*
      B: *WHAT IS LIFE*---Harrison---*4:18*

273. FEBRUARY 1971 (US MAIL ORDER) Do It Now
      Foundation LP 1001 (LP)
      Distributed by K-Tel
      by Various Artists
      DO IT NOW: 20 GIANT HITS
      side one
        cut one: *NOWHERE MAN*---*2:40*
          by The Beatles Prod: George Martin

274. FEB 15, 1971 (US) Apple 1828
      by George Harrison Prod: George Harrison and Phil Spector
      A: *WHAT IS LIFE*--Harrison---*4:18*
      B: *APPLE SCRUFFS*---Harrison---*3:03*

275. FEB 19, 1971 (UK) Apple R 5889
      FEB 22, 1971 (US) Apple 1829
      Recorded: Jan. 1971
      by Paul McCartney Prod: Paul McCartney
      A: Another Day--Mr. and Mrs. Paul McCartney---*3:41*
      B: Oh Woman, Oh Why---Paul McCartney---*4:55*

276. FEB 22, 1971 (US) Atlantic 2790
      MAY 7, 1971 (UK) Atlantic 2091-069
      by Steve Stills Prod: Steve Stills and Bill Halverson
      B: *WE ARE NOT HELPLESS*---Steve Stills---*4:17*
          Ringo: Drums
      A: *(love the one you're with)*

277. MAR 8, 1971 (US) Capitol 3060
      by Ashton, Gardner and Dyke   Prod: Ashton, Gardner & Dyke
      B: *I'M YOUR SPIRITUAL BREADMAN*---Tony Ashton---*3:16*
          George: Guitar
      A: *(ressurection shuffle)*

278. MAR 12, 1971 (UK) Apple R 5892
      A side recorded: Feb. 1971
      B side recorded: Feb. 1971 with vocals rerecorded in Early
       Mar. 1971
      by John Lennon Plastic Ono Band   Prod: John Lennon, Yoko
       Ono and Phil Spector (A side); Yoko Ono Plastic Ono Band
       Prod: John Lennon and Yoko Ono (B side)
      A: *Power To The People*---Lennon---*3:15*
      B: *Open Your Box* (later called: *Hirake*)---Yoko Ono---*3:23*

279. MAR 22, 1971 (US) Apple 1830
      by John Lennon Plastic Ono Band   Prod: John Lennon, Yoko
       Ono and Phil Spector (A side); Yoko Ono Plastic Ono Band
       Prod: John Lennon and Yoko Ono (B side)
      A: *Power To The People*---Lennon---*3:15*
      B: *TOUCH ME*---Yoko Ono---*3:40*

280. APR 9, 1971 (UK) Apple R 5898
      APR 16, 1971 (US) Apple 1831
      Recorded: Mar. 8, 1970
      by Ringo Starr   Prod: George Harrison (A side), Ringo Starr
       (B side)
      A: *It Don't Come Easy*---Starkey---*3:00*
      B: *Early 1970*---Starkey---*2:19*

281. APR 16, 1971 (UK) Apple 33
      APR 19, 1971 (US) Apple 1832
      Recorded: Late Feb. 1971
      by Ronnie Spector   Prod: George Harrison and Phil Spector
      A: Try Some, Buy Some---Harrison---*4:08*
      B: Tandoori Chicken---Harrison—Phil Spector---*2:14*

282. MAY 17, 1971 (US) Apple SMAS 3375 (LP)
      MAY 28, 1971 (UK) Apple PAS 1000 (LP)
      Recorded: Jan.–Mar. 1971
      by Paul and Linda McCartney

RAM   Prod: Paul and Linda McCartney
side one
Too Many People---Paul McCartney---*4:09*
3 Legs---Paul McCartney---*2:48*
Ram On---Paul McCartney---*2:30*
Dear Boy---Paul and Linda McCartney---*2:14*
Uncle Albert/Admiral Halsey---Paul and Linda McCartney---
---*4:50*
Smile Away---Paul McCartney---*4:01*
side two
Heart Of The Country---Paul and Linda McCartney---*2:22*
Monkberry Moon Delight---Paul and Linda McCartney---*5:25*
Eat At Home---Paul and Linda McCartney---*3:22*
Long Haired Lady---Paul and Linda McCartney---*6:06*
Ram On (version two)---Paul McCartney---*0:55*
The Back Seat Of My Car---Paul McCartney---*4:29*

283.   MAY 21, 1971   (US)   Apple SKAO 3376 (LP)
        MAY 28, 1971   (UK)   Apple SAPCOR 18 (LP)
        by The Radha Krsna Temple (London)
        THE RADHA KRSNA TEMPLE   Prod: George Harrison
        side one
        GOVINDA---Traditional--arr. Makunda Das Adhikary---*4:39*
        Sri Gurvastakam---Traditional--arr. Makunda Das Adhikary---
        3:07
        Bhaja Bhakata/Arati---Traditional--arr. Makunda Das Adhikary
        ---*8:28*
        HARE KRSNA MANTRA---Traditional--arr. Makunda Das
        Adhikary---*3:35*
        side two
        Sri Isopanisad---Traditional--arr. Makunda Das Adhikary---*4:00*
        Bhaja Hunre Mana---Traditional--arr. Makunda Das Adhikary
        ---*8:43*
        GOVINDA JAYA JAYA---Traditional--arr. Makunda Das
        Adhikary---*5:58*

284.   MAY 28, 1971   (UK)   A&M AMS 852
        by Gary Wright   Prod: Gary Wright
            George: Guitar
        A: Stand For Our Rights---Gary Wright---*3:32*
        B: Can't See The Reason---Gary Wright---*4:24*

285. JUN 18, 1971 (UK) Contour 287011 (LP)
by Tony Sheridan and The Beatles, and † The Beatles Prod:
Bert Kaempfert (Additional cuts by % Tony Sheridan and
The Beat Brothers)
THE EARLY YEARS
side one
†AIN'T SHE SWEET---Jack Yellen—Milton Ager---*2:12*
†CRY FOR A SHADOW---Lennon—Harrison---*2:22*
%(let's dance)
  MY BONNIE---Charles Pratt---*2:06*
  IF YOU LOVE ME, BABY---Charles Singleton—Waldenese
    Hall---*2:52*
%(what'd i say)
side two
  SWEET GEORGIA BROWN---Ben Bernie—Maceo Pinkard—
    Kenneth Casey---*2:03*
  THE SAINTS---P.D.---*3:19*
%(ruby baby)
  WHY---Tony Sheridan—Bill Crompton---*2:55*
  NOBODY'S CHILD---Mel Foree—Cy Coben---*2:58*
%(ya ya)

286. JUN 21, 1971 (US) Apple 1834
by Jackie Lomax Prod: George Harrison
A: SOUR MILK SEA---Harrison---*3:51*
B: I FALL INSIDE YOUR EYES---Jackie Lomax---*3:08*

287. JUL 7, 1971 (US) Apple 1835
JUL 16, 1971 (UK) Apple 36
by Bill Elliott and Elastic Oz Band Prod: John Lennon,
Yoko Ono, Mal Evans and Phil Spector (A side); John
Lennon and Elastic Oz Band Prod: John Lennon, Mal
Evans and Apple (B side)
*A: God Save Us---Lennon—Yoko Ono---*3:10*
*B: Do The Oz---Lennon—Yoko Ono---*3:09*

288. JUL 19, 1971 (US) United Artists UA 50809
by The Bonzo Dog Band Prod: Paul McCartney
A: I'M THE URBAN SPACEMAN---Neil Innes---*2:23*
B: (canyons of your mind)

289. JUL 26, 1971 (US) Chess CH 60008 (LP)
AUG 20. 1971 (UK) Rolling Stones Records COC 49101 (LP)
Recorded: Mid 1970
by Howlin' Wolf
THE LONDON HOWLIN' WOLF SESSIONS Prod: Norman
Dayron
side one
cut two: *I Ain't Superstitious*---Willie Dixon---*3:34*
Ringo (as Richie): Drums

290. JUL 28, 1971 (US) Apple 1836
JUL 30, 1971 (UK) Apple R 5912
Recorded: Mid July 1971
by George Harrison Prod: George Harrison and Phil Spector
*A: Bangla Desh---Harrison---3:52
*B: Deep Blue---Harrison---3:47

291. AUG 2, 1971 (US) Apple 1837
by Paul and Linda McCartney Prod: Paul and Linda McCartney
A: UNCLE ALBERT/ADMIRAL HALSEY---Paul and Linda
McCartney---*4:50*
B: TOO MANY PEOPLE---Paul McCartney---*4:09*

292. AUG 9, 1971 (US) Apple 1838
AUG 27, 1971 (UK) Apple 37
Recorded: Mid July 1971
by Ravi Shankar & Chorus (side one), and Ravi Shankar and
Ali Akbar Khan with Alla Rakah (side two) Prod: George
Harrison
side one
*Joi Bangla---Ravi Shankar---*3:18*
*Oh Bhaugowan--Ravi Shankar---*3:35*
side two
*Raga Mishra--Jhinjhoti---P.D.---*6:52*

293. AUG 13, 1971 (UK) Apple R 5914
by Paul and Linda McCartney Prod: Paul and Linda McCartney
A: THE BACK SEAT OF MY CAR---Paul McCartney---*4:29*
B: HEART OF THE COUNTRY---Paul and Linda McCartney
---*2:22*

294. AUG 16, 1971 (US) ABC 11310
by B. B. King Prod: Ed Michael and Joe Zagarino
A: *Ghetto Woman*—B. B. King—Dave Clark—*3:03*
      Ringo: Drums
B: *(seven minutes)*

295. SEP 9, 1971 (US) Apple SW 3379 (LP)
OCT 8, 1971 (UK) Apple PAS 10004 (LP)
Recorded: Early—Mid July 1971
by John Lennon Plastic Ono Band with The Flux Fiddlers
IMAGINE Prod: John Lennon, Yoko Ono and Phil Spector
side one
  Imagine—Lennon—*2:59*
  Crippled Inside—Lennon—*3:43*
  Jealous Guy—Lennon—*4:10*
  It's So Hard—Lennon—*2:22*
  I Don't Want To Be A Soldier Mama, I Don't Want To Die—
    Lennon—*6:01*
side two
  Give Me Some Truth—Lennon—*3:11*
  Oh My Love—Lennon—Yoko Ono—*2:40*
  How Do You Sleep?—Lennon—*5:29*
  How?—Lennon—*3:37*
  Oh Yoko!—Lennon—*4:18*

296. SEP 20, 1971 (US) Apple SVBB 3380 (2 LPs)
DEC 3, 1971 (UK) Apple SAPTU 101/2 (2 LPs)
New Songs Recorded: Aug. 1971
by Yoko Ono Plastic Ono Band with Joe Jones Tone Deaf
  Music Co.
FLY Prod: John Lennon and Yoko Ono
side one
  Midsummer New York—Yoko Ono—*3:50*
  Mind Train—Yoko Ono—*16:52*
side two
  Mind Holes—Yoko Ono—*2:45*
  DON'T WORRY KYOKO—Yoko Ono—*4:52*
  Mrs. Lennon—Yoko Ono—*4:10*
  HIRAKE (previously called: *Open Your Box*)—Yoko Ono—
    3:23
  Toilet Piece/Unknown—Yoko Ono—*0:30*
  O'Wind (Body Is The Scar Of Your Mind)—Yoko Ono—*5:22*

side three
Airmale (Tone Deaf Jam)—Yoko Ono—*10:40*
Don't Count The Waves—Yoko Ono—*5:26*
You—Yoko Ono—*9:00*
side four
Fly—Yoko Ono—*22:53*
Telephone Piece—Yoko Ono—*1:01*

297.   SEP 29, 1971   (US)   Apple 1839
OCT 29, 1971   (UK)   Apple 38
by Yoko Ono Plastic Ono Band   Prod: John Lennon and
Yoko Ono
A: *Mrs. Lennon*—Yoko Ono—*4:10*
B: *Midsummer New York*—Yoko Ono—*3:50*

298.   OCT 11, 1971   (US)   Apple 1840
by John Lennon Plastic Ono Band   Prod: John Lennon, Yoko
Ono and Phil Spector
A: *IMAGINE*—Lennon—*2:59*
B: *IT'S SO HARD*—Lennon—*2:22*

299.   OCT 11, 1971   (US)   ABC ABCX 730 (LP)
NOV 19, 1971   (UK)   Probe SPB 1041 (LP)
Recorded: June 9–16, 1971
by B. B. King
Ringo: Drums
B. B. KING IN LONDON   Prod: Ed Michael and Joe Zagarino
side two
cut one: *Ghetto Woman*—B. B. King–Dave Clark—*5:13*
cut two: *Wet Hayshark*—Gary Wright—*2:31*
cut three: *Part–Time Love*—Clay Hammond—*3:17*

300.   NOV 1, 1971   (US)   A&M SP 4296 (LP)
JAN 21, 1972   (UK)   A&M AMLS 64296 (LP)
by Gary Wright
FOOTPRINT   Prod: Gary Wright
George (as George O'Hara): Guitar, Slide Guitar
side one
Give Me The Good Earth—Gary Wright—*3:17*
Two Faced Man—Gary Wright—*3:40*
Love To Survive—Gary Wright—*4:48*
Whether It's Right Or Wrong—Gary Wright—*5:08*

STAND FOR OUR RIGHTS—Gary Wright—*3:32*
Fascinating Things—Gary Wright—*5:05*
Forgotten—Gary Wright—*4:02*
If You Treat Someone Right—Gary Wright—*4:50*

301. NOV 8, 1971 (US) A&M SP 3507 (LP)
      JAN 14, 1972 (UK) A&M AMLH 63507 (LP)
      Recorded: Aug.—Sept. 1971
      by Billy Preston
      I WROTE A SIMPLE SONG Prod: Billy Preston
      George (as George H.): Lead Guitar
      side one
      Should've Known Better—Billy Preston—Joe Greene—*2:28*
      I Wrote A Simple Song—Billy Preston—Joe Greene—*3:28*
      John Henry—Billy Preston—Robert Sam—*3:15*
      Without A Song—William Rose—Edward Eliscu—Vincent
          Youmans—*4:57*
      The Bus—Billy Preston—Joe Greene—*3:32*
      side two
      Outa—Space—Billy Preston—Joe Greene—*4:08*
      The Looner Tune—Billy Preston—Joe Greene—Jesse Kirkland
          —*2:47*
      You Done Got Older—Billy Preston—Bruce Fisher—*3:08*
      Swing Down Chariot—P.D.—*4:13*
      God Is Great—Billy Preston—Joe Greene—*3:32*
      My Country 'Tis Of Thee—P.D.—*4:27*

302. NOV 10, 1971 (US) Apple 1841
      by Badfinger   Prod: George Harrison
      A: *Day After Day*—Pete Ham—*3:02*
      B: *(money)*

303. DEC 1, 1971 (US) Apple 1842
      NOV 24. 1972 (UK) Apple R 5970
      Recorded: Oct.28—29, 1971
      by John Lennon and Yoko Ono Plastic Ono Band with The
        Harlem Community Choir (A side), and Yoko Ono Plastic
        Ono Band   Prod: John Lennon, Yoko Ono and Phil Spector
      A: *Happy Xmas (War Is Over)*—Lennon—Yoko Ono—*3:25*
     *B: *Listen, The Snow Is Falling*—Yoko Ono—*3:10*

304. DEC 7, 1971 (US) Apple SWAO 3384 (LP)
Most tracks recorded: Apr.–July 1968
by Ravi Shankar
RAGA (Original Soundtrack Album) Prod: George Harrison
side one
  Dawn To Dusk---Ravi Shankar---*3:38*
  Vedic Hymns---P.D.---*1:30*
  Baba Teaching---P.D.---*1:08*
  Birth To Death---Ravi Shankar---*3:10*
  Vinus House---Ravi Shankar---*2:37*
  Gurur Bramha---Ravi Shankar---*1:10*
  United Nations---Ravi Shankar–Yehudi Menuhin---*4:33*
side two
  medley: 4:31
    Raga Parameshwari---Ravi Shankar---*2:51*
    Rangeswhart---Ravi Shankar---*1:40*
  Banaras Ghat---Ravi Shankar---*2:45*
  Bombay Studio---Ravi Shankar---*2:45*
  Kinnara School---Ravi Shankar---*1:51*
  Frenzy And Distortion---Ravi Shankar---*1:06*
  Raga Desh---Ravi Shankar---*8:50*

305. DEC 7, 1971 (UK) Apple PCS 7142 (LP)
DEC 7, 1971 (US) Apple SW 3386 (LP)
Recorded: Early–Late Aug. 1971
by Wings
WILD LIFE Prod: Paul and Linda McCartney
side one
  Mumbo---Paul and Linda McCartney---*3:50*
  Bip Bop---Paul and Linda McCartney---*4:05*
  Love Is Strange---Ellis McDaniel–Mickey Baker---*4:45*
  Wild Life---Paul and Linda McCartney---*6:30*
side two
  Some People Never Know---Paul and Linda McCartney---*6:35*
  I Am Your Singer---Paul and Linda McCartney---*2:10*
  Bip Bop (reprise)---Paul and Linda McCartney---*0:48*
  Tomorrow---Paul and Linda McCartney---*3:17*
  Dear Friend---Paul and Linda McCartney—*5:42*

306. DEC 13, 1971 (US) Apple SW 3387 (LP)
FEB 11, 1972 (UK) Apple SAPCOR 19 (LP)
by Badfinger Prod: George Harrison

STRAIGHT UP
side one
cut five: *I'd Die Babe*---Joey Molland---*2:05*
cut six: *Name Of The Game*---Pete Ham---*5:49*
side two
cut one: *Suitcase*---Joey Molland---*2:53*
cut three: *Day After Day*---Pete Ham---*3:02*

307.   DEC 20, 1971   (US)   Apple STCX 3385   (3 LPs)
        JAN 10. 1972   (UK)   Apple STCX 3385   (3 LPs)
        Recorded Live: Aug. 1, 1971 at New York's Madison Square Garden
        by George Harrison and Friends
        THE CONCERT FOR BANGLA DESH   Prod: George Harrison and Phil Spector
        side one
        George Harrison/Ravi Shankar Introduction---*6:16*
        Bangla Dhun---*P.D.*---*16:19*
           Sitar And Sarod Duet
           Dadratal
           Teental
        side two
        Wah—Wah---Harrison---*3:15*
        My Sweet Lord---Harrison---*4:16*
        Awaiting On You All---Harrison---*2:37*
        That's The Way God Planned It---Billy Preston---*4:05*
           Billy Preston: Vocal Solo
        side three
        It Don't Come Easy---Starkey---*2:38*
           Ringo: Vocal Solo
        Beware Of Darkness---Harrison---*3:26*
           George and Leon Russell: Vocal Solos
        Introduction Of The Band---*3:00*
        While My Guitar Gently Weeps---Harrison---*4:39*
        side four
        medley: 9:11   Leon Russell: Vocal Solo
           Jumpin' Jack Flash---Mick Jagger—Keith Richard
           Youngblood---Jerry Leiber—Mike Stoller—Doc Pomus
        Here Comes The Sun---Harrison---*2:51*
        side five: Bob Dylan: Vocal Solos
        A Hard Rain's Gonna Fall---Bob Dylan---*5:04*
        It Takes A Lot To Laugh/It Takes A Train To Cry---Bob Dylan
           ---*2:54*

Blowin' In The Wind---Bob Dylan---*3:34*
Mr. Tambourine Man---Bob Dylan---*4:06*
Just Like A Woman---Bob Dylan---*4:14*
side six
Something---Harrison---*3:05*
Bangla Desh---Harrison---*4:14*

308.　　DEC 20, 1971　(US)　A&M 1320
　　　　JAN 21, 1972　(UK)　A&M AMS 877
　　　　by Billy Preston　Prod: Billy Preston
　　　　A: I WROTE A SIMPLE SONG---Billy Preston–Joe Greene---
　　　　　3:28
　　　　　　George: Lead Guitar
　　　　B: (outa–space)

Back Off Boogaloo/Blindman   Apple 1849 (45)

Woman Is The Nigger Of The World/   Apple 1848 (45)
  Sisters O Sisters

1972

Never Tell Your Mother She's Out Of Tune

309. JAN 14, 1972 (UK) Apple 40
by Badfinger Prod: George Harrison
A: *Day After Day*---Pete Ham---*3:02*
B: *(sweet tuesday morning)*

310. JAN 21, 1972 (UK) Apple 41
by Yoko Ono Plastic Ono Band Prod: John Lennon and Yoko
Ono (A side); John Lennon, Yoko Ono and Phil Spector
(B side)
A: *MIND TRAIN*---Yoko Ono
*B: *LISTEN, THE SNOW IS FALLING*---Yoko Ono---*3:10*

311. JAN 25, 1972 (US) ATCO 6873
by Jesse "Ed" Davis Prod: Jesse Davis and Albhy Galuten
A: *Sue Me, Sue You Blues*---Harrison---*2:45*
B: *(my captain)*

312. FEB 16, 1972 (US) Columbia C 31104 (LP)
JUN 2, 1972 (UK) CBS 64906 (LP)
by David Bromberg
DAVID BROMBERG Prod: David Bromberg
side two
cut four: *The Holdup*---Harrison—David Bromberg---*3:00*

313. FEB 18, 1972 (UK) Decca SKL 5098 (LP)
by The Rolling Stones Prod: Andrew Loog Oldham
MILESTONES
side one
cut six: *I WANNA BE YOUR MAN*---L-McC---*1:44*

314. FEB 25, 1972 (UK) Capitol CL 15712
     by The Steve Miller Band   Prod: Glyn Johns and Steve Miller
     side one
       MY DARK HOUR---Steve Miller---*3:05*
          Paul: Bass Guitar, Drums and Backing Vocal
     side two
       (the gangster is back)
       (song for our ancestors)

315. FEB 25, 1972 (UK) Apple R 5936
     FEB 28, 1972 (US) Apple 1847
     Recorded: Feb. 1, 1972
     by Wings   Prod: The McCartneys
     *A: Give Ireland Back To The Irish---McCartney & McCartney
          ---*3:42*
     *B: Give Ireland Back To The Irish (version)---McCartney &
          McCartney---*3:42*

316. MAR 6, 1972 (US) Apple 1845
     by Lon & Derrek Van Eaton   Prod: George Harrison
     A: Sweet Music---Lon & Derrek Van Eaton---*3:41*
     B: (song of songs)

317. MAR 6, 1972 (US) ATCO SD 33-382 (LP)
     MAY 19, 1972 (UK) Atlantic K 40329 (LP)
     by Jesse "Ed" Davis
     ULULU   Prod: Jesse Davis and Albhy Galuten
     side one
       cut four: *Sue Me, Sue You Blues*---Harrison---*2:45*

318. MAR 17, 1972 (UK) Apple R 5944
     MAR 20, 1972 (US) Apple 1849
     B side recorded: Sept. 1971
     by Ringo Starr   Prod: George Harrison (A side); Ringo Starr
       and Klaus Voorman (B side)
     A: Back Off Boogaloo---Starkey---*3:21*
     *B: Blindman---Starkey---*2:41*

319. APR 10, 1972 (US) ATCO SD 2-803 (2 LPs)
     JUL 7, 1972 (UK) Polydor 2659-012 (2 LPs)
     by Eric Clapton and Friends
       (By Cream   Prod: Felix Pappalardi; † Derek and The
       Dominoes   Prod: Phil Spector)

HISTORY OF ERIC CLAPTON
side two
   cut two: *BADGE*---Harrison—Eric Clapton---*2:45*
side four
   †cut one: *TELL THE TRUTH*---Eric Clapton—Bobby Whitlock
   ---*3:20*
   George: Guitar

320.   APR 24, 1972 (US) Apple 1848
      Recorded: Early Mar. 1972
      by John Lennon Plastic Ono Band with Elephant's Memory
      and The Invisible Strings (A side), and Yoko Ono Plastic
      Ono Band with Elephant's Memory and The Invisible
      Strings (B side) Prod: John Lennon, Yoko Ono and Phil
      Spector
      A: *Woman Is The Nigger Of The World*---Lennon—Yoko Ono
         ---*5:15*
      B: *Sisters, O Sisters*---Yoko Ono---*3:46*

321.   APR 28, 1972 (US) Apple SW 3391 (LP)
      by David Peel & The Lower East Side
      THE POPE SMOKES DOPE Prod: John Lennon and Yoko
      Ono
      side one
      I'm A Runaway---David Peel---*3:39*
      Everybody's Smoking Marijuana---David Peel---*4:06*
      F Is Not A Dirty Word---David Peel---*3:12*
      The Hippie From New York City---David Peel---*3:01*
      McDonald's Farm---David Peel---*3:13*
      The Ballad Of New York City—John Lennon/Yoko Ono---
         David Peel---*3:19*
      side two
      The Ballad Of Bob Dylan---David Peel---*4:12*
      The Chicago Conspiracy---David Peel---*3:47*
      The Hip Generation---David Peel---*1:50*
      I'm Gonna Start Another Riot---David Peel---*2:37*
      The Birth Control Blues---David Peel---*4:48*
      The Pope Smokes Dope---David Peel---*2:15*

322.   MAY 12, 1972 (UK) Apple R 5949
      MAY 29, 1972 (US) Apple 1851
      Recorded: Aug. 1971
      by Wings Prod: Paul McCartney
      A: Mary Had A Little Lamb---McCartney—McCartney---*3:30*
      B: Little Woman Love---McCartney—McCartney---*2:06*

323. MAY 15, 1972 (US) Columbia 45612
      by David Bromberg Prod: David Bromberg
      A: THE HOLDUP—Harrison—David Bromberg—*3:00*
      B: (suffer to sing the blues)

324. MAY 26, 1972 (UK) A&M AMLS 68099 (LP)
      JUL 10, 1972 (US) A&M SP 4348 (LP)
      Recorded: Nov. 1971—Feb. 1972
      by Peter Frampton
        Ringo: Drums
      WIND OF CHANGE Prod: Peter Frampton
      side two
        cut two: *The Lodger*—Peter Frampton—*5:40*
        cut four: *Alright*—Peter Frampton—*4:21*

325. JUN 12, 1972 (US) Apple SVBB 3392 (2 LPs)
      SEP 15, 1972 (UK) Apple PCSP 716 (2 LPs)
      Sides one and two recorded: Mar. 1—20, 1972
      Side three recorded live: Dec. 15, 1969 at London's Lyceum
        Ballroom
      Side four recorded live: June 6, 1971 at New York's Fillmore
        East
      by John Lennon and Yoko Ono Plastic Ono Band with
      Elephant's Memory and The Invisible Strings (sides one and
      two), John Lennon and Yoko Ono with The Plastic Ono
      Supergroup (side three) and John Lennon and Yoko Ono
      Plastic Ono Band with Frank Zappa and The Mothers Of
      Invention (side four)
      SOMETIME IN NEW YORK CITY Prod: John Lennon,
      Yoko Ono and Phil Spector
      side one
        Woman Is The Nigger Of The World—Lennon—Yoko Ono—
          5:15
        Sisters, O Sisters—Yoko Ono—*3:46*
        Attica State—Lennon—Yoko Ono—*2:52*
        Born In A Prison—Yoko Ono—*4:04*
        New York City—Lennon—*4:32*
      side two
        Sunday Bloody Sunday—Lennon—Yoko Ono—*5:00*
        The Luck Of The Irish—Lennon—Yoko Ono—*2:54*
        John Sinclair—Lennon—*3:28*
        Angela—Lennon—Yoko Ono—*4:08*
        We're All Water—Yoko Ono—*7:15*

record two: *Live Jam*
side three: *24:46*
  Cold Turkey---Lennon---*7:34*
  Don't Worry Kyoko---Yoko Ono---*17:12*
side four: *22:58*
  Well...(Baby Please Don't Go)---Walter Ward---*4:50*
  Jamrag---Lennon--Yoko Ono---*1:50*
  Scumbag---Lennon--Yoko Ono--Frank Zappa---*12:53*
  Au---Lennon--Yoko Ono---*3:25*

326.   JUL 7, 1972 (UK) Warner Brothers K 46141 (LP)
Recorded: Jan. 1972
by Bobby Keys
BOBBY KEYS Prod: Bobby Keys, Andy Johns and Jim
Gordon
Ringo: Drums; George: Guitar
side one
  Steal From A King---Dave Mason--Jim Gordon--Jim Price---
   3:49
  Smokefoot---Bobby Keys--Jim Gordon--Jim Price---*3:47*
  Bootleg---Charles Axton--Donald V. Dunn--Wayne Jackson--
   Isaac Hayes---*3:42*
  Altar Rock---Felix Pappalardi---*4:47*
side two
  Key--West---Bobby Keys--Jim Gordon--Jim Price--- *3:51*
  Command Performance---Jim Price---*4:06*
  Crispy Duck---Bobby Keys--Dave Mason--Jim Gordon--Jim
   Price---*3:03*
  Sand & Foam---Jim Gordon---*5:18*

327.   JUL 10, 1972 (US) RCA LSP 4717 (LP)
JUL 28, 1972 (UK) RCA SF 8297 (LP)
Recorded: Mid Mar.--Early May 1972
by Harry Nilsson
Ringo (as Richie Snare): Drums; † George (as George
Harrysong): Slide Guitar
SON OF SCHMILSSON Prod: Richard Perry
side one
  cut one: *Take 54*---Harry Nilsson---*4:22*
†cut five: *You're Breakin' My Heart*---Harry Nilsson---*3:10*
side two
  cut one: *Spaceman*---Harry Nilsson---*3:33*
  cut three: *At My Front Door*---Ewart G. Abner--John C.
   Moore---*2:46*

115

cut four: *Ambush*---Harry Nilsson---*5:35*
cut six: *The Most Beautiful World In The World*---Harry
Nilsson---*3:33*

328.   SEP 4. 1972 (US) RCA 74-0788
by Harry Nilsson   Prod: Richard Perry
A: SPACEMAN---Harry Nilsson---*3:33*
    Ringo: Drums
B: (turn on your radio)

329.   SEP 14, 1972 (UK) RCA 2266
by Harry Nilsson   Prod: Richard Perry
A: SPACEMAN---Harry Nilsson---*3:33*
    Ringo: Drums
B: YOU'RE BREAKIN' MY HEART---Harry Nilsson---*3:10*
    George: Slide Guitar

330.   SEP 18, 1972 (US) Apple SMAS 3389 (LP)
NOV 10, 1972 (UK) Apple SAPCOR 22 (LP)
by Elephant's Memory
ELEPHANT'S MEMORY   Prod: John Lennon and Yoko Ono
side one
    Liberation Special---Rick Frank—Stan Bronstein---*5:28*
    Baddest Of The Mean---Stan Bronstein—Rick Frank—Gary
      Van Scyoc—Adam Ippolito—Wayne Gabriel---*8:46*
    Cryin' Blacksheep Blues---Rick Frank—Stan Bronstein—
      D. Price---*4:27*
    Chuck 'n' Bo---Stan Bronstein—Rick Frank—Wayne Gabriel---
      4:33
side two
    Gypsy Wolf---Stan Bronstein—Rick Frank---*3:58*
    Madness---Adam Ippolito—Rick Frank—Stan Bronstein---*3:10*
    Life---Wayne Gabriel---*3:42*
    Wind Ridge---Gary Van Scyoc---*3:20*
    Power Boogie---Stan Bronstein—Rick Frank—Chris Robison
      ---*3:50*
    Local Plastic Ono Band---Rick Frank---*2:00*

331.   SEP 22, 1972 (US) Apple SMAS 3390 (LP)
FEB 9, 1973 (UK) Apple SAPCOR 25 (LP)
by Lon & Derrek Van Eaton   Prod: George Harrison; † Klaus
Voorman
Ringo: Drums

BROTHER
side one
    cut six: *SWEET MUSIC*---Lon & Derrek Van Eaton---*3:41*
side two
    cut five: *Another Thought*---Lon & Derrek Van Eaton---*3:41*

332.   SEP 25, 1972 (US) Apple SW 3395 (LP)
        NOV 24, 1972 (UK) Apple SAPCOR 23 (LP)
        by Mary Hopkin Prod: Paul McCartney
        THOSE WERE THE DAYS
        side one
            cut one: *THOSE WERE THE DAYS*---Gene Raskin---*5:06*
            cut two: *QUE SERA, SERA (WHATEVER WILL BE, WILL*
              BE)---Jay Livingston--Ray Evans---*3:04*
            cut three: *FIELDS OF ST. ETIENNE*---Bernard Gallagher--
              Graham Lyle---*3:12*
        side two
            cut three: *SPARROW*---Bernard Gallagher--Graham Lyle---*3:10*
            cut five: *GOODBYE*---L-McC---*2:23*

333.   OCT 9, 1972 (US) Polydor PD 3502 (2 LPs)
        APR 27, 1973 (UK) RSO 2659-022 (2 LPs)
        by Cream Prod: Felix Pappalardi
        HEAVY CREAM
        side one
            cut three: *BADGE*---Harrison--Eric Clapton---*2:45*

334.   OCT 9, 1972 (US) Polydor PD 3605 (2 LPs)
        APR 27, 1973 (UK) RSO 2659-024 (2 LPs)
        by Jack Bruce Prod: Felix Pappalardi
        JACK BRUCE AT HIS BEST
        side one
            cut one: *NEVER TELL YOUR MOTHER SHE'S OUT OF*
              TUNE--Jack Bruce--Peter Brown---*3:37*
            George: Rhythm Guitar

335.   NOV 3, 1972 (US) Elektra EKS 75049 (LP)
        DEC 15, 1972 (UK) Elektra K 42127 (LP)
        by Carly Simon
        NO SECRETS Prod: Richard Perry
        side two
            cut four: *Night Owl*---James Taylor---*3:47*
            Paul: Backing Vocal

336. NOV 6, 1972 (US) Capitol SVBB 11114 (2 LPs)
      FEB 9, 1973 (UK) Capitol E-ST SP 12 (2 LPs)
      by The Steve Miller Band   Prod: Glyn Johns and Steve Miller
      ANTHOLOGY
      side four
         cut four: *MY DARK HOUR*---Steve Miller---*3:05*
         Paul: Bass Guitar, Drums and Backing Vocal

337. NOV 13, 1972 (US) Apple 1854
      by Elephant's Memory   Prod: John Lennon and Yoko Ono
      A: *LIBERATION SPECIAL*---Rick Frank--Stan Bronstein---
         3:30
      B: *MADNESS*---Adam Ippolito--Rick Frank--Stan Bronstein
         ---*3:10*

338. NOV 13, 1972 (US) Apple 1853
      by Yoko Ono Plastic Ono Band (A side), and Yoko Ono
         Plastic Ono Band with Elephant's Memory (B side)   Prod:
         John Lennon and Yoko Ono
      A: *Now Or Never*---Yoko Ono---*4:57*
      B: *Move On Fast*---Yoko Ono---*3:40*

339. NOV 24, 1972 (UK) Ode 99001 (2 LPs)
      NOV 27, 1972 (US) Ode SP 99001 (2 LPs)
      Recorded: Sept. 1972
      by The London Symphony Orchestra and Chambre Choir with
         Guest Soloists
         Ringo: Vocal Solos
      TOMMY   Prod: Lou Reizner
      side two
         cut five: *Fiddle About*---John Entwistle---*1:23*
      side four
         cut three: *Tommy's Holiday Camp*---Keith Moon---*1:06*

340. DEC 1, 1972 (UK) Apple R 5973
      DEC 4, 1972 (US) Apple 1857
      Recorded: Late Oct. 1972
      by Wings Prod: Paul McCartney
      *A: *Hi, Hi, Hi*---Paul and Linda McCartney---*3:10*
      *B: *C Moon*---Paul and Linda McCartney---*4:33*

340a. DEC 4, 1972 (US) Apple 1854
by Elephant's Memory Prod: John Lennon and Yoko Ono
A: LIBERATION SPECIAL---Rick Frank–Stan Bronstein---
3:30
B: POWER BOOGIE---Stan Bronstein–Rick Frank–Chris
Robison---*3:50*

341. DEC 8, 1972 (UK) Apple 45
by Elephant's Memory Prod: John Lennon and Yoko Ono
A: POWER BOOGIE---Stan Bronstein–Rick Frank–Chris
Robison---*3:50*
B: LIBERATION SPECIAL---Rick Frank–Stan Bronstein---
5:28

341a. DEC 20, 1972 (US) London 2 PS 626/7 (2 LPs)
by The Rolling Stones Prod: Andrew Loog Oldham
MORE HOT ROCKS (BIG HITS AND FAZED COOKIES)
side two
  cut six: *WE LOVE YOU*---Mick Jagger–Keith Richard---*4:39*
John and Paul: Backing Vocals

**Band On
The Run**   Apple SO - 3415 (LP)

**Living In
The Material World**   Apple SMAS 3410 (LP)

**Photograph/
Down And Out**   Apple 1865 (45)

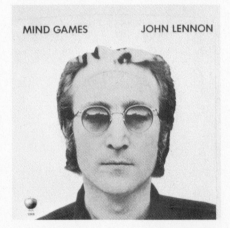

**Mind Games/
Meat City**   Apple 1868 (45)

1973
Wings Over Europe

342.   JAN 8, 1973   (US)   Apple SVBB 3399 (2 LPs)
FEB 16, 1973   (UK)   Apple SAPDO 1001 (2 LPs)
Recorded: Mid Oct.—Late Nov. 1972
by Yoko Ono Plastic Ono Band with Elephant's Memory, The
Endless Strings and Choir Boys
APPROXIMATELY INFINITE UNIVERSE   Prod: John
Lennon and Yoko Ono
side one
Yang Yang---Yoko Ono---*3:52*
Death Of Samantha---Yoko Ono---*6:23*
I Want My Love To Rest Tonight---Yoko Ono---*5:11*
What Did I Do!---Yoko Ono---*4:11*
Have You Seen A Horizon Lately---Yoko Ono---*1:55*
side two
Approximately Infinite Universe---Yoko Ono---*3:19*
Peter The Dealer---Yoko Ono---*4:43*
Song For John---Yoko Ono---*2:02*
Catman (The Rosies Are Coming)---Yoko Ono---*5:29*
What A Bastard The World Is---Yoko Ono---*4:33*
Waiting For The Sunrise---Yoko Ono---*2:32*
side three
I Felt Like Smashing My Face In A Clear Glass Window---
Yoko Ono---*5:07*
Winter Song---Yoko Ono---*3:37*
Kite Song---Yoko Ono---*3:19*
What A Mess---Yoko Ono---*2:41*
Shirankatta (I Didn't Know)---Yoko Ono---*3:13*
Air Talk---Yoko Ono---*3:21*
side four
I Have A Woman Inside My Soul---Yoko Ono---*5:31*
Move On Fast---Yoko Ono---*3:40*

Now Or Never---Yoko Ono---*4:57*
Is Winter Here To Stay?---Yoko Ono---*4:27*
Looking Over From My Hotel Window---Yoko Ono---*3:30*

343. JAN 22, 1973 (US) Apple SVBB 3396 (2 LPs)
      APR 13, 1973 (UK) Apple SAPDO 1002 (2 LPs)
      Recorded live: Oct. 8, 1972 at New York's Philharmonic Hall
      by Ravi Shankar and Ali Akbar Khan
      IN CONCERT 1972 Prod: George Harrison, Zakir Hussein
        and Phil McDonald
      side one
      Raga—Hem Bihag---Ravi Shankar—Ali Akbar Khan---*25:17*
      side two
      Raga—Manj Khamaj (Part One)---Ravi Shankar—Ali Akbar
        Khan---*26:16*
      side three
      Raga—Manj Khamaj (Part Two)---Ravi Shankar—Ali Akbar
        Khan---*25:06*
      side four
      Raga—Sindhi Bhairabi---Ravi Shankar—Ali Akbar Khan---*25:20*

344. FEB 26, 1973 (US) Apple 1859
      MAY 4, 1973 (UK) Apple 47
      by Yoko Ono Plastic Ono Band with Elephant's Memory, The
        Endless Strings and Choir Boys Prod: John Lennon and
        Yoko Ono
      A: DEATH OF SAMANTHA---Yoko Ono---*3:40*
      B: YANG YANG---Yoko Ono---*3:52*

345. MAR 23, 1973 (UK) Apple R 5985
      APR 9, 1973 (US) Apple 1861
      B side recorded live: Aug. 1972 in Europe
      by Paul McCartney and Wings Prod: Paul McCartney
      A: My Love---McCartney---*4:07*
      *B: The Mess---McCartney---*4:55*

346. APR 2, 1973 (US) Apple SKBO 3403 (2 LPs)
      APR 20, 1973 (UK) Apple PCSP 717 (2 LPs)
      by The Beatles (Additional instrumental cut † in US only by
        George Martin & Orchestra)
      THE BEATLES 1962–1966 Prod: George Martin
      side one
      LOVE ME DO---*2:19*
      PLEASE PLEASE ME---*2:00*
      FROM ME TO YOU---*1:49*

SHE LOVES YOU---2:18
I WANT TO HOLD YOUR HAND---2:24
ALL MY LOVING---2:04
CAN'T BUY ME LOVE---2:15
side two
A HARD DAY'S NIGHT---2:28
AND I LOVE HER---2:27
EIGHT DAYS A WEEK---2:43
I FEEL FINE---2:20
TICKET TO RIDE---3:03
YESTERDAY---2:04
side three
†(JAMES BOND THEME---Monty Norman---0:16)
HELP!---2:16
YOU'VE GOT TO HIDE YOUR LOVE AWAY---2:08
WE CAN WORK IT OUT---2:10
DAY TRIPPER---2:37
DRIVE MY CAR---2:25
NORWEGIAN WOOD (THIS BIRD HAS FLOWN)---2:00
side four
NOWHERE MAN---2:40
MICHELLE---2:42
IN MY LIFE---2:23
GIRL---2:26
PAPERBACK WRITER---2:25
ELEANOR RIGBY---2:11
YELLOW SUBMARINE---2:40

347. APR 2, 1973 (US) Apple SKBO 3404 (2 LPs)
APR 20, 1973 (UK) Apple PCSP 718 (2 LPs)
by The Beatles
THE BEATLES 1967–1970 Prod: George Martin; † George
Martin and Phil Spector
side one
STRAWBERRY FIELDS FOREVER---4:05
PENNY LANE---3:00
SGT. PEPPER'S LONELY HEARTS CLUB BAND---1:59
WITH A LITTLE HELP FROM MY FRIENDS---2:46
LUCY IN THE SKY WITH DIAMONDS---3:25
A DAY IN THE LIFE---5:03
ALL YOU NEED IS LOVE---3:57
side two
I AM THE WALRUS---4:35
HELLO GOODBYE---3:24
THE FOOL ON THE HILL---3:00

MAGICAL MYSTERY TOUR---2:48
LADY MADONNA---2:17
HEY JUDE---7:11
REVOLUTION---3:22
side three
BACK IN THE U.S.S.R.---2:45
WHILE MY GUITAR GENTLY WEEPS---Harrison---*4:46*
OB-LA-DI, OB-LA-DA---3:10
GET BACK---3:11
DON'T LET ME DOWN---3:34
THE BALLAD OF JOHN AND YOKO---2:58
OLD BROWN SHOE---Harrison---*3:16*
side four
HERE COMES THE SUN---Harrison---*3:04*
COME TOGETHER---4:16
SOMETHING---Harrison---*2:59*
OCTOPUS'S GARDEN---Starkey---*2:49*
LET IT BE---3:50
†ACROSS THE UNIVERSE---3:51
†THE LONG AND WINDING ROAD---3:40

348. APR 23, 1973 (US) Columbia KC 32074 (LP)
JUL 27, 1973 (UK) CBS 65416 (LP)
by Nicky Hopkins
George (as George O'Hara): Guitar
THE TIN MAN WAS A DREAMER Prod: Nicky Hopkins and
David Briggs
side one
cut two: *Waiting For The Band*---Nicky Hopkins---*2:15*
cut three: *Edward*---Nicky Hopkins---*5:20*
cut five: *Speed On*---Nicky Hopkins---Jerry Williams---*3:59*
side two
cut two: *Banana Anna*---Nicky Hopkins---Jerry Williams---*3:37*

349. APR 30, 1973 (US) Apple SMAL 3409 (LP)
MAY 4, 1973 (UK) Apple PCTC 251 (LP)
Recorded: Mar. and Oct. 1972
by Paul McCartney and Wings
RED ROSE SPEEDWAY Prod: Paul McCartney
side one
Big Barn Bed---McCartney---*3:48*
My Love---McCartney---*4:07*
Get On The Right Thing---McCartney---*4:15*
One More Kiss---McCartney---*2:27*
Little Lamb Dragonfly---McCartney---*6:18*

side two
Single Pigeon---McCartney---1:52
When The Night---McCartney---3:36
Loup (1st Indian On The Moon)---McCartney---4:21
medley: 11:14
   Hold Me Tight---McCartney---2:24
   Lazy Dynamite---McCartney---2:48
   Hands Of Love---McCartney---2:12
   Power Cut---McCartney---3:49

350.   MAY   7, 1973   (US)   Apple 1862
        MAY 25, 1973   (UK)   Apple R 5988
        Recorded during "Living In The Material World" album sessions
        by George Harrison   Prod: George Harrison
        A: *Give Me Love—(Give Me Peace On Earth)---Harrison---3:32*
      *B: *Miss O'Dell---Harrison---2:20*

351.   MAY 28, 1973   (US)   Columbia 45869
        AUG 10, 1973   (UK)   CBS 1328
        by Nicky Hopkins   Prod: Nicky Hopkins and David Briggs
        A: *SPEED ON---Nicky Hopkins—Jerry Williams---3:15*
               George (as George O'Hara): Guitar
        B: *(sundown in mexico)*

352.   MAY 30, 1973   (US)   Apple SMAS 3410 (LP)
        JUN 22, 1973   (UK)   Apple PAS 10006 (LP)
        Recorded: Jan.—April 1973, except instrumental track of †
        recorded in late February 1971
        by George Harrison
        LIVING IN THE MATERIAL WORLD   Prod: George Harrison
          except † George Harrison and Phil Spector
        side one
        Give Me Love—(Give Me Peace On Earth)---Harrison---3:32
        Sue Me, Sue You Blues---Harrison---4:43
        The Light That Has Lighted The World---Harrison---3:28
        Don't Let Me Wait Too Long---Harrison---2:54
        Who Can See It---Harrison---3:49
        Living In The Material World---Harrison---5:27
        side two
        The Lord Loves The One (That Loves The Lord)---Harrison---
          4:32
        Be Here Now---Harrison---4:07
        † Try Some, Buy Some---Harrison---4:06
        The Day The World Gets 'Round---Harrison---2:50
        That Is All---Harrison---3:40

353.   JUN 1, 1973 (UK) Apple R 5987
          JUN 18. 1973 (US) Apple 1863
          A side recorded: Oct. 1972
          by Wings Prod: George Martin (A side); Paul McCartney
           (B side)
          A: *Live And Let Die*—McCartney—*3:10*
        B: I Lie Around—McCartney—*5:00*

354.   JUL 2, 1973 (US) United Artists LA 100-G (LP)
          JUL 6, 1973 (UK) United Artists UAS 29475 (LP)
          by The George Martin Orchestra
           (By Paul McCartney and Wings; † B. J. Arnau)
          LIVE AND LET DIE (Original Soundtrack Album) Prod:
           George Martin
          side one
           cut one: *Live And Let Die (Main Title)*—Paul and Linda
             McCartney—*3:10*
          side two
          † cut two: *Live And Let Die*—Paul and Linda McCartney—*1:07*

355.   AUG 20, 1973 (US) Ode 66038
          by Cheech and Chong Prod: Lew Adler
          A: *Basketball Jones featuring Tyrone Shoelaces*—Richard
             "Cheech" Marin—Thomas Chong—*4:04*
             George: Guitar
          B: *(don't bug me)*

356.   AUG 27, 1973 (US) Ode SP 77019 (LP)
          SEP 28, 1973 (UK) Ode 77019 (LP)
          by Cheech and Chong
          LOS COCHINOS Prod: Lew Adler
          side two
           cut seven: *Basketball Jones featuring Tyrone Shoelaces*—
             Richard "Cheech" Marin—Thomas Chong—*4:04*
             George: Guitar

357.   SEP 7, 1973 (UK) Sunset SLS 50350 (LP)
          by The Bonzo Dog Band Prod: Paul McCartney
          I'M THE URBAN SPACEMAN
          side one
           cut six: *I'M THE URBAN SPACEMAN*—Neil Innes—*2:23*

358.   SEP 10, 1973 (US) RSO SO-877 (LP)
OCT 26, 1973 (UK) Polydor 2394-116 (LP)
Recorded live: Jan. 13, 1973 at London's Rainbow Theatre
Eric Clapton & Friends
ERIC CLAPTON'S RAINBOW CONCERT
side one
    cut one: *Badge*---Harrison—Eric Clapton---*3:29*

359.   SEP 24, 1973 (US) Apple 1865
OCT 19, 1973 (UK) Apple R 5992
Recorded during "Ringo" album sessions
by Ringo Starr   Prod: Richard Perry (A side); George Harrison
    and Richard Perry (B side)
A: Photograph---Starkey—Harrison---*3:58*
B: *Down And Out*---Starkey---*3:01*

360.   SEP 24, 1973 (US) Apple 1867
by Yoko Ono   Prod: Yoko Ono
A: Woman Power---Yoko Ono---*4:50*
      John: Guitar
B: Men, Men, Men---Yoko Ono---*4:01*
      John: Response Vocal

361.   OCTOBER 1973 (US MAIL ORDER) K-Tel TU 229 (LP)
by Various Artists
ORIGINAL HITS—ORIGINAL STARS
side one
    cut two: *MY BONNIE*---Charles Pratt---*2:06*
      by Tony Sheridan and The Beatles   Prod: Bert Kaempfert

362.   OCT 26, 1973 (UK) Apple R 5993
NOV 12, 1973 (US) Apple 1869
A side recorded: Sept. 1973
B side recorded: Oct. 1972
by Paul McCartney and Wings   Prod: Paul McCartney
A: Helen Wheels---McCartney---*3:45*
B: *Country Dreamer*---McCartney---*3:10*

363.   OCT 29, 1973 (US) Apple 1868
NOV 16, 1973 (UK) Apple R 5994
by John Lennon   Prod: John Lennon
A: Mind Games---Lennon---*4:10*
B: Meat City---Lennon---*2:52*

364. OCT 29, 1973 (US) Columbia KC 31721 (LP)
FEB 8, 1974 (UK) CBS 65258 (LP)
Recorded: July 1973
by Dave Mason
IT'S LIKE YOU NEVER LEFT Prod: Dave Mason
side one
cut three: *If You've Got Love*---Dave Mason---*3:19*
George (as Son of Harry): Guitar

365. NOV 2, 1973 (US) Apple SW 3412 (LP)
NOV 23, 1973 (UK) Apple SAPCOR 26 (LP)
by Yoko Ono Plastic Ono Band and Something Different
John (as John O'Cean): Guitar except † Response Vocal
FEELING THE SPACE Prod: Yoko Ono
side two
cut four: *She Hits Back*---Yoko Ono---*3:48*
cut five: *Woman Power*---Yoko Ono---*4:50*
†cut six: *Men, Men, Men*---Yoko Ono---*4:01*

366. NOV 2, 1973 (US) Apple SWAL 3413 (LP)
NOV 9, 1973 (UK) Apple PCTC 252 (LP)
Recorded: Mar.—July 1973
by Ringo Starr
"RINGO" Prod: Richard Perry
side one
I'm The Greatest---Lennon---*3:23*
Hold On (Have You Seen My Baby)---Randy Newman---*3:43*
Photograph---Starkey—Harrison---*3:58*
Sunshine Life For Me (Sail Away Raymond)---Harrison---*2:44*
You're Sixteen---Richard Sherman—Robert Sherman---*2:50*
side two
Oh My My---Starkey—Vini Poncia---*4:17*
Step Lightly---Starkey---*3:15*
Six O'Clock---Paul and Linda McCartney---*4:02*
Devil Woman---Starkey—Vini Poncia---*4:01*
You And Me (Babe)---Harrison—Mal Evans---*4:58*

367. NOV 2, 1973 (US) Apple SW 3414 (LP)
NOV 16, 1973 (UK) Apple PCS 7165 (LP)
Recorded: Sept. 1973
by John Lennon and The Plastic U.F.Ono Band

MIND GAMES   Prod: John Lennon
side one
  Mind Games---Lennon---*4:10*
  Tight A$---Lennon---*3:35*
  Aisumasen (I'm Sorry)---Lennon---*4:41*
  One Day (At A Time)---Lennon---*3:27*
  Bring On The Lucie (Freda Peeple)---Lennon---*4:11*
  Nutopian International Anthem---Lennon---*0:03*
side two
  Intuition---Lennon---*3:05*
  Out The Blue---Lennon---*3:19*
  Only People---Lennon---*3:21*
  I Know (I Know)---Lennon---*3:56*
  You Are Here---Lennon---*4:06*
  Meat City---Lennon---*2:52*

368.   NOV   2, 1973   (UK)   Chrysalis CHR 1054   (LP)
       DEC   7, 1973   (US)   Columbia KC 32729   (LP)
       Recorded: Aug. 1973
       by Alvin Lee and Mylon LeFevre
       ON THE ROAD TO FREEDOM   Prod: Alvin Lee
       side one
         cut three: *So Sad (No Love Of His Own)*---Harrison---*4:37*

369.   NOV   9, 1973   (UK)   Apple 48
       by Yoko Ono   Prod: Yoko Ono
       B: Men, Men, Men---Yoko Ono---*4:01*
             John: Response Vocal
       A: (run, run, run)

370.   NOV   9, 1973   (UK)   RCA 2439
       by Billy Lawrie   Prod: Billy Lawrie and Gary Osborne
       *A: Rock And Roller---Starkey–Billy Lawrie---*3:35*
       B: (shalee shala)

371.   DEC   3, 1973   (US)   Apple 1870
       FEB   8, 1974   (UK)   Apple R 5995
       by Ringo Starr   Prod: Richard Perry
       A: YOU'RE SIXTEEN---Richard Sherman–Robert Sherman
             ---*2:50*
       B: DEVIL WOMAN---Starkey–Vini Poncia---*4:01*

129

372.   DEC   5, 1973   (US)   Apple SO 3415   (LP)
         DEC   7, 1973   (UK)   Apple PAS 10007   (LP)
         Recorded: Sept. 1973
         by Paul McCartney and Wings
         BAND ON THE RUN   Prod: Paul McCartney
         side one
           Band On The Run—McCartney—*5:09*
           Jet—McCartney—*4:08*
           Bluebird—McCartney—*3:22*
           Mrs. Vandebilt—McCartney—*4:40*
           Let Me Roll It—McCartney—*4:51*
         side two (†included only on US album)
           Mamunia—McCartney—*4:51*
           No Words—McCartney–Denny Laine—*2:36*
         †HELEN WHEELS—McCartney—*3:45*
           Picasso's Last Words (Drink To Me)—McCartney—*5:48*
           Nineteen Hundred And Eighty Five—McCartney—*5:30*

372a.   DEC 17, 1973   (US)   Columbia 45987
         APR 19, 1974   (UK)   Chrysalis CHS 2035
         by Alvin Lee and Mylon LeFevre   Prod: Alvin Lee
         A: SO SAD (NO LOVE OF HIS OWN)—Harrison—*4:37*
         B: (riffin)

"WALKING IN THE PARK WITH ELOISE"

The Country Hams

Walking In The Park With Eloise/
Bridge Over The River Suite

EMI 3977 (45)

You're Sixteen/Devil Woman   Apple 1870   (45)

Only You/Call Me   Apple 1876   (45)

1974

A Dark Horse
At The White House

373.   JAN 7, 1974 (US) Columbia KC 32717 (LP)
Recorded: Aug. 17, 1972
by David Bromberg
WANTED—DEAD OR ALIVE Prod: David Bromberg
side one
    cut one: *The Holdup (version two)*—Harrison—David
      Bromberg—*3:03*

374.   JAN 28, 1974 (US) Apple 1871
by Paul McCartney and Wings Prod: Paul McCartney
A: JET—McCartney—*4:08*
B: MAMUNIA—McCartney—*4:51*

375.   FEB 15, 1974 (UK) Apple R 5996
FEB 18, 1974 (US) Apple 1871
by Paul McCartney and Wings Prod: Paul McCartney
A: JET—McCartney—*4:08*
B: LET ME ROLL IT—McCartney—*4:51*

376.   FEB 18, 1974 (US) Apple 1872
by Ringo Starr Prod: Richard Perry
A: OH MY MY—Starkey—Vini Poncia—*3:39*
B: STEP LIGHTLY—Starkey—*3:15*

377.   MAR 7, 1974 (US) Asylum 11027
by Jimmy Webb Prod: Jimmy Webb
  Ringo: Drums
A: Crying In My Sleep—Jimmy Webb—*4:10*
B: Ocean In His Eyes—Jimmy Webb—*4:27*

378.   MAR 25, 1974   (US)   Sire SAS 3702   (2 LPs)
       by Various Artists
       (By Peter and Gordon;   † The Silkie   Prod: John Lennon
         and Paul McCartney)
       HISTORY OF BRITISH ROCK
       side one
         cut four: *A WORLD WITHOUT LOVE*---L-McC---*2:38*
       side two
       † cut five: *YOU'VE GOT TO HIDE YOUR LOVE AWAY*---
         L-McC---2:20

379.   MAR 25, 1974   (US)   RCA APBO 0246
       JUN   7, 1974   (UK)   RCA APBO 0246
       by Harry Nilsson   Prod: Harry Nilsson
       A: Daybreak---Harry Nilsson---*2:43*
             Ringo: Drums;   George: Cowbell
       B: (down)

380.   MAR 29, 1974   (UK)   Arcade ADEP 9/10   (2 LPs)
       by Various Artists
       ALAN FREEMAN'S HISTORY OF POP VOL. 2
       side four
         cut one: *A WORLD WITHOUT LOVE*---L-McC---*2:38*
           by Peter and Gordon

381.   APR   1, 1974   (US)   Rapple ABL 1-0220   (LP)
       MAY 24, 1974   (UK)   RCA APL 1-0220   (LP)
       New Song † Recorded: Sept. 1972
       Dialogue % Recorded: Aug.–Oct. 1972
       by Harry Nilsson
       SON OF DRACULA (Original Soundtrack Album)   Overall
         production for album by Ringo Starr and Harry Nilsson.
         Music production by + Richard Perry and † Harry Nilsson.
       side one
       % It Is He Who Will Be King---Paul Buckmaster---*3:07*
       † Daybreak---Harry Nilsson---*2:43*
       + AT MY FRONT DOOR---Ewart G. Abner–John C. Moore---
         2:46
       % Count Down Meets Merlin And Amber---Paul Buckmaster---
         2:10
       +The Moonbeam Song---Harry Nilsson---*3:20*
       %Perhaps This Is All A Dream---Paul Buckmaster---*0:47*
       +Remember Christmas---Harry Nilsson---*4:09*

side two
%Intro---Paul Buckmaster---*0:20*
+Without You---Pete Ham--Tom Evans---*3:27*
% The Count's Vulnerability---Paul Buckmaster---*2:10*
+Down---Harry Nilsson---*3:07*
%Frankenstein, Merlin And The Operation---John Tavener---
   3:20
+Jump Into The Fire---Harry Nilsson---*3:16*
%The Abdication Of Count Down---Paul Buckmaster---*1:10*
  Medley: 0:49
   % The End---Paul Buckmaster
   + The Moonbeam Song---Harry Nilsson

382.   APR 8, 1974 (US) Apple 1873
        by Paul McCartney and Wings Prod: Paul McCartney
        A: BAND ON THE RUN---McCartney---*5:09*
        B: NINETEEN HUNDRED AND EIGHTY FIVE---McCartney
          --5:30

383.   MAY 24, 1974 (UK) United Artists UAD 60071/2 (2 LPs)
        SEP 9, 1974 (US) United Artists UA-LA 321-H2 (2 LPs)
        by The Bonzo Dog Band Prod: Paul McCartney
        THE HISTORY OF THE BONZOS
        side three
          cut one: *I'M THE URBAN SPACEMAN*---Neil Innes---*2:23*

384.   MAY 24, 1974 (UK) Warner Brothers K 16400
        JUL 29, 1974 (US) Warner Brothers 8001
        by Scaffold Prod: Paul McCartney
        A: Liverpool Lou---Dominic Behan---*2:58*
      *B: Ten Years After On Strawberry Jam---Paul and Linda
          McCartney---*2:52*

385.   JUN 3, 1974 (US) Asylum SD 5070 (LP)
        JUL 5, 1974 (UK) Asylum SYL 9014 (LP)
        Recorded: July--Aug. 1973
        by Jimmy Webb
        LAND'S END Prod: Jimmy Webb
         Ringo: Drums
        side one
         Ocean In His Eyes---Jimmy Webb---*4:27*
         Feet In The Sunshine---Jimmy Webb---*3:28*
         Cloud Man---Jimmy Webb---*3:45*
         Lady Fits Her Bluejeans---Jimmy Webb---*4:05*
         Just This One Time---Jimmy Webb---*4:58*

side two
Crying In My Sleep---Jimmy Webb---*4:10*
It's A Sin---Jimmy Webb---*3:06*
Alyce Blue Gown---Jimmy Webb---*4:58*
Land's End/Asleep On The Wind---Jimmy Webb---*9:07*

386.   JUN 17, 1974   (US)   ESP-DISK' ESP 45-63019
Recorded: Jan. 1971
by Thornton, Fradkin & Unger and The Big Band   Prod:
  Leslie Fradkin
A: God Bless California---Leslie Fradkin---*3:36*
      Paul: Bass Guitar and Backing Vocal
B: (sometimes)

387.   JUN 28, 1974   (UK)   Apple R 5997
by Paul McCartney and Wings   Prod: Paul McCartney
A: BAND ON THE RUN---McCartney---*5:09*
*B: Zoo Gang---McCartney---*1:55*

388.   JUN 28, 1974   (UK)   Polydor 2058-496
JUL 1, 1974   (US)   Capitol 3928
by John Christie   Prod: Dave Clark
*A: 4th Of July---Paul and Linda McCartney---*2:47*
B: (old enough to know better young enough to cry)

389.   JUN 28, 1974   (UK)   Warner Brothers K 56042 (LP)
JUL 2, 1974   (US)   Warner Brothers W 2794 (LP)
by James Taylor
 Paul: Backing Vocal
WALKING MAN   Prod: Dave Spinozza
side one
  cut two: *Rock 'n' Roll Is Music Now*---James Taylor---*3:25*
  cut three: *Let It All Fall Down*---James Taylor---*3:30*

390.   JUL 5, 1974   (UK)   Asylum AYM 529
by Jimmy Webb   Prod: Jimmy Webb
 Ringo: Drums
A: Feet In The Sunshine---Jimmy Webb---*3:28*
B: Ocean In His Eyes---Jimmy Webb---*4:27*

391.   JUL 8, 1974   (US)   Asylum 11042
by Jimmy Webb   Prod: Jimmy Webb
 Ringo: Drums
A: FEET IN THE SUNSHINE---Jimmy Webb---*3:28*
B: LADY FITS HER BLUEJEANS---Jimmy Webb---*4:05*

392.   JUL 8, 1974 (US) ESP-DISK' ESP 63019 (LP)
by Thornton, Fradkin & Unger and The Big Band   Prod:
  Leslie Fradkin
PASS ON THIS SIDE
side one
   cut one: *God Bless California*—Leslie Fradkin—*3:36*
     Paul: Bass Guitar and Backing Vocal

393.   JUL 8, 1974 (US) RCA PB 10001
SEP 13, 1974 (UK) RCA 2459
by Harry Nilsson   Prod: John Lennon
A: Many Rivers To Cross—Jimmy Cliff—*4:56*
B: Don't Forget Me—Harry Nilsson—*3:37*

394.   JUL 22, 1974 (US) Warner Brothers 8015
by James Taylor   Prod: Dave Spinozza
A: LET IT ALL FALL DOWN—James Taylor—*3:30*
     Paul: Backing Vocal
B: (daddy's baby)

395.   AUG 19, 1974 (US) RCA CPL 1-0570 (LP)
AUG 30, 1974 (UK) RCA APL 1-0570 (LP)
Recorded: Mar.—May 1974
by Harry Nilsson
PUSSY CATS   Prod: John Lennon
side one
  Many Rivers To Cross—Jimmy Cliff—*4:56*
  Subterranean Homesick Blues—Bob Dylan—*3:17*
  Don't Forget Me—Harry Nilsson—*3:37*
  All My Life—Harry Nilsson—*3:11*
  Old Forgotten Soldier—Harry Nilsson—*4:14*
side two
  Save The Last Dance For Me—Doc Pomus—Mort Shuman—
   4:25
  Medley: 3:43
   Mucho Mungo—Lennon
   Mt. Elga—Adapted by Harry Nilsson
  Loop De Loop—Ted Vann—*2:40*
  Black Sails—Harry Nilsson—*3:15*
  (We're Gonna) Rock Around The Clock—Jimmy DeKnight—
   Max Freedman—*3:12*

396.   SEP   2, 1974   (US)   Warner Brothers BS 2791 (LP)
          SEP 20, 1974   (UK)   Warner Brothers K 56054 (LP)
          by Adam Faith
            Paul: Synthesizer except † Backing Vocal
          I SURVIVE   Prod: Adam Faith and David Courtney
          side one
            cut five: *Change---Adam Faith--David Courtney---4:00*
          side two
            cut two: *Never Say Goodbye---Adam Faith--David Courtney*
              ---4:04
            cut three: *Goodbye---Adam Faith--David Courtney---4:01*
          † cut five: *Star Song---Adam Faith--David Courtney---5:58*

397.   SEP   6, 1974   (UK)   Warner Brothers K 16446
          OCT 28, 1974   (US)   Warner Brothers 8037
          Recorded during "McGear" album sessions
          by Mike McGear   Prod: Paul McCartney
          A: Leave It---McCartney---3:44
        *B: Sweet Baby---McCartney--Mike McGear---3:39

398.   SEP 13, 1974   (UK)   Dark Horse AMS 7133
          NOV   6, 1974   (US)   Dark Horse DH 10001
          by Ravi Shankar Family & Friends   Prod: George Harrison
          A: I Am Missing You---Ravi Shankar---3:40
          B: Lust---Ravi Shankar---3:12

399.   SEP 13, 1974   (UK)   Dark Horse AMS 7135
          NOV   7, 1974   (US)   Dark Horse DH 10002
          by Splinter   Prod: George Harrison
          A: Costafine Town---Robert J. Purvis--William Elliott---3:10
          B: Elly-May---Robert J. Purvis---2:43

400.   SEP 20, 1974   (UK)   Dark Horse AMLH 22001 (LP)
          SEP 25, 1974   (US)   Dark Horse SP 22001 (LP)
          by Splinter
          THE PLACE I LOVE   Prod: George Harrison
          side one
            Gravy Train---Robert J. Purvis---4:50
            Drink All Day (Got To Find Your Own Way Home)---Robert
              J. Purvis---3:20
            China Light---Robert J. Purvis--William Elliott---4:35
            Somebody's City---Robert J. Purvis---5:20

side two
 Costafine Town--Robert J. Purvis--William Elliott--*3:10*
 The Place I Love--Robert J. Purvis--*4:25*
 Situation Vacant--Robert J. Purvis--*4:00*
 Elly-May--Robert J. Purvis--*2:43*
 Haven't Got Time--Robert J. Purvis--*3:55*

401. SEP 20, 1974 (UK) Dark Horse AMLH 22002 (LP)
 OCT 7, 1974 (US) Dark Horse SP 22002 (LP)
 Recorded: April 1973–Early 1974
 by Ravi Shankar Family & Friends
 SHANKAR FAMILY & FRIENDS Prod: George Harrison
 side one
 I Am Missing You--Ravi Shankar--*3:40*
 Kahan Gayelava Shyam Salone--Ravi Shankar--*3:15*
 Supane Me Aye Preetam Sainya--Ravi Shankar--*4:44*
 I Am Missing You (reprise)--Ravi Shankar--*3:56*
 Jaya Jagadish Hare--P.D.--*4:50*
 side two: *Dream, Nightmare & Dawn (Music For A Ballet)*--
 Ravi Shankar--*29:13*
 Overture--Ravi Shankar--*2:28*
 Part One: Dream--*7:02*
  Festivity & Joy--Ravi Shankar--*3:52*
  Love-Dance Ecstasy--Ravi Shankar--*3:10*
 Part Two: Nightmare--*12:15*
  Lust--Ravi Shankar--*3:12*
  Dispute & Violence--Ravi Shankar--*3:05*
  Disillusionment & Frustration--Ravi Shankar--*2:51*
  Despair & Sorrow--Ravi Shankar--*3:07*
 Part Three: Dawn--*7:28*
  Awakening--Ravi Shankar--*3:07*
  Peace & Hope--Ravi Shankar--*4:21*

402. SEP 23, 1974 (US) Warner Brothers BS 2819 (LP)
 SEP 27, 1974 (UK) Warner Brothers K 56065 (LP)
 Recorded: July 1974
 by Ron Wood
 I'VE GOT MY OWN ALBUM TO DO Prod: Ron Wood and
 Gary Kellgren
 side one
  cut two: *Far East Man*--Harrison--Ron Wood--*4:40*

403. SEP 23, 1974 (US) Apple 1874
OCT 4, 1974 (UK) Apple R 5998
by John Lennon with The Plastic Ono Nuclear Band Prod:
 John Lennon
A: *Whatever Gets You Thru The Night*—Lennon—*3:24*
B: *Beef Jerky*—Lennon—*3:25*

404. SEP 26, 1974 (US) Apple SW 3416 (LP)
OCT 4, 1974 (UK) Apple PCTC 253 (LP)
Recorded: June—Aug. 1974
by John Lennon with The Plastic Ono Nuclear Band
WALLS AND BRIDGES Prod: John Lennon
side one
 Going Down On Love—Lennon—*3:53*
 Whatever Gets You Thru The Night—Lennon—*3:24*
 Old Dirt Road—Lennon—Harry Nilsson—*4:10*
 What You Got—Lennon—*3:06*
 Bless You—Lennon—*4:39*
 Scared—Lennon—*4:37*
side two
 No. 9 Dream—Lennon—*4:44*
 Surprise, Surprise (Sweet Bird Of Paradox)—Lennon—*2:33*
 Steel And Glass—Lennon—*4:35*
 Beef Jerky—Lennon—*3:25*
 Nobody Loves You (When You're Down And Out)—Lennon
  —*5:07*
 Ya Ya—Morris Robinson—Clarence Lewis—Lee Dorsey—*1:06*

405. SEP 27, 1974 (UK) Mercury 9104-001 (LP)
OCT 7, 1974 (US) Mercury SRM 1-1017 (LP)
Recorded: Jan.—Feb. 1974
by Rod Stewart
SMILER Prod: Rod Stewart
side two
 cut six: *Mine For Me*—McCartney—*4:02*

406. SEP 27, 1974 (UK) Warner Brothers K 56051 (LP)
OCT 14, 1974 (US) Warner Brothers BS 2825 (LP)
Recorded: Jan.—May 1974
by Mike McGear
MCGEAR Prod: Paul McCartney

side one
Sea Breezes—Bryan Ferry—*4:52*
What Do We Really Know?—McCartney—*3:28*
Norton—McCartney—Mike McGear—*2:35*
Leave It—McCartney—*3:44*
Have You Got Problems?—McCartney—Mike McGear—*6:16*
side two
The Casket—McCartney—Roger McGough—*4:19*
Rainbow Lady—McCartney—Mike McGear—*3:26*
Simply Love You—McCartney—Mike McGear—*2:47*
Givin' Grease A Ride—McCartney—Mike McGear—*5:35*
The Man Who Found God On The Moon—McCartney—Mike
   McGear—*6:26*

407.　OCT　1, 1974　(US)　RCA PB 10078
by Harry Nilsson　Prod: John Lennon
A: SUBTERRANEAN HOMESICK BLUES—Bob Dylan—*3:17*
B: MEDLEY: 3:43
     MUCHO MUNGO—Lennon
     MT. ELGA—Adapted by Harry Nilsson

408.　OCT　1, 1974　(US)　Atlantic SD 18108　(LP)
NOV　8, 1974　(UK)　Warner Brothers K 50064　(LP)
Recorded: Mid June 1974
by Peggy Lee　Prod: Paul McCartney
LET'S LOVE
side one
   cut one: *Let's Love*—Paul McCartney—*2:58*
side two
   cut six: *Let's Love (reprise)*—Paul McCartney—*1:20*

409.　OCT　7, 1974　(US)　Atlantic 3215
OCT 25, 1974　(UK)　Warner Brothers K 10527
by Peggy Lee　Prod: Paul McCartney
A: Let's Love—Paul McCartney—*2:58*
B: (always)

410.　OCT 18, 1974　(UK)　EMI 3977
DEC　2, 1974　(US)　EMI 3977
Recorded: June—July 1974
by The Country Hams　Prod: Paul McCartney
*A: Walking In The Park With Eloise—James McCartney—*3:07*
*B: Bridge Over The River Suite—Paul and Linda McCartney—
     3:08

411.   OCT 25, 1974   (UK)   Apple R 5999
       A and B sides reversed: Feb. 7, 1975
       NOV   4, 1974   (US)   Apple 1875
       A and B sides reversed: Jan. 20, 1975
       Recorded: June–July 1974
       by Paul McCartney and Wings   Prod: Paul McCartney
       A: Junior's Farm—McCartney—4:20
       B: Sally G—McCartney—3:37

412.   OCT 25, 1974   (UK)   Ronco RG 2009/10 (2 LPs)
       MAR 28, 1975   (US)   Arista AL 5000 (2 LPs)
       by Various Artists
       STARDUST (Original Soundtrack Album)
       side one
          cut six: *DO YOU WANT TO KNOW A SECRET—L-McC—
          1:59*
             by Billy J. Kramer with The Dakotas   Prod: George Martin

413.   NOV   4, 1974   (US)   Mercury 73636
       by Rod Stewart   Prod: Rod Stewart
       B: MINE FOR ME—McCartney—4:02
       A: (farewell)

414.   NOV 11, 1974   (US)   Apple 1876
       NOV 15, 1974   (UK)   Apple R 6000
       by Ringo Starr   Prod: Richard Perry
       *A: Only You (And You Alone)—Buck Ram—Ande Rand—
          3:16*
       B: Call Me—Starkey—3:57

415.   NOV 15, 1974   (UK)   Apple PCS 7168 (LP)
       NOV 18, 1974   (US)   Apple SW 3417 (LP)
       Recorded: Summer 1974
       by Ringo Starr
       GOODNIGHT VIENNA   Prod: Richard Perry
       side one
          (It's All Da-Da-Down To) Goodnight Vienna—Lennon—2:32
          Occapella—Allen Toussaint—2:55
          Oo-Wee—Starkey–Vini Poncia—3:42
          Husbands And Wives—Roger Miller—3:20
          Snookeroo—Elton John–Bernie Taupin—3:27

side two
All By Myself---Starkey--Vini Poncia---*3:20*
Call Me---Starkey---*3:57*
No No Song---Hoyt Axton--David P. Jackson---*2:30*
Only You (And You Alone)---Buck Ram--Ande Rand---*3:16*
Easy For Me---Harry Nilsson---*2:18*
Goodnight Vienna (reprise)---Lennon---*1:15*

416. NOV 15, 1974 (UK) DJM DJS 340
NOV 18, 1974 (US) MCA 40344
Recorded: Late Aug. 1974
by Elton John   Prod: Gus Dudgeon
John (as Dr. Winston O'Boogie): Guitars and (side A only)
    Backing Vocal
*A: *Lucy In The Sky With Diamonds*---L-McC---*5:59*
*B: *One Day At A Time*---Lennon---*3:47*

417. NOV 18, 1974 (US) Apple 1877
Recorded during "Dark Horse" album sessions
by George Harrison   Prod: George Harrison
A: *Dark Horse*---Harrison---*3:50*
*B: *I Don't Care Anymore*---Harrison---*2:40*

418. NOV 25, 1974 (US) Blue Sky PZ 33292 (LP)
FEB   7, 1975 (UK) Blue Sky 80586 (LP)
Recorded: Early Oct. 1974
by Johnny Winter
JOHN DAWSON WINTER III Prod: Shelly Yakus
side one
  cut one: *Rock & Roll People*---Lennon---*2:44*

419. DEC   2, 1974 (US) Sire SASH 3705 (2 LPs)
by Various Artists
  (By The Beatles   Prod: Bert Kaempfert; † Billy J. Kramer
    with The Dakotas   Prod: George Martin; % Badfinger
    Prod: Paul McCartney)
HISTORY OF BRITISH ROCK VOL. 2
side one
  cut one: *AIN'T SHE SWEET*---Jack Yellen--Milton Ager---*2:12*
†cut two: *BAD TO ME*---L-McC---*2:18*
side four
%cut one: *COME AND GET IT*---Paul McCartney---*2:21*

420. DEC 6, 1974 (UK) Warner Brothers K 16482
by Adam Faith   Prod: Adam Faith and David Courtney
A: *STAR SONG*---Adam Faith--David Courtney---*5:58*
       Paul: Backing Vocal
B: *(maybe)*

421. DEC 6, 1974 (UK) Apple R 6002
by George Harrison   Prod: George Harrison
A: *Ding Dong; Ding Dong*---Harrison---*3:39*
*B: *I Don't Care Anymore*---Harrison---*2:40*

422. DEC 9, 1974 (US) Apple SMAS 3418 (LP)
DEC 20, 1974 (UK) Apple PAS 10008 (LP)
Recorded: Sept.--Oct. 1974
by George Harrison
DARK HORSE Prod: George Harrison
side one
   Hari's On Tour (Express)---Harrison---*4:40*
   Simply Shady---Harrison---*4:36*
   So Sad---Harrison---*4:56*
   Bye Bye, Love---Felice Bryant--Boudleaux Bryant (Parody
      lyrics added by George Harrison)---*4:05*
   Maya Love---Harrison---*4:20*
side two
   Ding Dong; Ding Dong---Harrison---*3:39*
   Dark Horse---Harrison---*3:50*
   Far East Man---Harrison--Ron Wood---*5:47*
   It Is "He" (Jai Sri Krishna)---Harrison---*4:45*

423. DEC 9, 1974 (US) RCA PB 10139
by Harry Nilsson   Prod: John Lennon
A: *LOOP DE LOOP*---Ted Vann---*2:40*
B: *DON'T FORGET ME*---Harry Nilsson---*3:37*

424. DEC 16, 1974 (US) Apple 1878
JAN 31, 1975 (UK) Apple R 6003
by John Lennon   Prod: John Lennon
A: *NO. 9 DREAM*---Lennon---*4:44*
B: *WHAT YOU GOT*---Lennon---*3:06*

425. DEC 23, 1974 (US) Apple 1879
by George Harrison   Prod: George Harrison
A: *DING DONG; DING DONG*---Harrison---*3:39*
B: *HARI'S ON TOUR (EXPRESS)*---Harrison---*4:40*

Rock 'n' Roll   **Apple SK 3419 (LP)**

Listen To What The Man Said/   Capitol 4091 (45)
   Love In Song

Goodnight Vienna/Oo-Wee   Apple 1882 (45)

1975

You Should've Been There

426.   JAN 27, 1975   (US)   Apple 1880
        by Ringo Starr   Prod: Richard Perry
        A: *NO NO SONG*---Hoyt Axton–David P. Jackson---*2:30*
        A: *SNOOKEROO*---Elton John–Bernie Taupin---*3:27*

427.   JAN 31, 1975   (UK)   RCA 2504
        by Harry Nilsson   Prod: John Lennon
        A: *SAVE THE LAST DANCE FOR ME*---Doc Pomus–Mort
            Shuman---*4:25*
        B: *ALL MY LIFE*---Harry Nilsson---*3:11*

428.   FEB   7, 1975   (UK)   Warner Brothers K 56097   (LP)
        by Scaffold   Prod: Paul McCartney
        SOLD OUT
        side one
          cut one: *LIVERPOOL LOU*---Dominic Behan---*2:58*

429.   FEB   7, 1975   (UK)   Dark Horse AMS 5501
        by Splinter   Prod: George Harrison
        A: *DRINK ALL DAY (GOT TO FIND YOUR OWN WAY
            HOME)*---Robert J. Purvis---*3:20*
        B: *HAVEN'T GOT TIME*---Robert J. Purvis---*3:55*

430.   FEB   7, 1975   (UK)   Warner Brothers K 16520
        by Mike McGear   Prod: Paul McCartney
        A: *SEA BREEZES*---Bryan Ferry---*4:52*
        A: *GIVIN' GREASE A RIDE*---McCartney–Mike McGear---
            5:35

431. FEB 14, 1975 (US MAIL ORDER) Warner Brothers
PRO 596 (2 LPs)
by Various Artists
THE FORCE
side three
   cut six: *NORTON*—McCartney—Mike McGear—*2:35*
     by Mike McGear   Prod: Paul McCartney

432. FEB 17, 1975 (US) Apple SK 3419 (LP)
FEB 21, 1975 (UK) Apple PCS 7169 (LP)
Recorded: Oct. 21–25, 1974 except † Oct.–Dec. 1973
by John Lennon
ROCK 'N' ROLL   Prod: John Lennon except † Phil Spector
side one
   Be-Bop-A-Lula—Gene Vincent—Tex Davis—*2:36*
   Stand By Me—Ben E. King—Jerry Leiber—Mike Stoller—*3:29*
   Medley: 1:39
     Rip It Up—Robert Blackwell—John Marascalco—*1:06*
     Ready Teddy—Robert Blackwell—John Marascalco—*0:33*
   † You Can't Catch Me—Chuck Berry—*4:51*
   Ain't That A Shame—Antoine Domino—Dave Bartholomew
     —*2:31*
   Do You Want To Dance—Bobby Freeman—*2:53*
   †Sweet Little Sixteen—Chuck Berry—*3:00*
side two
   Slippin' And Slidin'—Richard Penniman—Edwin J. Bocage—
     Albert Collins—James Smith—*2:16*
   Peggy Sue—Jerry Allison—Norman Petty—Buddy Holly—*2:02*
   Medley: 3:40
     Bring It On Home To Me—Sam Cooke—*2:03*
     Send Me Some Lovin'—Lloyd Price—John Marascalco—*1:37*
   †Bony Moronie—Larry Williams—*3:50*
   Ya Ya—Morgan Robinson—Clarence Lewis—Lee Dorsey—*2:17*
   †Just Because—Lloyd Price—*4:25*

433. FEB 17, 1975 (US) Ring O' ST 11372 (LP)
APR 18, 1975 (UK) Ring O' 2320-101 (LP)
Recorded: Sept. 1974
by David Hentschel
STA*RTLING MUSIC   Prod: David Hentschel and John
  Gilbert
side one
   cut three: *Step Lightly*—Starkey—*3:39*
     Ringo (as R.S.): Finger Clicks

434. FEB 21, 1975 (UK) Dark Horse AMS 5502
by Splinter   Prod: George Harrison
A: CHINA LIGHT---Robert J. Purvis—William Elliott---*3:29*
*B: DRINK ALL DAY (GOT TO FIND YOUR OWN WAY
      HOME)*---Robert J. Purvis---*3:20*

435. FEB 21, 1975 (UK) Apple R 6004
by Ringo Starr   Prod: Richard Perry
A: SNOOKEROO---Elton John—Bernie Taupin---*3:27*
B: OO-WEE---Starkey—Vini Poncia---*3:42*

436. FEB 24, 1975 (US) MCA 40364
FEB 28, 1975 (UK) DJM DJS 354
*Recorded Live: Nov. 28, 1974 at New York's Madison Square
   Garden*
by The Elton John Band   Prod: Gus Dudgeon
*B: I Saw Her Standing There---L-McC---*3:53*
         John: Guitar and Vocal
A: (phildelphia freedom)

436a. FEB 28, 1975 (UK) Apple R 6001
by George Harrison   Prod: George Harrison
A: DARK HORSE---Harrison---*3:50*
B: HARI'S ON TOUR (EXPRESS)---Harrison---*4:40*

437. MAR 7, 1975 (US) Dark Horse DH 10003
by Splinter   Prod: George Harrison
A: CHINA LIGHT—Robert J. Purvis—William Elliott---*3:29*
B: HAVEN'T GOT TIME---Robert J. Purvis---*3:55*

438. MAR 10, 1975 (US) Apple 1881
APR 18, 1975 (UK) Apple R 6005
Recorded during "Rock 'n' Roll" album sessions
by John Lennon   Prod: John Lennon
A: STAND BY ME---Ben E. King—Jerry Leiber—Mike Stoller
      ---*3:29*
*B: Move Over Ms. L---Lennon---*2:56*

439. MAR 10, 1975 (US) RCA APL 1-0998 (LP)
MAR 28, 1975 (UK) RCA RS 1006 (LP)
Recorded: Jan. 1975
by David Bowie   Prod: David Bowie and Harry Maslin
YOUNG AMERICANS
side two
   cut three: *Across The Universe*---L-McC---*4:30*
      John: Guitar
   cut five: *Fame*---Lennon—David Bowie—Luther Andross---*4:12*

440.   MAR 10, 1975   (US)   RCA JB 10183
JUN 13, 1975   (UK)   RCA 2565
by Harry Nilsson   Prod: Harry Nilsson
A: Kojak Columbo---Harry Nilsson---*2:45*
      Ringo: Drums
B: (turn out the light)

441.   MAR 17, 1975   (US)   Track 2136   (LP)
MAY 23, 1975   (UK)   Polydor 2442-134   (LP)
Recorded: Sept.–Dec. 1974
by Keith Moon
TWO SIDES OF THE MOON   Prod: Mal Evans, Skip Taylor
  and John Stronach, except † Skip Taylor and John Stronach
side one
   cut two: *Solid Gold*---Nickey Barclay---*2:47*
      Ringo: Announcing
side two
   cut one: *Move Over Ms. L*---Lennon---*3:11*
†cut five: *Together*---Harry Nilsson---*3:03*
      Ringo: Drums and "Rap"

442.   MAR 21, 1975   (US)   RCA APL 1-0817   (LP)
MAR 28, 1975   (UK)   RCA 1008   (LP)
by Harry Nilsson
DUIT ON MON DEI   Prod: Harry Nilsson
side one
   cut four: *Kojak Columbo*---Harry Nilsson---*3:30*
      Ringo: Drums
side two
   cut five: *Good For God*---Harry Nilsson---*3:23*
      Ringo: Backing Vocal

443.   MAR 31, 1975   (US)   Track 40387
by Keith Moon   Prod: Mal Evans, Skip Taylor and John
  Stronach
A: SOLID GOLD---Nickey Barclay---*2:47*
      Ringo: Announcing
B: MOVE OVER MS. L---Lennon---*3:11*

444.   APR 21, 1975   (US)   Elektra 7E 1033   (LP)
JUN 6, 1975   (UK)   Elektra 52020   (LP)
by Carly Simon

PLAYING POSSUM   Prod: Richard Perry
side one
  cut four: *More And More*---Mac Rebbanack--Alvin Robinson
  ---4:02
  Ringo: Drums

445.   MAY 16, 1975   (UK)   Polydor 2058-584
     by Keith Moon   Prod: Skip Taylor and John Stronach
     B: *Together*---Harry Nilsson---*3:03*
        Ringo: Drums and "Rap"
     A: *(don't worry baby)*

446.   MAY 16, 1975   (UK)   Capitol R 6006
     MAY 23, 1975   (US)   Capitol 4091
     by Wings   Prod: Paul McCartney
     A: *Listen To What The Man Said*---McCartney---*3:59*
     B: *Love In Song*---McCartney---*3:05*

447.   MAY 27, 1975   (US)   Capitol SMAS 11419 (LP)
     MAY 30, 1975   (UK)   Capitol PCTC 254 (LP)
     Recorded: Mid Jan.--Early April 1975
     by Wings
     VENUS AND MARS   Prod: Paul McCartney
     side one
      Venus And Mars---McCartney---*1:16*
      Rock Show---McCartney---*5:32*
      Love In Song---McCartney---*3:05*
      You Gave Me The Answer---McCartney---*2:14*
      Magneto And Titanium Man---McCartney---*3:15*
      Letting Go---McCartney---*4:36*
     side two
      Venus And Mars--Reprise---McCartney---*2:03*
      Spirits Of Ancient Egypt---McCartney---*3:05*
      Medicine Jar---Jimmy McCulloch--Colin Allen--*3:37*
      Call Me Back Again---McCartney---*4:59*
      Listen To What The Man Said---McCartney---*3:59*
      Medley: 4:24
        Treat Her Gently---McCartney
        Lonely Old People---McCartney
      Crossroads Theme---Tony Hatch---*1:01*

448.   JUN 2, 1975 (US) Apple 1882
by Ringo Starr   Prod: Richard Perry
A: MEDLEY: 2:58
   (IT'S ALL DA-DA-DOWN TO) GOODNIGHT VIENNA
      --Lennon
   GOODNIGHT VIENNA—REPRISE---Lennon
B: OO-WEE---Starkey—Vini Poncia---*3:15*

449.   JUN 2, 1975 (US) RCA JB 10320
JUL 18, 1975 (UK) RCA 2579
by David Bowie   Prod: David Bowie and Harry Maslin
A: FAME---Lennon—David Bowie—Luther Andross---*3:30*
B: (right)

450.   JUN 20, 1975 (US) A&M SP 4532 (LP)
JUL 19, 1975 (UK) A&M AMLH 64532 (LP)
Recorded: Sept.—Oct. 1974
by Billy Preston
IT'S MY PLEASURE   Prod: Billy Preston, Malcolm Cecil and
   Robert Margouleff
side one
   cut three: *That's Life*---Billy Preston---*3:41*
      George (as Hari Georgeson): Guitar

451.   JUL 4, 1975 (UK) Warner Brothers K 16573
by Mike McGear   Prod: Paul McCartney
*A: Dance The Do---McCartney—Mike McGear---*2:59*
 B: NORTON---McCartney—Mike McGear---*2:35*

(Continued on page 369)

LINEAR
NOTES

The Album- & Song-Title Index

In order to provide the ability to cross reference, we have constructed an index of the song– and album – titles dealt with in the chronology, along with specific musician credits. This two–part index separates work done by the Beatles as a group, either for themselves or for others (in the form of a short section detailing those Lennon–McCartney songs written specifically for or "given" to other performers), from those sections covering the separate careers of John, Paul, George and Ringo as performers, producers, writers, or backing musicians for other artists.

When dealing with Beatle songs, we bothered to denote lead and backing vocalists. In the cases of individual efforts, the specific Beatle in question is presumed to be the lead vocalist unless otherwise indicated.

All songs in the Beatle index written by a member of the group have the initial of the *actual* author following the song. The term "Lennon–McCartney" was more often a legal device than a denotation of actual authorship between John and Paul.

Individual efforts are separated into material released under the name of an ex-Beatle (i.e. Lennon Index), and the instances in which they worked with other artists (i.e. Lennon For Others Index). We drew fine lines in the instances where the actual performer is a bit fuzzy. In dealing with John's collaborations with Yoko, we entered material written by John and Yoko or by John himself into the Lennon Index, while those written by Yoko are under Lennon For Others. We entered the Country Hams under the McCartney Index, and the Elastic Oz Band under the Lennon Index, since the names of these bands were mere pseudonyms. For the **Bangla Desh** album, we considered the lead vocalist as the performer, so *While My Guitar Gently Weeps* would be in the Harrison Index, but *That's The Way God Planned It* (sung by Billy Preston) is found under Harrison For Others.

Unless otherwise indicated, musician credits in the Beatle Index are: George Harrison–Lead Guitar, John Lennon–Rhythm Guitar, Paul McCartney–Bass and Ringo Starr–Drums.

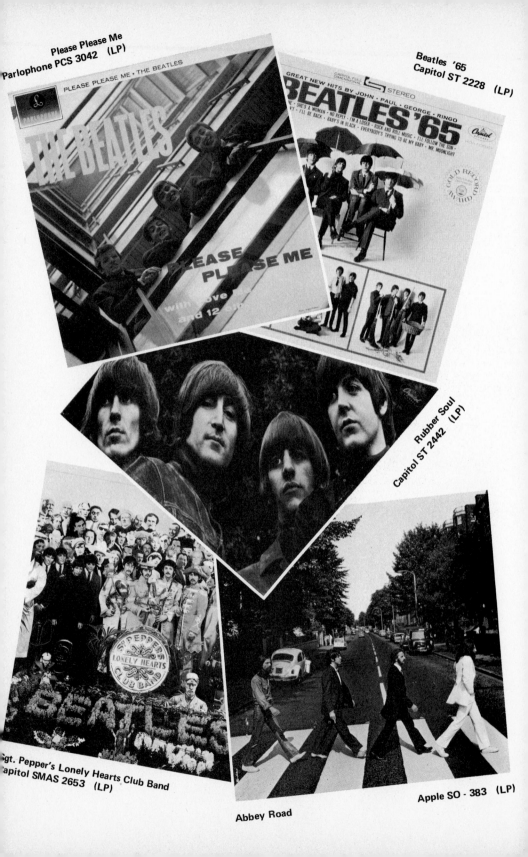

Please Please Me
Parlophone PCS 3042 (LP)

Beatles '65
Capitol ST 2228 (LP)

Rubber Soul (LP)
Capitol ST 2442

Sgt. Pepper's Lonely Hearts Club Band
Capitol SMAS 2653 (LP)

Abbey Road

Apple SO - 383 (LP)

By The Beatles

TITLE (Actual Author)	LEAD (Backing) VOCAL Backing Musicians	ENTRIES
Abbey Road (LP)		223
Across The Universe (J) (version one)	JOHN (Lizzie Bravo & Gayleen Pease John: Lead Guitar Paul: Piano John & George Martin: Organ	231
Across The Universe (J) (version two)	JOHN	248,347
Act Naturally	RINGO (Paul)	122,126,143,147
Ain't She Sweet (LP)		98
Ain't She Sweet	JOHN Pete Best: Drums	66,74,76,98,157, 247,285,419
All I've Got To Do (J)	JOHN (Paul)	28,34
All My Loving (EP)		42
All My Loving (P)	PAUL (John & George)	28,34,42,44,63, 346
All Together Now (P)	PAUL	193
All You Need Is Love (J)	JOHN Chorus: Mick Jagger, Gary Leeds, Keith Richard, Marianne Faithful, Jane Asher, Patti Boyd, Keith Moon and Graham Nash Studio Orchestra	169,174,193,347
The Amazing Beatles (LP)		157
And I Love Her (J+P)	PAUL George & Ringo: Claves & Bongos George: Acoustic Guitar Solo	75,77,83,84,103, 346
And Your Bird Can Sing (J)	JOHN (Paul & George)	147,150
Anna (Go To Him)	JOHN	9,15,23,32,36,52, 97,99,115
Another Beatles Christmas Record (1964) (J+P+G+R)		112,270
Another Girl (P)	PAUL (John & George) Paul: Lead Guitar	122,123
Any Time At All (J)	JOHN (Paul & George)	77,84,105
Ask Me Why (J)	JOHN	6,9,32,36,42,45, 52,97,99,115
Baby, It's You	JOHN (George & Paul) George Martin: Piano	9,15,32,36,97,99, 115
Baby, You're A Rich Man (J+P)	JOHN & PAUL	169,174
Baby's In Black (J+P)	JOHN & PAUL	108,110,118
Back In The USSR (P)	PAUL Paul: Lead Guitar George: Bass Guitar John: Six-string Bass	190,347

Bad Boy	JOHN	119,160
The Ballad Of John And	JOHN (Paul)	208,239,347
Yoko (J)	John: Guitar	
	Paul: Drums & Piano	
	George & Ringo not present	
The Beatles (LP)		190
The Beatles (EP)		52
The Beatles Again (LP)		239
(also called **Hey Jude**)		
The Beatles Christmas Album		270
(in UK: **From Then To Us**)		
The Beatles Christmas		30,270
Record (1963) (J+P+G+R)		
The Beatles First (LP)		74
Beatles For Sale (LP)		108
Beatles For Sale (EP)		116
Beatles For Sale No. 2 (EP)		118
The Beatles Fourth Christmas		161,270
Record (1966) (J+P+G+R)		
The Beatles Golden Discs (EP)		138
(also called **Beatles Million**		
Sellers)		
The Beatles Hits (EP)		20
The Beatles Million Sellers		138
(EP) (also called **Beatles**		
Golden Discs)		
The Beatles 1962–1966 (LP)		346
The Beatles 1967–1970 (LP)		347
The Beatles 1968 Christmas		192, 270
Record (J+P+G+R)		
The Beatles No. 1 (EP)		23
The Beatles Second Album		56
(LP)		
The Beatles Seventh Christmas		232,270
Record (1969) (J+P+G+R)		
Beatles VI (LP)		119
Beatles '65 (LP)		110
The Beatles Story (LP)		106
The Beatles Third Christmas		140,270
Record (1965) (J+P+G+R)		
The Beatles vs. The Four		97
Seasons (LP)		
The Beatles With Tony		41
Sheridan (LP)		
Beatlemania With The Beatles		28
(LP) Canada		
Because (J)	JOHN, PAUL & GEORGE	223
Being For The Benefit Of	JOHN	168
Mr. Kite (J)	John: Main Organ	
	George Martin: Harmony Organ	
	Mal Evans: Bass Harmonica	
The Big Hits From England		94
And The USA (LP)		
Birthday (J+P)	PAUL (Yoko Ono & Patti Harrison)	190
	George: Tambourine	
	Paul: Piano	
Blackbird (P)	PAUL	190
Blue Jay Way (G)	GEORGE (Paul)	174,175
Boys	RINGO	9,15,32,36,97,99,
		115,133

	John: Lead Guitar	
	Ringo: Timpani Drums	
	George not present	
First Vibration (LP)		206
Fixing A Hole (P)	PAUL	168
Flying (J+P+G+R)	INSTRUMENTAL	174,175
	John: Mellotron	
	J+P+G+R: Chanting	
The Fool On The Hill (P)	PAUL	174,175,347
	Paul: Piano, Flute & Recorder	
	George & John: Harmonicas	
For No One (P)	PAUL	150,154
	Paul: Piano	
	Alan Civil: Horn	
For You Blue (G)	GEORGE	248,249
	George: Acoustic Guitar	
	John: Steel Guitar	
	Paul: Piano	
Four By The Beatles (EP)		63
4 By The Beatles (EP)		113
From Me To You (J+P)	JOHN & PAUL	10,20,32,38,45,
		89,130,160,346
From Then to Us (in US: **The Beatles Christmas Album**		270
Get Back (P)	PAUL	202,347
(single version)	Billy Preston: Organ	
	John: Lead Guitar	
	George: Rhythm Guitar	
Get Back (P)	PAUL	248
(album version)	Billy Preston: Organ	
	John: Lead Guitar	
	George: Rhythm Guitar	
Getting Better (P)	PAUL	168
Girl (J)	JOHN (Paul & George)	136,137,346
Glass Onion (J)	JOHN	190
Golden Slumbers (P)	PAUL	223
Good Day Sunshine (P)	PAUL	150,154
	George Martin: Piano	
Good Morning, Good Morning (J)	JOHN	168
	With Sounds Inc.	
Good Night (J)	RINGO	190
	Thirty Piece Orchestra	
Got To Get You Into My Life (P)	PAUL	150,154
	Ian Hamer, Les Condon & Eddie Thornton: Trumpets	
	Alan Branscombe & Peter Coe: Tenor	
Happiness Is A Warm Gun (J)	JOHN	190
A Hard Day's Night (LP)		75(US),77(UK)
A Hard Day's Night—Film (EP)		103
A Hard Day's Night— Album (EP)		105
A Hard Day's Night (J)	JOHN (Paul)	75,77,78,80,160,
	George Martin: Piano	346
Hello Goodbye (P)	PAUL	173,174,347
	Paul: Piano	
	Ringo: Maracas	
Help! (LP)		122(UK),123(US)
Help! (J)	JOHN (George & Paul)	121,122,123,160,
		346
Helter Skelter (P)	PAUL	190

	Mal Evans: Trumpet John: Sax	
Her Majesty (P)	PAUL	223
Here Comes The Sun (G)	GEORGE	223,347
	George: Synthesizer	
Here There And Everywhere (P)	PAUL	150,154
Hey Bulldog (J)	JOHN	193
Hey-Hey-Hey-Hey!	PAUL (John & George)	108,119,133
Hey Jude (LP) (also called **The Beatles Again**)		239
Hey Jude (P)	PAUL (John & George) 40 Piece Orchestra	181,239,347
History Of British Rock Vol. 2 (LP)		419
History of British Rock Vol.3 (LP)		461
Hold Me Tight (J+P)	PAUL (John & George)	28,34
Honey Don't	RINGO	108,110,113
Honey Pie (P)	PAUL	190
	Paul: Piano John: Lead Guitar George: Bass	
I Am The Walrus (J)	JOHN	173,174,175,347
I Call Your Name (J)	JOHN	56,62,73
I Can Hear It Now— The Sixties (LP)		264
I Dig A Pony (J)	JOHN	248
I Don't Want To Spoil The Party (J)	JOHN & PAUL	108,114,118,119
I Feel Fine (J)	JOHN & PAUL John & George: Guitar Duet	107,110,138,160, 346
I Me Mine (G)	GEORGE	248
I Need You (G)	GEORGE (John & Paul)	122,123
I Saw Her Standing There (P)	PAUL (John)	9,15,23,33,34,36, 61,62,97,99
I Should Have Known Better (J)	JOHN	75,77,80,103, 239
I Wanna Be Your Man (J+P)	RINGO	28,34
	John: Hammond Organ	
I Want To Hold Your Hand (J+P)	JOHN & PAUL	29,33,34,61,62, 138,160,264, 346
I Want To Tell You (G)	GEORGE	150,154
	Paul: Piano	
I Want You (She's So Heavy) (J)	JOHN	223
	John: Lead Guitar	
I Will (P)	PAUL	190
If I Fell (J)	JOHN & PAUL	75,77,83,84,100, 103
If I Needed Someone (G)	GEORGE (John & Paul)	136,147
If You Love Me, Baby (also called *Take Out Some Insurance On Me, Baby*)	TONY SHERIDAN Pete Best: Drums	66,68,74,98,157, 159,247,285
I'll Be Back (J)	JOHN (Paul & George)	77,110
I'll Cry Instead (J)	JOHN & PAUL	75,77,82,84,105
I'll Follow The Sun (P)	PAUL	108,110,118
I'll Get You (J+P)	JOHN & PAUL	18,56,62,65
I'm A Loser (J)	JOHN (Paul)	108,110,113,116

I'm Down (P)	PAUL	121
	John: Hammond Organ	
I'm Happy Just To Dance With You (J)	GEORGE	75,77,82,84
I'm Looking Through You (P)	PAUL (John)	136,137
	Ringo: Hammond Organ	
I'm Only Sleeping (J)	JOHN (Paul & George)	147,150
I'm So Tired (J)	JOHN	190
In My Life (J+P)	JOHN (Paul)	136,137,346
	George Martin: Piano	
In The Beginning (LP)		247
The Inner Light (G)	GEORGE (John & Paul)	179
	Indian Musicians on all instruments	
Introducing The Beatles (LP)		15,36
It Won't Be Long (J)	JOHN	28,34
It's All Too Much (G)	GEORGE	193
It's Only Love (J)	JOHN (Paul)	122,137,143
I've Got A Feeling (J+P)	PAUL & JOHN	248
I've Just Seen A Face (P)	PAUL	122,137
Jolly What! (LP)		45
Julia (J)	JOHN	190
	John: Lead Acoustic Guitar	
Kansas City	PAUL (John & George)	108,119,133
Komm, Gib Mir Deine Hand (J+P)	JOHN & PAUL	49,84
Lady Madonna (P)	PAUL (John & George)	179,239,347
	Paul: Piano	
	Ronnie Scott, Harry Klein, Bill Povey & Bill Jackman: Sax	
Let It Be (LP)	Billy Preston: Organ	248
Let It Be (P)	PAUL	241,347
(single version)	Billy Preston: Organ	
	John: Bass	
	Paul: Piano	
Let It Be (P)	PAUL	248
(album version)	Billy Preston: Organ	
	John: Bass	
	Paul: Piano	
Let's Do The Twist... (LP)		60
Little Child (J+P)	JOHN & PAUL	28,34
	Paul: Piano	
	John: Harmonica	
The Long And Winding Road (P)	PAUL	248,249,347
	Strings, Voices, Harp & Drums: Overdubed	
	John: Bass	
	Paul: Piano	
Long Long Long (G)	GEORGE	190
	Paul: Hammond Organ	
	George: Acoustic Guitar	
Long Tall Sally (LP) Canada		62
Long Tall Sally (EP)		73
Long Tall Sally	PAUL	56,62,73
Love Me Do (P) (version one)	JOHN & PAUL (George)	5,7
Love Me Do (P) (version two)	JOHN & PAUL (George)	9,15,20,32,58,90,
	Ringo: Tambourine	115,129,346
	Andy White: Drums	
Love You Too (G)	GEORGE	150,154
	Anil Bhagwat: Tabla	
Lovely Rita (P)	PAUL	168

162

Lucy In The Sky With Diamonds (J)	JOHN	168,347
Maggie May	JOHN	248
Magical Mystery Tour (LP)		174
Magical Mystery Tour (EP)		175
Magical Mystery Tour (P)	JOHN & PAUL	174,175,347
Martha My Dear (P)	PAUL	190
	Paul: Piano	
Matchbox	RINGO	73,84,93
Maxwell's Silver Hammer (P)	PAUL	223
	George: Synthesizer & Acoustic Guitar	
	Ringo: Anvil	
Mean Mr. Mustard (J)	JOHN	223
Meet The Beatles (LP)		34
Michelle (J+P)	PAUL (John & George)	136,137,149,160, 346
Misery (J+P)	JOHN & PAUL	9,15,23,36,52,97, 99,132
Mr. Moonlight	JOHN	108,110,113
	Paul: Hammond Organ	
	George: African Drum	
Money (That's What I Want)	JOHN (George & Paul)	28,42,56
	George Martin: Piano	
Mother Nature's Son (P)	PAUL	190
	Paul: Acoustic Guitar	
	Horns	
	John, George & Ringo not present	
My Bonnie (LP)		4a
My Bonnie (EP)		2,13
My Bonnie	TONY SHERIDAN	1,2,3,4,4a,13,35,41,
	Pete Best: Drums	60,74,155,247, 285,361,461
The Night Before (P)	PAUL (George & John)	122,123
	John: Electric Piano	
No One's Gonna Change Our World		231
No Reply (J)	JOHN (Paul & George)	108,110,116
Nobody's Child	TONY SHERIDAN	40,74,76,98,157,
	Pete Best: Drums	247,285
Norwegian Wood (J)	JOHN (Paul)	136,137,346
	George: Sitar	
Not A Second Time (J)	JOHN	28,34
	George Martin: Piano	
Nowhere Man (EP)		149
Nowhere Man (J)	JOHN (Paul & George)	136,142,147,149, 206,273,346
Ob-la-di, Ob-la-da (P)	PAUL	190,347
Octopus's Garden (R)	RINGO	223,347
Oh! Darling (P)	PAUL	223
Old Brown Shoe (G)	GEORGE (Paul & John)	208,239,347
One After 909 (J)	JOHN & PAUL	248
Only A Northern Song (G)	GEORGE	193
The Original Discotheque Hits (LP)		159
Original Hits—Original Stars (LP)		361
P. S. I Love You (P)	JOHN & PAUL	5,7,9,15,32,42,58,
	Ringo: Maracas	90,115,129
	Andy White: Drums	

Paperback Writer (P)	PAUL (George & John)	145,160,239,346
Penny Lane (P)	PAUL	165,174,347
	Paul & George Martin: Pianos	
	John: Conga Drum	
	Frank Clarke: String Bass	
	David Mason: Sped-up Piccolo B Flat Trumpet	
	Philip Jones: Trumpet Solo	
Piggies (G)	GEORGE	190
	Chris Thomas: Harpsichord	
	Ringo: Tambourine	
Please Mr. Postman	JOHN (Paul & George)	28,31,56,62,63
Please Please Me (LP)		9
Please Please Me (J)	JOHN & PAUL (George)	6,9,20,32,36,38, 45,89,97,99,115, 130,346
Polythene Pam (J)	JOHN	223
Rain (J)	JOHN (Paul & George)	145,239
Revolution (J)	JOHN	181,239,347
Revolution 1 (J)	JOHN	190
	Paul: Piano	
Revolution 9 (J)	John, Ringo, George, Yoko and George Martin: Mixing, Editing and most vocals	190
Revolver (LP)		150(UK),154(US)
Rock And Roll Music	JOHN	108,110,116
	John, Paul and George Martin all on one Piano	
Rocky Racoon (P)	PAUL	190
	Paul: Acoustic Guitar	
	John: Harmonium	
	George Martin: Piano	
Roll Over Beethoven	GEORGE	28,31,56,62,63, 132
Rubber Soul (LP)		136(UK),137(US)
Run For Your Life (J)	JOHN (Paul & George)	136,137
The Saints (When The Saints Go Marching In)	TONY SHERIDAN Pete Best: Drums	1,2,3,4,4a,13,35,41, 60,74,155,247, 285
Sgt. Pepper's Lonely Hearts Club Band (LP)		168
Sgt. Pepper's Lonely Hearts Club Band (P)	PAUL	168,347
Sgt. Pepper's Lonely Hearts Club Band—Reprise (P)	PAUL (John & George)	168
Savoy Truffle (G)	GEORGE	190
Sexy Sadie (J)	JOHN	190
	Paul: Piano	
	John: Acoustic Guitar	
She Came In Through The Bathroom Window (P)	PAUL	223
She Loves You (J+P)	JOHN & PAUL	18,32,56,138,160, 346
She Said She Said (J)	JOHN	150,154
She's A Woman (P)	PAUL	107,110
	Paul: Piano	
She's Leaving Home (J+P)	PAUL	168
	Strings arranged by Mike Leander	
Sie Liebt Dich (J+P)	JOHN & PAUL	49,65
Slow Down	JOHN	73,84,93
Something (G)	GEORGE	223,224,347

Why Don't We Do It In The Road? (P)	PAUL Paul: Guitar, Piano, Bass & Drum	190
Wild Honey Pie (P)	PAUL Paul: Guitar, Bass, Drums	190
With A Little Help From My Friends (P)	RINGO	168,347
With The Beatles (LP)		28
Within You Without You (G)	GEORGE All music by George and Indian musicians John, Paul and Ringo not present	168
The Word (J+P)	JOHN, PAUL & GEORGE Paul: Piano George Martin: Harmonium	136,137
Words Of Love	JOHN, PAUL & GEORGE Ringo: Packing Case	108,118,119
Ya-Ya (EP)		5a
Yellow Submarine (LP)		193
Yellow Submarine (J+P)	RINGO (John, Paul & George) John: Blowing bubbles through a straw George: Swirling water in a bucket Chorus: Patti Harrison, Mal Evans, Neil Aspinal, George Martin, Geoffrey Emerick and studio staff Brass Band in studio	150,151,154,160, 193,346
Yer Blues (J)	JOHN	190
Yes It Is (J)	JOHN (Paul & George)	117,119
Yesterday (EP)		143
Yesterday (P)	PAUL Paul: Acoustic Guitar String Quartet John, George & Ringo not present	122,126,143,147, 160,346
Yesterday...And Today (LP)		147
You Can't Do That (J)	JOHN (Paul & George) George: 12 String Guitar	50,56,62,77,94
You Know My Name (Look Up My Number) (J)	JOHN Brian Jones: Sax Mal Evans: Background Vocal	241
You Like Me To Much (G)	GEORGE (Paul) John: Electric Piano Paul & George Martin: Steinway Piano	119,122,143
You Never Give Me Your Money (P)	PAUL	223
You Really Got A Hold On Me	JOHN & GEORGE (Paul) George Martin: Piano	28,56,62
You Won't See Me (P)	PAUL (George & John) Paul: Piano Mal Evans: Hammond Organ	136,137,149
Your Mother Should Know (P)	PAUL	174,175
You're Gonna Lose That Girl (J)	JOHN (Paul & George)	122,123
You've Got To Hide Your Love Away (J)	JOHN Flutes	122,123,346

Beatles
For Others

TITLE (Actual Author)	PERFORMER	ENTRIES
Bad To Me (J)	Billy J. Kramer with The Dakotas	16,22,37,54,71, 419
Do You Want To Know A Secret (J)	Billy J. Kramer with The Dakotas	12,22,37,71,412, 461
From A Window (P)	Billy J. Kramer with The Dakotas	81,92,96,104
Give Peace A Chance (J)	Plastic Ono Band	See Lennon Index
Goodbye (P)	Mary Hopkin	See McCartney For Others Index
Hello Little Girl (J)	The Fourmost	19,43
I Call Your Name (J)	Billy J. Kramer with The Dakotas	16,22,26,64,96
I Don't Want To See You Again (P)	Peter and Gordon	95,109,111,148, 167
I Saw Her Standing There (P)	Duffy Power with The Graham Bond Quartet	11
I Wanna Be Your Man (J+P)	The Rolling Stones	25,39,55,313
I'll Be On My Way (P)	Billy J. Kramer with The Dakotas	12,22,92,96
I'll Keep You Satisfied (P)	Billy J. Kramer with The Dakotas	24,51,71,79,96
I'm In Love (J)	The Fourmost	27,43
It's For You (J+P)	Cilla Black Johnny Pearson: Piano Judd Proctor: Guitar Kenny Clarke: Drums	87,101,188
Like Dreamers Do (P)	The Applejacks Arranged by Mike Leander	70
Love Of The Loved (P)	Cilla Black	21,57,188
Misery (J+P)	Kenny Lynch	8
Nobody I Know (P)	Peter and Gordon Eddie King: Guitar With Geoff Love's Music	67,86,94,109,139
One And One Is Two (P)	The Strangers with Mike Shannon	59
Step Inside Love (P)	Cilla Black	See McCartney For Others Index
That Means A Lot (P)	P. J. Proby Arranged and Conducted by George Martin	120,124,127,153
Thingumybob (P)	John Foster and Sons Ltd. Black Dyke Mills Band	See McCartney For Others Index
Tip Of My Tongue (P)	Tommy Quickly	17
A World Without Love (P)	Peter and Gordon With Geoff Love's Music	47,69,72,94,139, 148,378,380
A World Without Love (Live) (P)	Peter and Gordon	85

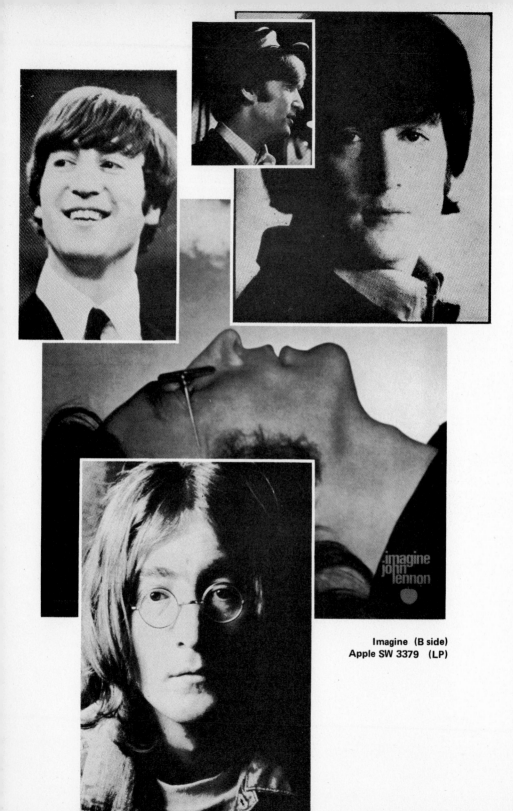

imagine
john
lennon

Imagine (B side)
Apple SW 3379   (LP)

By Lennon

TITLE	MUSICIANS	ENTRIES
Ain't That A Shame	See **Rock 'n' Roll**, Prod: Lennon	432
Aisumasen	See **Mind Games**	367
Amsterdam		227
Angela	See **Sometime In New York City**	325
Attica State	See **Sometime In New York City**	325
Au	See **Sometime In New York City** (Zappa)	325
Baby's Heartbeat		203
Be-Bop-A-Lula	See **Rock 'n' Roll**, Prod: Lennon	432
Beef Jerky	Instrumental	403,404
	John (as Dr. Winston and Booker Table and The Maitre d's) and Jesse Ed Davis: Guitars	
	Jim Keltner: Drums	
	Klaus Voorman: Bass	
	Arthur Jenkins: Percussion	
	Little Big Horns	
Bless You	John (as Rev. Fred Ghurkin) and Eddie Mottau: Acoustic Guitars	404
	Jesse Ed Davis: Guitar	
	Jim Keltner: Drums	
	Klaus Voorman: Bass	
	Ken Ascher: Electric Piano and Mellotron	
	Arthur Jenkins: Percussion	
Blue Suede Shoes	See **Live Peace In Toronto**	230
Bony Moronie	See **Rock 'n' Roll**, Prod: Spector	432
Bring It On Home To Me	See **Rock 'n' Roll**, Prod: Lennon	432
Bring On The Lucie	See **Mind Games**	367
Cambridge 1969	John & Yoko: Vocal	203
	John: Guitar	
	Mal Evans: Watch	
	John Tchikai: Sax	
	John Stevens: Percussion	
Cold Turkey	John & Eric Clapton: Guitars	226,458
	Ringo: Drums	
	Klaus Voorman: Bass	
Cold Turkey (Live No. 1)	See **Live Peace In Toronto**	230
Cold Turkey (Live No. 2)	John: Guitar & Vocal	325
	Yoko: Bag & Vocal	
	Jim Gordon & Keith Moon: Drums	
	George: Guitar	
	Eric Clapton: Guitar	
	Klaus Voorman: Bass	
	Bobby Keys: Sax	
	Nicky Hopkins: Overdubbed Electric Piano	
	Billy Preston: Organ	
	Delaney & Bonnie: Percussion	

	Steve Brendell: Maracas	
	King Curtis: Saxes	
I Found Out	See **John Lennon**	268
I Know (I Know)	See **Mind Games**	367
Imagine	Prod: John, Yoko Ono and Phil Spector	295
	Flux Fiddler String Orchestrations by Torrie Zito	
Imagine	John: Pianos	295,298,458,459
	Klaus Voorman: Bass	
	Andy White: Drums	
Instant Karma	John & George: Guitars	236,458
	Billy Preston: Organ	
	Klaus Voorman: Bass	
	Andy White: Drums	
	Mal Evans: Claps & Chimes	
	John & Klaus Voorman: Electric Pianos	
	George & Andy White: Grand Pianos	
	Chorus: The Above plus Allen Klein and The Patrons of London's Hatchett Club	
Intuition	See **Mind Games**	367
Isolation	See **John Lennon**	268
It's So Hard	John: Guitar	295,298
	Klaus Voorman: Bass	
	Jim Gordon: Drums	
	King Curtis: Sax	
Jamrag	See **Sometime In New York City** (Zappa)	325
Jealous Guy	John: Guitar & Whistling	295
	Klaus Voorman: Bass	
	Jim Keltner: Drums	
	John Barham: Harmonium	
	Andy White: Vibes	
John And Yoko		227
John Lennon/Plastic Ono Band	Prod: John, Yoko Ono & Phil Spector	268
	John: Guitar, Piano & Vocals	
	Yoko: Wind	
	Ringo: Drums	
	Klaus Voorman: Bass	
John Sinclair	John: Slide Guitar	325
	See **Sometime In New York City**	
Just Because	See **Rock 'n' Roll**, Prod: Spector	432
Life With The Lions (also called **Unfinished Music No. 2**)	Prod: John & Yoko Ono	203
Live Peace In Toronto	John: Guitar & Vocals	230
	Yoko: Vocals	
	Eric Clapton: Guitar	
	Klaus Voorman: Bass	
	Andy White: Drums	
Look At Me	See **John Lennon**	268
Love	See **John Lennon** except Piano by Phil Spector	268
Luck Of The Irish	See **Sometime In New York City**	325
Meat City	See **Mind Games** except Drums by Rick Marotta and Jim Keltner	363,367
Mind Games	Prod: John	367
	John: Vocals	
	Ken Ascher: Piano, Organ & Mellotron	
	David Spinozza: Guitar	
	Gordon Edwards: Bass	
	Jim Keltner: Drums	
	Michael Brecker: Sax	

(Continued on page 375)

Lennon
For Others

	Stan Bronstein, Gary Van Scyoc, Adam Ippolito, Rick Frank, Tex Gabriel, Yoko Ono and John: Vocals	
	John: Percussion	
Cryin' Blacksheep Blues	See **Elephant's Memory**	330
	Stan Bronstein, Gary Van Scyoc and John: Vocals	
	John: Guitar	
Death Of Samantha	See **Approximately Infinite Universe**	342,344
Don't Count The Waves	Yoko Ono: Voice & Claves	296
	Klaus Voorman: Percussion	
	Jim Keltner: Tuned Drum	
	John with The Joe Jones Tone Deaf Music Co.	
Don't Forget Me	Harry Nilsson: Vocal & Piano	393,395,423
	The Masked Alberts Orchestra	
Don't Worry Kyoko	Yoko Ono: Vocal	226,296
	John: Guitar	
	Eric Clapton: Lead Guitar	
	Klaus Voorman: Bass	
	Ringo: Drums	
Don't Worry Kyoko	Yoko Ono: Vocal	230
(Live No. 1)	John: Guitar	
	Eric Clapton: Lead Guitar	
	Klaus Voorman: Bass	
	Andy White: Drums	
Don't Worry Kyoko	Yoko Ono: Vocal	325
(Live No. 2)	John, George & Eric Clapton: Guitars	
	Keith Moon, Jim Gordon & Andy White: Drums	
	Klaus Voorman: Bass	
	Bobby Keys: Sax	
	Billy Preston: Organ	
	Delaney & Bonnie: Percussion	
	Nicky Hopkins: Overdubbed Electric Piano	
Elephant's Memory	Prod: John Lennon & Yoko Ono	330
	Stan Bronstein: Sax	
	Gary Van Scyoc: Bass	
	Adam Ippolito: Keyboard & Trumpet	
	Rick Frank: Drums & Percussion	
	Wayne 'Tex' Gabriel: Guitar	
Everybody's Smoking Marijuana	David Peel: Vocal	321
	See **Pope Smokes Dope**	
F Is Not A Dirty Word	David Peel: Vocal	321
	See **Pope Smokes Dope**	
Fame	David Bowie: Lead Vocal	439,449
	John, Carlos Alomar, David Bowie and Earl Slick: Guitars	
	Emir Kassan & Willie Weeks: Bass	
	Ralph McDonald, Pablo Rosario and Larry Washington: Percussion	
	Dennis Davis & Andy Newmark: Drums	
	John, David Bowie, Jean Fineberg and Jean Millington: Backing Vocals	
Fly	Prod: John Lennon & Yoko Ono	296
Fly	Yoko Ono: Vocal	296
	John: Guitar	
God Save Us	The Elastic Oz Band	287

	Prod: John, Yoko Ono, Mal Evans & Phil Spector	
	Bill Elliott: Lead Vocal	
(It's All Da-Da-Down To) Goodnight Vienna	John: Piano	See Starr Index
Goodnight Vienna—Reprise	John: Piano	See Starr Index
Greenfield Morning I Pushed An Empty Baby Carriage All Over The City	See **Yoko Ono**	269
Gypsy Wolf	See **Elephant's Memory**	330
	Stan Bronstein, Gary Van Scyoc, Adam Ippolito, Rick Frank, Tex Gabriel, Yoko Ono and John: Vocals	
	Rick Frank: Cherokee Indian Drum	
Have You Seen A Horizon Lately	See **Approximately Infinite Universe**	342
The Hip Generation	David Peel: Vocal	321
	See **Pope Smokes Dope**	
The Hippie From New York	David Peel: Vocal	321
	See **Pope Smokes Dope**	
Hirake (also called *Open Your Box*)	Yoko Ono: Vocals	278,296
	John: Guitars	
	Klaus Voorman: Bass	
	Jim Gordon: Drums	
I Felt Like Smashing My Face In A Clear Glass Window	See **Approximately Infinite Universe**	342
I Have A Woman Inside My Soul	See **Approximately Infinite Universe**	342
I Saw Her Standing There	The Elton John Band	436
	John: Vocal & Guitar	
	Elton John: Piano & Backing Vocal	
	Davey Johnstone: Guitar	
	Dee Murray: Bass	
	Ray Cooper: Percussion	
	Nigel Olsson: Drums	
	The Muscle Shoals Horns	
I Want My Love To Rest Tonight	See **Approximately Infinite Universe**	342
I'm A Runaway	David Peel: Vocal	321
	See **Pope Smokes Dope**	
I'm Gonna Start Another Riot	David Peel: Vocal	321
	See **Pope Smokes Dope**	
I'm The Greatest	John: Piano & Backing Vocal	See Starr Index
Is Winter Here To Stay	John (as Joel Nohnn): Guitar	342
	See **Approximately Infinite Universe**	
John John (Let's Hope For Peace)	Yoko Ono: Vocal	230
	John: Guitar	
	Eric Clapton: Lead Guitar	
	Klaus Voorman: Bass	
	Andy White: Drums	
Kite Song	See **Approximately Infinite Universe**	342
Liberation Special	See **Elephant's Memory**	330,337,340a,341
	Stan Bronstein, Gary Van Scyoc, Rick Frank, Tex Gabriel, Martha Valez, Toni Wine, Hilda Harris and Linda November: Vocal	
	Stan Bronstein: Percussion	
Life	See **Elephant's Memory**	330
	Tex Gabriel, Gary Van Scyoc, Martha Valez, Toni Wine, Hilda Harris and	

	Linda November: Vocals	
	Keith Johnson: Trumpet	
Listen The Snow Is Falling	Prod: John, Yoko Ono & Phil Spector	303,310
	Yoko Ono: Vocal	
	John, Klaus Voorman and Hugh McCracken: Guitars	
	Nicky Hopkins: Piano & Chimes	
Local Plastic Ono Band	See **Elephant's Memory**	330
	Rick Frank, John & Yoko, Tex Gabriel, Adam Ippolito, Gary Van Scyoc and Stan Bronstein: Vocals	
	Yoko Ono: Breath Rhythms	
	Stan Bronstein: Alto Sax & Percussion	
Looking Over From My Hotel Window	Yoko Ono: Piano	342
	See **Approximately Infinite Universe**	
Loop De Loop	Harry Nilsson: Vocal & Electric Piano	395,423
	Jesse Ed Davis & Danny Kootch: Guitars	
	Jane Getz: Piano	
	Jim Horn, Bobby Keys and Trevor Lawrence: Saxes	
	Chuck Findley: Trombone	
	Klaus Voorman: Bass	
	Keith Moon & Jim Keltner: Drums	
	Tony Jermano, Kristian Turner, Erik Mueller, Nathalie Altman, Peri Prestopino, Canty Turner, Phyllida Paterson, Rachel Mueller, Damon Vigiano, Susie Bell and David Steinberg: Backing Vocals	
Lucy In The Sky With Diamonds	Elton John: Piano & Vocals	416
	John: Guitar & Backing Vocals	
	Davey Johnstone: Guitar	
	Dee Murray: Bass	
	Ray Cooper: Percussion	
	Nigel Olsson: Drums	
McDonald's Farm	David Peel: Vocal	321
	See **Pope Smokes Dope**	
Madness	See **Elephant's Memory**	330,337
	Stan Bronstein, Gary Van Scyoc, Tex Gabriel, Martha Valez, Toni Wine, Hilda Harris and Linda November: Vocals	
Many Rivers To Cross	Harry Nilsson: Vocals	393,395
	Jesse Ed Davis & Danny Kootch: Guitars	
	Ken Ascher: Piano	
	Bobby Keys: Sax	
	Sneaky Pete: Pedal Steel Guitar	
	Willie Smith: Organ	
	Klaus Voorman: Bass	
	Ringo & Jim Keltner: Drums	
	The Masked Alberts Orchestra	
Men Men Men	Yoko Ono: Vocal	360,365,369
	John: Vocal Response	
	David Spinozza: Guitar	
	Ken Ascher: Piano	
	Gordon Edwards: Bass	
	Jim Keltner: Drums	
	Arthur Jenkins: Percussion	
Midsummer New York	Yoko Ono: Vocal	296,297
	John: Guitar & Piano	

	Klaus Voorman: Bass	
	Chris Osborne: Dobro	
	Jim Keltner: Drums & Percussion	
Mind Holes	Yoko Ono: Vocals	296
	John: Guitars	
Mind Train	Yoko Ono: Vocals	296,310
	John: Guitar	
	Klaus Voorman: Bass	
	Chris Osborne: Dobro	
	Jim Keltner: Drums	
Move On Fast	John (as Joel Nohnn): Guitar	338,342
	See **Approximately Infinite Universe**	
Move Over Ms. L	Keith Moon: Vocal & Drums	441,443
	Joe Walsh: Guitar Solo	
	Jesse Ed Davis: Guitar	
	David Foster: Piano	
	Ollie Mitchell & Steve Douglas: Horns	
	Paul Stallworth: Bass	
	Ron Grinel: Drums	
Mrs. Lennon	Yoko Ono: Vocal	296,297
	John: Piano & Organ	
	Klaus Voorman: Guitar, Bass & Bells	
Mucho Mungo/Mt. Elga	Harry Nilsson: Vocal	395,407
	Jesse Ed Davis & Danny Kootch: Guitars	
	Ken Ascher: Piano	
	Bobby Keys & Trevor Lawrence: Saxes	
	Keith Moon: Congas	
	Ringo & Cynthia Webb: Maracas	
	Klaus Voorman: Bass	
	Jim Keltner: Drums	
Now Or Never	See **Approximately Infinite Universe**	338,342
Old Forgotten Soldier	Harry Nilsson: Vocal & Piano	395
	Jesse Ed Davis: Guitar	
	Klaus Voorman: Bass	
One Day At A Time	Elton John: Piano & Vocals	416
	John: Guitar	
	Davey Johnstone: Guitar	
	Dee Murray: Bass	
	Ray Cooper: Percussion	
	Nigel Olsson: Drums	
Only You	John: Acoustic Guitar	See Starr Index
Open Your Box	Also called *Hirake*	278,296
O'Wind	Yoko Ono: Vocal	296
	John: Guitar	
	Jim Keltner: Drums & Tabla	
	Jim Gordon: Tabla	
	Klaus Voorman: Cymbal	
	Bobby Keys: Claves	
Paper Shoes	See **Yoko Ono**	269
Peter The Dealer	See **Approximately Infinite Universe**	342
The Pope Smokes Dope	David Peel	321
	Prod: John Lennon & Yoko Ono	
	Eddie Mottau & Chris Osborne: Guitars	
	Eddie Ryan: Drums	
	Lower East Side Friends Chorus	
The Pope Smokes Dope	David Peel: Vocal	321
	See **Pope Smokes Dope**	
Power Boogie	See **Elephant's Memory**	330,340a,341
	Stan Bronstein, Gary Van Scyoc, Adam Ippolito, Rick Frank, Tex Gabriel, John,	

Wind Ridge	See **Elephant's Memory**	330
	Gary Van Scyoc: Vocal & Acoustic Guitar	
	John: Electric Piano	
Winter Song	Yoko Ono: Vocal	342
	John & Mick Jagger: Guitars	
	See **Approximately Infinite Universe**	
Woman Power	Yoko Ono: Vocal	360,365
	John (as John O'Cean) & Dave Spinozza: Guitars	
	Ken Ascher: Piano	
	Sneaky Pete: Pedal Steel	
	Gordon Edwards: Bass	
	Arthur Jenkins: Percussion	
	Jim Keltner: Drums	
Yang Yang	See **Approximately Infinite Universe**	342,344
Yoko Ono/Plastic Ono Band	Prod: John & Yoko Ono	269
	Yoko Ono: Vocals	
	John: Guitar	
	Ringo: Drums	
	Klaus Voorman: Bass	
You	Yoko Ono: Voices	296
	The Joe Jones Tone Deaf Music Co.	
You've Got To Hide Your Love Away	The Silkie	125,134,378
	Prod: John & Paul	
	Paul: Rhythm Guitar	
	George: Tambourine	

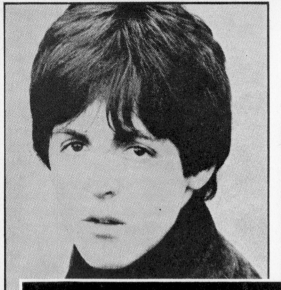

McCartney

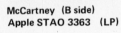

McCartney (B side)
Apple STAO 3363 (LP)

By McCartney

TITLE	MUSICIANS	ENTRIES
Another Day	Prod: Paul	275
	Dave Spinozza: Guitar	
Back Seat Of My Car	With The New York Philharmonic	282,293
	See **Ram**	
Band On The Run	Prod: Paul	372
	Paul: Guitars, Bass, Drums and Synthesizer	
	Linda: Keyboards & Percussion	
	Denny Laine: Guitar	
	Howie Casey: Sax Solos	
Band On The Run	See **Band On The Run**	372,382,387
Big Barn Bed	Paul: Vocal, Bass & Piano	349
	Denny Laine: Acoustic Guitar & Backing Vocal	
	Henry McCullough: Electric Guitar & Backing Vocals	
	Denny Seiwell: Drums	
	Linda: Backing Vocals	
Bip Bop (version one)	See **Wild Life**	305
Bip Bop (version two)	See **Wild Life**	305
Bluebird	See **Band On The Run**	372
Bridge Over The River Suite	Prod: Paul	410
	Paul with Wings (as The Country Hams)	
C Moon	Prod: Paul	340
	Paul: Piano	
	Denny Laine: Bass	
Call Me Back Again	See **Venus And Mars**	447
Country Dreamer	Prod: Paul	362
Crossroads Theme	See **Venus And Mars**	447
Dear Boy	See **Ram**	282
Dear Friend	Richard Hewson: String Arrangements	305
	See **Wild Life**	
Eat At Home	See **Ram**	282
Every Night	Paul: Vocal, Acoustic Guitars, Bass, and Drums	246
Get On The Right Thing	Paul: Vocal, Electric Guitar, Piano and Bass	349
	Dave Spinozza: Electric Guitar	
	Denny Seiwell: Drums	
	Linda: Backing Vocal	
Give Ireland Back To The Irish	Prod: The McCartneys	315
	Henry McCullough: Lead Guitar	
Give Ireland Back To The Irish—Version	Prod: The McCartneys	315
	Henry McCullough: Lead Guitar	

Glasses	Paul: Wine Glasses	246
Hands Of Love	Paul: Vocal & Acoustic Guitar	349
	Denny Laine: Electric Guitar	
	Henry McCullough: Percussion	
	Denny Seiwell: Drums & Percussion	
	Linda: Backing Vocal	
Heart Of The Country	See **Ram**	282,293
Helen Wheels	See **Band On The Run**	362,372
Hi Hi Hi	Prod: Paul	340
Hold Me Tight	Paul: Vocal, Piano & Bass	349
	Henry McCullough & Denny Laine:	
	Electric Guitar & Backing Vocals	
	Denny Seiwell: Drums & Backing Vocal	
	Linda: Backing Vocal	
Hot As Sun	Paul: Acoustic & Electric Guitars, Organ,	246
	Maracas, Bass, Bongos and Drums	
I Am Your Singer	See **Wild Life**	305
I Lie Around	Prod: Paul	353
Jet	See **Band On The Run**	372,374,375
Junior's Farm	Prod: Paul	411
Junk	Paul: Vocal, Acoustic Guitars, Bass,	246
	Xylophone and Bass Drum	
Kreen-Akrore	Paul: Piano, Guitar, Organ and Drums	246
	Paul & Linda: Breathing	
Lazy Dynamite	Paul: Vocal, Piano, Bass & Mellotron	349
	Henry McCullough: Electric Guitar	
	Denny Laine: Harmonica	
Let Me Roll It	See **Band On The Run**	372,375
Letting Go	See **Venus And Mars** except Geoff	447,452
	Britton: Drums	
Listen To What The Man Said	Tom Scott: Sax	446,447
	Dave Mason: Guitar	
	See **Venus And Mars**	
Little Lamb Dragonfly	Paul: Vocal & Bass	349
	Hugh McCracken: Electric Guitar	
	Denny Seiwell: Drums, Percussion &	
	Background Vocal	
	Linda: Dingers & Backing Vocal	
	Denny Laine: Backing Vocal	
Little Woman Love	Prod: Paul	322
Live And Let Die	Prod: George Martin	353,354
Lonely Old People	See **Venus And Mars**	447
Long Haired Lady	With The New York Philharmonic	282
	See **Ram**	
Loup	Paul: Guitar, Bass, Synthesizer & Chant	349
	Linda: Organ & Chant	
	Denny Laine: Electric Guitar & Chant	
	Henry McCullough: Electric Guitar &	
	Chant	
	Denny Seiwell: Drums & Chant	
Love In Song	See **Venus And Mars** except Geoff	446,447
	Britton: Drums	
Love Is Strange	See **Wild Life**	305
The Lovely Linda	Paul: Vocal, Guitars and Bass	246
McCartney	Prod: Paul	246
Magneto And Titanium Man	See **Venus And Mars**	447,460
Mamunia	See **Band On The Run**	372,374

186

Some People Never Know	See **Wild Life**	305
Spirits Of Ancient Egypt	See **Venus And Mars**	447
Suicide	Paul: Vocal & Guitar	246
Teddy Boy	Paul: Vocal, Guitar and Bass	246
	Paul & Linda: Backing Vocal	
That Would Be Something	Paul: Vocal, Guitars, Bass, Tom-Tom and Cymbal	246
3 Legs	See **Ram**	282
Tomorrow	See **Wild Life**	305
Too Many People	See **Ram**	282,291
Treat Her Gently	See **Venus And Mars**	447
Uncle Albert/Admiral Halsey	See **Ram**	282,291
Valentine Day	Paul: Guitars, Bass and Drums	246
Venus And Mars	Prod: Paul	447,460
	Arranged by Paul McCartney and Tony Dorsey	
	Paul: Vocal and Bass	
	Linda: Piano, Synthesizer & Backing Vocals Vocals	
	Jimmy McCulloch: Guitars & Vocals	
	Denny Laine: Guitars & Vocals	
	Joe English: Drums	
Venus And Mars	See **Venus And Mars**	447
Venus And Mars—Reprise	See **Venus And Mars**	447
Walking In The Park With Eloise	Prod: Paul	410
	Chet Atkins: Electric Guitar	
	Floyd Cramer: Piano	
	Geoff Britton: Drums	
	Paul with Wings (as The Country Hams)	
Wild Life	Prod: Paul	305
	Paul: Vocals, Guitar and Bass	
	Denny Laine: Guitar	
	Denny Seiwell: Drums	
	Linda: Keyboards & Backing Vocal	
Wild Life	See **Wild Life**	305
When The Night	Paul: Vocal & Piano	349
	Linda: Electric Bass Piano & Backing Vocal	
	Denny Laine & Henry McCullough: Acoustic Guitars & Backing Vocals	
	Denny Seiwell: Drums & Backing Vocals	
You Gave Me The Answer	See **Venus And Mars**	447,452
Zoo Gang	Prod: Paul	387
	Paul: Synthesizer	

McCartney For Others

TITLE	PERFORMER	ENTRIES
And The Sun Will Shine	Paul Jones Paul: Drums Jeff Beck: Guitar	178
Carolina In My Mind	James Taylor: Vocal & Guitar Prod: Peter Asher Paul: Bass Mick Wayne: Second Guitar Freddie Redd: Organ Bishop O'Brien: Drums Peter Asher: Tambourine Richard Hewson: String Arrangements James Taylor & Peter Asher: Backing Vocals	191,199,260
The Casket	See **McGear**	406
Catcall	Chris Barber Band	172,243
Change	Adam Faith Prod: Adam Faith & David Courtney Paul: Synthesizer Bob Henritt: Drums Dave Wintour: Bass Del Newman: String Arrangement	396
Come And Get It	Prod: Paul Pete Ham: Lead Guitar Tom Evans: Bass Mike Gibbons: Drums	229,233,237,419
Dance The Do	Mike McGear Prod: Paul	451
The Family Way	Prod: George Martin With The George Martin Orchestra	163
The Family Way Theme	Prod: George Martin With The George Martin Orchestra	162
Fields of St. Etienne	Mary Hopkin Prod: Paul	222,232
4th Of July	John Christie Prod: Dave Clark	388
From Head To Toe	The Escourts Prod: Paul Paul: Tambourine	158
The Game	George Martin: Piano See **Post Card**	195,197
Giving Grease A Ride	See **McGear**	406,430
God Bless California	Paul Thornton: Guitar & Vocals Leslie Fradkin: Lead Vocal & Guitar Bob Unger: Vocals Paul: Bass & Vocals Randy Edelman: Piano & Vocals Denny Seiwell: Drums Linda: Vocals	386,392

Goodbye	Mary Hopkin: Vocal & Guitar Prod: Paul Paul: Guitar	201,332
Goodbye	Adam Faith: Vocal Prod: Adam Faith & David Courtney Russ Ballard: Guitar & Piano Solo Paul: Synthesizer "Voices" Dave Wintour: Bass Bob Henritt: Drums	396
Got To Get You Into My Life	Cliff Bennett & The Rebel Rousers Prod: Paul	152,164
Happiness Runs (Pebble And *The Man)*	Mary Hopkin: Guitar See **Post Card**	195,197,216
Have You Got Problems	See **McGear**	406
The Honeymoon Song	With The Mike Cotton Band See **Post Card**	195,197
I Knew Right Away	Alma Cogan Paul: Tambourine	102
I'm The Urban Spaceman	The Bonzo Dog Band Prod: Paul (as Apollo C. Vermouth)	185,210,217,250, 251,288,357, 383
Inchworm	See **Post Card**	195,197
Is This What You Want	Paul: Bass	See Harrison For Others Index
Leave It	Tony Coe: Sax Denny Seiwell: Drums See **McGear**	397,406
Let It All Fall Down	James Taylor: Acoustic Guitar & Vocal Prod: Dave Spinozza Hugh McCracken: Electric Guitar Kenny Ascher: Electric Piano Andy Muson: Bass Ralph MacDonald: Percussion Rick Marotta: Drums Paul, Linda, James Taylor & Carly Simon: Backing Vocals	389,394
Let's Love	Peggy Lee: Vocals Prod: Paul Dave Grusin: Piano & Synthesizer Harvey Mason: Drums & Percussion Gene Cipriano: Oboe Peter Christlieb: Flute Chuck Rainey: Bass Erno Neufeld: Concert Master	408,409
Let's Love—Reprise	See *Let's Love*	408
Liverpool Lou	Scaffold Prod: Paul McCartney	384,428
Lord Of The Reedy River	Paul & Donovon: Guitars Donovon: Backing Vocal See **Post Card**	195,197
Love In The Open Air *(single version)*	Prod: George Martin With The George Martin Orchestra	162,166
Love In The Open Air *(album version)*	Prod: George Martin With The George Martin Orchestra	163
Love Is The Sweetest Thing	See **Post Card**	195,197
Lullaby Of The Leaves	See **Post Card**	195,197
The Man Who Found God On *The Moon*	Buzz Aldrin & Mission Control on Moon Benna & Theran: Hare Krishna Chant See **McGear**	406

McGear	Mike McGear: Vocals	406
	Prod: Paul	
	Paul: Bass, Piano & Backing Vocals	
	Linda: Synthesizer & Backing Vocals	
	Denny Laine: Electric Guitar & Backing Vocals	
	Jimmy McCullough: Electric Guitar	
	Brian Jones: Sax	
	Gerry Conway: Drums	
	Gerry Allison: String & Brass Arrangement	
	Paddy 'Pipes' Moloney: Aeolian Pipes	
	Derek Taylor: W.B. Giggling Gysmorchestra	
McGough & McGear	Roger McGough & Mike McGear	180
	Prod: Paul	
Mine For Me	Rod Stewart: Vocal	405,413
	Prod: Rod Stewart	
	M. Quittenton: Acoustic Guitar	
	Pete Sears: Piano	
	Dick Powell & Rick Gretch: Violins	
	Ray Cooper: Percussion	
	Spike Heatley: Bass	
	Kenny Jones: Drums	
	Paul: Backing Vocal	
	The Tropic Isle Steel Band	
My Dark Hour	Steve Miller: Vocal & Guitars	211,212,314,336
	Prod: Steve Miller & Glyn Johns	
	Paul (as Paul Ramon): Bass, Drums and Backing Vocals	
Never Say Goodbye	Adam Faith: Vocal	396
	Prod: Adam Faith & David Courtney	
	Paul: Synthesizer	
	David Courtney: Piano	
	Russ Ballard: Guitar	
	Dave Wintour: Bass	
	Bob Henritt: Drums	
Night Owl	Carly Simon: Vocal	335,467
	Prod: Richard Perry	
	Nicky Hopkins: Piano	
	Jimmy Ryan: Electric Guitar	
	Bobby Keys: Tenor Sax	
	Klaus Voorman: Bass	
	Ray Cooper: Congas	
	Jim Keltner: Drums	
	Paul & Linda, Doris Troy and Bonnie Bramlett: Backing Vocals	
Night Time	The Escourts	158
Norton	See **McGear**	406,431,451
Penina	Jotta Herre	271a
Post Card	Mary Hopkin: Vocals	195,197
	Prod: Paul McCartney	
Prince En Avignon	See **Post Card**	195,197
The Puppy Song	See **Post Card**	195,197
Que Sera Sera	Mary Hopkin	222,332
	Prod: Paul	
	Paul: Bass and Electric Guitar	
	Ringo: Drums	
Quelli Erand Giorni (Those Were The Days)	Mary Hopkin: Overdubbed Italian Vocal	186
	Prod: Paul	
Rainbow Lady	David Minns: Wine Glasses & Rainbow Box	406
	See **McGear**	

191

Rock 'n' Roll Is Music Now	James Taylor: Vocal & Acoustic Guitar	389
	Prod: Dave Spinozza	
	Hugh McCracken: Electric Guitar	
	Dave Spinozza: Electric Piano	
	Kenny Ascher: Piano	
	Andy Muson: Bass	
	Rick Marota: Drums	
	Paul & Linda, Carly Simon, James Taylor and Rick Marota: Backing Vocals	
	Howard Johnson: Tuba	
	Kenny Berger: Baritone Sax	
	Barry Rogers: Trombone	
	Michael Brecker: Tenor Sax	
	George Young: Alto Sax	
	Alan Rubin: Trumpet	
	Randy Brecker: Trumpet	
Rosetta	The Fourmost	196
	Prod: Paul	
Sea Breezes	See **McGear**	406,430
Simply Love You	See **McGear**	406,464
Six O'Clock	Paul: Piano, Synthesizer & Backing Vocal	See Starr Index
Someone To Watch Over Me	See **Post Card**	195
Sparrow	Mary Hopkin	201,332
	Prod: Paul	
Star Song	Adam Faith: Vocal	396,420
	Prod: Adam Faith & David Courtney	
	Russ Ballard: Guitar	
	David Courtney: Piano	
	Dave Wintour: Bass	
	Bob Henritt: Drums	
	Paul & Linda: Backing Vocals	
	Andrew Powell: String Arrangement	
Star Dust	Arranged: Paul	See Starr Index
Step Inside Love	Cilla Black	177,188
	Prod: George Martin	
	Arranged: Mike Vickers	
Sweet Baby	Mike McGear	397
	Prod: Paul	
	Same Musicians as **McGear**	
Ten Years After On Strawberry Jam	Scaffold	384
	Prod: Paul	
There's No Business Like Show Business	See **Post Card**	195,197
Thingumybob	John Foster & Sons Ltd. Black Dyke Mills Band	182
	Prod: Paul	
Those Were The Days	See **Post Card**	183,197,332,461
Thumbin' A Ride	Jackie Lomax: Vocal	209,235
	Prod: Paul	
	George: Guitar	
	Paul: Drums	
	Billy Preston: Piano & Organ	
	Klaus Voorman: Bass	
	George & Patti and The Rascals: Backing Vocals	
Turn! Turn! Turn!	Mary Hopkin	183,186
	Prod: Paul	

Voyage Of The Moon	Mary Hopkin: Vocal Paul & Donovon: Guitars See **Post Card**	195,197
We Love You	Paul: Backing Vocal	See Lennon For Others Index
What Do We Really Know?	See **McGear**	406,464
Woman	Peter & Gordon Arranged: Bob Peiper	141,144,146,148, 167,461
Y Blodyn Gwyn	See **Post Card**	195,197
Yellow Submarine	John Foster & Sons Ltd. Black Dyke Mills Band Prod: Paul	182
Young Love	With The Mike Cotton Band and The London Welsh Choir See **Post Card**	195,197
You're Sixteen	Paul: Kazoo	See Starr Index
You've Got To Hide Your Love Away	Paul: Rhythm Guitar	See Lennon For Others Index

GEORGE HARRISON
ALL THINGS MUST PASS

All Things Must Pass

Apple STCH 639 (LP)

By Harrison

TITLE	MUSICIANS	ENTRIES
All Things Must Pass	Prod: George & Phil Spector	265
	George, Eric Clapton & Dave Mason: Guitars	
	Gary Wright, Bobby Whitlock, Billy Preston and Gary Brooker: Keyboards	
	Pete Ham, Tom Evans, Joey Molland and Mike Gibbons: Rhythm Guitars and Percussion	
	Pete Drake: Pedal Steel Guitar	
	Bobby Keys: Tenor Sax	
	Jim Price: Trumpet	
	Klaus Voorman & Carl Radle: Bass	
	Mal Evans: Tambourine	
	Ringo, Jim Gordon & Alan White: Drums and Percussion	
	John Barham: Orchestral Arrangements	
	George and Phil Spector (as The George O'Hara-Smith Singers): Backing Vocals	
All Things Must Pass	See **All Things Must Pass**	265
Apple Scruffs	See **All Things Must Pass**	265,274
Art Of Dying	See **All Things Must Pass**	265
Awaiting On You All	See **All Things Must Pass**	265
Awaiting On You All—Live	See **Concert For Bangla Desh**	307
Ballad Of Sir Frankie Crisp	See **All Things Must Pass**	265
Bangla Desh	Prod: George & Phil Spector	290
	Ringo: Drums	
Bangla Desh—Live	Jim Horn: Sax	307
	See **Concert For Bangla Desh**	
Be Here Now	See **Living In The Material World**	352
Behind That Locked Door	See **All Things Must Pass**	265
Beware Of Darkness	See **All Things Must Pass**	265
Beware Of Darkness—Live	George & Leon Russell: Vocals	307
	Jim Horn: Sax	
	See **Concert For Bangla Desh**	
Bye Bye Love	George: Vocals and Everything Else	422,436a
Concert For Bangla Desh	Prod: George & Phil Spector	307
	George, Eric Clapton & Jesse Ed Davis: Guitars	
	Pete Ham, Tom Evans, Joey Molland and Mike Gibbons: Acoustic Guitars and Percussion	
	Billy Preston & Leon Russell: Keyboards	
	Chuck Findley, Jim Horn and Ollie Mitchell: Horns	
	Carl Radle & Klaus Voorman: Bass	

195

Ringo & Jim Keltner: Drums
Alan Beutler, Marlin Greene, Jeanie Greene,
    Joe Green, Dolores Hall, Jackie Kelso,
    Claudia Linnear, Lou McCreary, Don Nix
    and Don Preston: Chorus

Cowboy Museum	See **Wonderwall Music**	187
Crying	See **Wonderwall Music**	187
Dark Horse	Prod: George	422
Dark Horse	George & Robben Ford: Guitars	417,422,436a

Billy Preston: Electric Piano
Chuck Findley, Jim Horn & Tom Scott:
    Flutes
Willie Weeks: Bass
Emil Richards: Crochet
Jim Keltner: Hi-Hats
Andy Newmark: Drums
Olivia Arias, Lon & Derrek Van Eaton:
    Backing Vocals

The Day The World Gets 'Round	See **Living In The Material World**	352
Deep Blue	Prod: George & Phil Spector	290
Ding Dong; Ding Dong	George & Nick Jones: Guitars	421,422,425

George, Alvin Lee and Ron Wood:
    Electric Guitars
Gary Wright: Piano
Tom Scott: Horns
Klaus Voorman: Bass
Ringo & Jim Keltner: Drums

Don't Let Me Wait Too Long	See **Living In The Material World**	352
Dream Scene	See **Wonderwall Music**	187
Drilling A Home	See **Wonderwall Music**	187
Electronic Sound	Prod: George Harrison	204
Extra Texture	See page 373	
Fantasy Sequins	See **Wonderwall Music**	187
Far East Man	George: Guitars	422

Billy Preston: Electric Piano
Tom Scott: Horns
Willie Weeks: Bass
Andy Newmark: Drums

Give Me Love	See **Living In The Material World**	350,352
Glass Box	See **Wonderwall Music**	187
Greasy Legs	See **Wonderwall Music**	187
Guru Vandana	See **Wonderwall Music**	187
Hari's On Tour (Express)	Instrumental	422,425,436a

Tom Scott: Horns
Roger Kellaway: Piano
Max Bennett: Bass
John Guerin: Drums
George & Robben Ford: Guitars

Hear Me Lord	See **All Things Must Pass**	265
Here Comes The Sun	George: Vocal & Guitar	307

Pete Ham: Acoustic Guitar
Chorus

I Dig Love	See **All Things Must Pass**	265
I Don't Care Anymore	Prod: George	417,421
I Remember Jeep	Instrumental	265

George & Eric Clapton: Guitars
Billy Preston: Keyboards
Klaus Voorman: Bass
Ginger Baker: Drums

197

(Continued on page 375)

198

Harrison For Others

TITLE	PERFORMER	ENTRIES
Ain't That Cute	Doris Troy: Vocal Prod: George Peter Frampton: Guitar See **Doris Troy**	238,254
All That I've Got	Billy Preston: Vocal & Keyboard Prod: George	234
All Things (Must) Pass	See **Encouraging Words**	255
Awakening	See **Shankar Family & Friends**	401
Baba Teaching	Ustad Allauddin Khan: Voice See **Raga**	304
Baby You're A Lover	See **Is This What You Want**	200,207
Back Off Boogaloo	Prod: George	See Starr Index

Badge	Cream
	Prod: Felix Pappalardi
	Eric Clapton: Vocal & Guitar
	Felix Pappalardi: Piano & Mellotron
	George (as L'Angelo Misterioso): Rhythm
	  Guitar
	Jack Bruce: Bass
	Ginger Baker: Drums
		194,198,215,228,
		  319,333

Badge—Live	Eric Clapton: Guitar & Vocal
	With Peter Townsend, Rick Grech, Jim
	  Capaldi, Ronnie Wood, Stevie Winwood,
	  Jimmy Karstein and Rebop
		358

Banana Anna	Nicky Hopkins: Piano & Vocal Prod: Nicky Hopkins & David Briggs Jerry Williams: Vocals George (as George O'Hara): Guitar Prarie Prince: Drums Ray Cooper: Percussion & Congas Bobby Keys: Sax Klaus Voorman: Bass	348
Banaras Ghat	See **Raga**	304
Bangla Dhun	Ravi Shankar: Sitar Ali Akbar Khan: Sarod Alla Rakah: Tabla Kamala Chakrauarty: Tamboura	307
Basketball Jones	Cheech & Chong: Voices Prod: Lew Adler George: Guitar Carole King: Electric Piano Nicky Hopkins: Piano Tom Scott: Sax Billy Preston: Organ Klaus Voorman: Bass	355,356

	Jim Keltner: Percussion	
	George Bohanon, Dick Hyde and Paul Hubinon: Horns	
	Jim Karstein: Drums	
Bhaja Bhakata/Arati	See **Radha Krsna Temple**	283
Bhaja Hunre Mana	See **Radha Krsna Temple**	283
Birth To Death	See **Raga**	304
Blowin' In The Wind	Bob Dylan: Vocal, Harmonica & Acoustic Guitar	307
	George: Electric Guitar	
	Leon Russell: Bass	
	Ringo: Tambourine	
Bobby Keys	Instrumental	326
	Prod: Bobby Keys, Jim Gordon & Andy Johns	
	Bobby Keys & Jim Price: Horns	
	George, Eric Clapton, Dave Mason & Leslie West: Guitars	
	Klaus Voorman & Jack Bruce: Bass	
	Felix Pappalardi & Nicky Hopkins: Keyboards	
	Ringo & Jim Gordon: Drums	
Bombay Studio	See **Raga**	304
China Light	Splinter	400,434,437
	Prod: George	
	Bill Elliott & Bob Purvis: Vocals	
	George (as Hari Georgeson): Acoustic Guitar and Mandolin	
	Gary Wright: Piano	
	Billy Preston: Organ	
	Willie Weeks: Bass	
	Mike Kelly: Drums	
Cold Turkey (Live No. 2)	George: Guitar	See Lennon Index
Costafine Town	Splinter	399,400
	Prod: George	
	Bill Elliott & Bob Purvis: Vocals	
	George (as Hari Georgeson): Bass and 8-String Bass	
	George (as P. Roducer): Harmonium	
	George (as Jai Raj Harisein): Percussion	
	Gary Wright: Piano	
	Graham Maitland: Accordian	
	Mike Kelly: Drums	
Crippled Inside	George: Dobro	See Lennon Index
Dawn To Dusk	See **Raga**	304
Day After Day	Badfinger	302,306,309,461
	Prod: George	
Daybreak	George: Cow Bell	See Starr For Others Index
Despair And Sorrow	See **Shankar Family & Friends**	401
Disillusionment And *Frustration*	See **Shankar Family & Friends**	401
Dispute And Violence	See **Shankar Family & Friends**	401

Don't Worry Kyoko
  (Live No. 2)
	George: Guitar	See Lennon For
		  Others Index

Do What You Want	Billy Preston	219
	Prod: George	
Doris Troy	Prod: Doris Troy	254
	George, Eric Clapton, Steve Stills and Peter Frampton: Guitars	

200

	Billy Preston: Keyboards	
	Klaus Voorman: Bass	
	Delaney & Bonnie: Percussion	
	Ringo & Andy White: Drums	
Down And Out	Prod: George & Richard Perry	See Starr Index
Drink All Day	Splinter	400,429,434
	Prod: George	
	Bill Elliott & Bob Purvis: Vocals	
	George (as Hari Georgeson): 6 & 12	
	String Guitars and Dobro	
	George (as P. Roducer): Harmonium	
	and Jew's Harp	
	George (as Jai Raj Harisein): Percussion	
	Klaus Voorman: Acoustic Bass	
	Jim Keltner: Drums	
The Eagle Laughs At You	See **Is This What You Want**	184,200,207
Early 1970	George: Guitar	See Starr Index
Edward	Nicky Hopkins: Vocal & Piano	348
	Prod: Nicky Hopkins & David Briggs	
	George (as George O'Hara): Guitar	
	Bobby Keys: Sax	
	Klaus Voorman: Bass	
	Ray Cooper: Congas and Percussion	
	Prarie Prince: Drums	
Elly-May	Splinter	399,400
	Prod: George	
	Bill Elliott & Bob Purvis: Vocals	
	George (as Hari Georgeson): Acoustic	
	Guitar	
	George (as P. Roducer): Moog Synthesizer	
	Gary Wright: Piano	
	Klaus Voorman: Acoustic Bass	
	Mike Kelly: Drums	
Encouraging Words	Billy Preston	255
	Prod: George & Billy Preston	
Encouraging Words	See **Encouraging Words**	255
Everything's All Right	Billy Preston	219,225
	Prod: George	
Far East Man	Ron Wood: Vocal & Electric Guitar	402
	Prod: Ron Wood & Gary Kellgren	
	George: Guitar & Backing Vocal	
	Jean Roussel: Organ	
	Ian McLagan: Electric Piano	
	Mick Taylor: Bass	
	Andy Newmark: Drums	
Festivity And Joy	See **Shankar Family & Friends**	401
Footprint	Gary Wright: Keyboards	300
	Prod: Gary Wright	
	George (as George O'Hara), Hugh	
	McCracken and Jerry Donahue: Guitars	
	George (as George O'Hara): Slide Guitar	
	Bobby Keys: Tenor Sax	
	Jim Price: Trumpet & Trombone	
	Klaus Voorman: Bass	
	Alan White, Jim Keltner, Jim Gordon and	
	Collin Allan: Drums and Percussion	
	John Barham: String Arrangements	
	Doris Troy, Nannette Workman, Madeline	
	Bell, Liza Strike, Barry St. John, Pat	

How Do You Sleep	George: Slide Guitar	See Lennon Index
How The Web Was Woven	Jackie Lomax	235,242
	Prod: George	
	Leon Russell: Organ, Piano & Guitar	
Hummingbird	George: Guitar	244
	See **Leon Russell**	
I Am Missing You	See **Shankar Family & Friends**	398,401
I Am Missing You—Reprise	See **Shankar Family & Friends**	401
I Don't Want To Be A Soldier Mama	George: Slide Guitar	See Lennon Index
I Don't Want You To Pretend	See **Encouraging Words**	255
I Fall Inside Your Eyes	See **Is This What You Want**	200,205,207,242, 286
I Just Don't Know	See **Is This What You Want**	200,207
I Wrote A Simple Song	Billy Preston: Keyboards & Vocals	301
	Prod: Billy Preston	
	George (as George H.): Lead Guitar	
	David T. Walker: Guitar	
	Rocky Peoples: Tenor Sax	
	Charles Garnette: Trumpet	
	King Errison: Congas	
	Manuel Kellough: Drums	
	Quincy Jones: String & Horn Arrangements	
I Wrote A Simple Song	George: Guitar	301,308
	See **I Wrote A Simple Song**	
I'd Die Babe	Badfinger	306
	Prod: George	
I'm The Greatest	George: Guitar	See Starr Index
I'm Your Spiritual Breadman	Prod: Ashton, Gardner & Dyke	258,277
	George (as George O'Hara Smith): Electric Swivel Guitar	
	Eric Clapton: Electric Guitar	
If You've Got Love	Dave Mason: Vocal & Guitar	364
	Prod: Dave Mason	
	George (as Son Of Harry): Guitar	
	Mark Jordan: Piano	
	Carl Radle: Bass	
	Jim Keltner: Drums	
	Maxine Willard, Clydie King, Julia Tillman and Kathleen Saroyan: Background Vocals	
In Concert—1972	Prod: George, Zakir Hussein and Phil McDonald	343
	Ravi Shankar: Sitar	
	Ali Akbar Khan: Sarod	
	Alla Rakha: Tabla	
	Ashoka/Susan: Tambouras	
Instant Karma	George: Guitar & Piano	See Lennon Index
Is This What You Want	Jackie Lomax: Vocals	200,207
	Prod: George	
	George, Paul & Eric Clapton: Guitars	
	Nicky Hopkins: Keyboards	
	Klaus Voorman: Bass	
	Ringo, Bishop O'Brien & Hal Blaine: Drums	
	John Barham: String Arrangements	
	Along with Alan Branscombe, Pete Clark, Spike Heatley, Larry Knechtel, Tony Newman and Joe Osborn	
	Paul Beaver, Alan Pariser, Mal Evans and Bernie Krause: Special Effects	

205

Ronald Cohen: Sarangi
Ashish Khan & George Ruckert: Sarod
Ravi Shankar & Shubo Shankar: Sitars
Ravi Shankar: Surbahar
Lakshmi Shankar & Ashish Khan:
 Swarmandal
Fakir Muhammad & Nodu Mullick:
 Tamboura
L. Subramaniam: Violin
Bobby Bruce & Gordon Swift: Violins
Ray Pizzi: Bassoon
Hari Chaurasia, G. Sachdev & Sharad
 Kumar: Flutes
Tom Scott: Saxes and Boehm Flute
Gene Cipriano: Oboe
Ringo (as Billy Shears), Jim Keltner and
 Ed Shaunessey: Drums
Emil Richards: Marimbas
Palghat Ragho: Mridingam
Emil Richards: Percussion
Hari Chaurasia: Cow Bells
Vini Poncia: Tambourine
Alla Rakha: Tabla and Pakhavaj
Pranesh Khan & Harihar Rao: Dholak
Billy Preston & Fred Teague: Organ
Nicky Hopkins: Piano
Ravi Shankar, Paul Beaver, Malcolm
 Cecil and Robert Margouleff: Moog
 Synthesizer

She Belongs To Me	Billy Preston	219
	Prod: George	
Sing One For The Lord	See **Encouraging Words**	255
Situation Vacant	Splinter	400
	Prod: George	
	Bill Elliott & Bob Purvis: Vocals	
	George (as Hari Georgeson): Guitars	
	Gary Wright: Piano	
	Willie Weeks: Bass	
	Jim Keltner: Drums	
	Mel Collins: Horn Arrangements	
Somebody's City	Splinter	400
	Prod: George	
	Bill Elliott & Bob Purvis: Vocals	
	George (as Hari Georgeson): 6 String,	
	12 String and Electric Guitars	
	George (as Jai Raj Harisein): Percussion	
	Gary Wright: Piano	
	Klaus Voorman: Bass	
	Mike Kelly: Drums	
	Mel Collins: Horn Arrangements	
Sour Milk Sea	Jackie Lomax: Vocal	184,200,207,286
	Prod: George	
	George & Eric Clapton: Guitars	
	Nicky Hopkins: Piano	
	Eddie Clayton: Congas	
	Ringo: Drums	
So Sad	Mylon LeFevre: Lead Vocals & Harmonies	368,372a
	Alvin Lee: Guitars & Backing Vocals	
	Prod: Alvin Lee	

	George (as Hari Georgeson): Guitar, Slide Guitar, Bass & Backing Vocal	
	Ron Wood: 12 String Guitar	
	Mick Fleetwood: Drums	
Speak To Me	See **Is This What You Want**	200,207
Speed On	Nicky Hopkins: Piano & Vocal	348,351
	Prod: Nicky Hopkins & David Briggs	
	Jerry Williams: Vocal	
	George (as George O'Hara): Lead Guitar	
	Mick Taylor: Rhythm Guitar	
	Klaus Voorman: Bass	
	Bobby Keys & Jim Horn: Saxes	
	Jim Price: Trumpet	
	Ray Cooper: Percussion & Congas	
	Prarie Prince: Drums	
Sri Gurvastakam	See **Radha Krsna Temple**	283
Sri Isopanisad	See **Radha Krsna Temple**	283
Stand For Our Rights	Gary Wright: Keyboards	284,300
	Prod: Gary Wright	
	George & Hugh McCracken: Acoustic Guitars	
	Andy White: Harpsicord	
	King Curtis: Tenor Sax	
	Klaus Voorman: Bass	
	Jerry Donahue & Colin Allen: Percussion	
	Jim Gordon & Jim Keltner: Drums	
Sue Me Sue You Blues	Jesse Ed Davis: Guitar & Vocals	311,317
	Prod: Jesse Davis & Albhy Galuten	
	Mac Rebennack: Organ & Piano	
	Billy Rich: Fender Bass	
	Jim Keltner: Drums	
	Merry Clayton, Vanetta Fields, Clydie King and The Charles Chalmers Singers: Backing Vocals	
Suitcase	Badfinger	306
Sunset	See **Is This What You Want**	200,207
Sunshine Life For Me	George: Guitar & Backing Vocal	See Starr Index
Supane Me Aye Preetam Sai Sainya	See **Shankar Family & Friends**	401
Sweet Music	Lon Van Eaton: Piano & Vocal	316,331
	Derrek Van Eaton: Lead Vocals & Bass	
	Prod: George	
	Mike Hugg: Harmonium	
	Ringo & Jim Gordon: Drums	
Take My Word	See **Is This What You Want**	200,207
Tandoori Chicken	Ronnie Spector: Vocal	281
	Prod: George & Phil Spector	
	George: Guitar	
	Phil Spector & Leon Russell: Keyboards	
	Klaus Voorman: Bass	
	Jim Gordon: Drums	
Tell The Truth	Derek & The Dominoes	256,319
	Prod: Phil Spector	
	Eric Clapton: Guitar & Vocals	
	George: Guitar	
	Bobby Whitlock: Keyboards	
	Carl Radle: Bass	
	Jim Gordon: Drums	

(Continued on page 377)

By Starr

TITLE	MUSICIANS	ENTRIES

All By Myself	John Lennon & Alvin Robinson: Guitars
	Mac Rebennack: Piano
	Bobby Keys, Trevor Lawrence and Lou
	  McCreery: Horns
	Steve Madaio: Trumpet Solo
	Klaus Voorman: Bass
	Ringo & Jim Keltner: Drums
	Vini Poncia, Clydie King, Linda Lawrence,
	  Joe Greene and Richard Perry (Bass):
	  Backing Vocals
		415

Back Off Boogaloo	Prod: George George: Guitar Gary Wright: Keyboard Klaus Voorman: Bass Ringo: Drums Madeline Bell, Lesley Duncan and Jean Gilbert: Backing Vocals	318,466

Beaucoups Of Blues	Prod: Pete Drake
	Ringo: Acoustic Guitar, Drums & Vocals
	Charlie Daniels, Chuck Howard, Sorrells
	  Pickard and Jerry Reed: Guitars
	Pete Drake: Pedal Steel
	Charlie McCoy: Harmonica
	Roy Huskey: Bass
	Along with Buddy Harman, Dave Kirby,
	  Jerry Kennedy, Jerry Shook, George
	  Richey, Grover Lavender, Jim
	  Buchanan, D. J. Fontana, Ben Keith
	  and Jeannie Kendal
	The Four Jordanaires: Backing Vocals
		257

Beaucoups Of Blues	See **Beaucoups Of Blues**	257,259,466
Blast From Your Past		466
Blindman	Prod: Ringo & Klaus Voorman	318
Blue Turning Grey Over You	Arranged: Oliver Nelson See **Sentimental Journey**	245
Bye Bye Blackbird	Arranged: Maurice Gibb See **Sentimental Journey**	245

Call Me	Steve Cropper: Guitar
	David Foster: Piano
	Klaus Voorman: Bass
	Ringo: Drums
	Lon & Derrek Van Eaton, Vini Poncia,
	  Richard Perry, Klaus Voorman and
	  Cynthia Webb: Backing Vocals
		414,415

Coochy-Coochy	Prod: Pete Drake Ringo: Acoustic Guitar	259

Devil Woman	Jimmy Calvert: Guitar	366,371
	Tom Hensley: Piano	
	Tom Scott & Chuck Findley: Horns	
	Klaus Voorman: Bass	
	Milt Holland: Percussion	
	Ringo & Jim Keltner: Drums	
	Klaus Voorman & Richard Perry:	
	Backing Vocals	
Down And Out	Prod: George Harrison & Richard Perry	359
Dream	Arranged: George Martin	245
	See **Sentimental Journey**	
Early 1970	Prod: Ringo	280,466
	Ringo: Acoustic Guitar & Drums	
	George: Guitars	
Easy For Me	Lincoln Mayorga: Piano	415
	Strings Arranged By: Trevor Lawrence	
	and Vini Poncia	
	Strings Conducted By: Richard Perry	
Fastest Growing Heartache	See **Beaucoups Of Blues**	257
In The West		
Fiddle About	London Symphony Orchestra and	339
	Chambre Choir Conducted by David	
	Measham	
	Arranged By: Will Malone	
$15 Draw	See **Beaucoups Of Blues**	257
Goodnight Vienna	Prod: Richard Perry	415
Goodnight Vienna	John: Piano	415,448
	Lon Van Eaton & Jesse Ed Davis: Guitars	
	Billy Preston: Clavinet	
	Trevor Lawrence, Steve Madaio, Bobby	
	Keys and Lon Van Eaton: Horns	
	Carl Fortina: Accordian	
	Ringo & Jim Keltner: Drums	
	Clydie King and The Blackberries (Sherlie	
	Matthews, Venetta Fields and Flora	
	Williams): Backing Vocals	
Goodnight Vienna–Reprise	See *Goodnight Vienna*	415,448
Have I Told You Lately That	Arranged: Elmer Bernstein	245
I Love You	See **Sentimental Journey**	
Hold On (Have You Seen My	Marc Bolan: Guitar	366
Baby)	James Booker: Piano	
	Klaus Voorman: Bass	
	Tom Scott: Horns	
	Milt Holland: Percussion	
	Ringo & Jim Keltner: Drums	
Hunting Scene	Ringo & Peter Sellers: Voices	237
Husbands And Wives	Lon Van Eaton & Vini Poncia: Guitars	415
	Richard Bennett: Electric Guitar Solo	
	Tom Hensley: Electric Piano	
	Carl Fortina: Accordian	
	Vini Poncia: Backing Vocal	
I Wouldn't Have You Any	See **Beaucoups Of Blues**	257
Other Way		
I'd Be Talking All The Time	See **Beaucoups Of Blues**	257
I'm A Fool To Care	Arranged: Klaus Voorman	245
	See **Sentimental Journey**	
I'm The Greatest	John: Piano & Backing Vocal	366,466
	George: Guitars	
	Billy Preston: Organ	

	Klaus Voorman: Bass	
It Don't Come Easy	Ringo: Drums	
	Prod: George	280,466
	George: Guitars	
	Ron Cattermole: Sax & Trumpet	
	Ringo: Drums	
It Don't Come Easy—Live	Ringo: Vocals	See Harrison Index
	See **Concert For Bangla Desh**	Index
Let The Rest Of The World Go By	Arranged: Les Reed	245
	See **Sentimental Journey**	
Loser's Lounge	See **Beaucoups Of Blues**	257
Love Don't Last Long	See **Beaucoups Of Blues**	257
Love Is A Many Splendoured Thing	Arranged: Quincy Jones	245
	See **Sentimental Journey**	
Night And Day	Arranged: Chico O'Farrill	245
	See **Sentimental Journey**	
No No Song	Jesse Ed Davis: Electric Guitar	415,426,466
	Nicky Hopkins: Electric Piano	
	Trevor Lawrence & Bobby Keys: Horns	
	Klaus Voorman: Bass	
	Ringo: Drums & Percussion	
	Harry Nilsson: Backing Vocal	
Occapella	Lon Van Eaton & Jesse Ed Davis: Guitars	415
	Mac Rebennack: Piano	
	Trevor Lawrence, Steve Madaio, Lou McCreery and Bobby Keys: Horns	
	Klaus Voorman: Bass	
	Ringo & Jim Keltner: Drums	
	Jimmy Gilstrap, Joe Greene, Clydie King and Ira Hawkins: Backing Vocals	
Oh My My	Jimmy Calvert: Guitar	366,376,466
	Billy Preston: Piano & Organ	
	Jim Horn & Tom Scott (Solo): Horns	
	Klaus Voorman: Bass	
	Ringo & Jim Keltner: Drums	
	Vini Poncia: Harmony Vocal	
	Martha Reeves, Merry Clayton and Friends: Backing Vocal	
Only You	John: Acoustic Guitar	414,415,466
	Jesse Ed Davis & Steve Cropper: Electric Guitars	
	Billy Preston: Electric Piano	
	Ringo & Jim Keltner: Drums	
	Harry Nilsson: Backing Vocal	
Oo-Wee	Dennis Coffey: Guitar	415,435,448
	Mac Rebennack: Piano	
	Klaus Voorman: Bass	
	Trevor Lawrence, Steve Madaio, Lou McCreery and Bobby Keys: Horns	
	Ringo & Jim Keltner: Drums	
	Vini Poncia: Harmony Vocal	
	Clydie King and The Blackberries: Backing Vocal	
Photograph	George: 12 String Acoustic Guitar and Backing Vocal	359,366,466
	Nicky Hopkins: Piano	
	Vini Poncia & Jimmy Calvert: Acoustic Guitars	
	Lon & Derrek Van Eaton: Percussion	

	Bobby Keys: Tenor Sax Solo	
	Ringo & Jim Keltner: Drums	
	Orchestra & Chorus Arranged by: Jack Nitzche	
"Ringo"	Prod: Richard Perry	366
Sentimental Journey	Prod: George Martin	245
	With The George Martin Orchestra	
Sentimental Journey	Arranged: Richard Perry	245
	See **Sentimental Journey**	
Silent Homecoming	See **Beaucoups Of Blues**	257
Six O'Clock	Paul: Piano & Synthesizer	366
	Vini Poncia: Acoustic Guitar and Percussion	
	Klaus Voorman: Bass	
	Ringo: Drums	
	Paul & Linda McCartney: Backing Vocals	
	Strings and Flutes Arranged by Paul	
Snookeroo	Elton John: Piano	415,426,435
	Robbie Robertson: Guitar	
	James Newton Howard: Synthesizer	
	Trevor Lawrence, Steve Madaio, Bobby Keys and Chuck Findley: Horns	
	Klaus Voorman: Bass	
	Ringo & Jim Keltner: Drums	
	Linda Lawrence, Clydie King and Joe Greene: Backing Vocals	
Star Dust	Arranged: Paul McCartney	245
	See **Sentimental Journey**	
Step Lightly	Steve Cropper & Nicky Hopkins: Electric Guitars	366,376
	Jimmy Calvert: Acoustic Guitar	
	Clarinets Arranged by Tom Scott	
	Klaus Voorman: Bass	
	Ringo: Drums & Dancing Feet	
Sunshine Life For Me	George & Robbie Robertson: Guitars	366
	Rick Danko & David Bromberg: Fiddles	
	Levon Helm: Mandolin	
	Garth Hudson: Accordian	
	David Bromberg: Banjo	
	Klaus Voorman: Upright Bass	
	George & Vini Poncia: Backing Vocals	
	Ringo: Drums & Percussion	
Tommy's Holiday Camp	London Symphony Orchestra and Chambre Choir Conducted by David Measham	339
	Arranged by Will Malone	
Waiting	See **Beaucoups Of Blues**	257
Whispering Grass	Arranged: Ron Goodwin	245
	See **Sentimental Journey**	
Wine Women And Loud Happy Songs	See **Beaucoups Of Blues**	257
Without Her	See **Beaucoups Of Blues**	257
Woman Of The Night	See **Beaucoups Of Blues**	257
You Always Hurt The One You Love	Arranged: John Dankworth	245
	See **Sentimental Journey**	
You And Me (Babe)	George: Electric Guitar	366
	Vini Poncia: Acoustic Guitar	
	Nicky Hopkins: Electric Piano	
	Milt Holland: Marimba	

You're Sixteen   Tom Scott: Horn Arrangements
Jack Nitzche: String Arrangements
Ringo: Drums
Jimmy Calvert & Vini Poncia: Guitars   366,371,466
Nicky Hopkins: Piano
Paul: Kazoo
Klaus Voorman: Bass
Ringo & Jim Keltner: Drums
Harry Nilsson: Backing Vocals

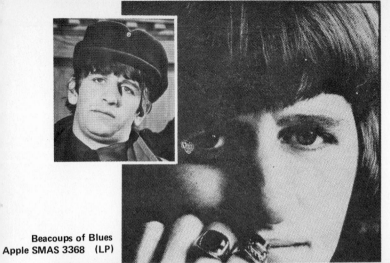

Beacoups of Blues
Apple SMAS 3368   (LP)

Beaucoups of Blues

Starr
For Others

TITLE	PERFORMER	ENTRIES
Ain't That Cute	Ringo: Drums	See Harrison For Others Index
All My Life	Ringo: Drums	See Lennon For Others Index
All Things Must Pass	Ringo: Drums & Percussion	See Harrison Index
Alright	Peter Frampton: Vocal, Guitar and Percussion	324
	Frank Carillo: Rhythm Guitar, Percussion & Backing Vocal	
	Billy Preston: Piano & Organ	
	Andrew Bown: Percussion and Backing Vocal	
	Klaus Voorman: Bass	
	Ringo: Drums	
Alyce Blue Gown	See **Land's End**	385
Ambush	Harry Nilsson: Vocals & Electric Piano	327
	Peter Frampton & Cris Spedding: Electric Guitars	
	Nicky Hopkins: Piano	
	Bobby Keys: Tenor Sax	
	Ray Cooper: Tambourine	
	John Uribe: Lead Guitar	
	Jim Price: Trumpet & Trombone	
	Klaus Voorman: Bass	
	Ringo (as Richie Snare): Drums	
Another Thought	Lon Van Eaton: Piano & Vocal	331
	Derrek Van Eaton: Lead Vocals	
	Prod: Klaus Voorman	
	T. J. Tindall: Guitar	
	Klaus Voorman: Bass	
	Ringo: Drums	
At My Front Door	Harry Nilsson: Vocals	327,381
	Peter Frampton & Cris Spedding: Electric Guitars	
	Nicky Hopkins: Piano	
	Bobby Keys: Tenor Sax	
	Ray Cooper: Congas	
	Klaus Voorman: Bass	
	Ringo (as Richie Snare): Drums	
Awaiting On You All—Live	Ringo: Drums	See Harrison Index
Bangla Desh	Ringo: Drums	See Harrison Index
Bangla Desh—Live	Ringo: Drums	See Harrison Index
Be Here Now	Ringo: Drums	See Harrison Index
Beware Of Darkness—Live	Ringo: Drums	See Harrison Index

Blowin' In The Wind	Ringo: Tambourine	See Harrison For Others Index
Bobby Keys	Ringo: Drums	See Harrison For Others Index
Cloud Man	See **Land's End**	385
Cold Turkey	Ringo: Drums	See Lennon Index
Count Down Meets Merlin And Amber	Ringo, Harry Nilsson and Suzanna Leigh: Voices	381
The Count's Vulnerability	Ringo: Voice	381
Crying In My Sleep	See **Land's End**	377,385
Daybreak	Harry Nilsson: Vocal & Piano	379,381
	George: Cow Bell	
	Peter Frampton: Guitar	
	Jim Price: Organ	
	Bobby Keys: Hi Sax	
	Cris Spedding: Bouzouki	
	Gene Cipriano: Horns	
	Ray Cooper: Percussion	
	Klaus Voorman: Bass	
	Ringo: Drums	
	Prod: Harry Nilsson	
The Day The World Gets 'Round	Ringo: Drums	See Harrison Index
Ding Dong; Ding Dong	Ringo: Drums	See Harrison Index
Don't Let Me Wait Too Long	Ringo: Drums	See Harrison Index
Don't Worry Kyoko	Ringo: Drums	See Lennon For Others Index
Doris Troy	Ringo: Drums	See Harrison For Others Index
The End	Ringo, Harry Nilsson: Voices	381
Feet In The Sunshine	See **Land's End**	385,390,391
Frankenstein, Merlin And The Operation	Ringo: Voice	381
Ghetto Woman	B. B. King: Vocal & Guitar	294,299
	Prod: Ed Michael & Joe Zagarino	
	Mac Rebennack: Guitar	
	Jim Price: Electric Piano	
	Gary Wright: Piano	
	Klaus Voorman: Bass	
	Ringo & Jim Gordon: Drums	
	Jimmie Haskell: String Arrangements	
Give Me Love	Ringo: Drums	See Harrison Index
God	Ringo: Drums	See Lennon Index
Gonna Get My Baby Back	See **Doris Troy**	254
Good For God	Harry Nilsson: Vocal	442
	Prod: Harry Nilsson	
	Jesse Ed Davis & Danny Kootch: Guitars	
	Trevor Lawrence & Bobby Keys: Sax	
	Gene Cipriano: Tenor Sax	
	Robert Greenidge: Steel Drums	
	Klaus Voorman: Bass	
	Jim Keltner: Drums	
	Pat Murphy & Carl McKnight: Percussion	
	Ringo & Harry Nilsson: Backing Vocals	
Greenfield Morning I Pushed An Empty Baby Carriage All Over The City	Ringo: Drums	See Lennon For Others Index
A Hard Rain's Gonna Fall	Ringo: Drums	See Harrison For Others Index

216

Hold On John	Ringo: Drums	See Lennon Index
Hummingbird	Ringo: Drums	See Harrison For Others Index
I Ain't Superstitious	Howlin' Wolf: Vocals	289
	Prod: Norman Dayron	
	Eric Clapton: Lead Guitar	
	Steve Winwood: Piano & Organ	
	Bill Wyman: Bass	
	Charlie Watts: Drums & Percussion	
	Hubert Sumlin: Rhythm Guitar	
	Joe Miller, Jordon Sandke, Dennis Lansing: Horns	
	Klaus Voorman: Bass	
	Ringo (as Richie): Drums	
I Found Out	Ringo: Drums	See Lennon Index
Isolation	Ringo: Drums	See Lennon Index
Is This What You Want	Ringo: Drums	See Harrison For Others Index
It Is He Who Will Be King	Ringo: Voice	381
It Takes A Lot To Laugh/It Takes A Train To Cry	Ringo: Tambourine	See Harrison For Others Index
It's A Sin	See **Land's End**	385
Jumpin' Jack Flash	Ringo: Drums	See Harrison For Others Index
Just Like A Woman	Ringo: Tambourine	See Harrison For Others Index
Just This One Time	See **Land's End**	385
Kojak Columbo	Harry Nilsson: Vocals	440,442
	Jesse Ed Davis & Danny Kootch: Guitars	
	Mac Rebbennack: Piano	
	Trevor Lawrence, Bobby Keys and Gene Cipriano: Saxes	
	Doug Dillard: Banjo	
	Joe De Aguero: Marimba	
	Pat Murphy: Congas	
	Klaus Voorman: Bass	
	Emmitt Kennedy & Milt Holland: Percussion	
	Ringo & Jim Keltner: Drums	
Lady Fits Her Bluejeans	See **Land's End**	385,391
Land's End	Prod: Jimmy Webb	385
	Jimmy Webb: Piano & Vocal	
	Fred Tackett, Dean Parks, Paul Keo and Jim Ryan: Guitars	
	B. J. Cole: Steel Guitar	
	Davey Johnstone: Mandolin	
	Tom Scott: Sax	
	David Hentschel: Synthesizer	
	Phillip Goodhand-Tait: Mellodiun	
	Dee Murray & Brian Hodges: Bass	
	Ringo, Nigel Olsson and Barry De Souza: Drums	
	David Katz: Concert Master	
	Joni Mitchell & Susan Webb: Backing Vocals	
Land's End/Asleep On The Wind	See **Land's End**	385
Leon Russell	Ringo: Drums	See Harrison For Others Index

217

Rock Around The Clock	Ringo: Drums	See Lennon For Others Index 370
Rock And Roller	Billy Lawrie: Vocal Ronnie Leahy: Keyboards Jimmy McCulloch: Guitars Colin Allen: Drums Steve Thompson: Bass Roger Ball and Malcolm Duncan: Horns Ray Cooper: Percussion Maggie Bell, Lulu and Liza Strike: Backing Vocals	
Save The Last Dance For Me	Ringo: Drums	See Lennon For Others Index
Shankar Family & Friends	Ringo (as Billy Shears): Drums	See Harrison For Others Index
Shoot Out On The Plantation	Ringo: Drums See **Leon Russell**	244
Solid Gold	Keith Moon: Vocals Prod: Mal Evans, Skip Taylor and John Stronach Ringo: Announcer Beau Guss: Guitar Solo Joe Walsh: Guitar & Synthesizer Patti Quatro: Guitar Nickey Barclay: Piano Paul Stallworth & Jean Millington: Bass Cam Davis: Drums Nickey Barclay, Patti Quatro, Jean Millington, Cam Davis, Sherlie Matthews, Lorna Willard and Julia Tillman: Backing Vocals	441,443
So Sad	Ringo: Drums	See Harrison Index
Son Of Dracula	Prod: Ringo & Harry Nilsson Incidental Music During Dialogue: Ann O'Dell: Piano Peter Robinson: Organ & Piano Diana Lewis: Harpsicord & Piano Barry Guy & Chris Lawrence: Bass Frank Riccotti & Ray Cooper: Percussion Morris Pert: Drums Martin Ford: Electric French Horn & Orchestral Arrangements	381
Sour Milk Sea	Ringo: Drums	See Harrison For Others Index
Spaceman	Harry Nilsson: Vocal & Electric Piano Prod: Richard Perry Peter Frampton, Cris Spedding and John Uribe: Acoustic Guitars Nicky Hopkins: Piano Klaus Voorman: Bass Richard Perry: Percussion Ringo (as Richie Snare): Drums Paul Buckmaster: Orchestral Arrangements	327,328,329
Step Lightly	Dick Hentschel: Synthesizer Ringo (as R. S.) & John Gilbert: Finger Clicks	433
Subterranean Homesick Blues	Ringo: Drums	See Lennon For Others Index
Sue Me Sue You Blues	Ringo: Drums	See Harrison Index
Sweet Music	Ringo: Drums	See Harrison For Others Index

An Index Of Friends

222

223

THE BEATLES FROM OTHERS

Slow Down/Dizzy, Miss Lizzy   Specialty 626 (45)

Slow Down/Match Box   Capitol 5255 (45)

THE BEATLES
FROM
OTHERS

"When we came over to America the first time, we were only coming over to buy LPs."
—John Lennon, August 1964

On June 1, 1956, *Heartbreak Hotel* by Elvis Presley had been number one for seven weeks. Carl Perkins' single *Blue Suede Shoes/ Honey Don't* had been out for six months; Little Richard's *Long Tall Sally* had been out for three months; and Chuck Berry's *Roll Over Beethoven*, one month. John Lennon had never met Paul McCartney. Richard Starkey was a messenger boy for the British Railways. And George Harrison was thirteen years old. They didn't know each other, but they all knew that music. It was the music they were listening to. It was the music they were growing up on. And when they themselves began performing, those were the songs they first played. When Lennon and McCartney started writing songs together, they were just expanding on the form set by Leiber and Stoller, Goffin and King, and Penniman and Marascalco.

Later, when they brought this music to a whole new generation of teenagers, it was christened "Beatlemusic." Very little attention was paid to the original sources of this so-called new sound, particularly in America where they suddenly erupted full-bloom on the *Ed Sullivan Show*. This is all the more surprising since the Beatles' music had its origins in the States.

By the summer of 1956, a new force was destroying the established patterns of American pop music. The hitherto repressed sound of black Rhythm and Blues was being adapted by white performers with backgrounds in Country and Western music. The music that resulted from this back and forth trading of styles was called "Rockabilly," which soon evolved into "Rock 'n' Roll." The sound had been around for a few years, in the R&B groups that arose after World War II. As with most black music it was mainly ignored by white America. It was only when white teenagers began showing interest in Rhythm and Blues songs that the music industry began to pay attention. Major record labels had white pop groups release toned-down, cleaned-up versions of songs by R&B artists that were beginning to receive pop attention. While by-passing the black performers, this policy wound up injecting the strains of Rhythm and Blues into the minds of most Americans. The final hurdle to mass acceptance was overcome when a white performer, Elvis Presley, presented almost unchanged the feelings of black Rhythm and Blues with white Country and Western undertones.

When Presley first appeared, English youth were busy playing skiffle—something akin to jugband music. Within months, hundreds of washboards had been returned to laundry rooms, and Britain was teaming with incipient rock 'n' rollers.

By the late 50's, every large American city had at least one or two full time Rock 'n' Roll stations. In England, however, the entire process by which teenagers listened to music was quite different. There was basically only one radio network with a few local branches. Rock 'n' Roll music was not at the top of the BBC's priority list for use of airtime. When it was on, programming was restricted to a few hours on the weekend. It was as if *American Bandstand* had been the only mass media outlet for Rock 'n' Roll music in the United States.

In spite of this, American Rockabilly and Rhythm and Blues music had a substantial and loyal following among British youth, but the radio played little part in its growth. The whole process resembled an underground society, at least to American eyes. The main place for exposure to this music was the local music hall or club (later to be called discotheques) where local disc jockeys would play records imported from America; or hometown bands, particularly in sea coast towns, would play numbers they learned of from records American seamen would bring with them.

It's probably for this reason that English fans thought of Rock 'n' Roll in terms of records, not songs. The flip side, usually ignored in America, was just as important as the hit side. The Beatles' choice of material from other artists makes sense, then, when you realize that many of the songs were flip sides of hit records.

In many ways, a lot of the Lennon/McCartney songs written after the Beatles became established stars, set the style for Rock in the 60's. But most of their early work was derived almost directly from the rockers of the 50's. However, the overflow of attention paid to the Beatles as performers, celebrities and symbols created the general impression that their style of music was totally self-created. But it's foolish to look at Beatle music as beginning in 1964, 1963 or even 1962. After all, they didn't write *Please Mr. Postman*—and neither did the Carpenters.

The easiest and best way to hear where the Beatles got their sound and what they did with it is to compare their versions of songs taken from other artists with the original versions. For example, when the Shirelles, a black American female group, sing the nonsense lyrics like *sha-la-la-la-la-la* in *Baby, It's You,* it seems much less incongruous than when it comes from the lips of young English boys. On the other hand, the Beatles sometimes made improvements on the originals. John's hysterical vocals and George's demonic guitar work say in sound what Larry Williams had to say in words—he's a "bad boy."

The following list traces the origins of the songs the Beatles released but didn't write. Many of the records listed are unavailable in their original form, but can be obtained as "Golden Oldies" or on "Best of..." compiliations. We have tracked down how the song appeared in its original form because in the era the Beatles were growing up, this is how the songs appeared. Beware of re-recordings on different labels, as an aging rock 'n' roller is wont to do anything when pressed for cash. For example, the albums released by Little Richard on Vee Jay and those by Chuck Berry on Mercury, both containing new but mediocre versions of their past hits, are best left forgotten.

Sample:

Song Title—Authors
   Release Date and Performer
   Label, Number and *Flip Side*

Key:

   All songs recorded by The Beatles except % Tony Sheridan and The Beatles, † John Lennon, $ George Harrison, * Ringo Starr, and + Paul McCartney.

Act Naturally—Johnny Russell—Vonie Morrison
   March 11, 1963 by Buck Owens
   Capitol 4937 b/w *Over And Over Again*

Ain't She Sweet—Jack Yellen—Milton Ager
   Originally Performed—Early 1927 by Paul Ash and Orchestra
   Vaudeville Hit—by Eddie Cantor

†*Ain't That A Shame*—Antoine Domino—Dave Bartholomew
   April 18, 1955 by Fats Domino
   Imperial 5348 b/w *La—La*

229

Anna (Go To Him)—Arthur Alexander
September 17, 1962 by Arthur Alexander
Dot 16387 b/w *I Hang My Head And Cry*

Baby, It's You—Mack David—Bert Bacharach—Barney Williams
December 4, 1961 by The Shirelles
Scepter 1227 b/w *The Things I Want To Hear*

Bad Boy—Larry Williams
January 19, 1959 by Larry Williams
Specialty 658 b/w *She Said "Yeah"*

*Beaucoups Of Blues—Buzz Rabin
Given to Ringo—1970
April 15, 1974 by Buzz Rabin
Elektra EKS 75076 (LP) **Cross Country Cowboy**

†*Be-Bop-A-Lula*—Gene Vincent—Tex Davis
May 28, 1956 by Gene Vincent
Capitol 3450 b/w *Woman Love*

†*Blue Suede Shoes*—Carl Perkins
January 2, 1956 by Carl Perkins
Sun 234 b/w *Honey Don't*

*Blue, Turning Grey Over You—Andy Razof—Thomas 'Fats' Waller
February 1, 1930 by Louis Armstrong and Orchestra
Okeh 4678 b/w *The Laughing Record*

†*Bring It On Home To Me*—Sam Cooke
May 14, 1962 by Sam Cooke
RCA 8036 b/w *Having A Party*

†*Bony Moronie*—Larry Williams
September 30, 1957 by Larry Williams
Specialty 615 b/w *You Bug Me, Baby*

Boys—Luther Dixon—Wes Farrell
November 7, 1960 by The Shirelles
Scepter 1211 b/w *Will You Still Love Me Tomorrow*

*Bye Bye Blackbird—Mort Dixon—Ray Henderson
Originally—Mid 1927 Vaudeville Theme for George Price
Hit—by Eddie Cantor

$Bye Bye, Love---Felix Bryant—Boudaloux Bryant
  May 15, 1957 by The Everly Brothers
  Cadence 1315 b/w *I Wonder If I Care Too Much*

Chains---Gerry Goffin—Carole King
  October 22, 1962 by The Cookies
  Dimension 1002 b/w *Stranger In My Arms*

(There's A) Devil In His Heart---Richard B. Drapkin
  August 6, 1962 by The Donays
  Brent 7033 b/w *Bad Boy*

Dizzy Miss Lizzie---Larry Williams
  February 24, 1958 by Larry Williams
  Specialty 626 b/w *Slow Down*

†*Do You Want To Dance*---Bobby Freeman
  March 3, 1958 by Bobby Freeman
  Josie 835 b/w *Big Fat Woman*

Dream---Johnny Mercer
  Originally—Theme for Mercer's 1945 CBS Radio Show
  Hit—January 20, 1945 by The Pied Pipers
    Capitol 185 b/w *Tabby The Cat*

Easy For Me---Harry Nilsson
  Given to Ringo—1974
  March 21, 1975 by Harry Nilsson
  RCA APL 1-0817 (LP) **Duit On Mon Dei**

Everybody's Trying To Be My Baby---Carl Perkins
  August 18, 1958 by Carl Perkins
  Sun 1225 (LP) **Teen Beat—Carl Perkins**

Fastest Growing Heartache In The West---Larry Kingston—Fred Dycus
  Given to Ringo—1970

Fiddle About---John Entwistle
  May 26, 1969 by The Who
  Decca DXSW 7205 (LP) **Tommy**

$15 Draw---Sorrells Pickard
  Given to Ringo—1970
  April 17, 1972 by Sorrells Pickard
  Decca DL 7-5338 (LP) **Sorrells Pickard**

Have I Told You Lately That I Love You?—Scott Wiseman
  Introduced—February 1945 by Lulu Belle and Scotty (Wiseman)
  First Recording—August 12, 1946 by Foy Willing and The Riders
    of The Purple Sage
  Majestic 6000 b/w *Cool Water*

Hey-Hey-Hey-Hey!—'Little' Richard Penniman
  January 13, 1958 by Little Richard
  Specialty 624 b/w *Good Golly, Miss Molly*

Hold On (Have You Seen My Baby)—Randy Newman
  March 2, 1970 by Randy Newman
  Reprise RS 6373 (LP) **12 Songs**

Honey Don't—Carl Perkins
  January 2, 1956 by Carl Perkins
  Sun 234 b/w *Blue Suede Shoes*

Husbands And Wives—Roger Miller
  January 31, 1966 by Roger Miller
  Smash 2024 b/w *I've Been A Long Time Learnin'*

I Wouldn't Have You Any Other Way—Chuck Howard
  Given to Ringo—1970

I'd Be Talking All The Time—Chuck Howard—Larry Kingston
  Given to Ringo—1970

I'm A Fool To Care—Ted Daffan
  Introduced—March 1941 by Ted Daffan
  Hit—June 7, 1954 by Les Paul and Mary Ford
    Capitol 2839 b/w *Auctioneer*

$*If Not For You*—Bob Dylan
  November 2, 1970 by Bob Dylan
  Columbia 30290 (LP) **New Morning**

†*Just Because*—Lloyd Price
  Originally Issued: January 28, 1957 by Lloyd Price
    KRC 300 b/w *Why*
  Reissued: February 18, 1957 by Lloyd Price
    ABC 9792 b/w *Why*

Kansas City—Jerry Leiber—Mike Stoller
  Originally *K.C. Loving*—December 29, 1952 by Little Willie Littlefield
    Federal 12110 b/w *Pleading At Midnight*
  Cover Model—March 9, 1959 by Little Richard
    Specialty 2104 (LP) **The Fabulous Little Richard**
  Hit—March 23, 1959 by Wilbur Harrison
    Fury 1023 b/w *Listen My Darling*

Let The Rest Of The World Go By—J. Keirn Brennan—Ernest K. Ball
  Introduced—September 1919 by George J. Trinkaus and Band
  Revived—1944 in a Film by E. K. Ball: *When Irish Eyes Are Smiling*
  Performed by Dick Haymes and a male quartet

Long Tall Sally—Enotris Johnson—Richard Penniman—Robert
  Blackwell
  March 12, 1956 by Little Richard
  Specialty 572 b/w *Slippin' And Slidin'*

Loser's Lounge—Bobby Pierce
  Given to Ringo—1970

Love Don't Last Long—Chuck Howard
  Given to Ringo—1970

Love Is A Many Splendored Thing—Paul Webster—Sammy Fain
  Originally—Theme to the 1955 Film: *Love Is A Many Splendored
    Thing,* sung by a chorus at the end
  Hit—July 11, 1955 by The Four Aces
    Decca 29625 b/w *Shine On Harvest Moon*

+*Love Is Strange*—Ellis McDaniel—Mickey Baker
  November 19, 1956 by Mickey and Sylvia
  Groove 0175 b/w *I'm Going Home*

Matchbox—Carl Perkins
  February 11, 1957 by Carl Perkins
  Sun 261 b/w *Your True Love*

Money (That's What I Want)—Berry Gordy—Janie Bradford
  December 10, 1959 by Barret Strong
  Anna 1111 b/w *Oh I Apologize*

Mr. Moonlight—Roy Lee Johnson
  January 15, 1962 by Dr. Feel Good and The Interns
  Okeh 7144 b/w *Doctor Feel Good*

233

%*My Bonnie (Lies Over The Ocean)*—Charles Pratt
  Originally Appeared—1881 in the Book: *Student Songs of 1881*
    (No Author Credited)
  First Published—1882 by Pratt, under the names J. T. Woods and
    H. J. Fuller

Night And Day—Cole Porter
  Originally—From 1932 Musical Play: *Gay Divorce,* sung by Fred
    Astaire and Claire Luce
  Hit—September 20, 1937 by Tommy Dorsey and Orchestra
    RCA 25657 b/w *Smoke Gets In Your Eyes*

%*Nobody's Child*—Mel Foree—Cy Coben
  December 12, 1949 by Hank Snow
  RCA 21-0143 b/w *The Only Rose*

No No Song—Hoyt Axton—David P. Jackson
  Given to Ringo—1974
  March 28, 1975 by Hoyt Axton
  A&M SP 4510 (LP) **Southbound**

Occapella—Allen Toussaint
  December 14, 1970 by Lee Dorsey
  Polydor 24-4042 (LP) **Yes We Can**

Only You (And You Alone)—Buck Ram—Ande Rand
  Original Version (Recorded before Hit Version)—November 23,
    1955 by The Platters
    Federal 12244 b/w *You Made Me Cry*
  Hit Version—July 5, 1955 by The Platters
    Mercury 70633 b/w *Bark Battle And Ball*

†*Peggy Sue*—Jerry Allison—Norman Petty—Buddy Holly
  September 23, 1957 by Buddy Holly
  Coral 61885 b/w *Everyday*

Please Mr. Postman—Brian Holland—Robert Bateman—Berry Gordy
  August 7, 1961 by The Marvellettes
  Tamla 54046 b/w *So Long Baby*

†*Ready Teddy*—Robert Blackwell—John Marascalco
  June 11, 1956 by Little Richard
  Specialty 579 b/w *Rip It Up*

234

†*Rip It Up*---Robert Blackwell--John Marascalco
   June 11, 1956 by Little Richard
   Specialty 579 b/w *Ready Teddy*

Rock And Roll Music---Chuck Berry
   September 30, 1957 by Chuck Berry
   Chess 1671 b/w *Blue Feeling*

Roll Over Beethoven---Chuck Berry
   May 14, 1956 by Chuck Berry
   Chess 1626 b/w *Too Much Monkey Business*

†*Send Me Some Lovin'*---Lloyd Price--John Marascalco
   February 25, 1957 by Little Richard
   Specialty 598 b/w *Lucille*

*Sentimental Journey---Bud Green--Les Brown--Ben Homer
   January 29, 1945 by Les Brown and Orchestra (Vocal: Doris Day)
   Columbia 36769 b/w *Twilight Time*

*Silent Homecoming---Sorrells Pickard
   Given to Ringo--1970

†*Slippin' And Slidin'*---Richard Penniman--Edwin J. Bocage--Albert
   Collins--James Smith
   March 12, 1956 by Little Richard
   Specialty 572 b/w *Long Tall Sally*

Slow Down---Larry Williams
   February 24, 1958 by Larry Williams
   Specialty 626 b/w *Dizzy Miss Lizzie*

*Snookeroo---Elton John--Bernie Taupin
   Given to Ringo--1974

†*Stand By Me*---Ben E. King--Jerry Leiber--Mike Stoller--Ollie Jones
   April 17, 1961 by Ben E. King
   ATCO 6194 b/w *On The Horizon*

*Star Dust---Hoagy Carmichael--words added by Mitchell Parish, 1929
   Introduced--1927 by Don Redman and Orchestra
   First Recording--October 31, 1927 by Emile Seidel and Orchestra
   (Piano: Hoagy Carmichael)
   Gennette 6311 b/w *One Night In Havana*

Hit—December 9, 1940 by Artie Shaw and Band
  RCA 27230 b/w *Temptation*

%*Sweet Georgia Brown*---Ben Bernie—Maceo Pinkard—Kenneth Casey
  Introduced—Spring 1925 by Ben Bernie and Orchestra

†*Sweet Little Sixteen*---Chuck Berry
  January 27, 1958 by Chuck Berry
  Chess 1683 b/w *Reelin' And Rockin'*

%*Take Out Some Insurance On Me, Baby*---Charles Singleton—
  Waldenese Hall
  April 13, 1959 by Jimmy Reed
  Vee Jay VJ 314 b/w *You Know I Love You*

 A Taste Of Honey---Ric Marlow—Bobby Scott
  Originally—From 1960 Play: *A Taste Of Honey*, performed by
    Bobby Scott and Combo
  First Recording—June 4, 1962 by The Victor Feldman Quartet
    Infinity 020 b/w *Valerie*
  Hit—June 18, 1962 by Martin Denny
    Liberty 55470 b/w *The Brighter Side*
  First Vocal Version—September 17, 1962 by Lenny Welch
    Cadence 1428 b/w *The Old Cathedral*

 'Till There Was You---Meredith Willson
  Originally—From 1957 Play: *The Music Man*, sung by Robert
    Preston and Barbara Cook
  First Recording—January 13, 1958 by Robert Preston and
    Barbara Cook
    Capitol WAO 990 (LP) **The Music Man** (Original Broadway Cast)
  Hit—May 18, 1959 by Anita Bryant
    Carlton 512 b/w *Little George*

*Tommy's Holiday Camp---Keith Moon
  May 26, 1969 by The Who
  Decca DXSW 7205 (LP) **Tommy**

 Twist And Shout---Bert Russell—Phil Medley
  May 7, 1962 by The Isley Brothers
  Wand 124 b/w *Spanish Twist*

*Waiting---Chuck Howard
  Given to Ringo—1970

236

†*Well...(Baby Please Don't Go)*---Walter Ward
June 23, 1958 by The Olympics
Demon 1508 b/w *Western Movies*

*Whispering Grass---Fred Fisher–Doris Fisher
August 19, 1940 by The Ink Spots
Decca 3258 b/w *Maybe*

%*Why (Can't You Love Me Again)*---Tony Sheridan–Bill Crompton
Original Recording–1958 demo tape by Tony Sheridan and The Shadows

**Wine, Women And Loud Happy Songs*---Larry Kingston
First Published–October 7, 1968
Given to Ringo–1970

*Without Her---Sorrells Pickard
Given to Ringo–1970
April 17, 1972 by Sorrells Pickard
Decca DL 7-5338 (LP) **Sorrells Pickard**

**Woman Of The Night*---Sorrells Pickard
Given to Ringo–1970

Words Of Love---Buddy Holly
June 17, 1957 by Buddy Holly
Coral 61852 b/w *Mailman Bring Me No More Blues*

†*Ya Ya*---Morgan Robinson–Clarence Lewis–Lee Dorsey
July 24, 1961 by Lee Dorsey
Fury 1053 b/w *Give Me You*

**You Always Hurt The One You Love*---Allan Roberts–Doris Fisher
May 22, 1944 by The Mills Brothers
Decca 18599 b/w *'Till Then*

†*You Can't Catch Me*---Chuck Berry
November 26, 1956 by Chuck Berry
Chess 1645 b/w *Havana Moon*

You Really Got A Hold On Me---William 'Smokey' Robinson
November 19, 1962 by The Miracles
Tamla 54073 b/w *Happy Landing*

You're Sixteen—Richard Sherman–Robert Sherman
   October 10, 1960 by Johnny Burnette
   Liberty 55285 b/w *I Beg Your Pardon*

The most obvious source of material available to someone studying a group of musicians is the records they released. It's the only place you find, captured in a static form, the group's vocal, musical and production techniques. If you dig a little deeper and do some reading on the individual members of the group, you can begin to understand what the group is trying to say and how its members see themselves in relation to other musicians. You can go to as many concerts as you can afford, read as many fan magazines as you wish, but in the end, their music exists only on record.

In the case of a group like the Beatles, who have either broken up or stopped performing live, their public image becomes synonymous with their image on record. And it becomes next to impossible to see behind that image to the musician who makes mistakes and sometimes just "sags off" in the studios.

By the late 60's, with very little new Beatle music likely to be released, the public's insatiable appetite for any "new" Beatle material prompted the fairly wide public distribution of a large body of old recordings, commonly called *bootlegs*. Through these recordings it is possible to preserve aspects of the Beatles' career which, in the case of less popular groups, would be lost after one performance.

The most interesting Beatle bootlegs are those from their early years of popularity, when their act still consisted largely of songs written by other people. Since they had few, if any, records on the market, it was not necessary to constantly plug the "latest single." Their stage act, then, consisted of a large number of early Rock 'n' Roll songs—a far greater number than the few they later released.

In preparing this section on musical influences, we felt that limiting ourselves to the songs the Beatles actually released would leave out a great deal of the story. However, tracking down every song they ever performed anywhere would have resulted in a virtual reprinting of the Top 100 songs of the 50's. Being compromisers at heart, we extracted forty songs (a Top 40 survey, if you will) that present a relatively balanced picture of the areas of music the Beatles were drawing from.

Angel Baby—Rose Hamlin
   November 21, 1960 by Rosie and The Originals
   Highland 1011 b/w *Give Me Love*

Be My Baby---Ellie Greenwich–Jeff Barry–Phil Spector
  August 12, 1963 by The Ronettes
  Philles 116 b/w *Tedesco And Pittman*

Besame Mucho---Consuelo Velazquez–Selig Shaftel
  December 17, 1943 by Jimmy Dorsey and Orchestra (Vocals:
    Bob Eberle and Kitty Kallen)
  Decca 18574 b/w *My Ideal*

Carol---Chuck Berry
  August 4, 1958 by Chuck Berry
  Chess 1700 b/w *Hey, Pedro*

Crying, Waiting, Hoping---Buddy Holly
  July 27, 1959 by Buddy Holly
  Coral 62134 b/w *Peggy Sue Got Married*

Don't Ever Change---Gerry Goffin–Carole King
  April 23, 1962 by The Crickets
  Liberty 55441 b/w *I'm Not A Bad Guy*

Glad All Over---Aaron Schroeder–Sid Tepper–Roy Bennett
  December 30, 1957 by Carl Perkins
  Sun 287 b/w *Lend Me Your Comb*

Good Golly, Miss Molly---Robert Blackwell–John Marascalco
  January 13, 1958 by Little Richard
  Specialty 624 b/w *Hey-Hey-Hey-Hey!*

Good Rockin' Tonight---Roy Brown
  Original–January 24, 1948 by Roy Brown
    Deluxe 3093 b/w *Lolly-Pop Mama*
  Hit–April 5, 1948 by Wynonie Harris
    King 4210 b/w *Good Morning Mr. Blues*

Hallelujah, I Love Her So---Ray Charles
  May 14, 1956 by Ray Charles
  Atlantic 1096 b/w *What Would I Do Without You*

Hi-Heel Sneakers---Robert Higgenbotham
  January 13, 1964 by Tommy Tucker
  Checker 1067 b/w *I Don't Want 'Cha*

Hippy Hippy Shake---Chan Romero
July 6, 1959 by Chan Romero
Del-Fi 4119 b/w *If I Had A Way*

The Honeymoon Song---Mikis Theodorakis—William Sansom
Originally—From 1959 Film: *Honeymoon*
First Recording—October 19, 1959 by Manuel
  Capitol 4306 b/w *Proud Matador*

Hound Dog---Jerry Leiber—Mike Stoller
Original—March 9, 1953 by Willie Mae 'Big Mama' Thornton
  Peacock 1612 b/w *Night Mare*
Hit—July 16, 1956 by Elvis Presley
  RCA 6604 b/w *Don't Be Cruel*

I Forgot To Remember To Forget---Stanley Kesler—Charles Feathers
August 15, 1955 by Elvis Presley
Sun 223 b/w *Mystery Train*

I Got A Woman---Ray Charles
December 27, 1954 by Ray Charles
Atlantic 1050 b/w *Come Back*

I Just Don't Understand---Marijohn Wilkin—Kent Westberry
June 5, 1961 by Ann-Margret
RCA 7894 b/w *I Don't Hurt Anymore*

I'm Gonna Sit Right Down And Cry (Over You)---Joe Thomas—
Howard Biggs
January 25, 1954 by Roy Hamilton
  Epic 9015 b/w *You'll Never Walk Alone*
Cover Model—September 10, 1956 by Elvis Presley
  RCA 6638 b/w *I'll Never Let You Go*

I'm Talking About You---Chuck Berry
February 6, 1961 by Chuck Berry
Chess 1779 b/w *Little Star*

Johnny B. Goode---Chuck Berry
March 31, 1958 by Chuck Berry
Chess 1691 b/w *Around And Around*

Lawdy Miss Clawdy---Lloyd Price
April 23, 1952 by Lloyd Price
Specialty 428 b/w *Mailman Blues*

Lend Me Your Comb—Kay Twomey—Fred Wise—Ben Weisman
December 30, 1957 by Carl Perkins
Sun 287 b/w *Glad All Over*

Little Queenie—Chuck Berry
March 9, 1959 by Chuck Berry
Chess 1722 b/w *Almost Grown*

Lonesome Tears In My Eyes—Johnny Burnette—Dorsey Burnette—
Paul Burlison—Al Mortimer
November 5, 1956 by The Johnny Burnette Trio
Coral CRL 57080 (LP) **Johnny Burnette And The Rock 'n' Roll
Trio**

Lucille—Richard Penniman—Albert Collins
February 25, 1957 by Little Richard
Specialty 598 b/w *Send Me Some Lovin'*

Memphis, Tennessee—Chuck Berry
June 22, 1959 by Chuck Berry
Chess 1729 b/w *Back In The USA*

Nothin' Shakin' (But The Leaves On The Trees)—Cirino Colacrai—
Eddie Fontaine—Dianne Lampert—Jack Cleveland
Original—June 16, 1958 by Eddie Fontaine
Sunbeam 105 b/w *Oh Wonderful Night*
Hit—July 28, 1958 by Eddie Fontaine
Argo 5309 b/w *Don't Ya Know*

Save The Last Dance For Me—Doc Pomus—Mort Shuman
August 15, 1960 by The Drifters
Atlantic 2071 b/w *Nobody But Me*

Shake Rattle And Roll—Charles Calhoun
Original—April 12, 1954 by Joe Turner
Atlantic 1026 b/w *You Know I Love You*
Hit—July 5, 1954 by Bill Haley And The Comets
Decca 29209 b/w *A.B.C. Boogie*

Sheila—Tommy Roe
May 28, 1962 by Tommy Roe
ABC 10329 b/w *Save Your Kisses*

(I Do The) Shimmy Shimmy—B. Massey—A. Sheubert
July 5, 1960 by Bobby Freeman
King 5373 b/w *You Don't Understand Me*

A Shot Of Rhythm And Blues—Terry Thompson
December 28, 1961 by Arthur Alexander
Dot 16309 b/w *You Better Move On*

Shout—Rudolph Isley—Ronald Isley—O'Kelly Isley
August 24, 1959 by The Isley Brothers
RCA 7588 b/w *Shout Part 2*

Some Other Guy—Jerry Leiber—Mike Stoller—Richard Barrett
April 9, 1962 by Richie Barrett
Atlantic 2142 b/w *Tricky Dicky*

So How Come (No One Loves Me)—Felix Bryant—Boudaloux Bryant
Original—May 9, 1960 by The Omegas
  Decca 31094 b/w *Study Hall*
Hit—November 1, 1960 by The Everly Brothers
  Warner Brothers WB 1395 (LP) **A Date With The Everly Brothers**

Soldier Of Love (Lay Down Your Arms)—Buzz Cason—Tony Moon
May 7, 1962 by Arthur Alexander
Dot 16357 b/w *Where Have You Been?*

Sure To Fall (In Love With You)—Carl Perkins
January 23, 1956 by Carl Perkins
Sun 235 b/w *Tennessee*

Three Cool Cats—Jerry Leiber—Mike Stoller
January 12, 1959 by The Coasters
ATCO 6132 b/w *Charlie Brown*

To Know Him Is To Love Him—Phil Spector
September 15, 1958 by The Teddy Bears
Dore 503 b/w *Don't You Worry My Little Pet*

You Win Again—Hank Williams
September 8, 1952 by Hank Williams
MGM 11318 b/w *Settin' The Woods On Fire*

BOOTLEGS

The Beatles' Story   Capitol STBO 2222
                                   (2 LPs)

The Beatles   Apple SWBO 101   (2 LPs)

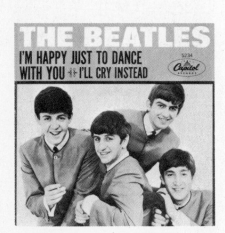

I'm Happy   Capitol 5234 (45)
Just To Dance With You/I'll
Cry Instead

Beatles   Parlophone PCS 3062 (LP)
For Sale (internal photo)

BOOTLEGS

Bootlegs generally fall into one of three categories: Recordings of Live Concerts, Recordings of Radio/Television/Film Appearances, or Studio Out-takes.

The first category is the most tantalizing, but usually the most disappointing. As there was never a live Beatles album issued, a great deal of interest has revolved around the few recordings made of the Beatles in concert. Unfortunately, most of the early recordings are of a limited technical proficiency, while the later ones are constantly marred by the sounds of thousands upon thousands of screaming voices.

The Beatles have always said that their stage act was at its best while they were playing in Hamburg and Liverpool's Cavern Club. Playing nightly for seven or eight hours at a time, they had to invent ways of keeping people's attention, either by fancy musicianship or eye-catching stage antics. In spite of the number of people who claimed to have seen greatness in the Beatles in those days, there are few, if any, recordings of note from this time. And those of us who weren't there must rely upon our imagination. When they first signed with Parlophone, George Martin was seriously considering recording a live album at the Cavern Club, but nothing came of it.

When the Beatles began playing large concerts in the major cities of the world, Martin also was considering an album of these shows. In fact, several were actually recorded. The main problem was always that the crowd noise level drowned out not only the sound of the music, but also impared the Beatles' own capability of hearing what they were playing. A live Beatle concert of these days was, really, more of an emotional than a musical event. And most of the bootleg recordings of this type are simply boring and hard to listen to.

The second category provides a bit more excitement. As the Beatles became known in Britain (in late 1962—early 1963) they, like any other group on the make, appeared on as many radio and television programs as they could. As their popularity grew, they were often the featured performers, taking time for interviews and singing more than just one or two songs per show. During the summer of 1963, the Beatles actually had their own weekly radio program on the BBC, during which they played a lot of their own songs and songs they took from others (some of which they never put on record). A great deal of material of this type still exists, and though sometimes repetitious (how many versions of *Long Tall Sally* do you really want to hear?), these are, in the end, the best opportunity we have to hear the Beatles playing spontaneously, without clean studio production. By 1965, they virtually ceased making live media appearances. For the next five years they appeared only in self-directed film clips, which appeared on television upon the release of each new single. Since the breakup of the group, most of the Beatles, especially John, have appeared on numerous interview and entertainment programs, occasionally performing as well.

From this second category we have limited ourselves to those media appearances most readily available among bootlegs, and to the ones which we feel to have some musical or historical interest.

The third and final category could, in the future, be the most important of all. Like any musical group, the Beatles recorded songs in the studio which, for various reasons, they decided not to release. A fair amount of material of both musical and historical interest presently exists in whichever vault EMI keeps such things. There is currently no hope of the public ever hearing them, but perhaps some day in the future, when legal and contractual situations change, some —if not all—may get out.

We have added our own fourth section, under the name bootlegs, since, particularly during the heyday of Beatlemania, many "records" were released that were bootlegs—if not in name, then surely in spirit. Enterprising and often self-seeking reporters packaged their own barely interesting interviews with the Beatles, or even their narration of Beatle events, into albums that put heavy emphasis on the name *Beatles*—often deceiving the naive record-buying public.

Finally, we have included a few items of Beatle-related material which, for various reasons, was never released. Those that did come out will be covered in a later section.

We have arranged this section chronologically, by recording date if possible. Otherwise, we have used the date of public performance. This was done for two reasons: It avoids the repetition inherent in cataloguing the many bootleg records available. More importantly, the very term *bootleg record* is a misnomer. Save for a handful of examples, none of the bootleg recordings were ever envisaged in the form they currently appear in, albums. Most of the performances contained were, in their original form, singular events: a TV show, a concert or a prospective record. Their inclusion and exclusion in the available bootleg albums are totally a result of the generally unknown people who pressed them.

1962

January 1, 1962–**Decca Audition Tapes.**

The Beatles' first audition for a major record label. Most attention was paid to their versions of old pop tunes (George singing lead on *The Sheik Of Araby* and Paul on *Red Sails In The Sunset*). They also did three Lennon-McCartney songs later given to other artists (*Like Dreamers Do, Hello Little Girl* and *Love Of The Loved*), plus six songs from the 50's (*'Till There Was You, Please Mr. Postman* and *Money*, which they later released; and *To Know Her Is To Love Her, Memphis* and *Three Cool Cats,* which they didn't release). Decca turned them down.

Early/Mid 1962–**Various Demo Tapes.**

Brian Epstein used parts of the Decca tapes along with some new, crude recordings to try and interest other companies in the Beatles. Several never–heard Lennon–McCartney songs were included in this new batch: *I Lost My Little Girl, Looking Glass, Thinking Of Linking, The Years Roll Along, Winston's Walk, Keep Looking That Way* and *Catswalk* (which was later given to the Chris Barber Band, under the name *Catcall*).

June 6, 1962–**Parlophone Audition Tape.**

The Beatles try out before George Martin doing early versions of *Love Me Do, P. S. I Love You, Ask Me Why* and *Hello Little Girl*; along with *Besame Mucho* and *Your Feet's Too Big.* Martin signed them up.

Summer 1962–**BBC Radio.**

This should be considered the Beatles' first album. It comes from one of their earliest radio performances, and contains fourteen songs written by other artists (only one ever appeared on a "real" Beatle album). It pre-dates the **Please Please Me** lp both by date and feel. In one performance, the Beatles presented a perfectly rounded collection of the different types of songs that were the basis for their own music.

John solos on five songs (*I Got A Woman, I Just Don't Understand, Slow Down, Lonesome Tears In My Eyes* and *I'm Gonna Sit Right Down And Cry Over You*), and Paul sings lead on three songs

(*Sure To Fall, To Know Her Is To Love Her* and *The Honeymoon Song*). John and Paul sing together on *Don't Ever Change* and *A Shot Of Rhythm And Blues*, while George sings lead on *Glad All Over, Nothin' Shakin', So How Come* and *Crying, Waiting, Hoping.*

George's songs are particular standouts due to both his sharp rockabilly guitar playing and the fact that he didn't do much singing on the early Beatle albums. John displays his already formed ability to sing fairly gutsy R&B songs, whether it be the very black *I Got A Woman* (from Ray Charles) or the blues-like *I Just Don't Understand* (from, of all people, Ann-Margret). Paul, while dabbling in rockabilly (*Sure To Fall*) is already singing ballads (*To Know Her Is To Love Her* and *The Honeymoon Song*).

A Shot Of Rhythm And Blues was one of Arthur Alexander's best records (better, in fact, than *Anna*), and the Beatles' version of it might have been a better lead-off single than *Love Me Do.*

An album of all fourteen songs is available under the names *Yellow Matter Custard* and *As Sweet As You Are.* Unfortunately, this recording, made from the radio, is far below studio quality.

Late August/Early September 1962—Granada TV Film Clip From The Cavern Club.

Granada Television was one of the first large broadcast companies to take note of the new musical sounds in Liverpool. A film crew captured the Beatles on stage soon after Ringo joined the group. The film clip was aired on the TV show *People And Places* on November 7, 1962. The earliest known sound film of the Beatles performing, it shows John singing Richie Barrett's *Some Other Guy.* Bootlegs of this song appeared as early as 1963.

September 11, 1962—First Parlophone Recording Session.

While recording their first single, the Beatles did an early version of *Please Please Me,* which was almost released as the B side of *Love Me Do.*

Fall 1962—BBC Radio.

In another of their early radio appearances the Beatles sang a song later given to Billy J. Kramer, *I'll Be On My Way.*

November 26, 1962—Studio Out-take.

Music publisher Dick James tried to get George Martin to have the Beatles record *How Do You Do It.* The group was more interested in doing their own compositions, and deliberately played poorly. That version wasn't issued, but the song later became a number one hit for Gerry and The Pacemakers.

Late December 1962—**Hamburg Star Club Tape.**

The only major recording of the Beatles' famed Hamburg days, recorded during one of their last visits there by Teddy Taylor.

Contents: *Be-Bop-A-Lula* (Vocal by German waiter, Horst Obber)/ *I Saw Her Standing There* (Paul)/*Hallelujah! I Love Her So* (Horst, again)/*My Girl Is Red Hot* (John)/*Sheila* (George)/*Kansas City* (Paul) /*Shimmy Shimmy* (Paul with John changing *m*'s to *t*'s)/*Red Sails In The Sunset* (Paul)/*Nothin' Shakin'* (Paul)/*Little Queenie* (Paul)/*Long Tall Sally* (Paul)/*'Till There Was You* (Paul)/*A Taste Of Honey* (Paul) /*Falling In Love Again* (The Marlene Dietrich hit by Paul)/*I Remember You* (Jolly What! The Frank Ifield hit by Paul)/*Ask Me Why* (Paul and John)/*Your Feet's Too Big* (Paul)/*Besame Mucho* (Paul)/ Two versions of *To Know Her Is To Love Her* (George)/Two versions of *Roll Over Beethoven* (George)/*Everybody's Trying To Be My Baby* (George)/*Sweet Little Sixteen* (John)/*Gonna Sit Right Down And Cry Over You* (John)/*I'm Talkin' About You* (John)/*Mr. Moonlight* (John)/*Matchbox* (Ringo).

They say this is a pretty good recording; it might make a great double album set someday.

Late 1962—**Studio Out-takes.**

Paul singing *I Forgot To Remember To Forget* and *Lucille,* while John sings an early version of *Dizzy Miss Lizzie.*

1963

January 18, 1963—**Radio Luxembourg.**

John sings lead on *Carol,* later a hit for the Rolling Stones, while Paul and George sing Carl Perkins' *Lend Me Your Comb.*

Terrible quality. A bad whine runs through the tape, which is very short anyway.

February 11, 1963—**"Please Please Me" Session Out-takes.**

Two tracks not included on their first Parlophone album. An early version of *Hold Me Tight* and John singing *Keep Your Hands Off My Baby.*

Early/Mid 1963—**BBC Radio.**

During the first half of the year the Beatles appeared on virtually every pop show on English radio, performing a lot of the songs that appeared on their first two albums.

Quality is fairly good and once again you can hear working, unproduced versions of familiar Beatle songs.

Contents: *Do You Want To Know A Secret, You Really Got A Hold On Me, Misery,* Two versions of *Money, 'Till There Was You, From Me To You, Roll Over Beethoven, Love Me Do, Kansas City,*

Long Tall Sally, Please Please Me, She Loves You, Words Of Love, Devil In Her Heart, Anna, There's A Place, Honey Don't (John on vocal, not Ringo), *Chains, I Saw Her Standing There* and *Boys* (all eventually released by the Beatles); plus *Hippy Hippy Shake* (Paul), *Sure To Fall* (Paul) and *Lucille* (Paul) (none ever released by the Beatles).

June/September 1963—Pop Go The Beatles.

For fifteen weeks during the summer, the Beatles hosted a weekly thirty minute radio show, featuring themselves and other guest artists.

Some material from these shows still available is: *Boys, There's A Place, Lend Me Your Comb, A Shot Of Rhythm And Blues, 'Till There Was You, Chains, Twist And Shout, Do You Want To Know A Secret, I'm Gonna Sit Right Down And Cry Over You* and *Crying, Waiting, Hoping,* along with the show's theme *Pop Go The Beatles.*

Mid 1963—Studio Out-takes.

A very nice version of John singing *I Got A Woman* and *Soldiers Of Love* (another Arthur Alexander record which had, for an early 60's song, surprisingly intriguing anti-war lyrics).

October 13, 1963—Sunday Night At The London Palladium.

The Beatles on their first major BBC TV show. They sang *I Want To Hold Your Hand, This Boy, All My Loving, Money* and *Twist And Shout.*

A lot of crowd noise, some dialogue, in a fair-quality recording.

October 30, 1963—Swedish TV Show "Drop In"

During their first foreign tour as celebrities, the Beatles performed six songs before a very appreciative audience. They may not have understood English, but the crowd certainly caught on to the music. The program was aired November 3, 1963.

Contents: *I Saw Her Standing There, From Me To You, Money, You Really Got A Hold On Me, She Loves You* and *Twist And Shout.*

Fall 1963—Studio Out-take.

The Beatles "gave" the song *Little Child* to Mike Hurst, who planned to release it as a single. It never came out and the Beatles put their own version on their second album.

November 4, 1963—Royal Variety Performance.

A possible marker of the beginning of Beatlemania in Britain, as the Beatles stole the show in England's top annual entertainment special. Filmed at the Prince of Wales Theatre and shown on television November 10, 1963. The Beatles sang *From Me To You, She Loves You, 'Till There Was You* and *Twist And Shout.*

This is a positively dreadful recording; somebody somewhere must have a better one. Besides, John's suggestion that the Royalty present "rattle their jewels" is not on it.

November 16, 1963—**Bournemouth Concert.**

For the first time Americans get to see the Beatles in action. Film crews from all three US TV networks filmed the Beatles' performance and the wild crowd reaction. Short film clips were seen on all three early the next week, while a longer segment was on the January 3, 1964 *Jack Paar Show* on NBC.

November 20, 1963—**Manchester Concert.**

An eight minute film was produced of the Beatles' performance, showing them singing *She Loves You* and *Twist And Shout.* The film was released December 22, 1963.

Late December 1963—**BBC Radio Show "From Us To You."**

The title of the Beatles' third single, *From Me To You,* was a take-off on a letter column in the weekly magazine *New Musical Express,* called "From Us To You." There was also a BBC show of the same name. When the Beatles appeared on the show, singing *Roll Over Beethoven, All My Loving* and *I Wanna Be Your Man,* they also changed lyrics and sang *From Us To You.*

1964

February 9, 1964—**The First "Ed Sullivan Show"**

The real beginning of Beatlemania in America, as millions of Americans saw the Beatles live, for the first time, on this CBS show. The Beatles sang *All My Loving, She Loves You, Till There Was You* and *This Boy.*

Fairly good quality recordings of this, and the February 16 show, exist. Unfortunately, most of Ed Sullivan's typical pithy remarks have been edited out.

February 11, 1964—**Washington DC Concert.**

The first outdoor Beatle concert in America (in the Washington Colosseum). A short film was made of the concert showing the Beatles singing *'Till There Was You* and *I Want To Hold Your Hand.*

The Carnegie Hall (New York) concert the next day, planned as a live album, was never recorded.

February 16, 1964—**The Second "Ed Sullivan Show"**

The Beatles sang six songs (*I Saw Her Standing There, I Want To*

Hold Your Hand, From Me To You, Twist And Shout, Please Please Me and *She Loves You,* again). Not bad, for newcomers, on the very time-conscious *Sullivan Show.*

February 29, 1964 (UK)–**Big Night Out (ABC TV).**
The Beatles appeared as a four man rock group (Plot sound familiar?), along with comedians Mike and Bernie Winters, in a number of fairly humerous skits.
Contents: Dialogue and *Please Mr. Postman, All My Loving, I Wanna Be Your Man* and *'Till There Was You.* All these are records— there was no live performance.

February 1964 (UK)–**Studio Out-take.**
Tony Sheridan, who was the lead singer on the Beatles' first recordings, was trying to draw some attention to his own career. He recorded, along with Bobby Patrick's Big Six, a song entitled *Tell Me If You Can,* which he *claimed* was a tune he co-wrote with Paul McCartney in Germany. For whatever reasons, it was never released.

March/April 1964–**A Hard Day's Night Soundtrack.**
The Beatles, appearing as a four man rock group, filmed their first feature movie at various points in England.
Fairly good quality dubs of the movie soundtrack (released in June) are not too hard to come across. They contain numerous gems of dialogue (Ringo being lectured by Paul's "Grandfather" and George telling off a snobby advertising man.)
Songs included: *A Hard Day's Night, I Should Have Known Better, I Wanna Be Your Man, Don't Bother Me, All My Loving, If I Fell, Can't Buy Me Love, And I Love Her, I'm Happy Just To Dance With You, This Boy, Tell Me Why* and *She Loves You,* plus instrumental music by George Martin. All songs are the tracks from the Beatles' albums.

May 6, 1964–**Around The Beatles.**
A one hour TV special on the Beatles in which, besides playing music, they appeared in a scene from Shakespear's *A Mid-Summer Night's Dream* (with Paul as Pyramus, John as Thisbe, George as Moonshine and Ringo as The Lion).
Music: Medley of *Love Me Do, Please Please Me* and *From Me To You;* and *She Loves You, I Want To Hold Your Hand, Can't Buy Me Love, Twist And Shout, Roll Over Beethoven, I Wanna Be Your Man, Long Tall Sally* and *Shout* (the only one in this group not on a Beatles record. It's a tremendously exciting version with George, John and Paul trading on vocals).
Portions of this show were seen in America on ABC TV on

252

November 15, 1964.

May 24, 1964—**The Ed Sullivan Show.**
The Beatles perform *You Can't Do That.*

June 9, 1964—**The Beatles American Tour With Ed Rudy (LP)**
News Documentary 2
When the Beatles first descended on America in February, their every movement was documented by reporters. Some decided that the usual channels of reporting were not enough. This "album" contains Rudy's ramblings on Beatle arrivals and departures, pointless interviews, excerpts from press conferences and Rudy's thick New York voice (run through an echo chamber) doing Armageddon announcing.

Sadly invaluable as an historical timepiece, it unknowingly captured the outer limits of fan worship. This was but the most popular of three albums by Rudy.

June 15, 1964—**Melbourne Australia Concert.**
Contents: *I Saw Her Standing There, You Can't Do That, All My Loving, She Loves You, 'Till There Was You, Roll Over Beethoven, Can't Buy Me Love* and *This Boy.*

Mid 1964—**Murray The K Fan Club Record.**
Famed New York disc jockey Murray the K, self-styled "friend" of the Beatles, was lucky enough to record fifteen minutes of interviews with the Beatles in the US in February and in Britain a short time later. The record also contains a very abbreviated version of *Shout* from *Around The Beatles.*

Mid 1964—**This Is The Savage Young Beatles (LP)**
Savage Records BM 69
A short album of dubious legality containing four tracks the Beatles recorded in Germany in 1961 with Tony Sheridan (*Cry For A Shadow, If You Love Me Baby, Sweet Georgia Brown* and *Why*), filled out by four non-Beatle Tony Sheridan cuts (*Let's Dance, What'd I Say, Ruby Baby* and *Ya Ya*), all of which were then available on an MGM album. This album resurfaced in 1966.

July 1964—**BBC Radio's "Top Of The Pops."**
One of the best recordings of the Beatles on radio. All four (but mainly John) engage host Brian Matthews in absurdist discussions, in between playing *Long Tall Sally, Things We Said Today* and *A Hard Day's Night* (containing a long fade-out to prove it wasn't a record).

August 7, 1964–**Studio Out-take.**

This was to have been the release date for Tommy Quickly's version of *No Reply* on Piccadilly Records. The single never came out, and the Beatles' own version of the song appeared on **Beatles For Sale.**

August 22, 1964–**Vancouver Concert.**

Contents: *Twist And Shout, You Can't Do That, She Loves You, Things We Said Today, Roll Over Beethoven, Can't Buy Me Love, Boys, A Hard Day's Night* and *Long Tall Sally.*

August 23, 1964–**Hollywood Bowl Concert.**

Contents: *Twist And Shout, You Can't Do That, All My Loving, She Loves You, Things We Said Today, Roll Over Beethoven, Can't Buy Me Love, If I Fell, I Want To Hold Your Hand, Boys, A Hard Day's Night* and *Long Tall Sally.*

The so-called live album that never was. The concert was recorded with the intention of producing a live LP. It is therefore better than most bootlegs. However, George Martin still felt there was much too much crowd noise, and that the music didn't sound that good–and this is one of the best bootlegs. A short excerpt of *Twist And Shout* did appear on Capitol's double LP **The Beatles' Story.**

September 2, 1964–**Philadelphia Concert.**

The so-called *Whiskey Flats* LP.

Contents: *Twist And Shout, You Can't Do That, All My Loving...* well, you get the idea. It was the same show as the Hollywood Bowl.

Fall 1964–**Hear The Beatles Tell All (LP) Vee Jay VJPRO 202**

A long playing promotional album recorded during the Beatles' tour of America in August. Side one, Jim Steck's interview with John Lennon, is–in total contrast to Ed Rudy's–one of the most intelligent of that time. Side two, in which Dave Hull interviews all four Beatles, is less revealing and closer to the average of that era.

Editing and background music was by Lou Adler.

Fall 1964–**Remember, We Don't Like Them, We Love Them.**

Another interview record (this time a 45) by an egocentric disc jockey/reporter (this time, Tom Clay) following the Beatles on their American tour. Clay seems more insistent than Rudy in acting as if he were a personal friend of the Beatles. His tenor prompted John Lennon to shoot off some pointed insults which apparently sailed right over Clay's head.

September/October 1964—**Studio Out-takes.**
While recording the LP **Beatles For Sale**, George recorded a song called *You'll Know What To Do,* while Paul sang *Always And Only.* Neither appeared on that or any other album.

October 9, 1964—**Granville Theatre In London.**
Before a live audience, the Beatles recorded three songs for the American TV show *Shindig.* Aired on January 20, 1965, the show included *Kansas City, Boys* and *I'm A Loser.*

October 1964—**Studio Out-takes.**
Beatles' manager Brian Epstein, who had just issued his auto-biography (*A Cellarful Of Noise*), planned on releasing an American album featuring segments of the book read by him. While recorded, the album was never released.

November 1964—**BBC Radio Show "Top Of The Pops."**
The Beatles, pushing their new single and album, appeared on the radio with Brian Matthews. George, who had a bad sore throat, was still able to sing *Everybody's Trying To Be My Baby.*

1965
February/March and April/May 1965—**Help Soundtrack.**
Filmed in the Bahamas, Austria and Britain, the second Beatles' film didn't quite equal their first, either in cinematic techniques or in dialogue. Like *A Hard Day's Night,* recordings of the soundtrack are easily available. But the script's many hackneyed cliches fail to overcome the loss of visuals. Songs included (all from records): *Help!, You're Gonna Lose That Girl, I Need You, She's A Woman, The Night Before, Another Girl, Ticket To Ride, You've Got To Hide Your Love Away* and instrumental music by George Martin.

April 3, 1965—**ITV's "Thank Your Lucky Stars."**
April 15, 1965—**BBC's "Top Of The Pops."**
Becoming more reclusive in their public appearances, the Beatles appeared on only two television shows to plug their new single, *Ticket To Ride.*

May/June 1965—**Studio Out-take.**
John tried once again to record *Keep Your Hands Off My Baby.* Once again, it was passed over.

June 20, 1965—**Paris Sports Stadium Concert.**
Contents: *I Feel Fine, Twist And Shout, She's A Woman, Ticket To Ride, Can't Buy Me Love, I'm A Loser, I Wanna Be Your Man,*

A Hard Day's Night, Baby's In Black, Rock And Roll Music, Everybody's Trying To Be My Baby and *Long Tall Sally*.

A fair quality recording, with the Beatles making lame attempts to speak French.

August 1, 1965—**Blackpool Night Out.**

The Beatles last live TV appearance for almost a year, in which they promoted their new single *Help!*. An added feature was a short film clip of them singing *I Do Like To Be Beside The Seaside.*

August 14, 1965—**Taping For "The Ed Sullivan Show."**

At the start of their second American tour, the Beatles recorded six songs before a live audience (*I Feel Fine, I'm Down, Ticket To Ride, Yesterday, Act Naturally* and *Help!*) for the September 12 *Ed Sullivan Show*. An intriguing moment is the crowd's reaction to *Yesterday*. They want to scream, but it's not a "screamer" song. Very unsure, the crowd quiets for the song, returning to its usual posture at the end.

August 15, 1965—**Shea Stadium Concert.**

A recording of (at that time) the largest concert ever held. This is the soundtrack to the film of the concert, first aired on BBC television May 1, 1966.

Contents: *I'm Down,* Dialogue, Introductions by Murry The K and Ed Sullivan, *Twist And Shout, I Feel Fine, Dizzy Miss Lizzie, Ticket To Ride, Act Naturally, Can't Buy Me Love, Baby's In Black, A Hard Day's Night* and *I'm Down* (with dialogue from Brian Epstein and George Harrison).

As this was held in the middle of a crowded baseball stadium, the resulting lack of fidelity is not surprising.

October/November 1965—**Studio Out-take.**

During the **Rubber Soul** sessions, Paul sang on an unreleased track *If You've Got Troubles,* which may or may not be an early version of *Have You Got Problems,* a song which appeared on brother Mike McGear's 1974 album.

December 2, 1965—**BBC's "Top Of The Pops."**

In the first of a series of personally directed pretaped appearances, the Beatles sang both sides of their single *Day Tripper/We Can Work It Out.*

Christmas 1965—**Paul's Christmas Album.**

Perhaps the rarest Beatle recording in existence. It's a special treat for the other three. Paul recorded a special album in which he appears as an announcer, a singer and a comedian. Only four copies were ever pressed.

1966

June 16, 1966–**BBC's "Top Of The Pops."**

Just before the Beatles began their final concert tour, they released a new single, *Paperback Writer/Rain.* They made a rare live appearance on television, during which they sang their new songs. At the same time, they continued their policy of filming specific clips to have inserted into musical TV programs. The film for this single was seen on the last *Thank Your Lucky Stars* on June 25, and on the *Ed Sullivan Show* in August.

June 26, 1966–**Hamburg Concert.**

During this last concert tour, they returned to Hamburg for the first time in over three years. A very poor quality recording exists of part of that concert.

Contents: *Rock And Roll Music, Baby's In Black, Nowhere Man, Yesterday, I Feel Fine* and *I'm Down.*

July 2, 1966–**Tokyo Concert.**

To transplant a popular phrase, this is the "finest *live* Beatles LP in existence." This is no cheap 'microphone in the balcony' job, but a totally audible, nicely mixed concert. There's just one problem...the Beatles didn't play very well. You can play *I Wanna Be Your Man* out of tune before a cheering throng without fear, because no one's gonna hear it anyway. However, when you perform a song like *Paperback Writer* out of tune *and* out of beat, you open yourself up to the question: What do these people think they're doing?

The fact is, the Beatles had begun to write songs which could not be easily performed on stage, if at all. Combine that with the general sloppiness of their stage act after playing for three years before crowds who really couldn't hear them, and you have an explanation for this very good, yet very bad, recording.

Contents: *Rock And Roll Music, She's A Woman, If I Needed Someone, Day Tripper, Baby's In Black, I Feel Fine, Yesterday, I Wanna Be Your Man, Nowhere Man, Paperback Writer* and *I'm Down.*

Perhaps the best packaged Beatle "black market" album, some people unfamiliar with bootlegging techniques might actually take it for a real album. After all, it even has song titles and times printed on the cover, along with a pretty label. But the unmistakable bootleg mentality shines through on the album's title: **Five Nights In A Judo Arena.** The Beatles played in Japan for just three days.

August 29, 1966—San Francisco Concert.

This was the Beatles' last live show, though few people suspected it at the time. On a suggestion from Paul, Beatles' aide Neil Aspinal made a crude recording of the concert on his cassette recorder by literally pointing it in the direction of the stage. This might be considered a classic example of something being of "purely historical interest."

Mid 1966—Studio Out-takes.

A very early version of a song George provisionally titled *Pink Litmus Paper Shirt,* while John sang lead on an unreleased track *Colliding Circles.*

1967

Late January 1967—Promotional Film.

Peter Goldmann directed two film clips of the Beatles performing *Strawberry Fields Forever* and *Penny Lane.* The sight of the four Beatles "playing" a song in the middle of an open field with no electric cords visible was clear notice to all interested that the Beatles' notion of public performance had gone through some changes. The two clips were seen on the *Ed Sullivan Show* in February.

Mid 1967—Studio Out-takes.

Now totally a studio band, the amount of Beatles' out-takes began increasing. Six are known to have come out of the year's recordings: *Not Unknown, Anything, India* (George on lead), *Annie* (Paul), *What's The News Maryjane* (John) and *Peace Of Mind.* Only the final two have appeared on bootlegs. *Peace Of Mind* contains intriguing lyrics woven around very complicated beat changes. In spite of the very bad recording available, it still deserves close attention.

June 25, 1967—"Our World" TV Broadcast.

The first live world-wide TV program contained, in a London segment, a view of the Beatles recording a new song, *All You Need Is Love.* Present and participating were a host of friendly rock 'n' rollers, and a large studio orchestra. While Lennon's vocal was later redone, the instrumental track was the one used on the record.

September/October 1967—"Magical Mystery Tour" Soundtrack.

The Beatles' own largely ad-libbed TV special, which was either extremely ahead of its time, extremely pointless or a bit of both. The soundtrack contains a number of worthwhile dialogue bits, though many come from the supporting cast.

Songs included are: *Magical Mystery Tour* (with a slightly different vocal) and (all from records) *The Fool On The Hill, Flying, I Am The Walrus, Blue Jay Way, Your Mother Should Know* and a short snippet of *Hello Goodbye*. Other highlights are the Bonzo Dog Band's rendition of *Death Cab For Cutie,* and the incidental background music. Amongst the latter were two original group compositions performed by an accordionist, Shirley Collins, *Shirley's Wild Accordion* and *Jessie's Dream*. The film premiered on BBC 1 on December 26, 1967, to nearly universal negative acclaim, much of which has been blunted by the passage of time.

November 10, 1967—**Promotional Film Clip.**

The Beatles had themselves filmed performing *Hello Goodbye* at London's Saville Theatre. The film showed the group not only in their Sgt. Pepper uniforms but also redonning their 1963 collarless jackets. Legal difficulties kept the clip off the November 23 *Top Of The Pops,* so its first airing was on the November 26 *Ed Sullivan Show.*

Late 1967/Early 1968—**Yellow Submarine Soundtrack.**

The Beatles really didn't have much to do with this film. Their song inspired it, and they contributed new songs to it. But they acted mostly as script advisors and appeared only briefly at the end. The main characters in the film are cartoon images of the four Beatles, using actors' voices.

Songs included (all from records): *Yellow Submarine, Eleanor Rigby,* bits of *Within You Without You* and *A Day In The Life, All Together Now, When I'm Sixty-Four, It's Only A Northern Song, Nowhere Man, Lucy In The Sky With Diamonds, Sgt. Pepper's Lonely Hearts Club Band, With A Little Help From My Friends, All You Need Is Love* and *Baby You're A Rich Man.* There is also a six second version of *Think For Yourself* (not from **Rubber Soul**) and *It's All Too Much* with a verse not on the album version. *Hey Bulldog,* never intended for the film, was added to fill out the album.

1968

January 1968—**Kenny Everett Interview.**

British radio personality Kenny Everett, always on fairly good terms with the Beatles, interviewed John Lennon, who had just returned from holiday in Morocco. Lennon happened to break out into a short, perverted version of the Ledbelly song *Cottonfields.* For reasons best left unspoken, many bootleggers have seen fit to include this twenty-three second "gem" on numerous albums.

February 1968—**Demo Tape.**
Paul, on piano, recorded a solo version of *Step Inside Love,* which he gave to Cilla Black as the theme for her new television program. Originally including only an opening and closing verse, the song elicited enough public response to prompt Paul to complete the tune, which Cilla issued as a single.

February 6, 1968—**"Cilla"**
Ringo made a solo guest appearance on Cilla Black's new TV show, during which they dueted on *Act Naturally.*

February 1968—**Promotional Film Clips.**
Two different film shorts were made for the release of *Lady Madonna,* the first of which aired on *Top Of The Pops* on March 14.

July/August 1968—**"Hey Jude" Rehearsal Film.**
While beginning to record *Hey Jude,* the Beatles were filmed, in rehearsal, for the program *Experiment In TV* (which was aired after the song was released).

Summer 1968—**Press Conference Ad-lib.**
During a meeting with reporters to discuss the new organization called Apple, John was asked to sing some new songs the group was working on. He responded with off-the-cuff acoustic versions of *Those Were The Days* and *Don't Let Me Down.*

September 4, 1968—**David Frost Show.**
Making a rare live appearance, the group performed an elongated version of *Hey Jude,* which wound up involving the whole audience. The show aired on September 8, 1968.

September 19, 1968—**BBC's "Top Of The Pops."**
Returning again to film, all four Beatles appeared singing *Revolution,* which contains a very nice McCartney harmony vocal.

Summer 1968—**Studio Out-take.**
While recording "The White Album," George (along with Eric Clapton) recorded *Not Guilty,* while Paul did an early version of *Junk* (then called *Jubilee*).

December 11, 1968—**"Rock And Roll Circus" Soundtrack.**
Michael Lindsay-Hogg produced a film of the Rolling Stones, containing many of the top names in rock music. One segment featured an eight and a half minute jam of *Yer Blues,* featuring John Lennon, Yoko Ono, Eric Clapton, Keith Richard, Mitch Mitchell and

Ivry Gitlis (on fiddle). The film had serious distribution problems (it was never finished).

1969

January 1969—"Let It Be" Soundtrack And Out-takes.

How many versions of *Get Back* do you think there are? Probably more than you'd want to hear. It's all part of the protracted and often confusing story of the project that came to be known as **Let It Be**.

After months of considering some form of live performance, the Beatles settled on having a documentary filmed of their recording activities. Consequently, there are 96 hours of sound film of the Beatles singing old Rock 'n' Roll standards, along with new group compositions (which wound up on the **Abbey Road** and **Let It Be** albums). It certainly was the best documented month in the Beatles' history; unfortunately, it was also one of their least creative. Once recorded, the tapes were virtually put on a shelf, as if they might go away.

The first plan was to issue an album of the Beatles redoing some vintage oldies. It was a common practice for the Beatles—and other groups—to warm up in the studio by playing old Rock 'n' Roll hits. During the month's filming, the Beatles sang, played, hummed or otherwise performed: *Stand By Me, Baby I Don't Care, Hippy Hippy Shake, Short Fat Fanny, A Fool Like Me, You Win Again, Turn Around, Lend Me Your Comb, Blue Suede Shoes, True Love, The Right String But The Wrong Yo-Yo, Sure To Fall, Thirty Days, Memphis Tennessee, Maybelline, Johnny B. Goode, Carol, Sweet Little Sixteen, Little Queenie, Roll Over Beethoven, Rock And Roll Music, Singing The Blues, The Midnight Special, The Rock Island Line, Michael Row The Boat Ashore, Devil In Her Heart, Hitch Hike, Money, Three Cool Cats, Yakety-Yak, Good Rockin' Tonight, All Shook Up, Don't Be Cruel, Lucille, Good Golly Miss Molly, Oh My Soul, Send Me Some Lovin', Dizzy Miss Lizzie, Bad Boy, Be-Bop-A-Lula, Save The Last Dance For Me, Besame Mucho, A Lotta Lovin', The House Of The Rising Sun, Tea For Two, Blowin' In The Wind, I Shall Be Released, All Along The Watchtower, I Threw It All Away, Momma You've Been On My Mind, Hi Heel Sneakers, It's Only Make Believe, C'mon Everybody, Somethin' Else, Third Man Theme, Piece Of My Heart, It's So Easy, Lawdy Miss Clawdy, Some Other Guy, Kansas City, You Really Got A Hold On Me, Shake Rattle And Roll, Stairway To Paradise, Whole Lotta Shakin' Goin' On* and *She Said She Said, You Can't Do That, Norwegian Wood* and *Love Me Do*. (Thank God K-Tel hasn't bought out Apple yet!)

After that plan was forgotten, a "normal" Beatle album was planned for release for the early summer. Like the finished **Let It Be** album, it was to have the studio talk and false starts left in. Copies were actually sent to radio stations, but at the last minute release was held up. These became the original *Let It Be* bootlegs. Appearing on the album were: *Let It Be, Save The Last Dance For Me/Don't Let Me Down, Maggie Mae, One After 909, Two Of Us, I Dig A Pony,* an elongated *Dig It, I've Got A Feeling The Long And Winding Road, For You Blue* and *Get Back,* along with an early version of Paul's *Teddy Boy* and a short piece called *The Walk* (which later surfaced as the opening bars to *3 Legs* on Paul's **Ram** album).

The album and the film, both delayed, finally came out in May 1970. The film's soundtrack contained numerous versions of songs from the **Let It Be** album (though none of the final album tracks were those heard in the film), but it also contained several elements worth preserving. Amidst the dialogue were group discussions on how to play the guitar, the effect of electricity on the human body and whether the Beatles should play before people again. A few songs that wound up on **Abbey Road** appeared in the film in early working versions (for example, *Maxwell's Silver Hammer* is followed from early chord work to a rejected finished version). Almost hidden inthe film were two group compositions which they even bothered to copyright: *Suzy Parker* (a Little Richard type rocker) and a "jazz" piano duet between Paul and Ringo. The soundtrack also allowed us to hear Paul at his Ricky Ricardo best. Perez Prado would blush at Paul's infectious version of *Besame Mucho* (*Why* wasn't that song released?).

The Beatles actually got around to only two live performances: singing *Two Of Us* and *Let It Be* before the cameras (these were shown on the March 1, 1970 *Ed Sullivan Show*), and their famed roof-top concert (January 30, 1969). Making their last public appearance as a group, the Beatles, along with Billy Preston, set up their equipment on the roof of their London studios, and sang *I've Got A Feeling, One After 909, I Dig A Pony* and *Get Back.*

A few years later, some other tapes from the **Let It Be** sessions reached the public. Commonly called *Sweet Apple Tracks*, the eight sides contain, aside from the expected workout of *Let It Be* songs, a fairly complete tracing of the evolution of *Get Back,* John's peculiar opus to Dick James (*Shakin' In The Sixties*) and Paul's own working version of *Penina.*

The amount of material available from this 28 day period could be considered the philosophy of bootlegging taken to its extreme. We are able to follow almost every step in the process of artistic creation. But in the end, it defeats the main purpose of recorded music by putting working versions on the same par as finished products. It's as if you were to read all an author's rough notes before you read the finished novel. The absurdity is compounded by the fact that the **Let It Be** album itself is, in reality, nothing but a glorified, Spector-ized rehearsal tape.

Early March 1969—**Studio Out-takes.**

Reunited in the studio after the nearly disasterous *Let It Be* sessions, the group recorded several tracks, none of which were ever released. Three songs which appeared on **Abbey Road** (*Maxwell's Silver Hammer, Polythene Pam* and *Octopus's Garden*) were actually finished at these sessions, though these versions were ultimately rejected.

The group recorded retakes of three songs originally done in 1967/1968. It was this version of John's *What's The News Maryjane* which almost came out as a single in December 1969. Paul tried again on *Jubilee,* as did George with *Not Guilty.* The final song has accumulated quite a reputation, quite a feat for a song hardly anyone has heard. To round out the foursome, Ringo sang on the oddly-named *I Should Like To Live Up A Tree.*

March 1969—**Studio Out-take.**

George, who was heavily involved in the career of fellow-Liverpudlian Jackie Lomax, co-produced with Jackie a song called *Goin' Back To Liverpool.* It was never released.

May 1969—**Studio Out-take.**

During this era, Apple Records was quite actively searching out new talent. One of the groups they found was a three man group from America called Mortimer. Paul, in an attempt to launch their career, "gave" them one of the songs from the Beatles' January recording sessions. At the time it was called *On Our Way Home,* but when the Beatles finally released their own version it was called *Two Of Us.* Mortimer's version never got out and nothing has been heard of them since.

Mid 1969—**Studio Out-take.**

Completing the list of known Beatle material yet unreleased are two songs from the *Abbey Road* era, *When I Come To Town* and *Four Nights In Moscow.*

Late October 1969—**Studio Out-take.**

Rick Grech, hoping for a solo album, gathered some musicians together to help out. Among those present were Eric Clapton, Denny Laine and George Harrison. Some songs were recorded, but when Grech's album came out sometime later, they weren't on it.

1970

February 12, 1970—BBC's "Top Of The Pops."
John, first of the Beatles to have a solo hit, made an appearance on television singing *Instant Karma!*.

February 1970—Studio Out-takes.
Two tracks left off Ringo's **Sentimental Journey** album of nostalgic favorites, *Autumn Leaves* and *I'll Be Looking At The Moon.*

March 15, 1970—Promotional Film Clip.
Ringo assembled quite a cast to sing *Sentimental Journey* (title track to his album). George Martin directed the Talk Of The Town Orchestra, while Doris Troy, Marsha Hunt and Madelene Bell sang back-up on this lovely *tour de force.* It was on the *Ed Sullivan Show* May 17, 1970.

Mid May 1970—Studio Out-take.
George flew to New York and recorded almost an album's worth of material with Bob Dylan which, sadly, has never been released.

June 30/July 1, 1970—Studio Out-takes.
Ringo's whirlwind recording sessions in Nashville almost resulted in two albums. Aside from the twelve songs released, there was a 20 minute "Nashville Jam" along with a 28 minute version of Ringo's song *Coochy-Coochy* (an edited version of which was released in America as a single).

Late 1970—Studio Out-take.
Ringo was apparently working with Bee Gee Maurice Gibb on an electronic "moog" album, which was never finished.

1971

January 1971—Studio Out-takes.
Two songs were recorded the day Denny Seiwell brought Paul and Linda McCartney to Leslie Fradkin's recording session. One (*God Bless California*) was released 3½ years later. The other (*Black Gypsy*) is supposed to be on Fradkin's next album. Paul plays bass and sings background on both.

February 1971—Studio Out-take.
Yoko's *Open Your Box* was planned as the flip side of *Power To The People.* However, last minute objections forced a re-recording of the song's vocal track. The song still had troubles and was only released in the United States later in the year under the name *Hirake.*

Spring 1971—**Brung To Ewe By Hal Smith (LP) Apple SPRO-6210**

A very strange collection of fifteen short skits featuring Paul and Linda McCartney, which were to be used to promote their new album **Ram**. The only recurrent themes are Paul singing *Now Hear This Song Of Mine,* and the repeated recorded bleat from some sheep. The production and mixing are rather poor, and it is very doubtful that these spots helped the album's sales very much.

Mid June 1971—**Studio Out-takes.**

Ringo spent one night at the sessions for a new Joe Cocker album. Also present were Stevie Winwood and Chris Stainton. Denny Cordell was the producer. Cocker's album was long delayed and, in the end, all the mid 1971 sessions were dumped.

Spring 1971—**Studio Out-take.**

John, at that time, got caught up in the obscenity trial of the publishers of *Oz Magazine.* A quick single, under the name Elastic Oz Band, was issued in July. Bill Elliot (later of the group Splinter) sang lead on the A side, while Lennon himself sang on the flip, *Do The Oz.* Two versions of that song exist, with the released one being much clearer (though it's not much of a tune).

August 1, 1971—**Bangla Desh Concert.**

George staged two shows to aid the residents of Bangla Desh. The evening show was, after lengthly disputes, released as a charity album, while the afternoon show, recorded on crude equipment, was quickly issued as a bootleg (to nobody's benefit).

Contents: *My Sweet Lord, While My Guitar Gently Weeps, Beware Of Darkness, Something, Bangla Desh, Mr. Tambourine Man, Just Like A Woman, That's The Way God Planned It, It Don't Come Easy* and *Jumpin' Jack Flash.*

September 9, 1971—**Dick Cavett Show.**

John and Yoko were the sole guests on Cavett's 90 minute show on ABC TV, September 21, 1971. For a late night talk show, the discussion was fairly interesting. The discussion centered on the Beatle years, Yoko's affect on the group and their current film-making projects. While there was no live music performed, excerpts from four films (*Imagine, Fly, Mrs. Lennon* and *Erection*) and their accompanying soundtracks were aired.

December 10, 1971—**Ann Arbor Concert.**

John and Yoko made a late-night appearance at a concert/rally for imprisoned radical John Sinclair. Aided by one of the most peculiar back-up bands in history (Jerry Rubin played bongos), John and

Yoko sang four of their new songs (*Attica State, Luck Of The Irish, Sisters O Sisters* and, of course, *John Sinclair*). A fairly good recording of these songs was almost issued as an EP on Apple.

1972

January 13,1972—**David Frost Show.**
February 14-18—**Mike Douglas Show.**
May 11, 1972—**Dick Cavett Show.**

Just as they were recording their new album, **Sometime In New York City**, John and Yoko toured the talk show circuit of American television with their new back-up band, Elephant's Memory. John and Yoko were actually the co-hosts of The Mike Douglas Show for an entire week. The high point of that week was the appearance of Chuck Berry. During an exciting duet, the "teacher" from St. Louis and his "pupil" from Liverpool rocked through *Memphis* and *Johnny B. Goode*. In their return to the Cavett show, John and Yoko performed their controversial new single, *Woman Is The Nigger Of The World*.

A bootleg album entitled *Telecasts* presents songs from all three shows on a fairly good quality recording. Contents: *John Sinclair, It's So Hard, Luck Of The Irish, Sisters O Sisters, We're All Water, Woman Is The Nigger Of The World, Attica State, Midsummer New York, Sakura* (a traditional Japanese folk song), *Memphis Tennessee, Johnny B. Goode* and *Imagine*.

August 22, 1972—**Brussels Concert.**

Paul, with his new group Wings, was the first of the former Beatles to launch a full-fledged tour. A fair-to-good recording of their Belgian concert is currently available.

Contents: *Lucille, Blue Moon Of Kentucky* (the Bill Monroe bluegrass standard), *Give Ireland Back To The Irish, Smile Away, Some People Never Know, Bip Bop, My Love* and *The Mess.*

August 30, 1972—**One To One Concert.**

John and Yoko and the "Plastic Ono Elephant's Memory Band" performed at a benefit in Madison Square Garden for the Willowbrook School for Children. The group performed fourteen numbers, and a live album was seriously considered. A cut-down of the concert was seen on ABC TV December 14, 1972.

Contents: *Sisters O Sisters, Instant Karma!, Come Together, Imagine, Cold Turkey, Hound Dog* and *Give Peace A Chance* (seen on the ABC show); *New York City, We're All Water, Woman Is The Nigger Of The World, Mother* and *Born In A Prison* (left out of the ABC show).

September 6, 1972–Jerry Lewis Muscular Dystrophy Telethon.
A welcome relief from the usual sort of guest Jerry Lewis had on his yearly show, John, Yoko and Elephant's Memory livened up the last part of the day-long telethon by singing *Now Or Never* and *Imagine.*

Early Fall 1972–Studio Out-takes.
George did some work with old friend Cilla Black, going so far as to donate two songs to her (*You've Gotta Stay With Me* and *When Every Song Is Sung*). The tracks were never quite completed and have yet to be released.

Late 1972–Studio Out-takes.
Four rejected Wings' tracks that almost appeared on an **Odds And Sods** type album called **Cold Cuts.**
Contents: *Momma's Little Girl, Tragedy* (the Thomas Wayne song), *I Don't Want To Smile* (drummer Denny Seiwell's song) and *Seaside Woman* (which was to be Linda's debut as a lead vocalist).

1973
Early 1973–The Beatles Alpha Omega (4 LPs)
Audio Tape Inc. ATRBH 3583
The unauthorized Beatle Anthology, which was advertised heavily on radio and television, prompting Apple to issue its own set in April. Unfortunately, this pirate edition has a much more representative sampling of songs than the "hit-oriented" Apple set. Its lack of any liner notes at all was an improvement over the grossly inaccurate time information on the legal album.
Contents: *Act Naturally, All I've Got To Do, All My Loving, And I Love Her, Baby's In Black, Yesterday, Ballad Of John And Yoko, Bangla Desh, Can't Buy Me Love, Come Together, Day Tripper, Do You Want To Know A Secret, Eight Days A Week, Eleanor Rigby, Uncle Albert/Admiral Halsey, I Should Have Known Better, It Won't Be Long, I Want To Hold Your Hand, Lady Madonna, Ticket To Ride, Lucy In The Sky With Diamonds, Michelle, Mr. Moonlight, I Feel Fine, If I Fell, I'll Be Back, Hey Jude, I'm A Loser, I'm Happy Just To Dance With You, I Saw Her Standing There, Nowhere Man, Ob-la-di Ob-la-da, Paperback Writer, Penny Lane, Help!, Roll Over Beethoven, Sgt. Pepper's Lonely Hearts Club Band, Get Back, Hello Goodbye, Revolution No. 1, Here Comes The Sun, I'll Follow The Sun, Imagine, Honey Don't, We Can Work It Out, With A Little Help From My Friends, Yellow Submarine, Baby You're A Rich Man, You Can't Do That, You've Got To Hide Your Love Away, Maybe I'm Amazed, A Hard Day's Night, She Loves You, Something, Strawberry Fields Forever, Tell Me Why, Long And Winding Road, Let It Be* and *Everybody's Trying To Be My Baby.*

March 10, 1973—**Public Service Announcement**

While in Los Angeles working on his new lp, Ringo supplied the no-nonsense vocal for a thirty second anti-drug public service announcement. His famous drumbeat passage from **Abbey Road** provided the musical backdrop. The spot was one cut (side 2, cut 10) of a 2-record package called **Get Off**.

March 18, 1973—**Taping Of "Live" Segments For McCartney TV Special**

Paul and his group Wings appeared before a live audience in ATV's Boreham Wood studios for use in Paul's upcoming TV special. Four songs were used: *Big Barn Bed, The Mess, Maybe I'm Amazed* and *Long Tall Sally.*

April 16, 1973 (US-ABC TV)

May 10, 1973 (UK-ATV)—**James Paul McCartney.**

Paul's one hour TV special dealing with...Paul. Though eagerly anticipated, the show was generally disappointing. The fantastic live segments only pointed out the lameness of Paul's run-throughs of *Blackbird/Bluebird, Michelle, Heart Of The Country, Yesterday, Mary Had A Little Lamb, Little Woman Love* and *C Moon.* The first part of the *Uncle Albert/Admiral Halsey* record was used during a short film clip.

The show highlighted Wings' then current single *My Love* and their upcoming movie theme *Live And Let Die.* Low moments were Paul's stilted guide to Liverpool, and his pink-tuxedoed, golden-slippered tap dance number *Gotta Sing Gotta Dance* (which he originally wrote for Twiggy).

May 22, 1973—**Edinburgh Concert.**

The main recording from Wings' first scheduled tour of England. It's a poor quality tape, which is a pity, since four of the songs have never been released by the group.

Contents: *Soily* (A Paul McCartney original), *Seaside Woman* (Linda on lead), *Go Now* (Denny Laine's hit with the original Moody Blues) and *Say You Don't Mind* (another Laine song, originally recorded by Colin Blunstone); and *Big Barn Bed, When The Night, Wild Life, Little Woman Love, C Moon, Live And Let Die, Maybe I'm Amazed, My Love, The Mess, Hi Hi Hi* and *Long Tall Sally.*

Mid 1973—**Studio Out-take.**

The "Ringo" album brought together all four ex-Beatles on the same record. One of Paul's contributions was his song *Six O'Clock.* Though originally five and a half minutes long, more than a minute of refrain was cut out at the last instant—too late to correct the label timing.

September 1973—**Studio Out-take.**

While in Lagos recording **Band On The Run,** Linda made another attempt at singing lead on *Oriental Nightfish.*

1974

January 1974—**Studio Out-takes.**

Since the early part of Wings' recording career, Paul has intended for Linda to release some songs on her own. His plans were closest to fulfillment during a short recording session in Paris, which also marked the formation of the "new" Wings (Jeff Britton on drums and Jimmy McCulloch on guitar, having just joined). Linda recorded two songs, one of which was called *Wide Prarie Maid.* These and her earlier unreleased recordings were to have come out under the name Suzie and The Red Stripes (named after a Jamaican beer). The world at large has yet to hear them.

May/June 1974—**Studio Out-take.**

In between recording sessions of his planned Oldies album, John produced an exciting version of Mick Jagger singing *Too Many Cooks.* Playing on the session were Bobby Keys and Jim Price (horns), Jim Keltner (drums), Jack Bruce (bass), and Billy Preston (keyboards). Recording companies and recording contracts being what they are, it is doubtful this shall ever be released.

Early Summer 1974—**Studio Out-takes.**

Paul and Linda spent some time in Nashville, soaking up its musical feeling and recording a few songs. The end result was two singles: *Junior's Farm/Sally G* and Paul's father's tune *Walking In The Park With Eloise,* released under the name Country Hams. Apparently some of the engineers have made free use of the rehearsal tapes, and early versions of all three songs are beginning to appear on bootlegs. Floyd Cramer, Chet Atkins and Pete Drake were helping out on the sessions.

August 1974—**George Harrison Interview Record (LP) Dark Horse**

A special promotional album sent to radio stations in mid October along with the first releases on George's Dark Horse label. Recorded in Los Angeles, the interview was conducted by Chuck Cassell, who questioned Harrison on matters ranging from the group Splinter through Ravi Shankar and Friends, and onto spiritualism. Excerpts from both Splinter's and Shankar's albums were included on the record.

November 4, 1974—**Seattle Concert.**

November 10, 1974—**Long Beach Concert.**

November 30, 1974—**Chicago Concert.**

There are currently three recordings available from George's less-than-universally-acclaimed concert tour of America.

Contents: *Hari's On Tour Express, While My Guitar Gently Weeps, Something, Sue Me Sue You Blues, For You Blue, Give Me Love, In My Life, Maya Love, Dark Horse, What Is Life* and *My Sweet Lord.*

1975

Early February 1975—**Roots (LP) Adam VIII Ltd. A 8018**

The complete story behind this briefly available album is clouded in legal briefs. Some of it is easy to explain. Fact: Morris Levy, owner of the publishing rights to Chuck Berry's song *You Can't Catch Me* claimed that John Lennon copied some lines from that song in *Come Together*. Fact: Partially to avoid suit, John recorded seven or eight oldies, including *You Can't Catch Me*, under Phil Spector's direction in October 1973. Fact: Spector took the master tapes and Lennon had some 'difficulty' getting them back. Fact: Lennon eventually rejected all but four of the old tracks and cut ten new ones in October 1974. Fact: Lennon presented Levy with an unpolished version of the album in late 1974. Fact: In early February 1975, ads began appearing on television promoting a mail-order album whose cover contained the specific statement that John Lennon and Apple records had authorized this enterprise. Fact: Both Lennon and Apple records denied that statement and rush released their own copy of the album, originally scheduled for April. Fact: Very soon thereafter, Adam VIII Ltd. stopped answering its phones and ceased distribution of their album.

The most obvious difference between the two versions is that the Adam VIII album contains two songs not included on the Apple LP, *Angel Baby* and *Be My Baby*. The latter, a Phil Spector song, is really quite good, with John injecting more real emotion into the lyrics than you might think possible. Other than that, the two albums are almost identical, with the Adam VIII LP tending to have slightly longer fade outs. On the Apple album, the first verse of *You Can't Catch Me* is abruptly edited into the middle of the song.

As this goes to print, the two sides have yet to resolve their claims.

February 12, 1975—**Studio Out-take.**

After taking part in New Orleans' Mardi Gras Celebration, Paul recorded the song *My Carnival,* which did not appear on the **Venus And Mars** album.

February 1975—**TV Videotape**

Paul and Wings recorded *Baby Face* (Paul on piano) with the Tuxedo Jazz Band, for a television appearance.

April 18, 1975—**"Old Gray Whistle Test" TV Special.**

John, still unable to leave the US due to immigration problems, appeared via film on British television singing his new single *Stand By Me*.

April 19/April 20, 1975—**George Harrison Interview by Dave Herman**

A two-hour interview recorded at Harrison's home in Los Angeles by Dave Herman of WNEW, New York. After dealing with the demise of Apple, the discussion turned to topics George was more anxious to discuss: the future of Dark Horse records. As in the 1974 interview, George introduced cuts from the Splinter and Shankar albums, while also providing information on Jiva, Dark Horse's first American group. Highlight of the program was the unearthing of some of George's musical roots. Recordings by English skiffle king Lonnie Donnegan and country star Slim Whitman were heard, with George even doing a lovely vocal segue into Slim's *Rose Marie*.

The two-hour program was first aired on WNEW on May 24, and was heard on the syndicated *King Biscuit Flower Hour* on August 17, 1975.

April 28, 1975—**Smothers Brothers Show.**

Ringo took part in a few comedy skits and sang *No No Song*, with Tom and Dick Smothers providing back-up vocals.

June 13, 1975—**"Salute To Sir Lew Grade" TV Special**

As part of a televised tribute program to British impresario Sir Lew Grade, John appeared singing *"Slippin' And Slidin' "* and *"Imagine"*. In a rare bit of visual "upstaging," his band (dubbed Etc.) drew almost as much attention as he did. Each member of the band appeared to be two-faced, thanks to masks worn on the back of their heads. The effect was particularly striking with the saxophone player, who seemed to be both playing and *not* playing at the same time.

November 14, 1975—**Melbourne Concert**

On their world tour, Paul and Wings (augmented by a four piece brass section) presented not only the expected work-out of tunes from their latest album, but also some old Beatles numbers.

Contents: *Venus And Mars, Rock Show, Jet, Let Me Roll It, Medicine Jar* (Jimmy), *Maybe I'm Amazed, Lady Madonna*, and the *Long And Winding Road*. An acoustic section of *Picasso's Last Words, Richard Corey* (the Paul Simon song, sung by Denny), *Bluebird, Blackbird, Yesterday* and *I've Just Seen A Face*. Back to rock with: *You Gave Me The Answer, Magneto and Titanium Man, Go Now* (Denny vocal), *Letting Go, Live And Let Die, Call Me Back Again, My Love, Listen To What The Man Said* and *Band On The Run*, with encores of *Hi Hi Hi* and *Soily*.

271

PANDEMONIUM SHADOW SHOW

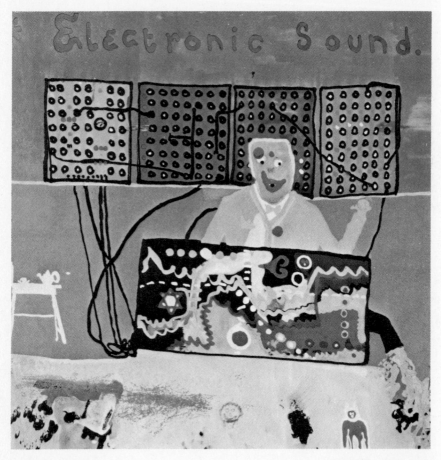

Electronic Sound   **Zapple ST - 3358 (LP)**

PANDEMONIUM
SHADOW
SHOW

Any discussion of Beatle-related records must, of necessity, be self-limited. At the outbreak of Beatlemania, hundreds of songs appeared "about the Beatles" (i.e. *All I Want For Christmas Is A Beatle* by Dora Bryan, *I Hate The Beatles* by Allan Sherman, *Ringo For President* by Rolf Harris, etc., etc., etc.), and since then many artists have done successful and sometimes even interesting cover versions of Beatle songs. Since the Beatles (either as a group or individually) had nothing to do with the actual production of these records, we have chosen to ignore all but a handful. The two main inclusions are the careers of Mike McGear (Paul's brother) and George Martin (their musical producer for eight years). The remaining few were included because of their deserved place in history (i.e. we felt like it).

MIKE MCGEAR
All selections by Scaffold except † by Mike McGear
MAY 6, 1966   (UK)   Parlophone R 5443
2 Days Monday/3 Blind Jellyfish

DEC 2, 1966   (UK)   Parlophone R 5548
Goodbat Nightman/Long Strong Black Pudding

NOV 4, 1967   (UK)   Parlophone R 5643
JAN 8, 1968   (US)   Bell 701
Thank U Very Much/I'd B The First

MAR 15, 1968   (UK)   Parlophone R 5679
MAY 27, 1968   (US)   Bell 724
Do You Remember/Carry On Know

MAY 17, 1968   (UK)   Parlophone PCS 7047   (LP)
MCGOUGH AND MCGEAR

JUN 14, 1968   (UK)   Parlophone R 5703
1-2-3/Today

JUL 5, 1968 (UK) Parlophone PCS 7051 (LP)
AN EVENING WITH SCAFFOLD

SEP 2, 1968 (US) Bell 6018 (LP)
THANK U VERY MUCH

OCT 18, 1968 (UK) Parlophone R 5734
DEC 16, 1968 (US) Bell 747
Lily The Pink/Buttons Of Your Mind

MAY 23, 1969 (UK) Parlophone PCS 7077 (LP)
L.P.

JUN 27, 1969 (UK) Parlophone R 5784
Charity Bubbles/Goose

OCT 17, 1969 (UK) Parlophone R 5812
Gin Gan Goolie/Liver Birds

JUN 5, 1970 (UK) Parlophone R 5847
All The Way Up/Please Sorry

OCT 23, 1970 (UK) Parlophone R 5866
Busdreams/If I Could Start All Over Again

OCT 1, 1971 (UK) Parlophone R 5922
Do The Albert/Commercial Break

APR 7, 1972 (UK) Island WIP 6131
†Woman/Kill

APR 21, 1972 (UK) Island ILPS 9191 (LP)
†WOMAN

MAY 25, 1973 (UK) Island ILPS 9234 (LP)
FRESH LIVER

NOV 2, 1973 (UK) EMI 2085
Lily The Pink/Do You Remember/Thank U Very Much

MAY 24, 1974 (UK) Warner Brothers K 16400
JUL 29, 1974 (US) Warner Brothers 8001
Liverpool Lou/Ten Years After On Strawberry Jam

SEP 6, 1974 (UK) Warner Brothers K 16446
OCT 28, 1974 (US) Warner Brothers 8037
†Leave It/Sweet Baby

SEP 27, 1974   (UK)   Warner Brothers K 56051 (LP)
OCT 14, 1974   (US)   Warner Brothers BS 2825 (LP)
†**MCGEAR**

DEC 7, 1974   (UK)   Warner Brothers K 16488
Mummy Won't Be Home For Christmas/The Wind Is Blowing

FEB 7, 1975   (UK)   Warner Brothers K 16520
†Sea Breezes/Givin' Grease A Ride

FEB 7, 1975   (UK)   Warner Brothers K 56067 (LP)
SOLD OUT

MAR 1, 1975   (UK)   Warner Brothers K 16521
Leaving Of Liverpool/Pack Of Cards

JUL 4,1975   (UK)   Warner Brothers K 16573
†Dance The Do/Norton

NOV 14, 1975   (UK)   Warner Brothers K 16658
†Simply Love You/What Do We Really Know

GEORGE MARTIN
MAY 8, 1964   (UK)   Parlophone R 5135
All My Loving/I Saw Her Standing There

JUN 26, 1964   (US)   United Artists UAS 6366 (LP)
A HARD DAY'S NIGHT (Original Soundtrack Album)
*I Should Have Known Better/And I Love Her/Ringo's Theme
(This Boy)/A Hard Day's Night*

JUL 10, 1964   (UK)   Parlophone PCS 3057 (LP)
AUG 3, 1964   (US)   United Artists UAS 6377 (LP)
OFF THE BEATLE TRACK
*All My Loving/Don't Bother Me/Can't Buy Me Love/All I've Got
To Do/I Saw Her Standing There/She Loves You/From Me To You/
There's A Place/This Boy/Please Please Me/Little Child/I Want To
Hold Your Hand*

JUL 31, 1964   (US)   United Artists 743
AUG 7, 1964   (UK)   Parlophone R 5166
Ringo's Theme (This Boy)/And I Love Her

SEP 21, 1964   (US)   United Artists 750
I Should Have Known Better/A Hard Day's Night

NOV 2, 1964   (US)   United Artists UAS 6383   (LP)
A HARD DAY'S NIGHT
I'll Cry Instead/Ringo's Theme (This Boy)/If I Fell/I'm Happy Just To Dance With You/A Hard Day's Night/I Should Have Known Better/I Want To Hold Your Hand/Can't Buy Me Love/She Loves You/And I Love Her/All My Loving/Don't Bother Me/Tell Me Why

FEB 19, 1965   (UK)   Parlophone GEP 8930   (EP)
MUSIC FROM "A HARD DAY'S NIGHT"
And I Love Her/Ringo's Theme (This Boy)/A Hard Day's Night/ If I Fell

MAR 19, 1965   (UK)   Parlophone R 5256
I Feel Fine/Niagra Theme

APR 12, 1965   (US)   United Artists UAS 6420   (LP)
GEORGE MARTIN SCORES INSTRUMENTAL VERSIONS OF THE HITS
I Feel Fine/P.S. I Love You/No Reply

AUG 13, 1965   (US)   Capitol SMAS 2386   (LP)
HELP! (Original Soundtrack Album)
James Bond Theme/From Me To You Fantasy/In The Tyrol/ Another Hard Day's Night/The Bitter End/You Can't Do That/The Chase

SEP   6, 1965   (US)   United Artists UAS 6448   (LP)
NOV 19, 1965   (UK)   Columbia TWO 102   (LP)
HELP!
Help!/Another Girl/You're Gonna Lose That Girl/I Need You/ You've Got To Hide Your Love Away/The Night Before/Ticket To Ride/Bahama Sound (UK only)*/Auntie Gin's Theme (I've Just Seen A Face)/That's A Nice Hat—CAP (It's Only Love)/Tell Me What You See/Scrambled Egg (Yesterday)*

NOV 12, 1965   (UK)   Parlophone R 5375
Yesterday/Another Girl

NOV 28, 1966   (US)   United Artists UAS 6539   (LP)
MAR 3, 1967   (UK)   United Artists SULP 1157   (LP)
THE BEATLE GIRLS
Girl/Eleanor Rigby/She Said She Said/I'm Only Sleeping/Anna (Go To Him)/Michelle/Got To Get You Into My Life/Woman/Yellow Submarine/Here There And Everywhere/And Your Bird Can Sing/ Good Day Sunshine

DEC 23, 1966   (UK)   United Artists UP 1165
Love In The Open Air/Theme From "The Family Way"

JAN 6, 1967   (UK)   Decca SKL 4847   (LP)
JUN 12, 1967   (US)   London MS 82007   (LP)
   THE FAMILY WAY (Original Soundtrack Album)
   Love In The Open Air

APR 24, 1967   (US)   United Artists UA 50148
Love In The Open Air/Bahama Sound

JAN 13, 1969   (US)   Apple SW 153   (LP)
JAN 17, 1969   (UK)   Apple PCS 7070   (LP)
   YELLOW SUBMARINE (Original Soundtrack Album)
   Pepperland/Sea Of Time/Sea Of Holes/Sea Of Monsters/March Of The Meanies/Pepperland Laid Waste/Yellow Submarine In Pepperland

DEC 11, 1970   (UK)   Sunset SLS 50182   (LP)
   BY GEORGE!
   Sgt. Pepper's Lonely Hearts Club Band/I Am The Walrus

JUL 2, 1973   (US)   United Artists LA 100-G   (LP)
JUL 6, 1973   (UK)   United Artists UAS 29475   (LP)
   LIVE AND LET DIE (Original Soundtrack Album)
   Bond Meets Solitaire/Whisper Who Dares/Snakes Alive/Baron Samedi's Dance Of Death/San Monique/Filet Of Soul—New Orleans/ Filet Of Soul—Harlem/Bond Drops In/If He Finds It, Kill Him/ Trespassers Will Be Eaten/Solitaire Gets Her Cards/Sacrifice/James Bond Theme

FRIENDS, RELATIVES AND TOTAL STRANGERS

JUL 3, 1964   (UK)   Decca F 11929
by The Pete Best Four
I'm Gonna Knock On Your Door/Why Did I Fall In Love With You
SUMMER 1965   (US)   Cameo 391
by Pete Best
Kansas City/Boys
SEP 20, 1965   (US)   Mr. Maestro Records 711
by Pete Best
I Can't Do Without You Now/Keys To My Heart
MID 1966   (US)   Savage BM 71   (LP)
by Pete Best
BEST OF THE BEATLES
   I Need Your Lovin'/Just Wait And See/Casting My Spell/Keys To

279

My Heart/Why Did You Leave Me Baby?/Shimmy Like My Sister Kate/I Can't Do Without You Now/I'm Blue/Some Other Guy/She's Allright/Nobody But You/Last Night

Best was drummer with the Beatles from mid 1960 until August 1962.

NOV 13, 1964 (UK) Parlophone
  by Rory Storme and The Hurricanes
America/Since You Broke My Heart

Ringo had played drums in Storme's group from mid 1960 until August 1962.

1965 (US) Recar 2012 (LP)
  by Louise Harrison Caldwell
ALL ABOUT THE BEATLES

Excerpts from interviews on five radio stations by George's sister.

DEC 31, 1965 (UK) Picadilly 7N 35290
MID FEB 1966 (US) Jerden JD 792
  by Freddie Lennon
That's My Life/The Next Time You Feel Important

John's father, who had seen his son only a few times since infancy.

JAN 1, 1965 (UK) Parlophone R 5212
  by Dick James
Sing A Song Of Beatles

The Beatles' music publisher, singing a medley of *From Me To You/I Want To Hold Your Hand/She Loves You/All My Loving/I Should Have Known Better/Can't Buy Me Love.*

JUN 3, 1963   (US)   Big Top 3152
  by Del Shannon
From Me To You/(two silhouettes)
OCT 28, 1963 (US) London 5202
  by Tony Newley
I Saw Her Standing There/(i love everything about you)

The only two artists to attempt a cover version of a Beatle song in America in the pre-*Ed Sullivan* days.

NOV 10, 1969　(US)　MGM K 14097
by The Mystery Tour
The Ballad Of Paul/The Ballad Of Paul (Follow The Bouncing Ball)
At last!　The real poop on all those nasty death rumors.

DEC 23, 1966　(UK)　Decca F 12536
by The Tudor Minstrels
Love In The Open Air/Young Love Theme From "The Family Way"
JAN 19, 1970　(US)　Commonwealth United CU 3006
by The Magic Christians
Come And Get It
Two cover versions of McCartney-authored film music.　Both
were attempts by the label which issued the original soundtrack to
have another group release a "quickie" hit.

NOV 8, 1974　(UK)　RSO 2394-141 (LP)
by The Original London Cast featuring Barbara Dickson
JOHN, PAUL, GEORGE, RINGO...AND BERT
*I Should Have Known Better/Your Mother Should Know/With A
Little Help From My Friends/Penny Lane/Here Comes The Sun/
Long And Winding Road/Help!/Lucy In The Sky With Diamonds/
You Never Give Me Your Money/Carry That Weight/We Can Work It
Out/A Day In The Life*
Music from a play loosely based on the history of the Beatles.

DEC 10, 1965　(UK)　Parlophone R 5393
JAN 31, 1966　(US)　Capitol 5580
by Peter Sellers
A Hard Day's Night/Help!
Two "send-ups" of popular Beatle songs which Sellers later
performed on one of the Beatles' TV specials.

OCT 1, 1965　(UK)　HMV 7EG 8887 (EP)
Devised: Fritz Spiegl;　Arranged: Harry Wild
EINE KLEINE BEATLEMUSIK
*She Loves You/A Hard Day's Night/All My Loving/Please Please
Me/I Want To Hold Your Hand/I'll Get You*
OCT 29, 1965　(UK)
THE BEATLE CRACKER SUITE
*It's For You/Help!/She Loves You/From Me To You/Ticket To
Ride/All My Loving*
Two of the earliest attempts to present Beatle music within a
classical framework.　Both arrangements were even copyrighted.

AUG 3, 1973 (UK) Wizard WIZ 104
by Denny Laine
Find A Way Somehow/Move Me To Another Place
NOV 30, 1973 (UK) Wizard SWZ 2001A (LP)
by Denny Laine
AHH...LAINE
*Big Ben/Destiny Unknown/Baby Caroline/Don't Try You'll Be
Refused/Talk To The Head/Sons Of Elton, Hays And Brown/Find
A Way Somehow/Having Heaven/On That Early Morn/The Blues/
Everybody/Move Me To Another Place*

Laine, formerly a member of the Moody Blues, was recording a
solo album in 1971 when he joined Paul's new group, Wings. The
album, long delayed, was finally finished in 1973.

JUN 29, 1973 (US) RCA APBO 0014
by B. J. Arnau
Live And Let Die/(in the night)

Arnau sang Paul's title song in the movie *Live And Let Die,* and
a truncated version of it appeared in the soundtrack.

MAY 24, 1974 (UK) Pye-Bradley BRAD 74071
by Jungle Juice
Zoo Gang/(monkey business)

An off-beat version of Paul's off-beat song, which came out one
month before Wings' own version.

OCT 23, 1967 (US) RCA LSP 3874 (LP)
by Harry Nilsson
PANDEMONIUM SHADOW SHOW
side one
cut five: *You Can't Do That*

A perfectly delightful medley of fifteen Beatle songs, weaving in
and out of the melody of *You Can't Do That.* It was this cut which
first brought Harry Nilsson to the attention of the Beatles.

NOV 10, 1975 (US) United Artists UALA 552-G (LP)
DEC 12, 1975 (UK) United Artists UAG 29902 (LP)
by Dr. John
HOLLYWOOD BE THY NAME
*New Island Soiree/Reggae Doctor/The Way You Do The Things You
Do/Swanee River Boogie/Yesterday/Babylon/Back By The River/It's
All Right With Me/Blue Skies/Will The Circle Be Unbroken/Hollywood
Be Thy Name/I Wanna Rock*

The Gumbo Doctor collected his musical friends in an LA studio to record a 'live' sounding album. Ringo acted as Master of Cere-
monies. Unfortunately, his no doubt memorable introductions were
left off the album, which is why you are reading about it here.

NO,
YOU'RE
WRONG

Red Rose Speedway   **Apple SMAL 3409 (LP)**

NO, YOU'RE WRONG

When you reach the outer limits of Beatle fandom, you come across a peculiar breed of human who feels a strange inner compulsion to get his hands on anything the Beatles ever touched. Often the gullible sort, they tend to accept a rumor that a Beatle had something to do with a record just on the off-chance that it might prove to be true.

In the early days, fly-by-night record companies tried to take advantage of this by subtly (or sometimes blatantly) implying they were putting out some sort of "Beatle" record. As the Beatles became more reclusive in the late 60's, keeping track of all their recorded appearances became much harder. In some cases people simply guessed wrong, attributing a Beatle presence where none existed. Stories like that tend to fester, and are still causing groundless worry among many collectors.

To relieve this pent-up tension among such fanatic fans, we hereby present a collection of discs which really, honest to god, THE BEATLES HAD NOTHING TO DO WITH.

C. 1965 *The Girl I Love* Quest 101
   by The Beatles
   Subtle. No, of course, it wasn't the Beatles (you can't believe everything you read on record labels). The song writing credit is to a Mr. Lemon, with publishing by familiar Maclen Music. This record is actually performed by a group called The Five Shits, a good name considering the quality of the disc.

OCT 8, 1965 (UK) London HLV 9997/(US) Tip 1021
   by John & Paul
   People Say/I'm Walking
   Now what do you think they're implying here? Could this be a rare recording by the Nurk Twins?
   For some unknown reason this record, which doesn't sound *at all* like Lennon and McCartney, has appeared on many Beatle bootleg

285

albums. Some people say it's really ex-drummer Pete Best singing, but it doesn't even sound like him.

FEB 20, 1970   (UK)   Punch Records
  by John Lennon and The Bleechers
  Ram You Hard
     No, of course, this isn't *the* John Lennon...

NOV 12, 1965   (ITALY)   Parlophone PMCQ 315006 (LP)
  by The Beatles
  THE BEATLES IN ITALY
  Twist And Shout/She's A Woman/I'm A Loser/Can't Buy Me Love/Baby's In Black/I Wanna Be Your Man/A Hard Day's Night/ Everybody's Trying To Be My Baby/Rock And Roll Music/I Feel Fine/Ticket To Ride/Long Tall Sally
     A perfect example of what rumors can do. In late 1965, when *Help!* was about to premiere in Italy, the local branch of Parlophone decided to issue a special album to accompany the film's opening. Some smart executive got the idea of putting together an album of all the songs the Beatles performed during their Italian concerts a few months earlier. The resulting album, made up of studio tracks taken from old records, didn't sell all that well and was soon pulled out of distribution.
     The story would have ended there, had it not been for an off-hand remark John Lennon made to an interviewer some years later. Lennon, who obviously knew very little of the album's existence, assumed that it was a tape of a Beatles' live performance. Though buried deep in an interview, the remark immediately caught the attention of many collectors. After a lengthly search, the actual album proved quite a disappointment to them. Since then, a number of bootleg albums have appeared, purporting to be the mythical live album (using various pirated live recordings).

JAN 27, 1967   (UK)   Decca F 12551
  by Peter Cook and Dudley Moore
  The LS Bumble Bee/Bee Side
     Cook and Moore, both very talented British humorists, put out a record spoofing the psychedelic craze. Six months *later,* with the release of **Sgt. Pepper**, a controversy erupted over the supposed LSD references in John's song *Lucy In The Sky With Diamonds.* Some-time later, some poor fool heard the Cook and Moore record and, obviously unfamiliar with their voices, assumed it to be Lennon in a put-down of the LSD charge. Since then, *The LS Bumble Bee* gained nearly universal acceptance as a true Beatle bootleg. Recently, however, the word got out that it was actually Cook and Moore. In

an effort to beat a dead horse, bootleggers now claim the song was written by John, a claim fervently denied by Cook and Moore, who have a warm spot in their hearts for this self-penned tune.

AUG   7, 1967   (US)   Capitol 5972
 by Lord Sitar
 Black Is Black/Have You Seen Your Mother Baby Standing In The Shadows

JUN 10, 1968   (US)   Capitol ST 2916   (LP)
AUG 16, 1968   (UK)   Columbia SCX 6256   (LP)
 by Lord Sitar
 LORD SITAR
 If I Were A Rich Man/Emerald City/Tomorrow's People/Daydream Believer/Like Nobody Else/I Am The Walrus/In A Dream/Eleanor Rigby/I Can See For Miles/Blue Jay Way/Black Is Black
   Oh, how tempting.   You hear stories of an entire album by George Harrison.   All the clues seem to point to corroboration.   The album would have come out just before George's **Wonderwall Music** (chock full of sitar sounds).   The name Lord Sitar, while a bit more subtle than George Harrysong, seems reasonable as a pseudonym. Then comes the climactic moment when you first hear a Lord Sitar track...George playing *If I Were A Rich Man*?
   No, folks; it's a great idea, but the album doesn't sound anything like the Indian-flavored music George has recorded.

DEC   6, 1967   (US)   London NPS 2   (LP)
DEC   8, 1967   (UK)   Decca TXS 103   (LP)
 by The Rolling Stones
 THEIR SATANIC MAJESTIES REQUEST
 Sing This All Together
   What with Mick Jagger singing in the chorus of *All You Need Is Love,* John and Paul singing on the Rolling Stones' *We Love You,* and the Beatles' own faces on the Stones' album cover, it wasn't very hard to believe that one of the many background voices on one cut was that of Paul McCartney.   Easy to believe, but not true.

1970   (UK)   Beacon 160
 by The Futz
 Have You Heard The Word/Futting
   A very peculiar record.   Released on a small British label around the time of the Beatles' break-up, rumors later claimed that this was the "last Beatles' recording session," or that it was the Beatles jamming with the Bee Gees, or it was John Lennon and a *few* Bee Gees—take your pick.   It's been widely bootlegged even to the extent

287

of reproducing the Beacon label. But, says Mal Evans, the former Beatles' road manager, none of it is true.

FEB 15, 1971   (US)   Capitol 6210
  by Hotlegs
  Neanderthal Man/You Didn't Like It Because You Didn't Think Of It
  A Top 40 Hit which, due to its peculiar sound, had many people convinced that Hotlegs was merely a cover name for some of the Beatles. The simple truth was that Hotlegs were a group of English musicians who, being influenced by the Beatles, reflected the Beatles' sound in their own recording. A few members of the group later joined the group 10cc.

LATE NOV 1969   (US)   Deity RS 6378   (LP)
  by The Masked Marauders
  THE MASKED MARAUDERS
  I Can't Get No Nookie/Duke Of Earl/Cow Pie/I Am The Japanese Sandman (Rang Tang Ding Dong)/The Book Of Love/Later/More Or Less Hudson's Bay Again/Season Of The Witch/Saturday Night At The Cow Palace
  Deity 0870
  by The Masked Marauders
  I Can't Get No Nookie/Cow Pie
  The only album to be recorded after it was reviewed! A tongue-in-cheek review in *Rolling Stone* of the ultimate supergroup jam (including Lennon, McCartney, Harrison, Dylan and Mick Jagger) prompted a public outcry for the album's release. As demand dictates supply, a record was quickly put together, following the outline in the review.
  It's really a very funny album. But how could anybody, after the final cut's declaration of illegitimacy, still believe that the album was for real? Yes, the album's liner notes clearly spell out it was a take-off. But, you know, there are still people who believe that all of the moon flights were staged on a secret desert base in Utah.

PRESSING
THE
PLASTIC

Hey Jude   **Apple SW - 385   (LP)**

Apple Albums

UK/US DATE	UK/US No.	ALBUM TITLE/ARTIST
11/ 1/68	SAPCOR 1	**Wonderwall Music** (Original Soundtrack)
12/ 2/68	ST 3350	by George Harrison *(187)*
11/29/68	SAPCOR 2	**Two Virgins**
11/11/68	T 5001	by John Lennon & Yoko Ono *(189)*
11/22/68	PCS 7067/8	**The Beatles**
11/25/68	SWBO 101	by The Beatles *(190)*
12/ 6/68	SAPCOR 3	**James Taylor**
2/17/69	SKAO 3352	by James Taylor

side one	side two
Don't Talk Now	*Carolina In My Mind*
Something's Wrong	*Brighten Your Night With My Day*
Knocking 'Round The Zoo	*Night Owl*
Sunshine Sunshine	*Rainy Day Man*
Taking It In	*Circle 'Round The Sun*
Something In The Way She Moves	*Blues Is Just A Bad Dream*

UK/US DATE	UK/US No.	ALBUM TITLE/ARTIST
12/ 6/68	SAPCOR 4	**Under The Jasmine Tree**
2/17/69	ST 3353	by The Modern Jazz Quartet

side one	side two
Blue Necklace	*Exposure*
Three Little Feelings	*Jasmine Tree*

UK/US DATE	UK/US No.	ALBUM TITLE/ARTIST
1/17/69	PCS 7070	**Yellow Submarine** (Original Soundtrack)
1/13/69	SW 153	by The Beatles *(193)*
2/21/69	SAPCOR 5	**Post Card**
3/ 3/69	ST 3351	by Mary Hopkin *(195,197)*

3/21/69 SAPCOR 6   **Is This What You Want**
5/19/69 ST 3354   by Jackie Lomax *(200,207)*

5/ 9/69 Zapple 01   **Life With The Lions**
5/26/69 Zapple ST 3357   by John Lennon & Yoko Ono *(203)*

5/ 9/69 Zapple 02   **Electronic Sound**
5/26/69 Zapple ST 3358   by George Harrison *(204)*

5/23/69 Zapple 03   **Listening to Richard Brautigan**
‑ ‑ ‑ ‑ ‑ ‑ ‑ ‑ ‑ ‑ ‑ ‑ ‑ ‑ ‑   by Richard Brautigan

side one	side two
The Telephone Door To Richard Brautigan	*Revenge Of The Lawn*
Trout Fishing In America	*The Telephone Door That Leads Eventually To Some Love Poems*
Love Poem	*In Watermelon Sugar*
A Confederate General From Big Sur	*Here Are Some More Sounds Of My Life*
Here Are The Sounds Of My Life In San Francisco	*Short Stories About California*
The Pill Versus The Springhill Mine Disaster	*Boo, Forever*

5/30/69 SAPCOR 7   **Accept No Substitute**
‑ ‑ ‑ ‑ ‑ ‑ ‑ ‑ ‑ ‑ ‑ ‑ ‑ ‑   by Delaney & Bonnie

side one	side two
Get Ourselves Together	*Love Me A Little Bit Longer*
Someday	*I Can't Take It Much Longer*
Ghetto	*Do Right Woman*
When The Battle Is Over	*Soldiers Of The Cross*
Dirty Old Man	*Gift Of Love*

6/20/69 SAPCOR 7   **White Trash**
‑ ‑ ‑ ‑ ‑ ‑ ‑ ‑ ‑ ‑ ‑ ‑ ‑ ‑   by Trash

7/ 4/69 SAPCOR 8   **Maybe Tomorrow**
7/14/69 ST 3355   by The Iveys

side one	side two
Maybe Tomorrow	*Fisherman*
See-Saw Granpa	*Sali Bloo*
Beautiful And Blue	*Angelique*
Dear Angie	*I'm In Love*
Think About The Good Times	*Knocking Down Our Home*
Yesterday Ain't Coming Back	*I've Been Waiting*

UK/US DATE	UK/US No.	ALBUM TITLE/ARTIST

8/22/69   SAPCOR 9
9/10/69   ST 3359

That's The Way God Planned It
by Billy Preston

side one
Do What You Want
I Want To Thank You
Everything's All Right
She Belongs To Me
It Doesn't Matter
Morning Star

side two
Hey Brother
What About You
Let Us All Get Together Right Now
This Is It
Keep To Yourself
That's The Way God Planned It

9/26/69   PCS 7088
10/ 1/69   SO 383

Abbey Road
by The Beatles *(223)*

11/ 7/69   SAPCOR 11
10/20/69   SMAX 3361

Wedding Album
by John Lennon & Yoko Ono *(227)*

10/24/69   SAPCOR 10
11/10/69   STAO 3360

Space
by The Modern Jazz Quartet

side one
Visitor From Venus
Visitor From Mars
Here's That Rainy Day

side two
Dilema
Adagio From Concertio De
   Aranjuez

12/12/69   CORE 2001
12/12/69   ST 3362

Live Peace In Toronto 1969
by Plastic Ono Band *(230)*

1/ 9/70   SAPCOR 12
2/16/70   ST 3364

Magic Christian Music*
by Badfinger

side one
Come And Get It
Crimson Ship
Dear Angie
Fisherman
Midnight Sun
Beautiful And Blue
Rock Of All Ages

side two
Carry On 'Til Tomorrow
I'm In Love
Walk Out In The Rain
Angelique
Knocking Down Our Home
Give It A Try
Maybe Tomorrow

------- -------

2/26/70   SW 385

Hey Jude
by The Beatles *(239)*

3/27/70   PCS 7101
4/24/70   SW 3365

Sentimental Journey
by Ringo Starr *(245)*

---

*In the U.S., *Angelique* and *Give It A Try* were removed, and *Fisherman* was shifted to side two, cut four.

| 4/17/70 | PCS 7102 | **McCartney** |
| 4/20/70 | STAO 3363 | by Paul McCartney *(246)* |

| 5/ 8/70 | PXS 1 | **Let It Be** (Original Soundtrack) |
| 5/18/70 | AR 34001 | by The Beatles *(248)* |

| 9/11/70 | SAPCOR 13 | **Doris Troy** |
| 11/ 9/70 | ST 3371 | by Doris Troy *(254)* |

| 9/11/70 | SAPCOR 14 | **Encouraging Words** |
| 11/ 9/70 | ST 3370 | by Billy Preston *(255)* |

| 9/25/70 | SAPCOR 15 | **The Whale** |
| 11/ 9/70 | SMAS 3369 | by John Tavener |

side one   **side two**

The Whale (Part One)   *The Whale (Concluded)*

| 9/25/70 | PAS 10002 | **Beaucoups Of Blues** |
| 9/28/70 | SMAS 3368 | by Ringo Starr *(257)* |

| 11/27/70 | SAPCOR 16 | **No Dice** |
| 11/ 9/70 | ST 3367 | by Badfinger |

side one   **side two**

I Can't Take It	*Blodwyn*
I Don't Mind	*Better Days*
Love Me Do	*It Had To Be*
Midnight Caller	*Waterford John*
No Matter What	*Believe Me*
Without You	*We're For The Dark*

| 11/30/70 | STCH 639 | **All Things Must Pass** |
| 11/27/70 | STCH 639 | by George Harrison *(265)* |

| 12/11/70 | PCS 7124 | **Plastic Ono Band** |
| 12/11/70 | SW 3372 | by John Lennon *(268)* |

| 12/11/70 | SAPCOR 17 | **Plastic Ono Band** |
| 12/11/70 | SW 3373 | by Yoko Ono *(269)* |

12/18/70	LYN 2154	**From Then To Us**
12/18/70	SBC 100	**The Beatles Christmas Album**
		by The Beatles *(270)*

UK/US DATE	UK/US No.	ALBUM TITLE/ARTIST
5/28/71	PAS 10003	**Ram**
5/17/71	SMAS 3375	by Paul & Linda McCartney *(282)*

5/28/71	SAPCOR 18	**Radha Krsna Temple**
5/21/71	SKAO 3376	by Radha Krsna Temple *(283)*

7/ 2/71 SAPCOR 20 — **Celtic Requiem**
by John Tavener

side one
Celtic Requiem

side two
Coplas
Nomine Jesu

10/ 8/71	PAS 10004	**Imagine**
9/ 9/71	SW 3379	by John Lennon *(295)*

9/17/71 SW 3377 — **Come Together** (Original Soundtrack)
by Stelvio Ciprioni

side one
Games People Play
Come Together (Arrival In Rome)
Love Is Blue
Fascinum
Monument To Love
Love Is Blue

side two
Love Is Blue/I Can Sing A Rainbow
Come Together
Love Is Blue
Bad Vibrations
Come Together/Get Together

12/ 3/71	SAPTU 101/2	**Fly**
9/20/71	SVBB 3380	by Yoko Ono *(296)*

10/ 1/71 SAPCOR 21 — **Earth Song—Ocean Song**
11/ 3/71 SMAS 3381 — by Mary Hopkin

side one
Earth Song
Ocean Song
International
How Come The Sun
There's Got To Be More

side two
Silver Birch And Weeping Willow
Martha
Streets Of London
Wind, Water, Paper And Clay

12/ 7/71 SWAO 3384 — **Raga** (Original Soundtrack)
by Ravi Shankar *(304)*

12/ 7/71	PCS 7142	**Wild Life**
12/ 7/71	SW 3386	by Wings *(305)*

2/11/72 SAPCOR 19
12/13/71 SW 3387

Straight Up
  by Badfinger

side one
Take It All
Baby Blue
Money
Flying
I'd Die, Babe
Name Of The Game

side two
Suitcase
Sweet Tuesday Morning
Day After Day
Sometimes
Perfection
It's Over

1/10/72 STCX 3385
12/20/71 STCX 3385

The Concert For Bangla Desh
  by George Harrison & Friends *(307)*

------- -------
12/27/71 SWAO 3388

El Topo (Original Soundtrack)
  by Alexandro Jodorowsky

side one
Entiero Del Primer Juguete
Bajo Tierra
La Cathedral De Los Puerlos
Los Mendigos Sagrados
La Muerte Es Un Nacimiento
Curios Mexicano
Valas Fatasma

side two
El Alma Nace En La Sangre
Topo Triste
Los Dioses De Azucar
Las Flores Nacen En El Barro
El Infierno De Las Angeleses
  Prostitutos
Marcha De Los O Jos En El
  Trianqulos
La Mieldel Dolor
300 Conejos
Conocimiento A Traves De La
  Musica
La Primera Flor Despues Del
  Diluvio

------- -------
4/28/72 SW 3391

The Pope Smokes Dope
  by David Peel *(321)*

9/15/72 PCSP 716
6/12/72 SVBB 3392

Sometime In New York City
  by John Lennon & Yoko Ono *(325)*

11/10/72 SAPCOR 22
9/18/72 SMAS 3389

Elephant's Memory
  by Elephant's Memory *(330)*

2/ 9/73 SAPCOR 25   **Brother**
9/22/72 SMAS 3390   by Lon & Derrek Van Eaton
side one   side two
Warm Woman   *Help Us All*
Sun Song   *Maybe There's Another*
More Than Words   *Ring*
Hear My Cry   *Sunshine*
Without The Lord   *Another Thought*
Sweet Music

11/24/72 SAPCOR 23   **Those Were The Days**
9/25/72 SW 3395   by Mary Hopkin
side one   side two
Those Were The Days   *Knock, Knock, Who's There*
Que Sera, Sera   *Heritage*
Fields Of St. Etienne   *Sparrow*
Kew Gardens   *Lontano Dagli Occhi*
Temma Harbour   *Goodbye*
Think About Your Children

12/ 8/72 APCOR 24   **Phil Spector's Christmas Album**
12/11/72 SW 3400   by Various Artists
side one   side two
White Christmas   *I Saw Mommy Kissing Santa Claus*
Frosty The Snowman   *Rudolph, The Red Nosed Reindeer*
Bells Of St. Mary   *Winter Wonderland*
Santa Claus Is Coming To   *Parade Of The Wooden Soldiers*
  Town   *Christmas (Baby Please Come*
Sleigh Ride   *Home)*
It's A Marshmallow World   *Here Comes Santa Claus*
                                Silent Night

2/16/73 SAPDO 1001   **Approximately Infinite Universe**
1/ 8/73 SVBB 3399   by Yoko Ono *(342)*

4/13/73 SAPDO 1002   **In Concert 1972**
1/22/73 SVBB 3396   by Ravi Shankar & Ali Akbar Khan *(343)*

4/20/73 PCSP 717   **1962–1966**
4/ 2/73 SKBO 3403   by The Beatles _ *(346)*

UK/US DATE	UK/US No.	ALBUM TITLE/ARTIST

4/20/73 PCSP 718   **1967–1970**
4/ 2/73 SKBO 3404   by The Beatles *(347)*

5/ 4/73 PCTC 251   **Red Rose Speedway**
4/30/73 SMAL 3409   by Paul McCartney & Wings *(349)*

6/22/73 PAS 10006   **Living In The Material World**
5/30/73 SMAS 3410   by George Harrison *(352)*

11/23/73 SAPCOR 26   **Feeling The Space**
11/ 2/73 SW 3412   by Yoko Ono

side one	side two
Growing Pain	*A Thousand Times Yes*
Yellow Girl (Stand By For Life)	*Straight Talk*
	Angry Young Woman
Coffin Car	*She Hits Back*
Woman Of Salem	*Woman Power*
Run, Run, Run	*Men, Men, Men*
If Only	

11/ 9/73 PCTC 252   **"Ringo"**
11/ 2/73 SWAL 3413   by Ringo Starr *(366)*

11/16/73 PCS 7165   **Mind Games**
11/ 2/73 SW 3414   by John Lennon *(367)*

3/ 8/74 SAPCOR 27   **Ass**
11/26/73 SW 3411   by Badfinger

side one	side two
Apple Of My Eye	*Constitution*
Get Away	*When I Say*
Icicles	*Cowboy*
The Winner	*I Can Love You*
Blind Owl	*Timeless*

12/ 7/73 PAS 10007   **Band On The Run**
12/ 5/73 SO 3415   by Paul McCartney & Wings *(371)*

10/ 4/74 PCTC 253   **Walls And Bridges**
9/26/74 SW 3416   by John Lennon *(404)*

UK/US DATE	UK/US No.	ALBUM TITLE/ARTIST
11/15/74	PCS 7168	**Goodnight Vienna**
11/18/74	SW 3417	by Ringo Starr *(415)*
12/20/74	PAS 10008	**Dark Horse**
12/ 9/74	SMAS 3418	by George Harrison *(422)*
2/21/75	PCS 7169	**Rock 'n' Roll**
2/17/75	SK 3419	by John Lennon *(432)*
10/ 3/75	PAS 1009	**Extra Texture**
9/22/75	SW 3420	by George Harrison *(455)*
10/24/75	PCS 7173	**Shaved Fish**
10/24/75	SW 3421	by John Lennon *(458)*
12/12/75	PCS 7170	**Blast From Your Past**
11/20/75	SW 3422	by Ringo Starr *(466)*

The Beatles Christmas Record (SBC 100) and LYN 2154) was released through the Fan Club, but not to the general public. The Iveys album (SAPCOR 8) was released in Europe only. The Delaney & Bonnie album was never released on Apple, but it was released on June 27, 1969 on Elektra (EKS 74039). The Trash album (SAPCOR 7) and the Richard Brautigan album (Zapple 03) were never released.

NOTE: In November 1971, all of the Beatle LPs and 45s issued by Capitol were printed with the Apple label (but with the original Capitol catalogue number).

Illustration: ©1929 The Saalfield Publishing Co., U.S.A.

C.M.Burd

Mary Had A Little Lamb
1851

Mary Had A Little Lamb/Little Woman Love   **Apple 1851   (45)**

Apple Singles

UK/US DATE	UK/US No.	ARTIST	A/B SIDE
8/30/68	5722	Beatles	*Hey Jude*
8/26/68	2276		*Revolution*
8/30/68	2	Mary Hopkin	*Those Were The Days*
8/26/68	1801		*Turn, Turn, Turn*
9/ 6/68	3	Jackie Lomax	*Sour Milk Sea*
8/26/68	1802		*The Eagle Laughs At You*
9/ 6/68	4	John Foster &	*Thingumybob*
8/26/68	1800	Sons Brass Band	*Yellow Submarine*
10/25/68	2	Mary Hopkin	*Quelli Erand Giorni*
------- -----			*Turn, Turn, Turn*
11/15/68	5	Iveys	*Maybe Tomorrow*
1/27/69	1803		*And Her Daddy's A Millionaire*
1/24/69	6	Trash	*Road To Nowhere*
3/ 3/69	1804		*Illusions*
3/ 7/69	7	Mary Hopkin	*Lontano Dagli Occhi*
------- -----			*The Game*
3/ 7/69	9	Mary Hopkin	*Prince En Avignon*
------- -----			*The Game*
------- -----		James Taylor	*Carolina In My Mind*
3/17/69	1805		*Taking It In*

301

UK/US DATE	UK/US No.	ARTIST	A/B SIDE
3/28/69 4/ 7/69	10 1806	Mary Hopkin	*Goodbye* *Sparrow*
4/11/69 5/ 5/69	5777 2490	Beatles with Billy Preston	*Get Back* *Don't Let Me Down*
5/ 9/69 -------	11 ----	Jackie Lomax	*New Day* *I Fall Inside Your Eyes*
5/16/69 -------	8 ----	Brute Force	*King Of Fuh* *Nobody Knows*
5/30/69 6/ 4/69	5786 2531	Beatles	*The Ballad Of John And Yoko* *Old Brown Shoe*
------- 6/ 2/69	---- 1807	Jackie Lomax	*New Day* *Thumbin' A Ride*
6/27/69 7/ 7/69	12 1808	Billy Preston	*That's The Way God Planned It* *What About You*
7/ 4/69 7/ 7/69	13 1809	Plastic Ono Band	*Give Peace A Chance* *Remember Love*
7/18/69 -------	14 ----	Iveys	*No Escaping Your Love* *Dear Angie*
7/18/69 -------	CT 1 ----	Iveys James Taylor Jackie Lomax Mary Hopkin	*Storm In A Teacup* *Something's Wrong* *Little Yellow Pills* *Happiness Runs*
8/29/69 8/22/69	15 1810	Radha Krishna Temple (London)	*Hare Krishna Mantra* *Prayer To The Spiritual Masters*
9/19/69 6/15/70	16 1823	Mary Hopkin	*Que Sera, Sera* *Fields Of St. Etienne*
10/ 3/69 10/15/69	17 1811	Trash	*Golden Slumbers/Carry That Weight* *Trash Can*

UK/US DATE	UK/US No.	ARTIST	A/B SIDE
10/31/69	5814	Beatles	*Something*
10/ 6/69	2654		*Come Together*
10/10/69	18	Hot Chocolate	*Give Peace A Chance*
10/17/69	1812	Band	*Living Without Tomorrow*
10/17/69	19	Billy Preston	*Everything's All Right*
10/24/69	1814		*I Want To Thank You*
10/24/69	1001	Plastic Ono Band	*Cold Turkey*
10/20/69	1813		*Don't Worry Kyoko*
12/ 5/69	1002	Plastic Ono Band	*You Know My Name*
-------	----		*What's The News Maryjane*
12/ 5/69	20	Badfinger	*Come And Get It*
1/12/70	1815		*Rock Of All Ages*
1/16/70	22	Mary Hopkin	*Temma Harbour*
1/29/70	1816		*Lontano Dagli Occhi*
1/30/70	21	Billy Preston	*All That I've Got*
2/16/70	1817		*As I Get Older*
2/ 6/70	23	Jackie Lomax	*How The Web Was Woven*
-------	----		*Thumbin' A Ride*
2/ 6/70	1003	John/Yoko with	*Instant Karma*
2/20/70	1818	Plastic Ono Band	*Who Has Seen The Wind*
2/13/70	24	Doris Troy	*Ain't That Cute*
3/16/70	1820		*Vaya Con Dios*
3/ 6/70	25	Radha Krishna	*Govinda*
3/24/70	1821	Temple (London)	*Govinda Jai Jai*
3/ 6/70	5833	Beatles	*Let It Be*
3/11/70	2764		*You Know My Name*
-------	----	Jackie Lomax	*How The Web Was Woven*
3/ 9/70	1819		*I Fall Inside Your Eyes*

UK/US DATE	UK/US No.	ARTIST	A/B SIDE
3/20/70 -------	26 ----	Mary Hopkin	*Knock Knock Who's There* *I'm Going To Fall In Love Again*
------- 5/11/70	---- 2832	Beatles	*The Long And Winding Road* *For You Blue*
8/28/70 9/21/70	28 1824	Doris Troy	*Jacob's Ladder* *Get Back*
9/ 4/70 -------	29 ----	Billy Preston	*My Sweet Lord* *Long As I Got My Baby*
------- 10/ 5/70	---- 2969	Ringo Starr	*Beaucoups Of Blues* *Coochy—Coochy*
------- 10/12/70	---- 1822	Badfinger	*No Matter What* *Carry On Till Tomorrow*
10/16/70 10/18/70	30 1825	Mary Hopkin	*Think About Your Children* *Heritage*
11/ 6/70 10/26/70	32 1805	James Taylor	*Carolina In My Mind* *Something's Wrong*
11/ 6/70 -------	31 ----	Badfinger	*No Matter What* *Better Days*
------- 11/23/70	---- 2995	George Harrison	*My Sweet Lord* *Isn't It A Pity*
------- 12/ 3/70	---- 1826	Billy Preston	*My Sweet Lord* *Little Girl*
------- 12/28/70	---- 1827	John/Yoko with Plastic Ono Band	*Mother* *Why*
1/15/71 -------	5884 ----	George Harrison	*My Sweet Lord* *What Is Life*
------- 2/15/71	---- 1828	George Harrison	*What Is Life* *Apple Scruffs*

UK/US DATE	UK/US No.	ARTIST	A/B SIDE
2/19/71	5889	Paul McCartney	*Another Day*
2/22/71	1829		*Oh Woman Oh Why*
3/12/71	5892	John/Yoko with	*Power To The People*
-------	----	Plastic Ono Band	*Open Your Box*
-------	----	John/Yoko with	*Power To The People*
3/22/71	1830	Plastic Ono Band	*Touch Me*
4/ 9/71	5898	Ringo Starr	*It Don't Come Easy*
4/16/71	1831		*Early 1970*
4/16/71	33	Ronnie Spector	*Try Some, Buy Some*
4/19/71	1832		*Tandoori Chicken*
6/18/71	34	Mary Hopkin	*Let My Name Be Sorrow*
-------	----		*Kew Gardens*
-------	----	Jackie Lomax	*Sour Milk Sea*
6/21/71	1834		*I Fall Inside Your Eyes*
7/16/71	36	Bill Elliott and	*God Save Us*
7/ 7/71	1835	Elastic Oz Band	*Do The Oz*
7/30/71	5912	George Harrison	*Bangla Desh*
7/28/71	1836		*Deep Blue*
-------	----	Paul & Linda	*Uncle Albert/Admiral Halsey*
8/ 2/71	1837	McCartney	*Too Many People*
8/27/71	37	Ravi Shankar	*Joi Bangla/Oh Bhaugowan*
8/ 9/71	1838	and Chorus	*Raga Mishra—Jhinjhoti*
8/13/71	5914	Paul & Linda	*Back Seat Of My Car*
-------	----	McCartney	*Heart Of The Country*
10/29/71	38	Yoko Ono with	*Mrs. Lennon*
9/29/71	1839	Plastic Ono Band	*Midsummer New York*
-------	----	John Lennon with	*Imagine*
10/11/71	1840	Plastic Ono Band	*It's So Hard*

UK/US DATE	UK/US No.	ARTIST	A/B SIDE
------- 11/10/71	---- 1841	Badfinger	*Day After Day* *Money*
11/24/72 12/ 1/71	5970 1842	John/Yoko with Plastic Ono Band	*Happy Xmas (War Is Over)* *Listen, The Snow Is Falling*
------- 12/ 1/71	---- 1843	Mary Hopkin	*Water Paper And Clay* *Streets Of London*
12/ 3/71 -------	39 ----	Mary Hopkin	*Water Paper And Clay* *Jefferson*
1/14/72 -------	40 ----	Badfinger	*Day After Day* *Sweet Tuesday Morning*
1/14/72 -------	5932 ----	Wings	*Love Is Strange* *I Am Your Singer*
1/21/72 -------	41 ----	Yoko Ono with Plastic Ono Band	*Mind Train* *Listen, The Snow Is Falling*
2/25/72 2/28/72	5936 1847	Wings	*Give Ireland Back To The Irish* *(version)*
3/10/72 3/ 6/72	42 1844	Badfinger	*Baby Blue* *Flying*
------- 3/ 6/72	---- 1845	Lon & Derrek Van Eaton	*Sweet Music* *Song Of Songs*
3/17/72 3/20/72	5944 1849	Ringo Starr	*Back Off Boogaloo* *Blindman*
------- 4/20/72	---- 6498 6499	David Peel and The Lower East Side	*F Is Not A Dirty Word* *The Ballad Of New York City/* *John Lennon—Yoko Ono*
5/12/72 4/24/72	5953 1848	John/Yoko with Elephant's Memory	*Woman Is The Nigger Of The World* *Sisters O Sisters*
6/ 9/72 5/ 3/72	43 1850	Chris Hodge	*We're On Our Way* *Supersoul*

UK/US DATE	UK/US No.	ARTIST	A/B SIDE
5/12/72	5949	Wings	*Mary Had A Little Lamb*
5/29/72	1851		*Little Woman Love*
-------	----	David Peel and	*Hippy From New York City*
6/16/72	6545	The Lower	*The Ballad Of New York City/*
	6546	East Side	*John Lennon—Yoko Ono*
11/24/72	44	Sundown Playboys	*Saturday Night Special*
9/26/72	1852		*Valse De Soleil Coucher*
-------	----	Mary Hopkin	*Knock Knock Who's There*
11/ 8/72	1855		*International*
-------	----	Yoko Ono with	*Now Or Never*
11/13/72	1853	Elephant's Memory	*Move On Fast*
-------	----	Elephant's Memory	*Liberation Special*
11/13/72	1854		*Madness*
12/ 1/72	5973	Wings	*Hi, Hi, Hi*
12/ 4/72	1857		*C Moon*
12/ 8/72	45	Elephant's Memory	*Power Boogie*
12/ 4/72	1854		*Liberation Special*
-------	----	Chris Hodge	*Goodbye Sweet Lorraine*
1/22/73	1858		*Contact Love*
5/ 4/73	47	Yoko Ono with	*Death Of Samantha*
2/26/73	1859	Elephant's Memory	*Yang Yang*
3/ 9/73	46	Lon & Derrek	*Warm Woman*
-------	----	Van Eaton	*More Than Words*
3/23/73	5985	Paul McCartney	*My Love*
4/ 9/73	1861	and Wings	*The Mess*
5/25/73	5988	George Harrison	*Give Me Love*
5/ 7/73	1862		*Miss O'Dell*
6/ 1/73	5987	Wings	*Live And Let Die*
6/18/73	1863		*I Lie Around*

UK/US DATE	UK/US No.	ARTIST	A/B SIDE
10/19/73 9/24/73	5992 1865	Ringo Starr	*Photograph* *Down And Out*
------- 9/24/73	---- 1867	Yoko Ono	*Woman Power* *Men, Men, Men*
10/26/73 11/12/73	5993 1869	Paul McCartney and Wings	*Helen Wheels* *Country Dreamer*
11/16/73 10/29/73	5994 1868	John Lennon	*Mind Games* *Meat City*
11/ 9/73 -------	48 ----	Yoko Ono	*Run, Run, Run* *Men, Men, Men*
2/ 8/74 12/ 3/73	5995 1870	Ringo Starr	*You're Sixteen* *Devil Woman*
3/ 8/74 12/17/73	49 1864	Badfinger	*Apple Of My Eye* *Blind Owl*
------- 1/28/74	---- 1871	Paul McCartney and Wings	*Jet* *Mamunia*
2/15/74 2/18/74	5996 1871	Paul McCartney and Wings	*Jet* *Let Me Roll It*
------- 2/18/74	---- 1872	Ringo Starr	*Oh My My* *Step Lightly*
------- 4/ 8/74	---- 1873	Paul McCartney and Wings	*Band On The Run* *Nineteen Hundred Eighty Five*
6/28/74 -------	5997 ----	Paul McCartney and Wings	*Band On The Run* *Zoo Gang*
10/ 4/74 9/23/74	5998 1874	John Lennon	*Whatever Gets You Thru The Night* *Beef Jerky*
10/25/74 11/ 4/74	5999 1875	Paul McCartney and Wings	*Junior's Farm* *Sally G*
11/15/74 11/11/74	6000 1876	Ringo Starr	*Only You* *Call Me*

308

UK/US DATE	UK/US No.	ARTIST	A/B SIDE
11/22/74	6001	George Harrison	*Dark Horse*
11/18/74	1877		*I Don't Care Anymore*
12/ 6/74	6002	George Harrison	*Ding Dong Ding Dong*
- - - - - - -	- - - -		*I Don't Care Anymore*
1/31/75	6003	John Lennon	*No. 9 Dream*
12/16/74	1878		*What You Got*
- - - - - - -	- - - -	George Harrison	*Ding Dong Ding Dong*
12/23/74	1879		*Hari's On Tour (Express)*
- - - - - - -	- - - -	Ringo Starr	*No No Song*
1/27/75	1880		*Snookeroo*
2/21/75	6004	Ringo Starr	*Snookeroo*
- - - - - - -	- - - -		*Oo—Wee*
2/28/75	6001	George Harrison	*Dark Horse*
- - - - - -	- - - -		*Hari's On Tour (Express)*
4/18/75	6005	John Lennon	*Stand By Me*
3/10/75	1881		*Move Over Ms. L*
- - - - - - -	- - - -	Ringo Starr	*It's All Down To Goodnight Vienna*
6/ 2/75	1882		*Oo—Wee*
- - - - - - -	- - - -	John Lennon	*Slippin' And Slidin'*
6/ 2/75	1883		*Ain't That A Shame*
9/12/75	6007	George Harrison	*You*
9/15/75	1884		*World of Stone*
10/24/75	6009	John Lennon	*Imagine*
- - - - - - -	- - - -		*Working Class Hero*
2/ 6/76	6012	George Harrison	*This Guitar*
12/ 8/75	1885		*Maya Love*

Apple 1002, 5932 and 6001 (11/22/74) were never released. Apple 8 and 1883 were never released, but DJ copies were sent out. Apple 6498 & 6499, 6545 & 6546 were two special DJ singles never intended for general release. Apple CT1 was a special promotional record for a business firm. Apple 7 was released in Italy, Apple 9 in France, Apple 14 in Europe.

Dark Horse (B side)   **Apple SMAS 3418 (LP)**

Dark Horse

UK/US DATE	UK/US No.	ALBUM TITLE/ARTIST
9/20/74	AMLH 22001	**The Place I Love**
9/25/74	SP 22001	by Splinter *(400)*
9/20/74	AMLH 22002	**Shankar Family & Friends**
10/ 7/74	SP 22002	by Ravi Shankar & Friends *(401)*

UK/US DATE	UK/US No.	ARTIST	A/B SIDE
9/13/74	AMS 7133	Ravi Shankar	*I Am Missing You*
11/ 6/74	DH 10001	& Friends	*Lust*
9/13/74	AMS 7135	Splinter	*Costafine Town*
11/ 7/74	DH 10002		*Elly-May*
2/ 7/75	AMS 5501	Splinter	*Drink All Day*
------	-------		*Haven't Got Time*
2/21/75	AMS 5502	Splinter	*China Light*
------	-------		*Drink All Day*
------	-------	Splinter	*China Light*
3/ 7/75	DH 10003		*Haven't Got Time*

(Continued on page 379)

Sta*rtling Music   Ring O' ST - 11372 (LP)

Ring O' Records

UK/US DATE	UK/US No.	ALBUM TITLE/ARTIST
4/18/75	2320-101	Sta*rtling Music
2/17/75	ST 11372	by David Hentschel

side one	side two
Devil Woman	*Photograph*
Six O'Clock	*Have You Seen My Baby*
Step Lightly	*I'm The Greatest*
Oh My My	*Sunshine Life For Me (Sail Away*
You're Sixteen (I)	*Raymond)*
You're Sixteen (II)	*You And Me (Babe)*

UK/US DATE	UK/US No.	ARTIST	A/B SIDE
3/21/75	2017101	David Hentschel	*Oh My My*
2/17/75	11372		*Devil Woman*
9/ 5/75	2017102	Bobby Keys	*Gimmie The Key*
8/25/75	4129		*Honky Tonk (Parts 1 & 2)*
11/14/75	2017103	Carl Groszmann	*I've Had It*
- - - - - - - -	- - - - - - -		*C'mon And Roll*
11/21/75	2017104	Colonel (Doug Bogie)	*Away In A Manger*
- - - - - - - -	- - - - - - - -		*Cokey Cokey*

An elongated 'disco' version of *Gimmie The Key* was issued on Ring O' SPRO 8193. The Colonel (Doug Bogie) single was not released on Ring O' in the U.S., but it was released on December 8, 1975 by ABC Records (ABC 12148).

YES
I'M GONNA BE
A STAR

Help!   Parlophone PCS 3071   (LP)

Help!   Capitol 2386   (LP)

A Hard   Parlophone PCS 3058   (LP)
Day's Night

Yellow   Apple PCS 7070   (LP)
Submarine

The Beatles
On Film

A Hard Day's Night   (87 Minutes)
 Starring The Beatles
 Filmed: March–April 1964
 Screenplay: Alun Owen
 Directed: Richard Lester
 Produced: Walter Shenson
 Distributed: United Artists
 World Premiere: July 6, 1964 (London)
 New York Premiere: August 11, 1964

Help!   (90 Minutes)
 Starring The Beatles
 Filmed: February–May 1965
 Screenplay: Marc Behm and Charles Wood
 From a story by Marc Behm
 Directed: Richard Lester
 Produced: Walter Shenson
 Distributed: United Artists
 World Premiere: July 29, 1965 (London)
 New York Premiere: August 23, 1965

The Beatles At Shea Stadium   (50 Minutes)
 A Documentary Starring The Beatles
 Filmed Live At New York's Shea Stadium August 15, 1965
 World Premiere: May 1, 1966 (BBC TV)

The Family Way   (115 Minutes)
 Music by Paul McCartney
 Screenplay: Bill Naughton
 From Bill Naughton's play *All In Good Time*
 Produced and Directed: John and Roy Boulting
 Associate Producer: Dennis O'Dell
 Distributed: Warner Brothers
 World Premiere: December 18, 1966 (London)
 New York Premiere: June 28, 1967

How I Won The War   (109 Minutes)
   Featuring John Lennon as Musketeer Gripweed
   Filmed: September–October 1966
   Screenplay: Charles Wood
   Based on a novel by Patrick Ryan
   Produced and Directed: Richard Lester
   Distributed: United Artists
   World Premiere: October 18, 1967 (London)
   New York Premiere: November 8, 1967

Magical Mystery Tour   (54 Minutes)
   Starring The Beatles
   Filmed: September–October 1967
   Produced and Directed: The Beatles
   World Premiere: December 26, 1967 (BBC-1 TV)

Wonderwall   (92 Minutes)
   Music by George Harrison
   Story: Gerard Brach
   Screenplay: G. Cain
   Directed: Joe Massot
   Produced: Andrew Braunsberg
   Distributed: Cinecenta
   World Premiere: May 17, 1968 (Cannes Film Festival)
   London Pemiere: January 20, 1969

Yellow Submarine   (85 Minutes)
   Cartoon Featuring The Beatles
   Screenplay: Lee Minoff, Al Brodax, Jack Mendelsohn and Erich
      Segal
   From an original story by Lee Minoff
   Based on the song by John Lennon and Paul McCartney
   Animation designed by Heinz Edelmann
   Directed: George Dunning
   Produced: Al Brodax
   Distributed: United Artists
   World Premiere: July 17, 1968 (London)
   New York Premiere: November 13, 1968

Candy   (119 Minutes)
   Featuring Ringo as Emmanuel the Gardener
   Filmed: Late November–Mid December 1967
   Screenplay: Buck Henry
   From a novel by Terry Southern and Mason Hoffenberg
   Directed: Christian Marquand

Produced: Robert Hagglas
Distributed: Cinerama Releasing Corporation
New York Premiere: December 17, 1968
London Premiere: February 20, 1969
Soundtrack Album featuring The Byrds and Steppenwolf. Music
    composed and conducted by Dave Grusin
    US: December 30, 1968 ABC OC-9
    UK: March 14, 1969 Stateside SSL 10276

Rock 'n' Roll Circus
    Featuring John Lennon and Yoko Ono
    Filmed: December 11, 1968
    Produced: Michael Lindsay-Hogg
    Never commercially released

The Magic Christian   (92 Minutes)
    Featuring Ringo Starr as Youngman Grand
    Filmed: March–May 1969
    Screenplay: Terry Southern, Joseph McGrath and Peter Sellers
    From the novel by Terry Southern
    Directed: Joseph McGrath
    Produced: Dennis O'Dell
    Distributed: Commonwealth United Films
    World Premiere: December 12, 1969 (London)
    New York Premiere: February 11, 1970

Let It Be   (88 Minutes)
    A Documentary Featuring The Beatles
    Filmed: January 1969
    Directed: Michael Lindsay-Hogg
    Produced: Neil Aspinal
    Distributed: United Artists
    New York Premiere: May 13, 1970
    London Premiere: May 20, 1970

200 Motels   (99 Minutes)
    Featuring Ringo Starr as Frank Zappa and The Dwarf
    Story and Screenplay: Frank Zappa
    Animation: Chuck Swenson
    Directed: Tony Palmer
    Produced: Jerry Good and Herb Cohen
    Distributed: United Artists
    New York Premiere: November 10, 1971

Soundtrack Album by Frank Zappa and The Mothers Of Invention
US: October 18, 1971 United Artists UAS 9956 (2 LPs)
UK: November 12, 1971 United Artists UDF 50003 (2 LPs)

Raga   (96 Minutes)
Featuring George Harrison
Screenplay: Nancy Becal
Produced and Directed: Howard Worth
Distributed: Apple Films
New York Premiere: November 23, 1971

Blindman   (105 Minutes)
Featuring Ringo as Candy
Filmed: June—August 1971
Directed: Ferdinando Baldi
Produced: Saul Swimmer
World Premiere: November 15, 1971 (Rome)
American Premiere: January 12, 1972 (Chicago)

The Concert For Bangla Desh   (140 Minutes)
A Documentary Featuring George Harrison and Ringo Starr
Filmed Live At New York's Madison Square Garden August 1, 1971
Directed: Saul Swimmer
Produced: George Harrison and Allen Klein
Distributed: 20th Century Fox
New York Premiere: March 23, 1972
London Premiere: July 1, 1972

Born To Boogie
Filmed: March—April 1972
Directed: Ringo Starr
London Premiere: December 18, 1972
Theme Song by T. Rex
UK: December 1, 1972 MARC 3 b/w *Solid Gold Easy Action*
US: June 11, 1973 Reprise 1161 b/w *The Groover*

That'll Be The Day   (90 Minutes)
Featuring Ringo
Filmed: October 1972—January 1973
Story and Screenplay: Ray Connolly
Directed: Claude Whatham
Produced: David Puttnam and Sanford Lieberson
Distributed: Mayfair Films
World Premiere: April 12, 1973 (London)
US Premiere: October 29, 1973 (Los Angeles)
Soundtrack Album featuring Various Artists
UK: May 25, 1973 Ronco Records

Live And Let Die (121 Minutes)
   Title Music by Paul McCartney
   Screenplay: Tom Mankiewicz
   From a book by Ian Fleming
   Directed: Guy Hamilton
   Produced: Albert Broccoli and Harry Saltzman
   New York Premiere: June 29, 1973
   London Premiere: July 5, 1973

Son Of Dracula (90 Minutes)
   Featuring Ringo as Merlin
   Filmed: August–October 1972
   Screenplay: Jay Fairbank
   Directed: Freddie Francis
   Produced: Ringo Starr
   Distributed: Cinemation Industries
   World Premiere: Mid May 1974 (Atlanta)

Little Malcolm And His Struggle Against The Eunuchs
   Executive Producer: George Harrison
   Featuring Bob Purvis and Bill Elliott (Splinter) singing Mal Evans'
      song *Lonely Man*
   World Premiere: Berlin Film Festival 1974

Lisztomania (105 Minutes)
   Featuring Ringo as The Pope
   Written and Directed: Ken Russell
   Produced: Roy Baird and Dave Puttnam
   Distributed: Warner Brothers
   New York Premiere: October 10, 1975
   London Premiere: November 13, 1975
   Soundtrack Album featuring Roger Daltry and Rick Wakeman
      with The English Rock Ensemble, John Forsythe, George
      Michie, The National Philharmonic Orchestra and David Wilde.
      US: October 13, 1975 A&M SP 4546 (LP)
      UK: October 24, 1975 A&M AMLH 64546 (LP)

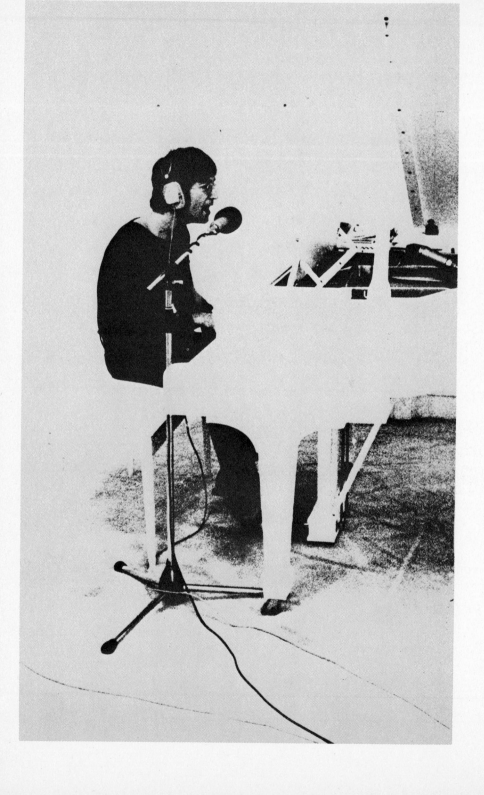

John And Yoko
On Film

Rape (Film No. 6) (73 Minutes)
 Produced: Hans Preiner, John Lennon and Yoko Ono
 World Premiere: March 31, 1969 (Austrian National Television)

An Evening With John & Yoko
 Mid September 1969 at London's New Cinema Club
 Featuring Four John & Yoko Films
  1. *Two Virgins* (19 Minutes)
  2. *Smile* (52 Minutes)
  3. *Honeymoon* (Filmed in Amsterdam)
  4. *Self Portrait*

Filmmaker's Fortnight Festival (Cannes , France)
 May 15, 1971 Featuring Two John & Yoko Films
  1. *Apotheosis (Balloon)* (18 Minutes)
   Produced: Nick Knowland
  2. *Fly* (50 Minutes)

London's Art Spectrum
 Early September 1971 at London's Alexander Palace
 Featuring Five John & Yoko Films
  1. *Cold Turkey*
  2. *Ballad Of John And Yoko*
  3. *Give Peace A Chance*
  4. *Instant Karma*
  5. *Up Your Legs*

Erection 1972
 No, it's not what you're thinking (that's *Self Portrait*). It's a time-elapsed view of a building's construction.

Imagine
 World Premiere: December 23, 1972

323

BOOKS
FOR BOYS
AND GIRLS
OF ALL AGES

WEDDING
ALBUM

Wedding Album   Apple SMAX 3361 (LP)

BOOKS
FOR BOYS
AND GIRLS
OF ALL AGES

All Together Now
  Harry Castleman and Wally Podrazik   Pierian; Ballantine Books
    1976
Apple To The Core
  Peter McCabe and Robert Schonfeld   Pocket Books   1972
As Time Goes By
  Derek Taylor   Straight Arrow   1973
The Beatles: An Illustrated Record
  Roy Carr and Tony Tyler   Harmony   1975
The Beatles: The Fabulous Story of John, Paul, George and Ringo
  Robert Burt and Jeremy Pascall   Octopus   1975
The Beatles—The Authorized Biography
  Hunter Davies   McGraw--Hill; Dell   1968
The Beatles—The Real Story
  Julius Fast   Putnam; Berkley   1968
The Beatles Book
  Edward Davis, Editor   Cowles   1968
The Beatles Illustrated Lyrics
  Alan Aldridge, Editor   Delacorte; Dell   1969
The Beatles Illustrated Lyrics—Volume 2
  Alan Aldridge, Editor   Delacorte   1971
The Beatles Lyrics Illustrated
  Dell   1975
A Cellarful of Noise
  Brian Epstein and Derek Taylor   Doubleday; Pyramid   1964
The Compleat Beatles Quiz Book
  Edwin Goodgold and Dan Carlinsky   Warner   1975
Get Back
  Jonathan Cott and David Dalton   Apple Publishing   1970
A Hard Day's Night
  John Burke   Dell   1964

Help!
  Al Hine   Dell   1965
In His Own Write
  John Lennon   Simon & Schuster; New American Library   1964
John Lennon—One Day At A Time
  Anthony Fawcett   Grove Press   1976
The Lennon Play: In His Own Write
  John Lennon, Andrienne Kennedy and Victor Spinetti   Simon &
    Schuster   1968
Lennon Remembers: The Rolling Stone Interviews
  Jann Wenner   Straight Arrow; Popular Library   1971
Linda's Pictures
  Linda McCartney   Knopf   1976
The Longest Cocktail Party
  Richard DiLello   Playboy Press   1972
Love Me Do
  Michael Braun   Penguin   1964
The Man Who Gave The Beatles Away
  Allan Williams and William Marshall   Macmillan   1975
Out Of His Head: The Sound Of Phil Spector
  Richard Williams   Outerbridge & Lizard   1972
The Paul McCartney Story
  George Tremlett   Futura   1974
The Penguin John Lennon
  In His Own Write and *A Spaniard In The Works* in one
  paperback volume   Penguin   1966
A Spaniard In The Works
  John Lennon   Simon & Schuster   1965
Twilight Of The Gods: The Beatles In Retrospect
  Wilfred Howard Mellers   Viking; Schirmer   1973
Yellow Submarine
  Lee Minoff, Al Brodax, Jack Mendelsohn and Erich Segal
    Signet   1969

When two publishers are given (separated by a semi-colon), the first
refers to the hardbound edition, the second the paperback edition.

NUMBER ONE WITH A BULLET

The Beatles' Hits   **Parlophone GEP 8880 (EP)**

The Beatles' Million Sellers   **Parlophone GEP 8946 (EP)**

Solid Gold --
Rock 'n' Roll

The following Beatle records have been certified by the Record Industry Association of America (R.I.A.A.) as Gold Records.

Date Awarded	Title
February 3, 1964	Meet The Beatles
February 3, 1964	*I Want To Hold Your Hand*
March 31, 1964	*Can't Buy Me Love*
April 13, 1964	The Beatles' Second Album
August 24, 1964	Something New
August 25, 1964	*A Hard Day's Night*
December 31, 1964	*I Feel Fine*
December 31, 1964	Beatles '65
December 31, 1964	The Beatles' Story
July 1, 1965	Beatles' VI
August 23, 1965	Help!
September 2, 1965	*Help!*
September 16, 1965	*Eight Days A Week*
October 20, 1965	*Yesterday*
December 24, 1965	Rubber Soul
January 6, 1966	*We Can Work It Out*
April 1, 1966	*Nowhere Man*
July 8, 1966	"Yesterday"...And Today
July 14, 1966	*Paperback Writer*
August 22, 1966	Revolver
September 12, 1966	*Yellow Submarine*
March 20, 1967	*Penny Lane*
June 15, 1967	Sgt. Pepper's Lonely Hearts Club Band
September 11, 1967	*All You Need Is Love*
December 15, 1967	Magical Mystery Tour
April 8, 1968	*Lady Madonna*
September 13, 1968	*Hey Jude*
November 20, 1968	*Those Were The Days* (by Mary Hopkin)

Date Awarded	Title
December 6, 1968	**The Beatles**
February 5, 1969	**Yellow Submarine**
May 19, 1969	*Get Back*
July 16, 1969	*The Ballad Of John And Yoko*
October 27, 1969	**Abbey Road**
October 27, 1969	*Something/Come Together*
March 6, 1970	**Hey Jude**
March 17, 1970	**Live Peace In Toronto** (Lennon)
March 17, 1970	*Let It Be*
April 30, 1970	**McCartney** (McCartney)
May 26, 1970	**Let It Be**
December 14, 1970	*Instant Karma!* (Lennon)
December 14, 1970	*My Sweet Lord* (Harrison)
December 17, 1970	**All Things Must Pass** (Harrison)
January 28, 1971	**Plastic Ono Band** (Lennon)
June 9, 1971	**Ram** (McCartney)
August 3, 1971	*It Don't Come Easy* (Starr)
September 21, 1971	*Uncle Albert/Admiral Halsey* (McCartney)
October 1, 1971	**Imagine** (Lennon)
January 4, 1972	**Concert For Bangla Desh** (Harrison)
January 13, 1972	**Wild Life** (McCartney)
March 4, 1972	*Day After Day* (by Badfinger)
April 13, 1973	**The Beatles 1962–1966**
April 13, 1973	**The Beatles 1967–1970**
May 25, 1973	**Red Rose Speedway** (McCartney)
June 1, 1973	**Living In The Material World** (Harrison)
July 6, 1973	*My Love* (McCartney)
August 31, 1973	*Live And Let Die* (McCartney)
November 8, 1973	**"Ringo"** (Starr)
November 30, 1973	**Mind Games** (Lennon)
December 7, 1973	**Band On The Run** (McCartney)
December 28, 1973	*Photograph* (Starr)
January 8, 1974	**The Early Beatles**
January 31, 1974	*You're Sixteen* (Starr)
June 4, 1974	*Band On The Run* (McCartney)
October 22, 1974	**Walls And Bridges** (Lennon)
December 9, 1974	**Goodnight Vienna** (Starr)
December 16, 1974	**Dark Horse** (Harrison)
June 2, 1975	**Venus And Mars** (McCartney)
September 5, 1975	*Listen To What The Man Said* (McCartney)
November 11, 1975	**Extra Texture** (Harrison)

Top Of The Pops

The following are the weekly chart positions of Beatle records in Britain, taken from *Melody Maker's* weekly record charts. Both singles and albums from 1962–1975 are included in this listing. Additionally, the weekly positions of Beatle-related records are also listed.

All records are by the Beatles unless otherwise indicated. The following abbreviations are used to identify the other artists:

Aj–Applejacks
Bf–Badfinger
BJK–Billy J. Kramer with
    The Dakotas
BP–Billy Preston
CB–Cilla Black
CBn–Cliff Bennett and
    The Rebel Rousers
Cm–Cream
DBw–David Bowie
EC–Eric Clapton
EJ–Elton John
Fm–Fourmost
G–George Harrison
J–John Lennon

J/Y–John Lennon and
    Yoko Ono
MH–Mary Hopkin
P–Paul McCartney
PJ–P. J. Proby
P/G–Peter and Gordon
P/W–Paul McCartney & Wings
R–Ringo Starr
RdS–Rod Stewart
RKT–Radha Krsna Temple
RS–The Rolling Stones
RW–Ron Wood
Sf–Scaffold
Sk–Silkie
Sp–Splinter

All chart positions are taken from the *Melody Maker* Top 30 Singles Charts and Top 30 Albums Charts. The total number of records listed on these charts varied over the years as follows: The Top 20 Singles became the Top 30 on April 14, 1962; this became the Top 50 on September 15, 1962. It returned to a Top 30 on April 1, 1967.

The Top 10 Albums became the Top 20 on October 5, 1968; it expanded to the Top 30 Albums on February 7, 1970.

Beatles For Sale No. 2   **Parlophone GEP 8938   (EP)**

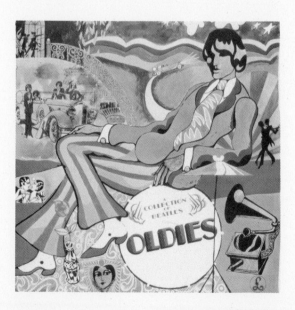

A Collection   **Parlophone PCS 7016   (LP)**
** Of Beatles Oldies**

Melody Maker Charts

1962 **1963**

	OCT	NOV	NOV	NOV	NOV	DEC	DEC	DEC	DEC	JAN	JAN	JAN
	27	3	10	17	24	1	8	15	22	5	12	19
Love Me Do	48	40	30	28	26	26	24	24	22	21	21	26
Please Please Me												47

	FEB	FEB	FEB	FEB	FEB	MAR	MAR	MAR	MAR	MAR	APR	APR
	26	2	9	16	23	2	9	16	23	30	6	13
Love Me Do	34	37	41	43								
Please Please Me	39	21	9	2	2	*1	*1	2	4	7	13	17
Please Please Me (LP)											10	7

		MAY	MAY	MAY	MAY		JUN	JUN	JUN	JUN		JUL
	20	27	4	11	18	25	1	8	15	22	29	6
Please Please Me	23	28	41	40	49							
From Me To You	19	3	*1	*1	*1	*1	*1	*1	3	3	5	8
My Bonnie									38	46		
Please Please Me (LP)	5	3	*1	*1	*1	*1	*1	*1	*1	*1	*1	*1
(Do You...Know A Secret–BJK)		47	19	9	6	2	2	*1	4	7	9	

				AUG	AUG	AUG	AUG	AUG	SEP	SEP	SEP	SEP
	13	20	27	3	10	17	24	31	7	14	21	28
From Me To You	12	16	16	19	24	28	35	43				
Twist & Shout (EP)		14	6	4	2	3	4	9	12	11	20	
She Loves You									12	*1	*1	*1
The Beatles Hits (EP)												44
Please Please Me (LP)	*1	*1	*1	*1	*1	*1	*1	*1	*1	*1	*1	*1
(Do You...Know A Secret–BJK)	14	18	20	28	41	43						
(Bad To Me–BJK)				31	11	4	*1	*1	2	2	3	4
(Hello Little Girl–Fm)											41	26

	OCT	OCT	OCT	OCT	NOV	NOV	NOV	NOV	NOV	DEC	DEC	DEC
	5	12	19	26	2	9	16	23	30	7	14	21
Twist & Shout (EP)	29	31	33	38	38	32	25	15	14	11	12	13
She Loves You	*1	3	4	3	3	2	2	*1	*1	2	2	2
The Beatles Hits (EP)	37	29	31	35	31	23	24	18	15	17	14	17
The Beatles No. 1 (EP)					40	27	22	21	19	23	25	
I Want To Hold Your Hand										*1	*1	*1
Please Please Me (LP)	*1	*1	*1	*1	*1	*1	*1	*1	2	2	2	2
With The Beatles (LP)									*1	*1	*1	*1
(Bad To Me–BJK)	11	22	25	43	44							
(Hello Little Girl–Fm)	22	12	11	9	10	12	18	27	34	43		
(Love Of The Loved–CB)					41	34	31	35	39	48	49	
(I'll Keep You Satisfied–BJK)						24	10	4	4	6	11	14
(I Wanna Be Your Man–RS)							46	34	30	21	17	15

	JAN				FEB					MAR	
	28	4	11	18	25	1	8	15	22	29	7	14
Twist & Shout (EP)		16	19	23	23	30	39	39	49	48		
She Loves You		3	6	7	10	13	22	26	27	33	38	40
The Beatles' Hits (EP)		24	20	28	33	47						
The Beatles No. 1 (EP)		31	29	38	46	48						
I Want To Hold Your Hand		*1	2	2	3	6	9	14	15	20	25	29
All My Loving (EP)							42	20	13	12	16	19
Please Please Me (LP)	2	2	2	2	2	2	2	2	2	2	3	2
With The Beatles (LP)	*1	*1	*1	*1	*1	*1	*1	*1	*1	*1	*1	*1
(I'll Keep You Satisfied–BJK)		20	24	32	41							
(I Wanna Be Your Man–RS)		10	11	12	17	21	24	31	33	42		
(I'm In Love–Fm)		50	31	27	19	15	15	16	21	25	34	39

			APR				MAY					JUN
	21	28	4	11	18	25	2	9	16	23	30	6
She Loves You	46	47	47									
I Want To Hold Your Hand	31	37	38	45								
All My Loving (EP)	20	24	23	28	33	38						
Can't Buy Me Love		*1	*1	*1	2	3	5	9	14	19	25	28
Please Please Me (LP)	2	2	3	2	2	2	4	5	5	7	5	8
With The Beatles (LP)	*1	*1	*1	*1	*1	*1	2	2	2	2	2	2
(World Without Love–P/G)	30	15	6	2	*1	*1	2	2	7	11	20	26
(Nobody I Know–P/G)												45

			JUL				AUG					
	13	20	27	4	11	18	25	1	8	15	22	29
Can't Buy Me Love	34	45	47									
Ain't She Sweet	36	27	24	28	33	47						
Long Tall Sally (EP)				20	15	14	17	22	25	27	30	35
A Hard Day's Night						*1	*1	*1	*1	2	2	4
Please Please Me (LP)	6		10									
With The Beatles (LP)	2	2	2	2	2	3	3	4	6	7	5	7
A Hard Day's Night (LP)						*1	*1	*1	*1	*1	*1	*1
(World Without Love–P/G)	37	48										
(Nobody I Know–P/G)	20	12	6	9	11	16	21	29	36	44		
(Like Dreamers Do–Aj)	41	33	26	18	18	17	23	23	30	41		
(From A Window–BJK)							27	19	16	12	12	17
(It's For You–CB)									27	14	9	9

	SEP				OCT					NOV		
	5	12	19	26	3	10	17	24	31	7	14	21
Long Tall Sally (EP)	44	39	47	49								
A Hard Day's Night	7	9	12	19	28	30	37	50				
With The Beatles (LP)	8	8	10									
A Hard Day's Night (LP)	*1	*1	*1	*1	*1	*1	*1	*1	*1	*1	*1	*1
(From A Window–BJK)	23	30	36	50								
(It's For You–CB)	8	11	16	25	29	42						

1965

	DEC					JAN					FEB	
	28	5	12	19	26	2	9	16	23	30	6	13
A Hard Day's Night—film (EP)	48	34	41	44								
I Feel Fine		*1	*1	*1	*1	*1	*1	2	5	13	21	25
A Hard Day's Night (LP)	*1	*1	2	3	2	3	4	3	3	4	4	5
Beatles For Sale (LP)			*1	*1	*1	*1	*1	*1	*1	*1	*1	2

			MAR				APR				MAY	
	20	27	6	13	20	27	3	10	17	24	1	8
I Feel Fine	40	49										
Ticket To Ride									*1	*1	*1	*1
A Hard Day's Night (LP)	7	8	9									
Beatles For Sale (LP)	2	2	2	2	2	2	2	2	2	*1	*1	*1

				JUN				JUL				
	15	22	29	5	12	19	26	3	10	17	24	31
Ticket To Ride	*1	3	9	13	24	40	46	49				
Help!												*1
Beatles For Sale (LP)	*1	*1	*1	3	3	4	5	6	6	8	8	9

	AUG				SEP				OCT			
	7	14	21	28	4	11	18	25	2	9	16	23
Help!	*1	*1	*1	2	3	4	9	17	19	29	35	38
Beatles For Sale (LP)		9	10	10								
Help! (LP)		*1	*1	*1	*1	*1	*1	*1	*1	*1	2	*1
(Hide Your Love Away—Sk)								37	33	27	24	24
(That Means A Lot—PJ)								46	38	34	25	26

1966

	NOV					DEC				JAN		
	30	6	13	20	27	4	11	18	25	1	8	15
We Can Work It Out/Day Trip.							3	*1	*1	*1	*1	2
Help! (LP)	*1	*1	*1	*1	*1	2	3	4	3	4	5	4
Rubber Soul (LP)							*1	*1	*1	*1	*1	*1
(Hide Your Love Away—Sk)	33											
(That Means A Lot—PJ)	34											

		FEB				MAR				APR		
	22	29	5	12	19	26	5	12	19	26	2	9
We Can Work It Out/Day Trip.	2	4	9	18	33							
Help! (LP)	5	5	6	9		10						
Rubber Soul (LP)	*1	*1	*1	*1	*1	*1	*1	2	2	2	2	2
(Woman—P/G)						47	30	23	22	21	29	34

			MAY				JUN				JUL	
	16	23	30	7	14	21	28	4	11	18	25	2
Paperback Writer										*1	*1	*1
Rubber Soul (LP)	2	2	3	3	3	4	3	3	5	6	7	8
(Woman—P/G)	45											

					AUG				SEP			
	9	16	23	30	6	13	20	27	3	10	17	24
Paperback Writer	*1	8	15	19	23	32	35					
Yellow Sub./Eleanor Rigby						4	*1	*1	*1	2	2	5
Rubber Soul (LP)	8											
Revolver (LP)						*1	*1	*1	*1	*1	*1	*1
(*Get You Into My Life*—CBn)							43	31	18	10	6	10

	OCT					NOV				DEC		
	1	8	15	22	29	5	12	19	26	3	10	17
Yellow Sub./Eleanor Rigby	10	16	19	31	38							
Revolver (LP)	*1	*1	2	2	2	2	2	5	5	5	6	6
Beatle Oldies (LP)												7
(*Get You Into My Life*—CBn)	17	21	31	48								

1967

	JAN					FEB				MAR		
	24	31	7	14	21	28	4	11	18	25	4	11
Penny Lane/Straw. Fields										3	*1	*1
Revolver (LP)	9											
Beatle Oldies (LP)	5	4	4	6	10							

			APR					MAY				JUN
	18	25	1	8	15	22	29	6	13	20	27	3
Penny Lane/Straw. Fields	*1	4	9	11	15	19	27					
Sgt. Pepper (LP)												*1

			JUL					AUG				
	10	17	24	1	8	15	22	29	5	12	19	26
All You Need Is Love						3	*1	*1	*1	2	2	4
Sgt. Pepper (LP)	*1	*1	*1	*1	*1	*1	*1	*1	*1	*1	*1	*1

	SEP					OCT				NOV		
	2	9	16	23	30	7	14	21	28	4	11	18
All You Need Is Love	10	13	17	22								
Sgt. Pepper (LP)	*1	*1	*1	*1	*1	*1	*1	*1	*1	2	2	2

1968

	DEC					JAN				FEB		
	25	2	9	16	23	6	13	20	27	3	10	17
Hello Goodbye		3	*1	*1	*1	*1	3	5	7	15	21	
Magical Mystery Tour (EP)				17	10	4	*1	2	7	14	17	21
Sgt. Pepper (LP)	2	2	2	2	2	2	3	3	3	2	2	4

	MAR					APR				MAY
	24	2	9	16	23	30	6	13	20	27	4
Magical Mystery Tour (EP)	25										
Lady Madonna					3	2	2	5	6	17	25
Sgt. Pepper (LP)	4	5	6	8	10						
(*Step Inside Love*—CB)					14	10	7	7	10	14	24

NO RECORDS ON CHARTS: **May 11, 1968—Aug. 31, 1968**

SEP / OCT / NOV

	7	14	21	28	5	12	19	26	2	9	16	23
	SEP				OCT				NOV			
Hey Jude	*1	*1	*1	*1	2	3	3	2	6	11	13	21
Sgt. Pepper (LP)						20						
(Those Were The Days–MH)	23	8	2	2	*1	*1	*1	*1	*1	4	6	8
(Urban Spaceman–BDB)												29

1969

DEC / JAN / FEB

	30	7	14	21	4	11	18	25	1	8	15	22
	DEC				JAN				FEB			
Hey Jude	28											
The Beatles (LP)	3	*1	*1	*1	*1	*1	*1	*1	*1	*1	*1	2
Yellow Submarine (LP)									14	5	4	4
(Those Were The Days–MH)	12	16	21	23	27							
(Urban Spaceman–BDB)	20	15	11	7	5	4	8	9	13	22		
(Best Of Cilla Black (LP)–CB)					18	17						

MAR / APR / MAY

	1	8	15	22	29	5	12	19	26	3	10	17
	MAR				APR				MAY			
Get Back									2	*1	*1	*1
The Beatles (LP)	4	3	7	9	10	12	14	19	18			
Yellow Submarine (LP)	4	4	8	11	17	19						
(Goodbye–MH)						16	8	3	2	2	2	4
(Badge–Cm)										29	26	22
(Goodbye (LP)–Cm)			2	2	*1	*1	*1	*1	2	*1	3	6
(Post Card (LP)–MH)			15	8	7	6	9	13	11	10	13	13

JUN / JUL / AUG

	24	7	14	21	28	5	12	19	26	2	9	16
		JUN				JUL				AUG		
Get Back	*1	2	4	5	12	19	27	30				
Ballad Of John And Yoko		15	2	*1	*1	*1	3	6	13	17	22	
Give Peace A Chance–J							30	9	3	2	2	2
The Beatles (LP)	14	19										
(Goodbye–MH)	9	16	23									
(Badge–Cm)	21	24										
(God Planned It–BP)							23	14	7	9	11	14
(Goodbye (LP)–Cm)	8	12	14	12	15							
(Post Card (LP)–MH)	16											

SEP / OCT / NOV

	23	30	6	13	20	27	4	11	18	25	1	8
			SEP				OCT				NOV	
Give Peace A Chance–J	6	13	22	28								
Something											26	
Cold Turkey–J											27	
Abbey Road (LP)							*1	*1	*1	*1	*1	*1
(God Planned It–BP)	22	30										
(Hare Krishna Mantra–RKT)						30	19	14	11	15	20	26
(Best Of Cream (LP)–Cm)												17

1970

	DEC			JAN							
	15	22	29	6	13	20	3	10	17	24	31
Something	12	5	4	6	8	11	14	19	27		
Cold Turkey–J	19	13	12	17	23						
Abbey Road (LP)	*1	*1	*1	*1	*1	*1	*1	*1	*1	*1	*1
(*Come & Get It*–Bf)									20	7	4
(Best Of Cream (LP)–Cm)	13	7	11	5	7	8	8	9	10	12	11

	FEB				MAR				APR		
	7	14	21	28	7	14	21	28	4	11	18
Instant Karma–J			17	6	4	5	6	11	15	25	
Let It Be						15	3	3	6	10	13
Abbey Road (LP)	*1	*1	2	3	4	6	6	5	7	7	9
(*Come & Get It*–Bf)	4	5	10	15	23	29					
(*Temma Harbour*–MH)	16	7	4	7	8	12	21	27			
(*Knock Knock*–MH)							22		5	3	5
(*Govinda*–RKT)											26
(Best Of Cream (LP)–Cm)	12	14	15	15	22	20	29	26			

	MAY						JUN				JUL
	25	2	9	16	23	30	6	13	20	27	4
Let It Be	20	28									
Abbey Road (LP)	10	9	13	12	17	18		23			
McCartney (LP)–P		10	2	2	2	2	3	3	3	3	4
Sentimental Journey (LP)–R		29	20	20	27	26					
Let It Be (LP)					3	3	*1	*1	*1	*1	*1
(*Knock Knock*–MH)	6	9	17	23							
(*Govinda*–RKT)	27										

	AUG								SEP		
	11	18	25	1	8	15	22	29	5	12	19
McCartney (LP)–P	3	8	6	7	6	9	9	11	12	12	17
Let It Be (LP)	*1	*1	*1	2	2	2	2	3	3	5	4

	OCT						NOV				DEC
	26	3	10	17	24	31	7	14	21	28	5
McCartney (LP)–P	14	16	28								
Let It Be (LP)	5	8	9	9	13	17	19		20	26	18
(*Think About...Children*–MH)								26	20	21	24

1971

	JAN							FEB			
	12	19	26	9	16	23	30	6	13	20	27
My Sweet Lord–G						17	*1	*1	*1	*1	*1
Let It Be (LP)	18	20		22	17	18	21	22			
All Things Must Pass (LP)–G			20	10	5	5	3	*1	*1	*1	*1
Plastic Ono Band (LP)–J	23	15	16	23	15	16	19	8	13	20	20
(*No Matter What*–Bf)						26	19	13	6	6	7

	MAR				APR				MAY			
	6	13	20	27	3	10	17	24	1	8	15	22
My Sweet Lord–G	*1	*1	3	8	10	15	22	28				
Another Day–P	14	4	2	2	2	5	9	14	18	23		
Power To The People–J			28	13	7	6	12	18	19	26		
It Don't Come Easy–R								17	9	5	5	6
All Things Must Pass (LP)–G	*1	*1	*1	*1	2	3	4	10	9	10	17	15
Plastic Ono Band (LP)–J	14	22	23	25								
(*No Matter What*–Bf)	9	18	22									

	JUN				JUL						AUG	
	29	5	12	19	26	3	10	17	24	31	7	14
It Don't Come Easy–R	8	12	21	28								
Bangla Desh–G												29
All Things Must Pass (LP)–G	21	22	30									
Ram (LP)–P		6	6	2	2	2	2	*1	2	*1	2	*1

	SEP						OCT					NOV
	21	28	4	11	18	25	2	9	16	23	30	6
Bangla Desh–G	18	15	13	12	21	23	29					
Ram (LP)–P	3	4	5	4	6	8	8	8	10	14	16	25
Imagine (LP)–J											10	5

1972

	DEC			JAN						FEB		
	13	20	27	4	11	18	25	8	15	22	29	5
Ram (LP)–P	30		29									
Imagine (LP)–J	2	2	2	2	*1	*1	*1	3	4	4	3	4
Wild Life (LP)–P/W					16	18	13	16	15	16	26	
Bangla Desh (LP)–G										26	10	5

	MAR					APR						
	12	19	26	4	11	18	25	1	8	15	22	29
Give Ireland Back–P/W				28	23	18	20	23	30			
Back Off Boogaloo–R								30	16	11	4	3
Imagine (LP)–J	5	6	7	7	5	8	9	11	13	13	12	14
Bangla Desh (LP)–G	4	5	4	6	10	10	17	15	21			
(*Day After Day*–Bf)	25	15	11	9	12	16	21	28				

	MAY				JUN				JUL			
	6	13	20	27	3	10	17	24	1	8	15	22
Back Off Boogaloo–R	3	5	10	22								
Mary Had A Little Lamb–P/W					24	13	9	6	7	9	14	21
Imagine (LP)–J	21	14	17	16	18	24				30		

	AUG				SEP						OCT	
	29	5	12	19	26	2	9	16	23	30	7	14
Mary Had A Little Lamb–P/W	28											
Imagine (LP)–J									19	25		
Sometime In NYC (LP)–J/Y											28	16
(**History Of Clapton** (LP)–Cm)								22	20	20	24	

	NOV						DEC				JAN	
	21	28	4	11	18	25	2	9	16	23	6	13
Happy Xmas–J/Y									16	16	10	15
Hi, Hi, Hi/C Moon–P/W									25	19	17	9
Sometime In NYC (LP)–J/Y	16	14	19	13	24	30						

	FEB						MAR				APR
	20	27	3	10	17	24	3	10	17	24	31	7
Happy Xmas–J/Y	22											
Hi, Hi, Hi/C Moon–P/W	5	5	7	14	21	29						
Imagine (LP)–J	26	26	27	25								

			MAY				JUN				
	14	21	28	5	12	19	26	2	9	16	23	30
My Love–P/W	28	22	15	10	11	10	10	14	26			
Give Me Love–G									22	14	9	8
Live And Let Die–P/W										25	15	10
Beatles, 1967–1970 (LP)				8	8	2	2	2	3	3	3	2
Beatles, 1962–1966 (LP)				9	9	4	3	3	2	*1	2	3
Red Rose Speedway (LP)–P/W						26	9	6	5	6	6	9
Material World (LP)–G												26

	JUL				AUG				SEP			
	7	14	21	28	4	11	18	25	1	8	15	22
Give Me Love–G	7	9	17	23								
Live And Let Die–P/W	8	11	11	17	24	24	27					
Beatles, 1967–1970 (LP)	*1	*1	2	5	5	5	11	9	11	14	12	10
Beatles, 1962–1966 (LP)	3	6	8	8	8	7	13	16	22	22	23	24
Red Rose Speedway (LP)–P/W	10	11	17	19	28	24						
Material World (LP)–G	11	5	5	6	11	11	25		29			

		OCT				NOV				DEC		
	29	6	13	20	27	3	10	17	24	1	8	15
Photograph–R						23	20	13	7	5	7	14
Helen Wheels–P/W							30	27	23	13	13	11
Mind Games–J											29	23
Beatles, 1967–1970 (LP)	12	12	16	25	23	27	21					
Beatles, 1962–1966 (LP)	23		24		30		26	24	26	20	24	
"Ringo" (LP)–R										29	15	6
Mind Games (LP)–J											25	15
(Rainbow Concert (LP)–EC)							20		21			

	JAN				FEB				MAR			
	22	12	19	26	2	9	16	23	2	9	16	23
Photograph–R	25											
Helen Wheels–P/W	18											
Mind Games–J	28											
You're Sixteen–R								24	10	5	3	4
Jet–P/W									21	14	9	7
Beatles, 1967–1970 (LP)		23	15	29	23				30			
Beatles, 1962–1966 (LP)		27	20		19	27	24					
"Ringo" (LP)–R	9	17	25	21	29		20	30	26			
Mind Games (LP)–J	6	14	18	12	18	22						
Band On The Run (LP)–P/W	14	13	12	9	7	9	9	10	8	9	7	8

	APR					MAY				JUN		
	30	6	13	20	27	4	11	18	25	8	15	22
You're Sixteen–R	5	9	15	23								
Jet–P/W	4	11	19	26								
Beatles, 1967–1970 (LP)						29		29	28			
Band On The Run (LP)–P/W	4	2	2	2	3	4	5	4	4	5	7	7
(*Liverpool Lou*–Sf)										25	16	7
(History of Pop (LP)–P/G)	26	19	10	11	12	20	29					

	JUL					AUG				SEP		
	29	6	13	20	27	3	10	17	24	31	7	14
Band On The Run–P/W			17	7	3	2	5	10	12	22	30	
Beatles, 1967–1970 (LP)								24	26			
Beatles, 1962–1966 (LP)	25											
Band On The Run (LP)–P/W	6	7	4	4	2	*1	*1	*1	*1	*1	*1	2
Sgt. Pepper (LP)						28						
(*Liverpool Lou*–Sf)	11	12	16									

	OCT					NOV				DEC		
	21	28	5	12	19	26	2	9	16	23	30	7
Junior's Farm–P/W									27	19	16	19
Only You–R												30
Band On The Run (LP)–P/W	2	3	3	4	4	3	6	4	5	7	14	12
Walls And Bridges (LP)–J					29	16	8	11	9	15	22	
(*Costafine Town*–Sp)									23	18	20	22
(*Lucy In The Sky*–EJ/J)											19	13
(Smiler (LP)–RdS)						6	6	*1	*1	*1	*1	4	5
(Stardust (LP)–BJK)									18	21	26	19	22

1975

	JAN					FEB				MAR		
	14	21	11	18	25	1	8	15	22	1	8	15
Junior's Farm–P/W	28											
Only You–R			26	27								
No. 9 Dream–J									30	27	23	23
Band On The Run (LP)–P/W	16	20	21	22	17			28	23	23	21	24
Beatles, 1962–1966 (LP)				30	29	30						
Rock 'n' Roll (LP)–J											30	12
(*Lucy In The Sky*–EJ/J)	10	3	14	19	24							
(Smiler (LP)–RdS)	8	9	10	10	8	10	20	19				
(Stardust (LP)–BJK)			29	21	12	18	12	15	13	15	20	
(My Own Album (LP)–RW)			27									

	MAR		APR				MAY				JUN	
	22	29	5	12	19	26	3	10	17	24	31	7
No. 9 Dream–J	25											
Listen What Man Said–P/W												23
Rock 'n' Roll (LP)–J	11	10	17	20	28						24	30
(Stardust (LP)–BJK)	22	29										
(Young Americans (LP)–DBw)			15	7	6	*1	5	12	13	19		

(Continued on page 385)

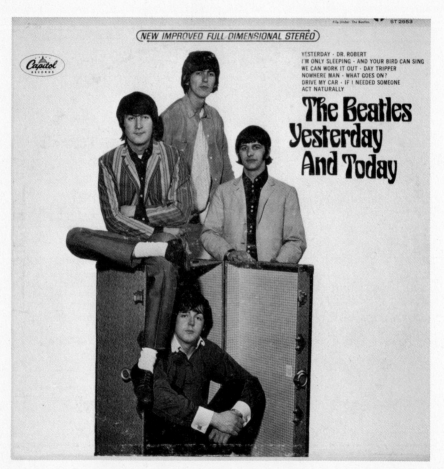

Yesterday And Today   Capitol ST 2553 (LP)

American Top 40

The following are the weekly chart positions of Beatle records in the United States, taken from *Billboard Magazine's* weekly record charts. Singles and albums are listed separately. Additionally, both lists also include the weekly positions of Beatle-related singles and albums which hit the charts.

All records are by the Beatles unless otherwise indicated. The following abbreviations are used to identify the other artists listed:

A/M—Alvin Lee & Mylon LeFevre
Bf—Badfinger
BJK—Billy J. Kramer with
    The Dakotas
BP—Billy Preston
CB—Cilla Black
CH—Chris Hodge
Cm—Cream
DB—David Bromberg
DBw—David Bowie
DP—David Peel
EC—Eric Clapton
EJ—Elton John
EM—Elephant's Memory
ER—Ed Rudy
G—George Harrison
GM—George Martin
HN—Harry Nilsson
Iv—Iveys
J—John Lennon

JL—Jackie Lomax
JT—James Taylor
JW—Johnny Winter
J/Y—John & Yoko
KM—Keith Moon
LS—London Symphony Orch.
MH—Mary Hopkin
P—Paul McCartney
P/G—Peter and Gordon
PL—Peggy Lee
P/W—Paul McCartney & Wings
R—Ringo Starr
RdS—Rod Stewart
RSh—Ravi Shankar
RSp—Ronnie Spector
Sdtk—Soundtrack
Sk—Silkie
Sp—Splinter
T—Trash
Y—Yoko Ono

All chart positions are taken from *Billboard's* Hot 100 Singles Charts and Top LP Charts. Additionally, records listed as "bubbling under" either chart have also been listed.

Meet the Beatles!   **Capitol ST 2047   (LP)**

Something New   **Capitol ST 2108   (LP)**

Billboard
Singles Charts

1963

AUG

	3	10	17
From Me To You	125	116	124

NO RECORDS ON CHARTS: August 24, 1963–January 11, 1964

1964

	JAN		FEB					MAR			APR	
	18	25	1	8	15	22	29	7	14	21	28	4
I Want To Hold Your Hand	45	3	*1	*1	*1	*1	*1	*1	*1	2	2	4
She Loves You		69	21	7	2	2	2	2	2	*1	*1	3
Please Please Me			68	57	45	29	6	4	3	3	4	5
I Saw Her Standing There			117	68	54	35	28	18	15	14	26	31
My Bonnie				107	67	54	42	31	26	42		
From Me To You						120	101	86	73	58	50	41
Twist And Shout									55	7	3	2
Roll Over Beethoven								102	79	75	68	
Can't Buy Me Love										27	*1	
All My Loving										71	58	
Do You...Know A Secret										78	46	
You Can't Do That										115	65	
Thank You Girl											79	

	APR			MAY					JUN			
	11	18	25	2	9	16	23	30	6	13	20	27
I Want To Hold Your Hand	7	19	24									
She Loves You	4	8	19	36								
Please Please Me	9	16	29									
I Saw Her Standing There	38	45										
From Me To You	52											
Twist And Shout	2	2	2	7	11	20	41					
Roll Over Beethoven	78											
Can't Buy Me Love	*1	*1	*1	*1	5	11	23	42				
All My Loving	50	48	45	59								
Do You...Know A Secret	14	5	3	3	2	5	12	19	36			
You Can't Do That	48	55	60									
Thank You Girl	61	49	37	40	35	49						
There's A Place	74		120									
Love Me Do	81	73	67	32	12	3	2	*1	2	4	7	11
Why	131	88										
P. S. I Love You					64	33	15	11	10	15	22	37
Sie Liebt Dich								108	108	102	101	97
Four By The Beatles (EP)									105	97	97	92

	APR 11	18	25	MAY 2	9	16	23	30	JUN 6	13	20	27
(World Without Love–P/G)				105	76	30	10	7	6	2	2	*1
(Bad To Me–BJK)							120	71	61	26	16	9

	JUL 4	11	18	25	AUG 1	8	15	22	29	SEP 5	12	19
Love Me Do	19	24										
A Hard Day's Night			21	2	*1	*1	3	3	4	8	8	12
Ain't She Sweet			90	67	40	25	22	19	24	30	37	
I Should Have Known Better				119	75	66	59	53				
And I Love Her				80	65	40	27	17	13	12	12	28
I'll Cry Instead				115	62	44	34	29	25	34	36	
I'm Happy Just To Dance				113	95	104	102	118	116	112		
If I Fell					92	87	72	57	54	53	59	55
Matchbox										81	42	32
Slow Down										99	67	55

	JUL 4	11	18	25	AUG 1	8	15	22	29	SEP 5	12	19
(World Without Love–P/G)	6	8	22	28								
(Bad To Me–BJK)	9	11	18	24	35							
(I'll Keep You Satisfied–BJK)				85	54	46	35	30	36	51		
(Ringo's Theme–GM)				94		81	65	56	55	55	53	57
(And I Love Her–GM)						105						
(From A Window–BJK)								92	79	64	51	37
(It's For You–CB)									128			84

	SEP 26	OCT 3	10	17	24	31	NOV 7	14	21	28	DEC 5	12
A Hard Day's Night	19	24	50									
If I Fell	59											
Matchbox	23	18	18	17	52							
Slow Down	32	27	25	39								
I Feel Fine											22	5
She's A Woman											46	29

	SEP 26	OCT 3	10	17	24	31	NOV 7	14	21	28	DEC 5	12
(From A Window–BJK)	30	23	23	27	50							
(It's For You–CB)	82	79	115	120								
(I Don't Want To See You–P/G)		84	61	48	27	20	16	24	26	33		
(I Should Have Known...–GM)		114	111									
(Hard Day's Night–GM)		122										

1965

	DEC 19	26	JAN 2	9	16	23	30	FEB 6	13	20	MAR 27	6
I Feel Fine	2	*1	*1	*1	2	4	11	22	40			
She's A Woman	14	4	4	11	12	14	37					
Eight Days A Week										53	19	5
I Don't Want To Spoil The Party										81	59	47
4 By The Beatles (EP)											81	77

	MAR 13	20	27	APR 3	10	17	24	MAY 1	8	15	22	29
Eight Days A Week	*1	*1	4	7	11	17	38					
I Don't Want To Spoil The Party	44	39	44									
4 By The Beatles (EP)	73	70	68									
Ticket To Ride							59	18	3	3	*1	2
Yes It Is								115	71	57	46	54

	JUN				JUL
	5	12	19	26	3
Ticket To Ride	5	9	11	20	47

NO RECORDS ON CHARTS: July 10, 1965–July 24, 1965

	JUL	AUG				SEP				OCT		
	31	7	14	21	28	4	11	18	25	2	9	16
Help!	110	41	14	3	2	*1	*1	*1	5	11	15	22
I'm Down		118	105	105	102	102	101	114				
Yesterday								106	45	3	*1	*1
Act Naturally								109	87	72	51	49
(Hide Your Love Away—Sk)											104	81

1966

	OCT		NOV				DEC				JAN	
	23	30	6	13	20	27	4	11	18	25	1	8
Help!	29	32										
Yesterday	*1	*1	3	11	13	26	45					
Act Naturally	47	47	54									
Boys		102										
We Can Work It Out							101	36	11	2	*1	
Day Tripper							103	56	28	18	10	
(Hide Your Love Away—Sk)	61	51	39	20	12	10	14	27	31			

	JAN			FEB				MAR			APR
	15	22	29	5	12	19	26	5	12	19	26	2
We Can Work It Out	*1	2	*1	4	5	13	24	48			
Day Tripper	6	5	13	22	36	47					
Nowhere Man								25	7	4	3	6
What Goes On								118	89	81		
(Woman—P/G)				83	61	55	43	26	20	15	14	

	APR			
	9	16	23	30
Nowhere Man	6	11	13	28
(Woman—P/G)	19	18	23	24

NO RECORDS ON CHARTS: May 7, 1966–June 4, 1966

	JUN			JUL					AUG			
	11	18	25	2	9	16	23	30	6	13	20	27
Paperback Writer	28	15	*1	2	*1	5	6	12	18	37		
Rain	72	42	29	24	23	23	34					
Yellow Submarine											52	8
Eleanor Rigby											101	65

	SEP				OCT		
	3	10	17	24	1	8	15
Yellow Submarine	5	3	2	4	8	16	32
Eleanor Rigby	47	26	14	11	11	21	37

NO RECORDS ON CHARTS: October 22, 1966–February 11, 1967

1967

	FEB		MAR				APR				
	18	25	4	11	18	25	1	8	15	22	29
Penny Lane	116	83	36	5	*1	3	3	6	12	21	25
Strawberry Fields Forever	118	85	45	16	11	11	8	15	21	28	

NO RECORDS ON CHARTS: **May 6, 1967–July 15, 1967**

	JUL		AUG				SEP				
	22	29	5	12	19	26	2	9	16	23	30
All You Need Is Love	71	29	3	2	*1	2	2	6	8	24	48
Baby You're A Rich Man	115	64	41	34	38	41					

NO RECORDS ON CHARTS: **October 7, 1967–November 25, 1967**

1968

	DEC					JAN				FEB	
	2	9	16	23	30	6	13	20	27	3	10
Hello Goodbye	45	8	3	3	*1	*1	*1	3	6	12	31
I Am The Walrus	102	64	57	56	75						

NO RECORDS ON CHARTS: **February 17, 1968–March 16, 1968**

	MAR		APR				MAY				JUN
	23	30	6	13	20	27	4	11	18	25	1
Lady Madonna	23	9	7	6	4	4	4	10	15	31	44
The Inner Light	117	96	107								

NO RECORDS ON CHARTS: **June 8, 1968–September 7, 1968**

	SEP		OCT				NOV					
	14	21	28	5	12	19	26	2	9	15	23	30
Hey Jude	10	3	*1	*1	*1	*1	*1	*1	*1	*1	*1	2
Revolution	38	12	12	12	15	17	17	19	19	20	29	
(Those Were The Days–MH)		132	70	54	18	13	4	2	2	2	3	4
(Sour Milk Sea–JL)			117	117								
(Eagle Laughs At You–JL)							125	125	125			

1969

	DEC				JAN		
	7	14	21	28	4	11	18
Hey Jude	2	6	11	15	23	30	38

NO RECORDS ON CHARTS: **January 25, 1969–February 8, 1969**

	FEB		MAR			
	15	22	1	8	15	22
(Maybe Tomorrow–Iv)	89	75	73	68	67	69

NO RECORDS ON CHARTS: **March 29, 1969**

	APR				MAY					JUN		
	5	12	19	26	3	10	17	24	31	7	14	21
Get Back						10	3	*1	*1	*1	*1	*1
Don't Let Me Down						40	36	35	42			
Ballad Of John And Yoko											71	24
(*Badge*–Cm)	87	76	68	68	60							
(*Goodbye*–MH)			86	64	27	24	14	14	13	16	17	
(*Carolina In My Mind*–JT)			118									

	JUN	JUL				AUG					SEP	
	28	5	12	19	26	2	9	16	23	30	6	13
Get Back	3	6	12	16	27							
Ballad Of John And Yoko	11	11	8	8	8	10	29					
Give Peace A Chance–J					62	43	23	20	15	15	14	29
(*God Planned It*–BP)					103	84	76	71	62	65	65	

	SEP
	20
Give Peace A Chance–J	34

NO RECORDS ON CHARTS: **September 27, 1969–October 11, 1969**

1970

	OCT		NOV					DEC				JAN
	18	25	1	8	15	22	29	6	13	20	27	3
Something	20	11	11	9	3	3						
Come Together	23	13	10	3	2	7						
Something/Come Together							*1	3	4	6	7	12
Cold Turkey–J					86	74	47	44	39	35	33	33
(*Golden Slumbers/Weight*–T)					112							

	JAN				FEB				MAR			
	10	17	24	31	7	14	21	28	7	14	21	28
Something/Come Together	16	20	22	29								
Cold Turkey–J	33	30	32	46								
Instant Karma–J								85	33	15	4	3
Let It Be											6	2
(*Come And Get It*–Bf)					92	89	54	41	38	32	23	10
(*Temma Harbour*–MH)						112	97	79	52	52	51	39
(*All That I've Got*–BP)											108	110

	APR				MAY					JUN		
	4	11	18	25	2	9	16	23	30	6	13	20
Instant Karma–J	3	3	4	4	5	8	18	27				
Let It Be	2	*1	*1	2	2	3	4	6	10	21	23	44
Long & Winding/For You Blue								35	12	10	*1	*1
(*Come And Get It*–Bf)	9	8	7	7	8	18	29					
(*Temma Harbour*–MH)	39	41										

	JUN	JUL				AUG
	27	4	11	18	25	1
Long & Winding/For You Blue	4	4	8	20	21	
(Que Sera Sera—MH)		118	98	95	86	77

NO RECORDS ON CHARTS: August 8, 1970–October 17, 1970

1971

	OCT		NOV				DEC				JAN	
	24	31	7	14	21	28	5	12	19	26	2	9
Beaucoups Of Blues—R	126	121	100	96	94	87	87					
My Sweet Lord/Isn't A Pity—G						72	13	6	2	*1	*1	*1
Mother—J												87
(No Matter What—Bf)	101	79	57	42	36	24	8	8	10	10	13	21
(Carolina In My Mind—JT)				99	89	80	77	70	70	67		
(Think About Children—MH)				99	99	97	87					

	JAN			FEB				MAR				APR
	16	23	30	6	13	20	27	6	13	20	27	3
My Sweet Lord/Isn't A Pity—G	*1	2	2	3	6	16	36					
Mother—J	60	45	43	43	55							
What Is Life—G								66	27	19	15	10	14
Another Day/Oh Woman—P								55	36	20	14	10
Power To The People—J												73
(No Matter What—Bf)	30											
(My Sweet Lord—BP)		116	120	116	94	94	90	110				

	APR			MAY				JUN				
	10	17	24	1	8	15	22	29	5	12	19	26
What Is Life—G	14	18	33									
Another Day/Oh Woman—P	8	5	5	8	14	20	39					
Power To The People—J	40	28	15	11	11	15	31	37				
It Don't Come Easy—R				49	24	13	8	5	4	4	5	7
(Try Some Buy Some—RSp)					87	79	77	77				

	JUL		
	3	10	17
It Don't Come Easy—R	10	12	28

NO RECORDS ON CHARTS: July 24, 1971–August 7, 1971

	AUG			SEP				OCT				
	14	21	28	4	11	18	25	2	9	16	23	30
Uncle Albert/Adm. Halsey—P	65	21	12	*1	5	5	6	6	7	7	13	18
Bangla Desh/Deep Blue—G	67	43	31	24	23	23	31					
Imagine—J											20	6

1972

	NOV				DEC				JAN			
	6	13	20	27	4	11	18	25	1	8	15	22
Uncle Albert/Adm. Halsey—P	26											
Imagine—J	4	3	3	6	10	13	23					
(Day After Day—Bf)					74	51	39	26	17	16	14	5

352

	JAN	FEB				MAR				APR		
	29	5	12	19	26	4	11	18	25	1	8	15
Give Ireland Back—P/W							78	63	37	22	21	30
Back Off Boogaloo—R										88	42	31
(Day After Day—Bf)	5	4	10	12	17	26						
(Baby Blue—Bf)										78	42	26	19

	APR		MAY				JUN			JUL		
	22	29	6	13	20	27	3	10	17	24	1	8
Give Ireland Back—P/W	30	35										
Back Off Boogaloo—R	19	11	10	9	9	23	47					
Woman Is The Nigger—J					76	65	61	57	71			
Mary Had A Little Lamb—P/W										85	58	43	38
(Baby Blue—Bf)	15	14	14	22	31	69						
(We're On Our Way—CH)						105	90	69	56	51	47	44
(The Way God Planned It—BP)												98

	JUL			AUG				SEP	
	15	22	29	5	12	19	26	2	9
Mary Had A Little Lamb—P/W	29	28	35						
(The Way God Planned It—BP)	96	96	95	78	69	68	65	65	67

NO RECORDS ON CHARTS: September 16, 1972—November 18, 1972

1973

	NOV	DEC					JAN				FEB	
	25	2	9	16	23	30	6	13	20	27	3	10
Hi Hi Hi—P/W				100	42	27	22	18	12	11	10	17
(Knock Knock—MH)	110	105	97	94	92	92						

	FEB	
	17	24
Hi Hi Hi—P/W	24	38

NO RECORDS ON CHARTS: March 3, 1973—April 7, 1973

	APR			MAY				JUN				
	14	21	28	5	12	19	26	2	9	16	23	30
My Love—P/W	73	62	36	26	13	6	2	*1	*1	*1	*1	2
Give Me Love—G						59	34	14	13	8	5	*1

	JUL				AUG				SEP			
	7	14	21	28	4	11	18	25	1	8	15	22
My Love—P/W	3	9	21	31	40	59						
Give Me Love—G	4	5	6	10	31	45	57					
Live And Let Die—P/W	69	44	29	21	3	2	2	2	5	7	9	17

	SEP	OCT				NOV				DEC		
	29	6	13	20	27	3	10	17	24	1	8	15
Live And Let Die–P/W	27	36										
Photograph–R		74	60	29	18	11	6	4	*1	2	5	8
Mind Games–J							76	60	41	30	24	20
Helen Wheels–P/W									66	42	31	24
You're Sixteen–R												75

1974

	DEC		JAN				FEB				MAR	
	22	29	5	12	19	26	2	9	16	23	2	9
Photograph–R	13	28	32	45	74							
Mind Games–J	19	18	25	29	34	44	60					
Helen Wheels–P/W	20	16	12	10	12	17	20	37	58			
You're Sixteen–R	50	27	16	6	5	*1	2	3	3	9	11	20
Jet–P/W								69	47	27	20	14
Oh My My–R												65
(Apple Of My Eye–Bf)								105	102	103	105	

	MAR			APR				MAY				JUN
	16	23	30	6	13	20	27	4	11	18	25	1
You're Sixteen–R	34	47										
Jet–P/W	10	8	7	11	14	27	38	47	48			
Oh My My–R	44	28	19	12	9	6	5	13	17	26	31	38
Band On The Run–P/W						68	41	22	14	7	5	2

	JUN				JUL				AUG		
	8	15	22	29	6	13	20	27	3	10	17
Oh My My–R	52										
Band On The Run–P/W	*1	5	6	8	17	15	26	40	60	70	95

NO RECORDS ON CHARTS: August 24, 1974–September 21, 1974

	SEP	OCT				NOV					DEC	
	28	5	12	19	26	2	9	16	23	30	7	14
Whatever Gets Thru Night–J	53	33	24	18	12	6	3	*1	12	21	40	40
Junior's Farm/Sally G–P/W							59	43	28	15	12	10
Only You–R								63	53	34	25	18
Dark Horse–G									69	53	43	32
(Mine For Me–RdS)								104	104	102	93	
(Lucy In The Sky–EJ/J)										48	36	9
(Costafine Town–Sp)											110	96

1975

	DEC		JAN				FEB				MAR	
	21	28	4	11	18	25	1	8	15	22	1	8
Whatever Gets Thru Night—J	56	64	79									
Junior's Farm/Sally G—P/W	8	6	4	3	7	17						
Sally G/Junior's Farm—P/W							66	50	45	39	64	
Only You—R	14	9	7	6	12	27	35	56				
Dark Horse—G	24	20	16	15	33	49						
No. 9 Dream—J	68	58	47	35	29	21	17	13	10	9	13	47
Ding Dong; Ding Dong—G				81	59	46	38	36	49			
No No Song/Snookeroo—R								78	58	40	31	25
(Mine For Me—RdS)	91											
(Lucy In The Sky—EJ/J)	6	2	*1	*1	5	11	20	32	41	52	71	
(Costafine Town—Sp)	93	87	85	83	82	77	100					

	MAR			APR				MAY				
	15	22	29	5	12	19	26	3	10	17	24	31
No No Song/Snookeroo—R	14	9	6	3	3	4	24	51	67			
Stand By Me—J	78	67	52	36	30	24	20	20	49			
Listen What The Man Said—P/W												65

	JUN			JUL				AUG			
	7	14	21	28	5	12	19	26	2	9	16	23
Listen What The Man Said—P/W	35	22	9	7	3	3	*1	5	8	12	17	44
Goodnight Vienna/Oo-Wee—R		82	63	52	39	31	31	63				
(Fame—DBw)				90	78	67	55	45	39	35	30	24

	AUG	SEP				OCT				NOV		
	30	6	13	20	27	4	11	18	25	1	8	15
Listen What The Man Said—P/W	57											
You—G				75	49	41	33	25	23	20	20	39
Letting Go—P/W						74	54	42	39	39	64	
Venus And Mars Rock Show—P/W										82	60	36
(Fame—DBw)	11	7	5	*1	2	*1	3	12	29	31	41	97

	NOV		DEC			
	22	29	6	13	20	27
You—G	91					
Venus And Mars Rock Show—P/W	27	17	14	12	36	97

355

Revolver

Capitol ST 2576 (LP)

Billboard
Album Charts

1964

	FEB					MAR				APR		
	1	8	15	22	29	7	14	21	28	4	11	18
Meet The Beatles	92	3	*1	*1	*1	*1	*1	*1	*1	*1	*1	*1
Introducing The Beatles		59	22	3	2	2	2	2	2	2	2	2
The Beatles And Guests			147	147	142	128	121	103	87	77	70	68
Jolly What!										135	112	104

	APR	MAY					JUN				JUL	
	25	2	9	16	23	30	6	13	20	27	4	11
Meet The Beatles	*1	2	2	3	5	5	6	7	9	9	14	14
Introducing The Beatles	2	4	7	7	8	10	11	12	14	17	17	20
The Beatles And Guests	68	83	106	146								
Jolly What!	105	113	119									
Beatles' Second Album	16	*1	*1	*1	*1	*1	4	4	4	4	4	5
(Beatles' American Tour—ER)							96	61	38	31	29	29
(Little Children—BJK)									149	124	99	91
(World Without Love—P/G)										114	87	48

	JUL		AUG					SEP				OCT
	18	25	1	8	15	22	29	5	12	19	26	3
Meet The Beatles	18	25	31	32	43	46	48	49	56	54	46	44
Introducing The Beatles	26	31	33	37	48	56	61	73	72	75	70	67
Beatles' Second Album	7	9	9	9	11	17	20	25	26	35	30	29
A Hard Day's Night	12	*1	*1	*1	*1	*1	*1	*1	*1	*1	*1	*1
Something New				125	6	2	2	2	2	2	2	2
(Beatles' American Tour—ER)	24	20	20	25	29	45	85					
(Little Children—BJK)	68	59	57	57	53	49	49	48	53	87	122	
(World Without Love—P/G)	23	22	21	26	26	40	55	69	127	135	134	142
(Off The Beatle Track—GM)								130	121	111	111	118

	OCT				NOV				DEC			
	10	17	24	31	7	14	21	28	5	12	19	26
Meet The Beatles	52	53	57	57	56	55	60	64	65	62	69	72
Introducing The Beatles	78	82	93	96	97	99	104	107	111	112	142	142
Beatles' Second Album	37	39	42	48	61	63	69	73	75	71	70	65
A Hard Day's Night	*1	*1	*1	3	3	3	3	4	4	8	10	7
Something New	2	2	4	4	4	5	6	6	7	10	14	14
Beatles vs. Four Seasons	147	142	145									
Songs Pictures and Stories				121	115	87	76	71	63	66	97	109
Beatles' Story										97	20	8
(Off The Beatle Track—GM)	114	118	125	125	125							

1965

	JAN					FEB				MAR		
	2	9	16	23	30	6	13	20	27	6	13	20
Meet The Beatles	73	69	65	57	56	52	51	49	50	66	67	71
Introducing The Beatles	141	146										
Beatles' Second Album	70	70	72	69	64	62	62	63	69	72	80	85
A Hard Day's Night	6	6	5	5	6	11	11	13	14	18	21	21
Something New	14	13	17	21	23	27	27	31	41	44	44	47
Songs Pictures and Stories	117	138										
Beatles' Story	7	7	7	7	16	16	29	46	62	86	86	94
Beatles '65	98	*1	*1	*1	*1	*1	*1	*1	*1	*1	3	3
(I Don't Want To See...–P/G)	133	106	100	98	95	99	98	107	108	110	116	

	MAR	APR				MAY					JUN	
	27	3	10	17	24	1	8	15	22	29	5	12
Meet The Beatles	81	83	100	104	109	118	120	116	114	114	121	
Beatles' Second Album	89	91	94	96	100	105	112					
A Hard Day's Night	23	28	37	40	44	51	49	48	48	50	64	74
Something New	49	54	61	74	87	90	117	121				
Beatles' Story	102	108										
Beatles '65	3	3	3	7	9	12	13	12	13	17	21	22
The Early Beatles					132	110	91	76	58	54	46	43

	JUN		JUL					AUG			SEP
	19	26	3	10	17	24	31	7	14	21	28	4
A Hard Day's Night	100	124	134									
Beatles '65	30	33	29	25	23	28	28	33	35	38	38	39
The Early Beatles	45	56	55	53	58	69	83	90	109	113	124	130
Beatles VI		149	48	*1	*1	*1	*1	*1	*1	2	2	4
Help!											148	61

	SEP			OCT					NOV			
	11	18	25	2	9	16	23	30	6	13	20	27
Beatles '65	37	36	39	43	48	51	56	59	61	76	86	87
The Early Beatles	130	136	142	145	147	148	144	137	134	121	121	118
Beatles VI	8	9	10	10	18	19	21	21	19	25	26	32
Help!	*1	*1	*1	*1	*1	*1	*1	*1	*1	2	3	4

1966

	DEC				JAN					FEB		
	4	11	18	25	1	8	15	22	29	5	12	19
Beatles '65	107	110	110	113	98	96	145	147	147	143	136	131
The Early Beatles	125	128										
Beatles VI	51	48	52	54	57	66	70	72	74	79	84	80
Help!	4	7	9	11	15	17	18	16	11	14	17	22
Rubber Soul				106	60	*1	*1	*1	*1	*1	*1	2

	FEB	MAR				APR					MAY	
	26	5	12	19	26	2	9	16	23	30	7	14
Beatles '65	121	101	104	104	106	110	113	113	110	133	146	
Beatles VI	78	75	70	84	86	123						
Help!	26	28	30	31	28	27	28	29	31	42	45	57
Rubber Soul	2	3	4	4	5	7	7	12	14	18	19	16
(Woman–P/G)								133	115	104	100	90

	MAY		JUN				JUL				AUG	
	21	28	4	11	18	25	2	9	16	23	30	6
Help!	78	80	91	93	95	128						
Rubber Soul	18	18	18	17	16	17	24	24	27	31	34	36
Yesterday And Today								120	18	2	*1	*1
(Woman–P/G)	85	74	62	60	63	72	78	82	141			
(Best Of–P/G)											130	115

	AUG			SEP				OCT				
	13	20	27	3	10	17	24	1	8	15	22	29
Rubber Soul	36	31	29	31	31	33	36	35	58	82	88	95
Yesterday And Today	*1	*1	*1	2	7	8	15	19	30	39	39	42
Revolver				45	*1	*1	*1	*1	*1	*1	2	2
(Best Of–P/G)	100	83	81	76	72	79	81	109	112	113		

1967

	NOV				DEC					JAN		
	5	12	19	26	3	10	17	24	31	7	14	21
Rubber Soul	105	106	101	110	113	119						
Yesterday And Today	48	45	49	51	56	63	72	108	118	130	132	134
Revolver	5	8	7	8	6	9	13	13	12	17	18	20

	JAN	FEB				MAR				APR		
	28	4	11	18	25	4	11	18	25	1	8	15
Yesterday And Today	138	136										
Revolver	23	24	27	29	48	51	52	72	78	77	69	65

	APR		MAY				JUN				JUL	
	22	29	6	13	20	27	3	10	17	24	1	8
Revolver	60	60	65	90	135	135	130	128	123	123	135	138
Sgt. Pepper										8	*1	*1

	JUL			AUG				SEP				
	15	22	29	5	12	19	26	2	9	16	23	30
Revolver	138	159	160	157	156	155	153	146	143	134	137	136
Sgt. Pepper	*1	*1	*1	*1	*1	*1	*1	*1	*1	*1	*1	*1

	OCT				NOV				DEC			
	7	14	21	28	4	11	18	25	2	9	16	23
Revolver	136	131	128	123	121	122	135	136	142	143	146	151
Sgt. Pepper	*1	2	3	2	2	2	2	2	4	4	3	3
Magical Mystery Tour												157

1968

	DEC	JAN				FEB				MAR		
	30	6	13	20	27	3	10	17	24	2	9	16
Revolver	153	153	152	154	157	161	163	159				
Sgt. Pepper	3	5	5	6	6	6	13	12	17	17	16	16
Magical Mystery Tour	4	*1	*1	*1	*1	*1	*1	*1	*1	3	4	4

	MAR		APR				MAY				JUN	
	23	30	6	13	20	27	4	11	18	25	1	8
Sgt. Pepper	14	14	28	29	35	33	42	51	52	47	45	43
Magical Mystery Tour	6	6	15	15	20	21	19	19	17	15	25	25

	JUN			JUL				AUG				
	15	22	29	6	13	20	27	3	10	17	24	31
Sgt. Pepper	38	34	33	31	29	27	33	34	37	37	39	45
Magical Mystery Tour	30	32	32	33	34	36	75	79	82	80	92	95

	SEP			OCT				NOV				
	7	14	21	28	5	12	19	26	2	9	16	23
Sgt. Pepper	52	47	46	42	41	55	64	51	59	59	70	71
Magical Mystery Tour	95	93	92	82	71	91	92	100	100	101	101	99

1969

	NOV	DEC				JAN				FEB		
	30	7	14	21	28	4	11	18	25	1	8	15
Sgt. Pepper	73	74	71	62	63	66	56	65	65	87	113	131
Magical Mystery Tour	98	91	91	85	85	71	75	109	112	132		
The Beatles			11	2	*1	*1	*1	*1	*1	*1	2	*1
Wonderwall Music—G							197	189	149	72	58	56
Yellow Submarine											86	6
Two Virgins—J/Y											158	149
(Goodbye—Cm)												107

	FEB	MAR					APR				MAY	
	22	1	8	15	22	29	5	12	19	26	3	10
Sgt. Pepper	166											
The Beatles	*1	*1	2	3	3	5	17	17	18	18	18	22
Wonderwall Music—G	51	49	49	62	65	70	72	86	104	158		
Yellow Submarine	3	2	4	6	7	12	22	19	19	24	34	48
Two Virgins—J/Y	147	147	126	126	124	125						
(Goodbye—Cm)	20	9	3	2	2	3	4	10	10	14	17	24
(Post Card—MH)						104	48	29	28	28	33	33

	MAY			JUN				JUL			AUG	
	17	24	31	7	14	21	28	5	12	19	26	2
The Beatles	24	34	39	52	49	45	58	58	57	65	72	72
Yellow Submarine	46	54	54	77	75	78	83	107	112	122		
Life With The Lions—J/Y								197	194	190	179	184	174
Electronic Music—G								192	191			
(Goodbye—Cm)	26	28	44	54	54	53	63	65	66	78	80	98
(Post Card—MH)	36	36	45	55	58	57	77	103	105	111	122	161
(Is This What You Want—JL)							178	151	147	147	145	142	187
(Best Of—Cm)										60	25	7

	AUG			SEP				OCT			
	9	16	23	30	6	13	20	27	4	11	18	25
The Beatles	70	66	66	67	67	69	80	89	97	93	90	96
Life With The Lions—J/Y	174	179										
Abbey Road											178	4
(Goodbye—Cm)	111											
(Post Card—MH)	166											
(Is This What You Want—JL)	187	183										
(Best Of—Cm)	7	6	4	4	4	3	7	6	6	7	9	9

1970

	NOV					DEC				JAN		
	1	8	15	22	29	6	13	20	27	3	10	17
The Beatles	102	95	101	97	96	86	87	84	79	85	101	117
Abbey Road	*1	*1	*1	*1	*1	*1	*1	*1	2	*1	*1	2
Sgt. Pepper			124	118	111	110	110	107	104	101	115	120
Magical Mystery Tour			146	134	129	129	127	120	113	109	123	127
Wedding Album–J/Y							182	180	178			
Live Peace In Toronto–J/Y											136	71
(Best Of–Cm)	20	16	16	21	26	42	40	46	45	48	55	55

	JAN		FEB				MAR				APR	
	24	31	7	14	21	28	7	14	21	28	4	11
The Beatles	133	133	151	177	178	169	172					
Abbey Road	*1	2	2	2	2	2	3	3	6	7	7	7
Sgt. Pepper	118	117	115	129	129	133	160	148	150	165	166	
Magical Mystery Tour	127	127	126	124	124	190	187					
Live Peace In Toronto–J/Y	17	14	10	10	16	20	22	18	18	17	24	24
Hey Jude									3	2	2	2
(Best Of–Cm)	60	63	66	78	81	96	135	136	154	161	163	161
(Magic Christian–Sdtk)									185	145	136	115
(Magic Christian Music–Bf)									89	73	68	

	APR		MAY					JUN				JUL
	18	25	2	9	16	23	30	6	13	20	27	4
Abbey Road	8	9	15	20	29	30	34	51	50	50	53	53
Live Peace In Toronto–J/Y	29	41	42	54	87	90	90	89	92	99	119	174
Hey Jude	2	3	3	3	4	6	7	35	32	25	24	32
McCartney–P				14	3	*1	*1	*1	2	2	2	2
Sentimental Journey–R					51	26	25	28	28	22	34	58
In The Beginning					145	142	142	154	117	117	149	
Let It Be							104	2	*1	*1	*1	*1
(Best Of–Cm)	161	159	167	178	178							
(Magic Christian–Sdtk)	106	110	108	132	131	156	156	185				
(Magic Christian Music–Bf)	56	55	70	70	68	81	80	80	88	106	120	165

	JUL			AUG					SEP			
	11	18	25	1	8	15	22	29	5	12	19	26
Abbey Road	49	54	52	52	55	68	71	76	80	93	108	105
Live Peace In Toronto–J/Y	174	171	167	168	175	179						
Hey Jude	38	53	57	77	76	78	78	75	90	110	112	107
McCartney–P	3	3	3	5	5	12	13	16	19	18	25	48
Sentimental Journey–R	89	120	128	130	142	144						
Let It Be	2	2	2	6	4	11	11	12	14	26	24	33
Sgt. Pepper			159	160	163	161						
Magical Mystery Tour			194	192								
(Magic Christian Music–Bf)	172	187										

	OCT					NOV				DEC		
	3	10	17	24	31	7	14	21	28	5	12	19
Abbey Road	122	123	122	119	134	126	123	127	131	131	138	140
Hey Jude	143	147	144	151	160							
McCartney—P	48	68	61	68	70	83	88	88	99	103	110	111
Let It Be	37	40	40	50	46	57	56	82	79	75	74	86
Beaucoups Of Blues—R		141	92	75	73	71	65	76	84	99	99	
All Things Must Pass—G												5
(James Taylor—JT)	127	121	167	93	85	80	74	66	62	73	66	79
(No Dice—Bf)									74	37	34	28

1971

	DEC	JAN					FEB				MAR	
	26	2	9	16	23	30	6	13	20	27	6	13
Abbey Road	136	136	137	131	124	122	122	126	136	138	142	142
McCartney—P	105	101	100	100	101	105	104	112	121	131	123	119
Let It Be	83	90	94	99	93	93	94	98	115	111	107	112
Beaucoups Of Blues—R	112	164	182	184	189							
All Things Must Pass—G	2	*1	*1	*1	*1	*1	*1	*1	3	6	7	11
John Lennon—J	14	12	9	9	8	6	12	12	12	29	32	36
(James Taylor—JT)	84	88	85	81	81	89	93	101	105	122	120	126
(No Dice—Bf)	28	34	45	52	50	60	60	78	99	105	146	
(Yoko Ono—Y)							199	182	185			

	MAR		APR				MAY					JUN
	20	27	3	10	17	24	1	8	15	22	29	5
Abbey Road	152	151	166	174	169	175	174	171	176			
McCartney—P	120	124										
Let It Be	117	122	124	132	142	168	170	160	166	162	160	155
All Things Must Pass—G	9	9	13	15	19	24	37	40	38	45	56	53
John Lennon—J	44	42	60	63	93	88	106	109	112	131		
Ram—P												6
(James Taylor—JT)	142	139	189	176								

	JUN		JUL						AUG			
	12	19	26	3	10	17	24	31	7	14	21	28
Let It Be	164											
All Things Must Pass—G	73	87	119	132	130	152	152	165	160	160	154	180
Ram—P	4	3	3	4	4	5	5	4	3	4	2	2

	SEP				OCT					NOV		
	4	11	18	25	2	9	16	23	30	6	13	20
All Things Must Pass—G	176											
Ram—P	3	5	5	4	5	6	7	9	9	9	9	19
Imagine—J		163	134	10	3	2	2	*1	4	4	4	
John Lennon—J												162
(Fly—Y)										202	199	199

1972

	NOV 27	DEC 4	11	18	25	JAN 1	8	15	22	29	FEB 5	12
Ram–P	19	22	28	52	56	69	89	84	93	104	128	144
Imagine–J	4	6	7	9	18	22	29	35	39	48	54	61
John Lennon–J	114	114	149	163								
Wild Life–P/W					25	13	11	11	10	10	19	22
Concert For Bangla Desh–G						14	4	2	2	2	2	2
(Earth Song/Ocean Song–MH)		207	205	204								
(Straight Up–Bf)					138	65	60	59	51	49	47	44

	FEB 19	26	MAR 4	11	18	25	APR 1	8	15	22	MAY 29	6
Imagine–J	73	86	84	92	89	101	128	175				
Wild Life–P/W	25	34	51	51	53	59	58	81	101	148		
Concert For Bangla Desh–G	2	3	2	3	9	11	11	18	20	20	19	19
(Straight Up–Bf)	34	32	31	50	51	51	51	50	57	57	54	55
(David Bromberg–DB)							194	194	216	204		
(History Of Eric Clapton–Cm)									168	39	32	23

	MAY 13	20	JUN 27	3	10	17	24	JUL 1	8	15	22	29
Concert For Bangla Desh–G	17	24	21	25	33	42	43	45	58	57	70	84
Sometime In New York–J/Y								190	90	65	58	50
(Straight Up–Bf)	66	65	62	74	85	89	89	105	120	153	158	170
(History Of Eric Clapton–Cm)	15	14	14	10	8	7	7	6	6	12	17	20
(Pope Smokes Dope–DP)			208	192	191	191						
(The Way God Planned It–BP)					147	140	138	133	133	128	127	127

	AUG 5	12	19	26	SEP 2	9	16	23	30	OCT 7	14	21
Concert For Bangla Desh–G	101	106	107	107	112	112	113	123	141	150	171	
Sometime In New York–J/Y	49	48	48	56	61	88	88	91	103	117	132	142
(History Of Eric Clapton–Cm)	24	31	31	32	30	32	32	46	52	52	54	67
(The Way God Planned It–BP)	135	141	161	181								
(Heavy Cream–Cm)											211	

1973

	OCT 28	NOV 4	11	18	25	DEC 2	9	16	23	30	JAN 6	13
(History Of Eric Clapton–Cm)	67	75	104	106	103	103	107	128	149	160	163	166
(Heavy Cream–Cm)	162	156	145	141	136	136	135	148	165	193		
(Elephant's Memory–EM)	213	208	205									
(Those Were The Days–MH)						205	202	202	201	201		
(Tommy–LS/R)							136	73	32	21	13	10

	JAN 20	27	FEB 3	10	17	24	MAR 3	10	17	24	31	APR 7
(History Of Eric Clapton–Cm)	172	174										
(Tommy–LS/R)	7	5	5	5	6	11	21	27	34	49	57	69
(Approx. Infinite Univ.–Y)						209	198	194	194	193	217	

	APR			MAY				JUN				
	14	21	28	5	12	19	26	2	9	16	23	30
The Beatles 1962–1966	94	23	9	6	4	3	3	5	5	5	11	13
The Beatles 1967–1970	97	24	10	7	5	2	*1	3	2	2	5	6
Red Rose Speedway–P/W					127	32	13	*1	*1	*1	2	2
Living In The Material World–G										11	*1	*1
(Tommy–LS/R)	78	80	108	146	153	170						

	JULY				AUG				SEP			
	7	14	21	28	4	11	18	25	1	8	15	22
The Beatles 1962–1966	17	17	20	21	24	29	39	49	47	49	52	57
The Beatles 1967–1970	8	11	14	17	21	24	26	35	35	39	42	54
Red Rose Speedway–P/W	3	5	5	10	19	21	22	31	32	48	48	63
Living In The Material World–G	*1	*1	*1	3	4	14	17	21	31	36	38	39
(Live & Let Die–Sdtk/P/W)				93	62	27	21	18	17	21	31	33
(Rainbow Concert–EC)												115

	SEP	OCT			NOV					DEC		
	29	6	13	20	27	3	10	17	24	1	8	15
The Beatles 1962–1966	60	64	68	72	84	86	88	111	111	110	124	123
The Beatles 1967–1970	57	61	62	68	75	82	87	86	88	88	89	89
Red Rose Speedway–P/W	66	84	85	94	98	112	140	167	163	191	188	
Living In The Material World–G	38	69	72	73	94	100	134	136	143	149	184	
"Ringo"–R									15	3	2	2	4
Mind Games–J									16	11	9	9
(Live & Let Die–Sdtk/P/W)	48	79	83	111	150	178						
(Rainbow Concert–EC)	43	26	26	18	18	24	32	48	70	111	142	158
(Ass–Bf)												180

1974

	DEC	JAN					FEB				MAR	
	22	29	5	12	19	26	2	9	16	23	2	9
The Beatles 1962–1966	120	115	113	109	108	119	122	124	126	129	129	134
The Beatles 1967–1970	87	85	81	79	81	87	96	98	108	109	112	114
"Ringo"–R	3	6	8	9	13	13	15	15	15	20	22	25
Mind Games–J	9	10	18	19	24	29	34	41	49	72	85	118
Band On The Run–P/W	33	21	14	13	9	8	7	9	8	9	9	8
(Rainbow Concert–EC)	198											
(Ass–Bf)	154	129	122	126	158	164	184					
(The Road To Freedom–A/M)			182	153	143	138	145	151	177	184		
(Wanted: Dead Or Alive–DB)						220	207	206	192	175	169	

	MAR			APR				MAY				JUN
	16	23	30	6	13	20	27	4	11	18	25	1
The Beatles 1962–1966	137	131	125	119	111	116	123	120	128	144	140	132
The Beatles 1967–1970	115	109	102	101	95	97	101	104	119	128	125	119
"Ringo"–R	29	40	42	44	44	45	49	49	50	51	52	62
Mind Games–J	149	187										
Band On The Run–P/W	8	7	5	2	*1	2	4	7	7	6	4	2
(Wanted: Dead Or Alive–DB)	167	198										

364

	JUN 8	15	22	29	JUL 6	13	20	27	AUG 3	10	17	24
The Beatles 1962–1966	134	130	126	128	124	118	123	132	136	129	126	137
The Beatles 1967–1970	119	115	117	111	104	98	105	107	110	120	124	129
"Ringo"–R	66	76	94	117	150	160	171	193				
Band On The Run–P/W	*1	*1	2	2	*1	4	4	7	8	10	10	10

	AUG 31	SEP 7	14	21	28	OCT 5	12	19	26	NOV 2	9	16
The Beatles 1962–1966	147	154	181	193	200							
The Beatles 1967–1970	140	146	162	172	195							
Band On The Run–P/W	13	14	24	38	48	45	42	61	70	82	103	126
Walls And Bridges–J							72	21	12	4	2	*1
(Pussy Cats–HN)		158	148	136	124	100	89	78	67	60	77	120
(Smiler–RdS)									90	42	34	18
(The Place I Love–Sp)								173	162	149	137	
(Shankar Family–RSh)										203		
(Let's Love–PL)												209

1975

	NOV 23	30	DEC 7	14	21	28	JAN 4	11	18	25	FEB 1	8
Band On The Run–P/W	141	134	159	164	178	183	191	186	196	199	200	200
Walls And Bridges–J	6	4	4	10	20	29	42	62	73	97	97	93
Goodnight Vienna–R		70	29	21	13	10	9	8	8	10	22	36
Dark Horse–G						58	21	13	5	4	7	6
(Pussy Cats–HN)	138											
(Smiler–RdS)	14	13	30	54	63	102	116	122	147	155		
(The Place I Love–Sp)	116	105	93	82	82	81	123	130	156	192		
(Shankar Family–RSh)									181	176	188	
(John Dawson Winter III–JW)			139	96	80	78	78	92	85	92	90	108
(Hist. British Rock-II–Bf,BJK)					182	172	162	151	146	141	147	193

	FEB 15	22	MAR 1	8	15	22	29	APR 5	12	19	26	MAY 3
Band On The Run–P/W	195	194	185	195	198	196	199	196	197	199	196	199
Walls And Bridges–J	98	89	81	119	130	164	189	186	186			
Goodnight Vienna–R	40	38	45	64	60	56	50	65	90	103	104	118
Dark Horse–G	5	11	22	45	50	79	101	122	147	158		
Rock 'n' Roll–J			47	18	12	10	8	7	6	9	14	
(John Dawson Winter III–JW)	117	148										
(Hist. British Rock-II–Bf,BJK)	199	199	195									
(Young Americans–DBw)		141					14	10	9	9	11	11
(Two Sides Of The Moon–KM)								167	155	155		
(Tommy–LS/R)								189	178	167	157	146
(Stardust–BJK)											210	208

	MAY				JUN				JUL		
	10	17	24	31	7	14	21	28	5	12	19
Band On The Run—P/W	197	199									
Goodnight Vienna—R	144	170									
Rock 'n' Roll—J	37	52	64	84	105	128					
Venus And Mars—P/W						25	2	2	2	2	*1
(Young Americans—DBw)	22	36	47	54	74	82	93	117	111	105	93
(Tommy—LS/R)	134	124	113	102	91	91	101	139	171		
(Stardust—BJK)	206										

	JUL	AUG					SEP				OCT
	26	2	9	16	23	30	6	13	20	27	4
Venus And Mars—P/W	2	5	6	11	15	18	26	37	45	63	99
(Young Americans—DBw)	82	72	62	51	40	32	28	24	21	19	17

	OCT			NOV					DEC			
	11	18	25	1	8	15	22	29	6	13	20	27
Venus And Mars—P/W	99	95	93	87	80	76	59	47	35	32	32	48
Extra Texture—G	34	10	8	8	8	9	12	59	106	176	178	
Shaved Fish—J					97	37	21	16	13	12	29	47
Blast From Your Past—R									176	59	48	39
(Young Americans—DBw)	17	34	54	83	106	106	102	110	197			
(Harder To Live—Sp)					207	208	208	203	209	207	207	207
(Hist. British Rock - III)							190	180	175	170	159	149

BUT ANYWAY, BYE BYE

In the few months since the main body of the book was prepared, some new material has been released. Since we were unable to place this latest information in the appropriate chapters, we created the following addenda.

1975

You Should've Been There

(Continued from page 152)

452. SEP 5, 1975 (UK) Capitol R 6008
SEP 29, 1975 (US) Capitol 4145
by Wings   Prod: Paul McCartney
A: *LETTING GO*---McCartney---*3:30*
B: *YOU GAVE ME THE ANSWER*---McCartney---*2:14*

453. SEP 12, 1975 (UK) Apple R 6007
SEP 15, 1975 (US) Apple 1884
by George Harrison   Prod: George Harrison
A: *You*---Harrison---*3:40*
B: *World Of Stone*---Harrison---*4:46*

454. SEP 15, 1975 (US) Elektra 45278
by Carly Simon   Prod: Richard Perry
A: *MORE AND MORE*---Mac Rebbanack—Alvin Robinson---
3:35
Ringo: Drums
B: *(love out in the street)*

455. SEP 22, 1975 (US) Apple SW 3420 (LP)
OCT 3, 1975 (UK) Apple PAS 10009 (LP)
*Recorded: May—June 1975, except the instrumental track
of † mostly recorded in Feb. 1971*
by George Harrison
EXTRA TEXTURE – READ ALL ABOUT IT   Prod: George
Harrison (as OHNOTHIMAGEN)
side one
† *You*---Harrison---*3:40*
The Answer's At The End---Harrison---*5:30*
This Guitar (Can't Keep From Crying)---Harrison---*4:11*
Ooh Baby (You Know That I Love You)---Harrison---*3:50*
World Of Stone---Harrison---*4:46*
side two
† *A Bit More Of You*---Harrison---*0:45*

Can't Stop Thinking About You---Harrison---*4:30*
Tired Of Midnight Blue---Harrison---*4:50*
Grey Cloudy Lies---Harrison---*3:41*
His Name Is Legs (Ladies & Gentlemen)---Harrison---*5:45*

456. SEP 26, 1975 (UK) Island ILPS 9352 (LP)
by Peter Skellern
HARD TIMES Prod: Meyer Schagaloff
side two
    cut two: *Make Love Not War*---Peter Skellern—John Burrows---
      John Harding---*3:16*
    George: Guitar

457. OCT 6, 1975 (US) Dark Horse SP 22006 (LP)
OCT 24, 1975 (UK) Dark Horse AMLH 22006 (LP)
Recorded: Early 1974
by Splinter Prod: George Harrison and Tom Scott
HARDER TO LIVE
side two
    cut four: *Lonely Man*---Robert J. Purvis—Mal Evans---*5:34*

458. OCT 24, 1975 (US) Apple SW 3421 (LP)
OCT 24, 1975 (UK) Apple PCS 7173 (LP)
*New Song Recorded Live: Aug. 30, 1972 at New York's
   Madison Square Garden*
by John Lennon
SHAVED FISH Prod: John Lennon, Yoko Ono and Phil
Spector except †John Lennon; % John and Yoko; $ Phil
Spector
side one
%GIVE PEACE A CHANCE---L-McC---*0:59*
COLD TURKEY---Lennon---*4:59*
$INSTANT KARMA! (WE ALL SHINE ON)---Lennon---*3:12*
POWER TO THE PEOPLE---Lennon---*3:04*
MOTHER---Lennon---*5:03*
WOMAN IS THE NIGGER OF THE WORLD---Lennon—Yoko
  Ono---*4:37*
side two
IMAGINE---Lennon---*2:59*
†WHATEVER GETS YOU THRU THE NIGHT---Lennon---*3:04*
†MIND GAMES---Lennon---*4:10*
†NO. 9 DREAM---Lennon---*4:44*
Medley: 4:15
    HAPPY XMAS (WAR IS OVER)---Lennon—Yoko Ono---*3:25*
†Give Peace A Chance---L-McC---*0:50*

459. OCT 24, 1975 (UK) Apple R 6009
by John Lennon Prod: John Lennon, Yoko Ono and Phil
Spector
A: IMAGINE---Lennon---2:59
B: WORKING CLASS HERO---Lennon---3:44

460. NOV 28, 1975 (UK) Capitol R 6010
OCT 27, 1975 (US) Capitol 4175
by Wings Prod: Paul McCartney
A: MEDLEY: 3:39
VENUS AND MARS---McCartney---1:05
ROCK SHOW---McCartney---2:34
B: MAGNETO AND TITANIUM MAN---McCartney---3:15

461. OCT 27, 1975 (US) Sire SASH 3712-2 (2 LPs)
by Various Artists
(By Tony Sheridan and The Beatles Prod: Bert Kaempfert;
† Billy J. Kramer with The Dakotas Prod: George Martin;
% Peter and Gordon; $ Badfinger Prod: George Harrison;
+ Mary Hopkin Prod: Paul McCartney)
HISTORY OF BRITISH ROCK, VOL. 3
side one
†cut four: *DO YOU WANT TO KNOW A SECRET---L-McC---1:59*
cut five: *MY BONNIE---Charles Pratt---2:06*
side two
%cut seven: *WOMAN---Paul McCartney---2:21*
side three
$cut one: *DAY AFTER DAY---Pete Ham---3:02*
side four
+cut six: *THOSE WERE THE DAYS---Gene Raskin---5:06*

462. NOV 7, 1975 (UK) Atlantic K 60063 (2 LPs)
by Steve Stills
Ringo: Drums
2 ORIGINALS OF STEVE STILLS (1 & 2) Prod: Steve Stills
and Bill Halverson
side two
cut two: *TO A FLAME---Steve Stills---3:10*
cut five: *WE ARE NOT HELPLESS--Steve Stills---4:17*

463. NOV 14, 1975 (UK) Decca ROST 1/2 (2 LPs)
by The Rolling Stones   Prod: Andrew Loog Oldham
ROLLED GOLD–THE VERY BEST OF THE ROLLING STONES
side one
   cut two: *I WANNA BE YOUR MAN*—L-McC—*1:44*
side three
   cut five: *WE LOVE YOU*—Mick Jagger—Keith Richard—*4:39*
    John and Paul: Backing Vocals

464. NOV 14, 1975 (UK) Warner Brothers K 16658
by Mike McGear   Prod: Paul McCartney
A: SIMPLY LOVE YOU—McCartney—Mike McGear—*2:47*
B: WHAT DO WE REALLY KNOW?—McCartney—*3:28*

465. NOV 14, 1975 (UK) Charisma CB 268
by Monty Python   Prod: George "Onothimagen" Harrison
A: Lumberjack Song—Monty Python—*3:17*
B: (spam song)

466. NOV 20, 1975 (US) Apple SW 3422 (LP)
DEC 12, 1975 (UK) Apple PCS 7170 (LP)
by Ringo Starr
BLAST FROM YOUR PAST Prod: Richard Perry except
   † George Harrison; % Pete Drake; and $ Ringo Starr
side one
   YOU'RE SIXTEEN—Richard Sherman—Robert Sherman—*2:50*
   NO NO SONG—Hoyt Axton—David P. Jackson—*2:30*
   †*IT DON'T COME EASY*—Starkey—*3:00*
   PHOTOGRAPH—Starkey—Harrison—*3:58*
   †*BACK OFF BOOGALOO*—Starkey—*3:22*
side two
   ONLY YOU (AND YOU ALONE)—Buck Ram—Andy Rand—*3:16*
   %*BEAUCOUPS OF BLUES*—Buzz Rabin—*2:33*
   OH MY MY—Starkey—Vini Poncia—*4:17*
   $*EARLY 1970*—Starkey—*2:19*
   I'M THE GREATEST—Lennon—*3:23*

467. NOV 24, 1975 (US) Elektra 7E 1048 (LP)
DEC 19, 1975 (UK) Elektra K 52025 (LP)
by Carly Simon   Prod: Richard Perry
BEST OF CARLY SIMON
side two
   cut three: *NIGHT OWL*—James Taylor—*3:47*
    Paul: Backing Vocal

468.   DEC 8, 1975   (US)   ODE SP 77033   (LP)
APR 2, 1976   (UK)   ODE 77033   (LP)
Recorded: August 25-29, 1975
by Tom Scott
NEW YORK CONNECTION   Prod: Tom Scott and Hank Cicalo
side two
   cut three: *Appolonia (Fostrata)*---Tom Scott---*3:59*
      George: Slide Guitar

469.   DEC   8, 1975   (US)   Apple 1885
FEB 6, 1976   (UK)   Apple R 6012
by George Harrison   Prod: George Harrison
A: THIS GUITAR (CAN'T KEEP FROM CRYING)---Harrison---*3:49*
B: MAYA LOVE---Harrison---*4:20*

By Lennon
(Continued from page 175)

TITLE	MUSICIANS	ENTRIES
Give Peace A Chance (Live No. 2)	John Lennon, Yoko Ono and Stevie Wonder with the Elephant's Memory Band, Sha-Na-Na and Roberta Flack	458

By Harrison
(Continued from page 198)

TITLE	MUSICIANS	ENTRIES
The Answer's At The End	George: Guitar & Vocals Jim Keltner: Drums Paul Stallworth: Bass David Foster: Piano Gary Wright: Organ Norm Kinney: Percussion David Foster: String Arrangement	455
A Bit More Of You	See *You*	455
Can't Stop Thinking About You	George: Guitar & Vocals Jim Keltner: Drums Klaus Voorman: Bass Nicky Hopkins: Piano David Foster: Electric Piano Gary Wright: Arp Strings Jesse Ed Davis: Guitar Paul Stallworth: Backing Vocals David Foster: String Arrangement	455
Extra Texture – Read All About It	Prod: George (as Ohnothimagen)	455

Grey Cloudy Lies	George: Guitar, Arp, Bass Moog & Vocal	455
	Jim Keltner: Drums	
	David Foster: Piano	
	Jesse Ed Davis: Guitar	
His Name Is Legs (Ladies & Gentlemen)	George: Acoustic Piano, Guitar & Vocal	455
	Andy Newmark: Drums	
	Willie Weeks: Bass	
	Billy Preston: Electric Piano	
	David Foster: Tack Piano	
	Tom Scott & Chuck Findley: Horns	
	"Legs" Larry Smith: Guest Vocal	
Ooh Baby (You Know That I Love You)	George: Guitar & Vocal	455
	Jim Keltner: Drums	
	Klaus Voorman: Bass	
	Gary Wright: Electric Piano	
	Jesse Ed Davis: Guitar	
	Tom Scott & Chuck Findley: Horns	
This Guitar (Can't Keep From Crying)	George: Acoustic & Electric Guitars, Arp Bass & Vocals	455,469
	Jim Keltner: Drums	
	David Foster: Piano	
	Jesse Ed Davis: Guitar	
	Gary Wright: Arp Strings	
	David Foster: String Arrangement	
Tired Of Midnight Blue	George: Guitars & Vocals	455
	Jim Keltner: Drums & Percussion	
	Paul Stallworth: Bass	
	Leon Russell: Piano	
World Of Stone	George: Guitar & Vocal	453,455
	Jim Keltner: Drums	
	Klaus Voorman: Bass	
	David Foster: Piano & Arp Strings	
	Gary Wright: Organ	
	Jesse Ed Davis: Guitar	
You	George: Guitar & Vocals	453,455
	Jim Gordon & Jim Keltner: Drums	
	Carl Radle: Bass	
	Leon Russell: Piano	
	Gary Wright: Electric Piano	
	David Foster: Organ & Arp Strings	
	Jim Horn: Sax	

Harrison
For Others

(Continued from page 208)

TITLE	MUSICIANS	ENTRIES
Appolonia	Tom Scott: Soprano Sax, Flute and Lyricon George: Slide Guitar Ralph McDonald: Percussion Gary King: Bass Steve Gadd: Drums Richard Teli: Keyboards Bob James: Electric Piano Hugh McCracken: Guitar Eric Gale: Guitar	468
Lonely Man	Splinter Prod: George & Tom Scott Bill Elliott & Bob Purvis: Vocals George (as Hari Georgeson): Guitars Billy Preston: Organ Jim Keltner: Drums Bill Dickinson: Bass John Taylor: Fender Rhodes	457
Lumberjack Song	Prod: George Arranged by Fred Tomlinson with the Voices and Feet of the Fred Tomlinson Mounted Singers and Monty Python's Flying Circus (in alphabetical order: Graham Chapman, John Cleese, Terry Gilliam, Eric Idle, Terry Jones, and Michael Palin with Carol Cleveland and Neil Innes	465
Make Love Not War	Peter Skellern George: Guitar Rob Townsend: Drums George Ford: Bass Mick Greene & Brian Alterman: Guitars Chris Perrin: Tabla	456
You've Got Me Thinking	Jackie Lomax Jackie Lomax & Eric Clapton: Guitars Klaus Voorman: Bass Guitar Ringo: Drums	200,207

You/World Of Stone (B side)   Apple 1884 (45)

Dark Horse

(Continued from page 311)

UK/US DATE	UK/US No.	ALBUM TITLE/ARTIST
10/24/75	AMLH 22006	**Harder To Live**
10/ 6/75	SP 22006	by Splinter

side one	side two
Please Help Me	*Berkley House Hotel*
Sixty Miles Too Far	*After Five Years*
Harder To Live	*Green Line Bus*
Half Way There	*Lonely Man*
Which Way Will I Get Home	*What Is It (If You Never Ever Tried It Yourself)*

UK/US DATE	UK/US No.	ALBUM TITLE/ARTIST
10/31/75	AMLH 22003	**Jiva**
10/ 6/75	SP 22003	by Jiva

side one	side two
Something's Goin' On Inside L.A.	*World Of Love*
The Closer I Get	*What You're Waiting For*
Love Is A Treasure	*It's Time You Know*
Take My Love	*Don't Be Sad*
Hey Brother	*All Is Well*

UK/US DATE	UK/US No.	ALBUM TITLE/ARTIST
10/24/75	AMLH 22005	**Mind Your Own Business**
10/20/75	SP 22005	by Henry McCullough

side one	side two
You'd Better Run	*Lord Knows*
Sing Me A Song	*Down The Mine*
I Can Drive A Car	*Oil In My Lamp*
Baby What You Do To Me	*Mind Your Own Business*
Country Irish Rose	*I'm In Heaven*

UK/US DATE	UK/US No.	ARTIST	A/B SIDE
11/ 7/75	AMS 5503	Splinter	*Which Way Will I Get Home*
--------	---------		*Green Line Bus*
1/30/76	AMS 5505	Stairsteps	*From Us To You*
12/ 3/75	DH 10005		*Time*
2/13/76	AMS 5504	Attitudes	*Ain't Love Enough*
12/ 9/75	DH 10004		*The Whole World's Crazy*

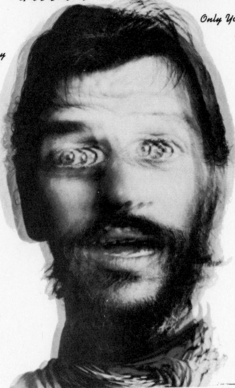

BLAST FROM YOUR PAST
RINGO STARR

You're Sixteen
No No Song
It Don't Come Easy
Photograph
Back Off Boogaloo

Only You (And You Alone)
Beaucoups Of Blues
Oh My My
Early 1970
I'm The Greatest

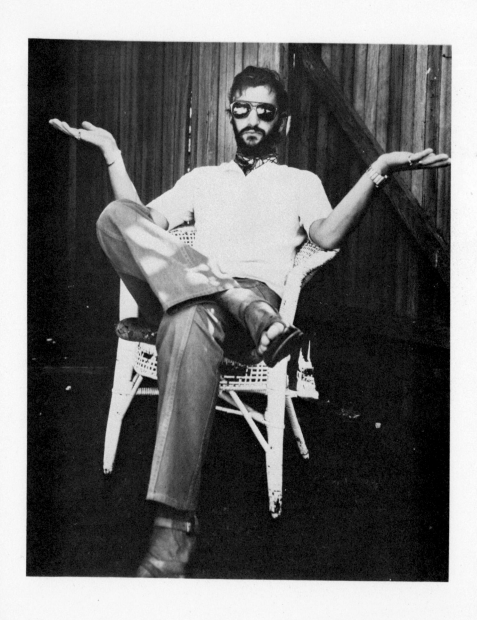

OH, REALLY?

Since first publication of this book, the world at large has come to know what we both knew long ago: we're not perfect. We made a few mistakes. We even (gasp!) left a few things out. For this new printing we cleaned up all the known mistakes and left this space for the few items that have recently been brought to our attention.

BEACH BOYS
SEP 18, 1967 (US)   Brother ST 9001 (LP)
NOV 20, 1967 (UK)   Brother ST 9001 (LP)
Recorded: April 11, 1967
by The Beach Boys   Prod: The Beach Boys and Paul McCartney
SMILEY SMILE
side one
   cut two: *Vegetables*---Brian Wilson—Van Dyke Parks---*2:05*

OCT 28, 1974 (US)   Reprise 2MS 2167 (2 LPs)
by The Beach Boys   Prod: The Beach Boys and Paul McCartney
FRIENDS/SMILEY SMILE
record two: Smiley Smile
   cut two: *VEGETABLES*---Brian Wilson—Van Dyke Parks---*2:05*

At the time of this recording, the Beach Boys were: Al Jardine, Mike Love, Brian Wilson, Carl Wilson, Dennis Wilson and (not yet an 'official' member) Bruce Johnston.

DONOVAN
NOV 22, 1968 (UK) PYE 7N 17660
Recorded: November 1968
by Donovan   Prod: Mickie Most
A: Atlantis---Donovan Leitch---*4:58*
   Paul: Tambourine and Backing Vocal
B: (i love my shirt)

JAN 20, 1969 (US) Epic 5-10434
by Donovan   Prod: Mickie Most
B: *Atlantis*—Donovan Leitch—*4:58*
  Paul: Tambourine and Backing Vocal
A: *(to susan on the west coast waiting)*

AUG 11, 1969 (US) Epic BN 26481 (LP)
by Donovan   Prod: Mickie Most
BARABAJAGAL
side two
  cut three: *ATLANTIS*—Donovan Leitch—*4:58*
  Paul: Tambourine and Backing Vocal

SEPT 19, 1975 (US) Epic BG 33731 (2 LPs)
by Donovan   Prod: Mickie Most
BARABAJAGAL/HURDY GURDY MAN
record one: Barabajagal
side two
  cut three: *ATLANTIS*—Donovan Leitch—*4:58*
  Paul: Tambourine and Backing Vocal

  Musicians: Donovan: Guitar and Vocals; Danny Thompson: Bass; Tony Carr: Drums; and Alan Hawkshaw: Piano.

BOBBY HATFIELD
MAR 1, 1972 (US) Warner Brothers WB 7566
MAR 10, 1972 (UK) Elektra K 16163
Recorded: Jan. 1972
by Bobby Hatfield   Prod: Richard Perry
A: *Oo Wee Baby, I Love You*—Richard Parker—*3:35*
  Ringo: Drums
B: *(rock 'n' roll woman)*

  Musicians: Bobby Hatfield: Vocal; Chris Stainton: Keyboards; Klaus Voorman: Bass.

384

Melody Maker Charts

(Continued from page 343)

	JUN			JUL				AUG				
	14	21	28	5	12	19	26	2	9	16	23	30
Listen What Man Said –P/W	10	6	6	8	7	24						
Venus And Mars (LP)–P/W	16	10	5	2	*1	*1	*1	*1	*1	*1	*1	2
Beatles, 1967–1970 (LP)							26		23	26	25	29
Band On The Run (LP)–P/W										28	27	22
(Fame –DBw)												28

	SEP				OCT				NOV			
	6	13	20	27	4	11	18	25	1	8	15	22
You –G									29			
Imagine –J										30	14	5
Venus And Mars (LP)–P/W	4	4	4	7	8	11	8	11	13	23		
Band On The Run (LP)–P/W	17	22	19		25							
Extra Texture (LP)–G								20				
Shaved Fish (LP)–J												17
(Fame –DBw)	26	27										

	NOV	DEC		
	29	6	13	20
Imagine –J	6	7	14	18
Shaved Fish (LP)–J	9	6	5	7
(Rolled Gold –RS)	29	11	10	8

The Beatles/1967--1970   Apple SKBO 3404 (2 LPs)

ABOUT THE AUTHORS

Harry Castleman was born in Salem, Massachusetts in 1953 and is currently out of work.

Wally Podrazik was born in Chicago in 1952 and is still living.